MEDIA COMPOSER® 6:

PART 1—EDITING ESSENTIALS

Mary Plummer

Course Technology PTR

A part of Cengage Learning

COURSE TECHNOLOGY
CENGAGE Learning®

Australia, Brazil, Japan, Korea, Mexico, Singapore, Spain, United Kingdom, United States

Media Composer® 6:
Part 1—Editing Essentials
Mary Plummer

Publisher and General Manager,
Course Technology PTR:
Stacy L. Hiquet

Associate Director of Marketing:
Sarah Panella

Manager of Editorial Services:
Heather Talbot

Senior Marketing Manager:
Mark Hughes

Acquisitions Editor:
Dan Gasparino

Project Editor:
Kate Shoup

Technical Reviewer:
Bryan Castle

Copy Editor:
Tonya Cupp

Interior Layout:
Shawn Morningstar

Cover Designer:
Avid Technology, Mike Tanamachi

DVD-ROM Producer:
Avid Technology, Brandon Penticuff

Indexer:
Valerie Haynes Perry

Proofreader:
Kate Shoup

Printed in the
United States of America
1 2 3 4 5 6 7 14 13 12

Library of Congress Control Number: 2011942192

ISBN-13: 978-1-133-72798-9

ISBN-10: 1-133-72798-0

Course Technology, a part of Cengage Learning
20 Channel Center Street
Boston, MA 02210 USA

Cengage Learning is a leading provider of customized learning solutions with office locations around the globe, including Singapore, the United Kingdom, Australia, Mexico, Brazil, and Japan. Locate your local office at:
international.cengage.com/region

Cengage Learning products are represented in Canada by Nelson Education, Ltd.

For your lifelong learning solutions, visit **courseptr.com.**

Visit our corporate Web site at **cengage.com.**

This book includes material that was developed in part by the Avid Technical Publications department and the Avid Training department.

To Klark and to Katie, my one-in-a-million girl.

Acknowledgments

My sincerest gratitude to the companies who provided us with the amazing footage to use for the exercises in this book: NEHST and Allentown Productions for the *Running the Sahara* trailer footage, First Tracks Productions for the use of their demo footage, and Upper Ground Enterprises/Hell's Kitchen post team for the *Hell's Kitchen* footage.

Thank you to Bryan Castle for all of your assistance, knowledge, and help in crafting and finishing this book. Huge thanks to my dear friend Mr. D for lending your talents and time to bring this project to fruition. A bow to the amazing team at Cengage for their Herculean efforts in getting to the finish line. Finally, thanks to Patty for the opportunity and for making it all happen.

About the Author

Mary Plummer has been editing film and video professionally for more than 20 years, including film, online, offline, linear, and non-linear editing systems. Her freelance experience includes music videos, documentaries, promos, trailers, pilots, show intros, commercials, and independent feature films. The first feature film that she edited was finished on the original Avid Media Composer in the early 1990s. Since then, her knowledge and experience has evolved in tandem with the professional non-linear editing tools. In addition to her editing career, she is also a Master Trainer and author of numerous film and television industry books, including *Title Design Essentials for Film and Video*.

Contents

Exercise 3
Organizing and Consolidating Your Media   127

Lesson 4
Manual Timeline Editing   131

Exercise 4
Building a Storyboard and Montage   169

Lesson 5
Refining the Edit   173

Exercise 5
Making Further Refinements   225

Lesson 6
Refining and Mixing Audio   229

Exercise 6
Setting Levels   259

Lesson 7
Customizing Media Composer   261

Exercise 7
Customizing Your Media Composer Setup   283

Exercise 10
Preparing and Exporting a Sequence   349

Appendix A
Technical Fundamentals   351

Appendix B
Capturing Tape-Based Media   373

Appendix C
Outputting to Tape   397

Appendix D
Glossary   409

Appendix E
Answers to Review/Discussion Questions   429

Index   437

Introduction

Welcome to *Media Composer 6: Part 1–Editing Essentials* and the Avid Learning Series. Whether you are interested in self study or would like to pursue formal certification through an Avid Learning Partner, this book provides the first step toward developing your core skills and introduces you to the power of Media Composer 6. In addition, *Media Composer 6: Part 1–Editing Essentials* is the first course of study for those pursuing Media Composer User certification.

The material in this book covers the basic principles you need to complete a Media Composer project, from initial setup to final mixdown. Whether your project involves editing corporate industrials, television programming, or independent films, *Media Composer 6: Part 1–Editing Essentials* will teach you what you need to know to be successful with Media Composer.

Using This Book

This book has been designed to familiarize you with the practices and processes you will use to complete a Media Composer project. Each lesson focuses on a phase of the editing process, starting with organizing media, assembling a sequence, refining a sequence, creating titles and effects, and finally outputting your program so others can view it. Using real-world projects from Media Composer editors, the lessons provide information not only on how the features operate but also the concepts behind them. Media Composer projects and media are provided on the DVD, allowing you to follow step-by-step exactly how to perform each task. At the end of each lesson, review questions can help you retain the knowledge you've learned along the way. Additional exercises are also provided, giving you an extra opportunity to explore each feature and technique.

Using the DVD

The DVD-ROM included with this book contains projects and media files for the exercises in the book. These must be installed before you can use them.

If you purchased an ebook version of this book, you may download the contents from www.courseptr.com/downloads. Please note that you will be redirected to the Cengage Learning site.

Please follow these installation instructions exactly or you may not have access to all the project files and media associated with this course.

Installation Instructions

1. Make sure Media Composer 6 is installed and that you have opened the application at least once. Opening the application creates important folders that you will use during this installation.

2. Insert the accompanying DVD into your Windows or Macintosh computer's disc drive.

3. View the contents of the DVD. There are two folders on the DVD, and each folder must be copied to specific locations.

4. Drag the **MC6 Editing Book Files** folder to your desktop.

5. The **Avid MediaFiles** folder on the DVD contains the individual media files you'll use for this book. This folder should be copied to the top level of your hard drive. If you've already used Media Composer on this system, it is possible that you have an existing Avid MediaFiles folder, which you should not delete.

6. Navigate to the root level of the hard drive where you want to store the media files. This may be your internal drive, in which case navigate to **C drive:** (Windows) or **Macintosh HD** (Mac). If you have a locally attached external hard drive you want to use, navigate to the root level of the external hard drive.

Note: The root level of a hard drive is also called the top level. It is the highest level in the hierarchy of folders on your computer.

7. Make sure at the top level of your hard drive that there is no existing Avid MediaFiles folder. If there is no existing Avid MediaFiles folder, drag the entire **Avid MediaFiles** folder from the DVD onto the top level of your hard drive. If an Avid MediaFiles folder does exist on the top level of your hard drive, double-click it to reveal the MXF folder.

8. On the DVD, double-click the **Avid MediaFiles** folder and then double-click the **MXF** folder.

9. Inside the DVD's **MXF** folder are four numbered folders: **0101, 0102, 0103,** and **0104**. Drag all four numbered folders from the DVD into the **MXF** folder on your hard drive.

Caution: Do not rename the folders named OMFI MediaFiles or Avid MediaFiles located on the media drive. Media Composer uses the folder names to locate the media files.

Prerequisites

This course is designed for those who are new to professional video editing as well as experienced professional editors who are completely unfamiliar with Media Composer software. Although this book is not aimed at teaching the theory behind film and television editing, the content of this course does provide some background on the craft of editing, making it appropriate for students or people new to the art. At the same time, its primary focus is on how Media Composer works, making it a perfect introduction to the software for skilled professionals.

System Requirements

This book assumes that you have a system configuration suitable to run Media Composer 6. To verify the most recent system requirements, visit www.avid.com/US/products/media-composer and click the System Requirements tab.

Becoming Avid Certified

Avid certification is a tangible, industry-recognized credential that can help you advance your career and provide measurable benefits to your employer. When you're Avid certified, you not only help to accelerate and validate your professional development, but you can also improve your productivity and project success.

Avid offers programs supporting certification in dedicated focus areas including Media Composer, Sibelius, Pro Tools, Worksurface Operation, and Live Sound.

To become certified in Media Composer, you must enroll in a program at an Avid Learning Partner, where you can complete additional Media Composer coursework if needed and take your certification exam. To locate an Avid Learning Partner, visit www.avid.com/training.

Media Composer Certification

Avid offers two levels of Media Composer certification:

- Avid Media Composer User Certification
- Avid Media Composer Professional Certification

User Certification

The Avid Media Composer Certified User Exam is the first of two certification exams that allow you to become Avid certified. The two combined certifications offer an established and recognized goal for both academic users and industry professionals.

The Avid Media Composer User Certification requires that you display a firm grasp of the core skills, workflows, and concepts of non-linear editing on the Media Composer system.

Courses/books associated with User certification include the following:

- *Media Composer 6: Part 1–Editing Essentials* (MC101)
- *Media Composer 6: Part 2–Effects Essentials* (MC110)

These core courses can be complemented with *Color Grading with Media Composer 6 and Symphony 6.*

Professional Certification

The Avid Media Composer Professional Certification prepares editors to competently operate a Media Composer system in a professional production environment. Professional certification requires a more advanced understanding of Media Composer, including advanced tools and workflows involved in creating professional programs.

Courses/books associated with Professional certification include the following:

- *Media Composer 6: Professional Picture and Sound Editing* (MC201)
- *Media Composer 6: Professional Effects and Compositing* (MC205)

These Professional courses can be complemented with *Color Grading with Media Composer 6 and Symphony 6.*

For more information about Avid's certification program, please visit www.avid.com/US/support/training/certification.

Exploring the Interface and Preparing to Edit

In this lesson, you'll follow a real-world workflow to preview and organize clips in a project. This is a crucial step for any long form project such as a documentary or feature length film.

Media Used: Running the Sahara

Duration: 45 minutes

GOALS

- Launch Media Composer and open a project
- Identify the basic elements of the Media Composer interface
- Explore the Project window
- Work with folders and bins
- Change bin views
- Create new bins
- Duplicate and organize clips
- Save your work

Starting the System

The first step to working with Media Composer is, of course, to start your system. It is important to power up all hardware correctly to ensure that Media Composer recognizes your external drives, decks, and hardware. In this section, you will turn on your system and launch Media Composer. Chances are, your computer is already up and running while you read this, but in case it isn't follow the steps in this section.

To turn on your system and launch Media Composer:

1. Turn on all peripheral hardware, such as Avid I/O boxes, monitors, and speakers.

2. Turn on all external drives and wait about 15 to 20 seconds for them to get up to speed.

Note: **In a workgroup environment, you might need to launch and log on to Client Manager on ISIS or Connection Manager on Avid Unity Media Network.**

3. Turn on your computer.

4. Log on to your system (if necessary).

5. On your computer, launch Avid Media Composer. To do so, choose START > AVID > AVID MEDIA COMPOSER (Windows) or click on the AVID MEDIA COMPOSER icon on the Dock (Mac), as shown in Figure 1.1. You can also launch Media Composer from within the Macintosh folder hierarchy. To do so, choose APPLICATIONS > AVID MEDIA COMPOSER > AVID MEDIA COMPOSER. The Select Project dialog box, shown in Figure 1.2, will appear.

Figure 1.1
Launching Media Composer from the Dock on a Mac.

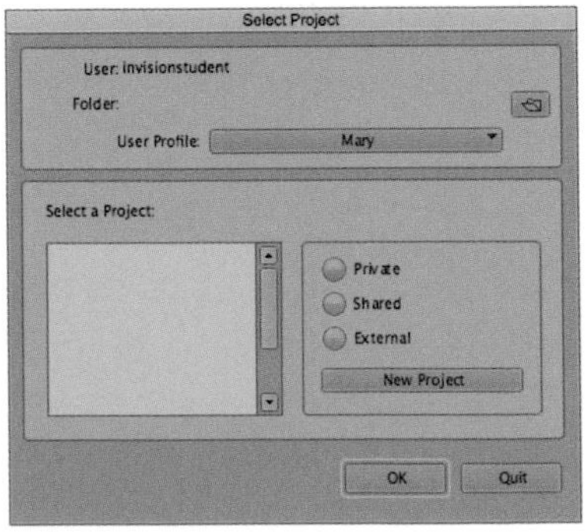

Figure 1.2
The Select Project dialog box.

Depending on your system settings, you may see one of the following before the Select Project dialog box appears:

- If you are working on a Macintosh computer and it is set to sleep when idle, you may see a dialog box warning you that this could reduce performance. Click the Continue button. If you don't want to see this dialog box on a regular basis, click the Don't Warn Me Again check box to select it first.

- If the Avid License Agreement appears (it appears the first 10 times you launch the application), click the Accept or Accept and Don't Show Again button.

Opening a Project

When you launch Media Composer, the Select Project dialog box appears automatically. This dialog box is where you create a new project or select an existing project that you want to open. You also choose the user profile. If you are already working in Media Composer and want to select a different project (or create a new one), you can access the Select Project dialog box by selecting the Project window and choosing File > Close Project. You'll try that method in Lesson 3, "Ingesting File-Based Media," when you create a new project. For now, you'll work with the primary book project, MC6 Editing.

Before opening a project, let's import the user profile that you will be using for most of this book. Your Media Composer user profile makes it easy to customize the Media Composer interface and tools. These user settings are useful for customizing your workspace, and they are particularly important if you share a computer with others and wish to maintain your personal Media Composer settings. You will create a new user profile and customize user settings in Lesson 7, "Customizing Media Composer." For now, you can work with the user profile designed by Avid for new users, called Training User.

To import a user profile:

1. In the Select choose Project dialog box, click the **USER PROFILE** drop-down menu and choose **IMPORT USER OR USER PROFILE**.

2. When the Select User Directory window opens, choose **DESKTOP** > **MC6 EDITING BOOK FILES** > **TRAINING USER** (as shown in Figure 1.3). Then click the **OPEN** button. The Training User profile is now in the list, but still needs to be selected.

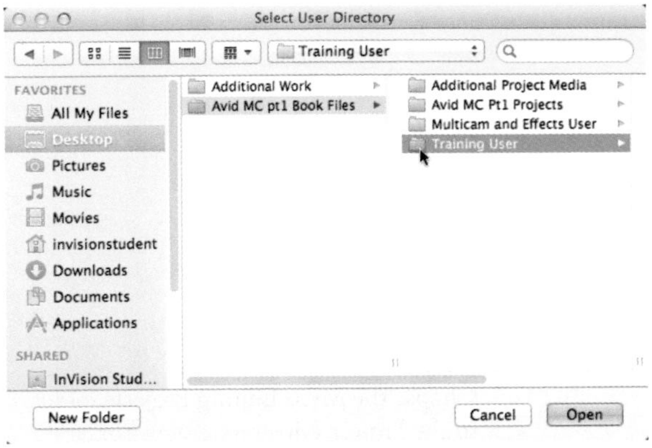

Figure 1.3

Choose Training User in the
Select User Directory dialog box.

Note: If you get a warning dialog box indicating that the user profile already
exists, that just means that someone else (or you) already imported the
Training User profile. In that case, click OK in the warning dialog box;
then select Training User from the User Profile drop-down menu.

Once the user profile had been selected, you are ready to open a project.

To open a project:

1. Choose from one of three project locations:

    • **Private.** Only you (based on your login ID) have access to these projects.

    • **Shared.** All users on this computer have access to these projects.

    • **External.** Select this option to choose a project stored outside the Avid
    Projects folder.

    In this example, click the **EXTERNAL** button. You can now choose a project
    from any location on your computer or an external drive. In this case
    you'll choose a project from the MC6 Editing Book Files folder on your
    desktop.

2. Click the folder in the top-right corner of the Select Project dialog box.
    The Project Directory dialog box opens. In the Project Directory dialog
    box, navigate to **DESKTOP** > **MC6 EDITING BOOK FILES** > **MC6 EDITING
    PROJECTS**, as shown in Figure 1.4. This folder contains all of the projects
    for the lessons in this book.

3. Click the **OPEN** button. A list of the projects in the selected location
    appears on the left side of the Select Project dialog box. (See Figure 1.5.)

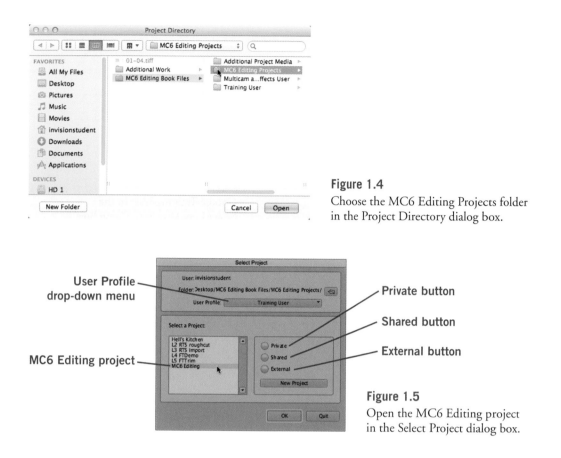

Figure 1.4
Choose the MC6 Editing Projects folder in the Project Directory dialog box.

Figure 1.5
Open the MC6 Editing project in the Select Project dialog box.

4. Select the **MC6 Editing** project in the list and click the **OK** button to open the project. The project opens in Media Composer, with the three primary interface windows showing: the Project window, the Composer window, and the Timeline window (see Figure 1.6). (Note that your windows may fit the screen differently, depending on your computer's resolution settings.)

Tip: You can also double-click a project's name in the Select Project dialog box to open the project.

That's it. You successfully launched Media Composer, imported a user profile, and opened a project.

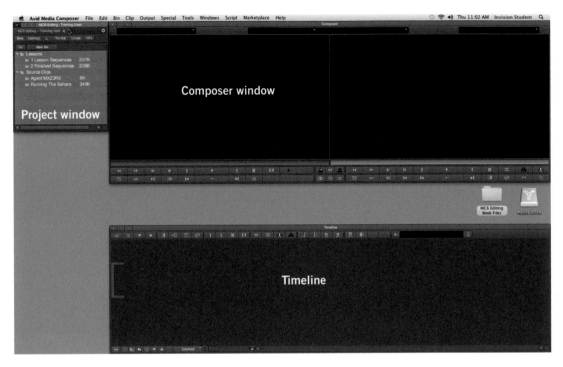

Figure 1.6
The project opens in Media Composer.

Exploring the Workspace

When you open a project in Media Composer, the arrangement of the workspace is based on settings in the user profile. For example, as you saw in Figure 1.6, the Training User default workspace is the Source/Record Editing layout, which includes the three primary editing interface components:

- **The Composer window.** This is the window you'll use to view your clips and your edited sequence. As you can see in Figure 1.7, the Composer window is split into two sections: the Source monitor on the left and the Record monitor on the right.

- **The Project window.** The Project window, shown in Figure 1.8, is the central location for important information about your project such as settings and the project format. It also contains all of the bins, clips, and sequences for your current project. You'll work with the Project window more in the next section.

- **The Timeline.** The Timeline is where you build your sequence. As shown in Figure 1.9, it contains clips, titles, and effects. It shows the clips in order over time, hence the name *Timeline*.

Figure 1.7
The Composer window.

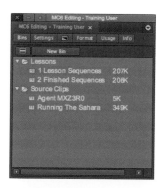

Figure 1.8
The Project window.

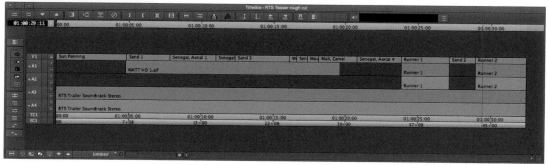

Figure 1.9
The Timeline.

In Media Composer, a *workspace* is a pre-built collection of windows designed to give you the tools you need for common editing tasks. Workspaces are fully customizable. You can change the window arrangement, change the tools displayed, and even link them to other user settings such as a customized view of the Timeline.

Let's take a look at some of the workspace presets.

1. Choose **WINDOWS > WORKSPACES > AUDIO EDITING**. As shown in Figure 1.10, the workspace changes to the Audio preset, which includes the Audio Mixer tool. You'll use the Audio Editing workspace in Lesson 6, "Refining and Mixing Audio."

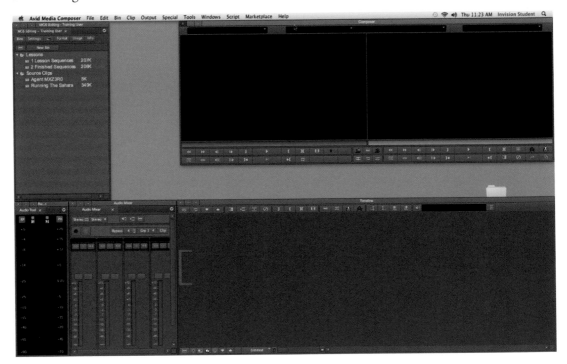

Figure 1.10
The Audio Editing workspace.

2. Choose **WINDOWS > WORKSPACES > CAPTURE**. This workspace includes the Capture tool, which you need if you are capturing video from a deck (see Figure 1.11). You'll learn more about the Capture workspace in Appendix B, "Capturing from Tape."

Tip: Choosing Windows > Workspaces > Source/Record Editing is a quick way to return your windows to the default editing workspace. This is especially handy to clean up your window arrangement if you have inadvertently cluttered, overlapped, moved, or lost windows in your current layout.

3. To return to the Source Record workspace, which you will use for most of this book, choose **WINDOWS > WORKSPACES > SOURCE/RECORD EDITING**.

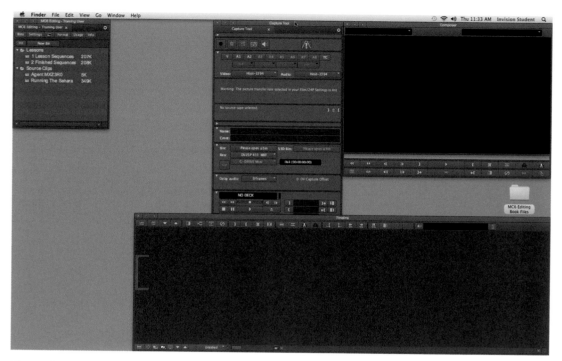

Figure 1.11
The Capture workspace.

4. Before moving on, let's resize the Timeline window so it fills the empty space below the Composer window. If needed, drag the top edge of the Timeline window upward until it touches the bottom of the Composer window.

Workspaces involve more than just the window arrangements. They can include other tools and can be linked to user settings, such as Timeline layouts and bin views. Don't worry if you don't detect all the Training User workspace features at first glance; they will become more apparent as you learn Media Composer.

Tip: Windows in the Media Composer workspace can—and often do—overlap one another. So how do you identify the active window? Simple. The × (Close), – (Minimize), and + (Zoom) buttons appear colored on the active window only. On inactive windows, these buttons appear gray. (See Figure 1.12.)

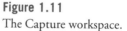 Active    Inactive

Figure 1.12
Look at these buttons to determine which window is active.

Understanding the Project Window

The Timeline and the Composer windows are the same for every project. The Project window, however, is unique for each project, based on the project's format, contents, and organization. Think of the Project window—which is named after the current project and user (in this case, MC6 Editing–Training User)—as the central headquarters for a project. It contains all the important information about your current job, with buttons for Bins, Settings, Effects, Format, Usage, and Info (see Figure 1.13).

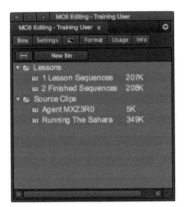

Figure 1.13
The Project window for the current project:
MC6 Editing–Training User.

The Project window includes buttons for each of its six different panes. These are as follows:

■ **Bins pane.** The Bins pane lists all the bins and folders for the project. These contain all your project assets, including audio and video clips, sequences, images, sound effects, and more.

■ **Settings pane.** This is the central location where you can find all of the settings in Media Composer. These settings can be used to control everything from the look of the interface, to media formats, to the configuration of external hardware. You'll explore this pane more fully in Lesson 7.

■ **Effect Palette.** The Effect Palette includes all the effects and effect presets that can be applied to transitions or to segments.

■ **Format pane.** This lets you view basic project information such as the video format. This information correlates with the options you select in the New Project dialog box when creating a new project. You'll work with this pane in Lesson 3.

■ **Usage pane.** This pane includes the Statistics feature, which gathers and reports information on system usage based on the project.

■ **Info pane.** The Info pane is handy when you need information about the system memory, or need access to the Hardware tool.

Let's take a moment to look at the Settings pane. There are three types of settings: Project, Site, and User. You'll explore these settings more in Lesson 7. For now, let's look at one example, the Keyboard settings.

To explore the Keyboard settings:

1. Click the **Settings** button to show the Settings pane. As shown in Figure 1.14, the settings are listed in alphabetical order, enabling you to easily scroll through the list to find the specific setting you want to view or customize.

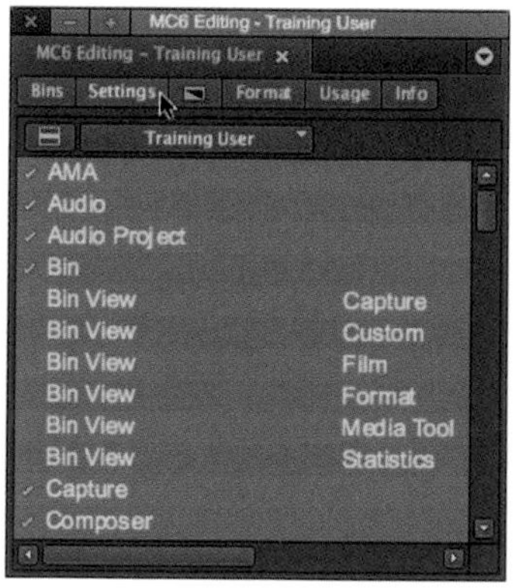

Figure 1.14
The Project window's Settings pane.

Note: Media Composer is fully customizable, making it is quite user friendly. Many of the features that you are familiar with in your computer operating system are also available in Media Composer. For example, there are at least three ways to accomplish almost everything in Media Composer: by using a menu, by clicking a button, and by pressing a keyboard shortcut.

2. Because the settings you are going to look at are the Keyboard settings, why not use the keyboard to get there? Press the **K key** on your keyboard to instantly highlight the first setting in the list that begins with the letter K. (This happens to be the Keyboard setting.) Media Composer also conveniently scrolls the list up so that the letter you selected appears at the top of the Settings pane.

3. Double-click the word Keyboard in the list. As shown in Figure 1.15, the Keyboard window opens.

Figure 1.15
Opening the Keyboard window.

Note: **The Keyboard window shows the shortcuts for the standard keyboard and those that use the Shift modifier. You will learn to customize the keyboard and buttons in Lesson 7.**

4. The Keyboard window, shown in Figure 1.16, is a mini-map of the keyboard, with icons that represent the Media Composer functions or shortcuts assigned to each key. (Note that the keyboard in the Keyboard window is mapped to the settings established for the Training User user profile.) These icons also appear in the interface as buttons. To see the keyboard shortcuts for the Shift key, press and hold down the **SHIFT KEY** on your computer's keyboard.

Figure 1.16
The Keyboard window.

Tip: **Studying the Keyboard window is a great way to become familiar with the keyboard shortcuts as you learn Media Composer.**

5. Press **CTRL+W** (Windows) or **COMMAND+W** (Mac) to close the Keyboard window. Alternatively, click the red × (**CLOSE**) button.

6. In the Project window, click the **BINS** button.

You'll spend much of the rest of this project in the Bins pane, where you'll discover how projects are organized.

Working with Bins and Folders in the Project Window

Welcome to the Bins pane, shown in Figure 1.17. Think of the Project window—which is named after the current project and user (in this case, MC6 Editing–Training User)—as the central headquarters for a project containing the reference library for every piece of media in your project. The actual media remains safely stored in the Avid Media Files folder on your media drive or server. Media Composer only points to the media, with reference files—more commonly referred to as *clips*. Clips contain data and information about the original media, and can be played, edited, and even deleted without ever actually touching the original media. In other words, the editing process is *nondestructive*.

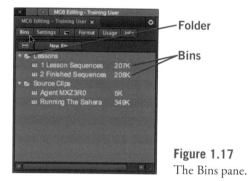

—Folder

—Bins

Figure 1.17
The Bins pane.

All of the clips and sequences for your project are stored and organized in the Bins pane. Just as pieces of film have been stored in bins since the advent of film editing, master clips and sequences in Media Composer are stored in bins. Bins, in turn can remain at the root level of the Bins pane, or be further organized into folders.

Let's take a look at the current project and see how it is organized. As you can see, there are two folders: Lessons and Media. Inside those folders are bins. To open or close a folder, you can either double-click the folder or click the triangle located to the left of the folder.

To see how a project is organized:

1. Click the triangle to the left of the Lessons folder to close the folder.
   As shown in Figure 1.18, the triangle changes from a downward-pointing shape to one that points to the right, and the bins in the folder are hidden.

2. Double-click the **LESSONS** folder to open it again. Notice that the Lessons folder contains two bins: 1 Lesson Sequences and 2 Finished Sequences.

Figure 1.18
Hide the contents of the Lessons folder.

3. Double-click the **1 LESSON SEQUENCES** bin. As shown in Figure 1.19, the
    Lesson Sequences bin opens as a separate window named after the bin.
    Inside the 1 Lesson Sequences bin window are sequences that you will be
    working with throughout this book. Notice that the sequence icon looks
    like a filmstrip, or a series of clips side by side.

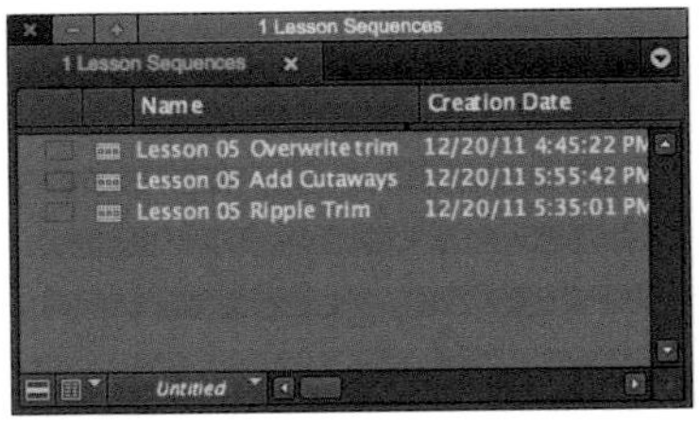

Figure 1.19
Opened bin, with lesson sequences
listed alphanumerically.

Note: **Although bins can hold both clips and sequences, this bin only contains
sequences to help keep your lesson elements separated as you work your
way through the lessons in this book.**

4. Click the × (**CLOSE**) button in the upper-left corner of the open bin to
    close the 1 Lesson Sequences bin.

5. Let's make two new bins and use one of them for the sequences you will
    create in this project. To begin, click twice on the **NEW BIN** button in the
    Project window's Bins pane. As shown in Figure 1.20, two new bins
    appear at the root level of the Bins pane. In addition, two windows open,
    representing the two new bins. By default, Media Composer names all
    new bins after the project. Don't worry if you accidentally created too
    many bins. You'll learn to delete them shortly.

6. We actually only need one new bin at the moment, so let's rename one of
    them, and throw the other in the trash. To rename a bin, first click once
    on its name in the Bins pane—in this example, **MC6 EDITING BIN**—to
    highlight it, as shown in Figure 1.21.

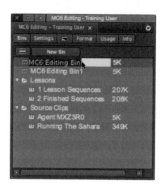

Figure 1.20
Creating two new bins.

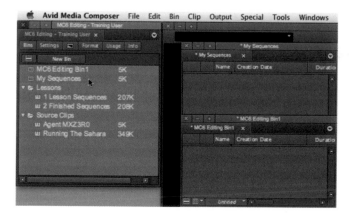

Figure 1.21
Selecting the bin's name.

7. Type **My Sequences** and press **Enter** (Windows) or **Return** (Mac).
   The name on the bin and in the title bar of the bin's window changes to
   My Sequences, as shown in Figure 1.22.

Figure 1.22
Renaming the bin.

8. Next, delete the remaining new bin. To begin, click the icon (not the name)
   for the other new bin, **MC6 Editing Bin1**, in the Project window's Bins pane

Note: **Clicking on an icon selects the item. Clicking on the name highlights the name field and makes it active. This is true for folders, bins, sequences, and master clips in Media Composer.**

9. Press the **DELETE** or **BACKSPACE KEY** to delete the bin. Alternatively, right-click the bin and choose **DELETE SELECTED BINS** from the menu that appears. A red Trash bin appears at the bottom of the Project window, with your deleted bin inside (see Figure 1.23).

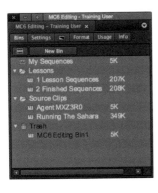

Figure 1.23
Deleting a bin.

Note: **The Trash bin stays with your project for the life of the project—unless it is emptied. This is a terrific safety net because in the editing world, people are known to change their minds. In fact, most professional editors don't empty their Trash bin until they are completely finished with a project. If you ever need to open a bin that is in the Trash bin, you will need to drag it out of the Trash bin first.**

10. Close the **MY SEQUENCES** bin window.

11. The My Sequences bin is still at the root level of the Bins pane, above the Lessons folder. To keep things organized, move it to the Lessons folder. Simply drag the icon for the **MY SEQUENCES** bin down to the **LESSONS** folder icon, as shown in Figure 1.24. Figure 1.25 shows the result of the move.

Figure 1.24
Dragging a bin to move it.

Figure 1.25
The bin is moved.

12. Close the **Lessons** folder.

Moving and Resizing a Bin

In this section, you'll see the footage for the theatrical trailer of a documentary film called *Running the Sahara*. First, you'll open the bin containing the media for the trailer and identify the different types of master clips. Then you'll resize the bin and explore the different bin views. Rather than double-click to open the bin, this time you'll try the menu method.

To open a bin via the menu method:

1. In the Bins pane, click the **Running the Sahara** bin icon, as shown in Figure 1.26.

Figure 1.26
The Running the Sahara bin icon.

2. Instead of double-clicking the bin to open it, right-click it and choose **Open Selected Bins** from the menu that appears, as shown in Figure 1.27. (If you don't have a mouse with a right-click button, double-click the bin icon to open it.) The Running the Sahara bin window opens. As shown in Figure 1.28, the Running the Sahara bin has more than 50 video and audio clips, which are currently displayed in Text view. This current

view includes columns of information about the clips. (You'll learn more about the different views in the next section.)

Figure 1.27
Choosing Open Selected Bins from the context menu.

Figure 1.28
The Running the Sahara bin window.

Note: Keep in mind that due to the consolidation of the media for this book to fit on the DVD, the exact number of clips in your bin may be different from that shown in the screen shots.

3. Let's go ahead and move the bin window under the Project window and resize it before exploring the different bin views. To move the bin window, drag its header (where it says Running the Sahara) and place it directly under the Project window. When the bin window is in place, drag the lower-right corner of the bin window down and to the right to enlarge the bin until it covers the lower half of the screen as shown in Figure 1.29.

Now is a good time to identify the different clip icons, located in the Icon column on the far left side of the bin window. Bins contain either clips or sequences. You've already worked with sequences, so you are familiar with their icon. Four different types of clips appear in Text view, each with their own icons: master clips including video, master clips with audio only, subclips, and AMA-linked clips.

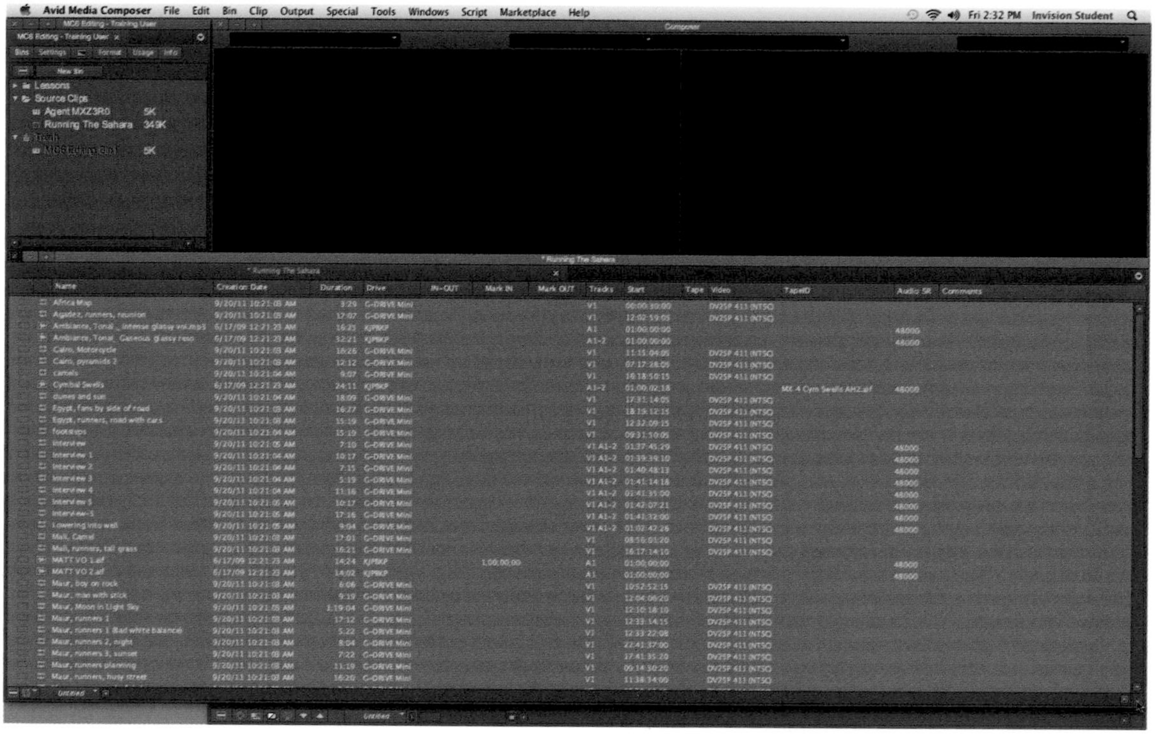

Figure 1.29
The bin window, moved and resized.

You'll work with subclips and AMA-linked media in Lesson 3, "Ingesting File-Based Media," and Lesson 4, "Editing with Subclips and Storyboards." For now, you'll focus on the two most common types of clips, audio and video, whose icons are shown in Figure 1.30.

RTS Trailer Soundtrack   **Audio**   Cairo, Motorcycle   **Video**

Figure 1.30
Clip icons in Text view.

Changing the Bin View

Media Composer offers three bin views: Text, Frame, and Script. In addition, the program supports a variety of Text view presets. In this section, you'll look at the different bin views to determine which bin view will work best for previewing and organizing this project's clips.

To change the bin view:

1. Click the **BIN VIEW MENU** button (the down arrow) in the lower-left
    corner of the bin window and choose **FRAME** (see Figure 1.31). As shown
    in Figure 1.32, the items in your bin now appear as images that display the
    first frame of each clip. This is not only a handy way to visually identify
    the content of each clip, but it also makes it very apparent which clips are
    video and which are audio only.

Figure 1.31
Switching to Frame view.

Figure 1.32
Clips in Frame view.

2. Click the **BIN VIEW MENU** button and choose **SCRIPT**. As shown in Figure
    1.33, the Script view is like the best of both worlds. You get a frame to
    identify the clip visually, plus some columns of information. There is even
    a large Comment text field, where you can write comments for clips as
    needed. (Any comments you type will also appear in the Comments column
    in Text view.)

Figure 1.33
Clips in Script view.

Note: **The columns in Script view are based on the current Text view columns. To see different columns in Script view, simply change the Text view column preset before switching views. You'll work with this in Lesson 3.**

3. Now that you have seen all three bin views, let's go back to Text view and resize the window. Then you'll be ready to preview a clip in the Source monitor. Click the **Bin View Menu** button and choose **Text**.

4. Finally, drag the lower-right corner of the open bin to the left until it fits in the empty space next to the Composer and Timeline windows.

Exploring the Editing Interface

Let's spend a few minutes working with each window to understand each one's part in the editing process. Along the way, you'll also discover some of the added features and tricks built into Media Composer to enhance your editing experience.

The editing process begins with the Project window because that is where you access your clips. Clips are then opened in the Composer window—specifically, the Source monitor located on the left side of the window.

You can open a clip by either double-clicking the clip icon or dragging the clip to the Source monitor.

To open clips:

1. Double-click the **CAIRO, PYRAMIDS 2** clip (icon). As shown in Figure 1.34, the Composer window becomes active, with the Cairo, pyramids 2 clip loaded and ready to play in the Source monitor. Alternatively, you can drag the clip icon from the open bin to the Source monitor to load the clip. The clip opens in the Composer window's Source monitor.

Source monitor

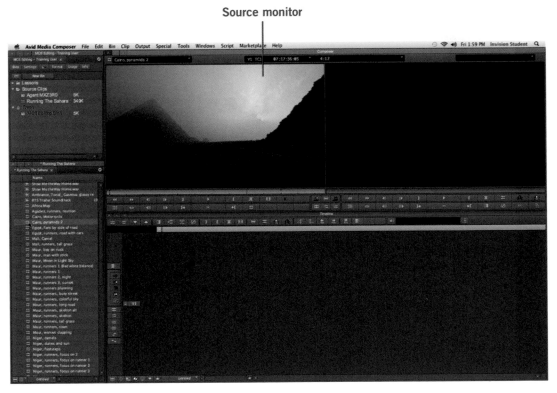

Figure 1.34
The clip opens in the Source monitor.

2. In the Timeline window, locate the **V1 SOURCE TRACK** button (refer to Figure 1.34). The Source Track buttons correspond with the tracks in the Source monitor.

3. Let's take a look at a clip with three tracks: Video (V1) and Audio (A1–2). In the Running the Sahara bin, double-click the **SAND 1** icon to load it into the Source monitor. The Timeline window now has three Source Track buttons, representing each of the tracks in the Source monitor. (See Figure 1.35.)

V1 (video) Source Track button   A1 and A2 (audio) Source Track buttons

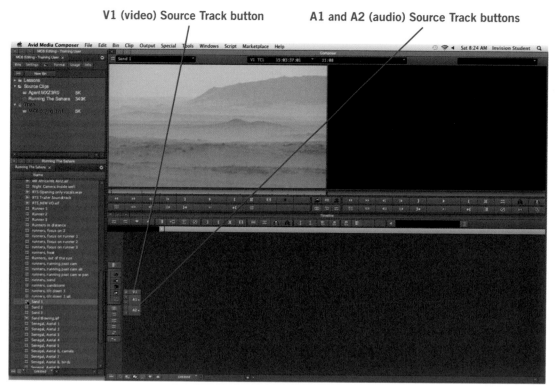

Figure 1.35
The Sand 1 clip in the Source monitor, and the V1, A1, and A2 Source Track buttons in the Timeline.

Note: You can see which tracks are included with a clip in the Track column of
the Text bin view.

It is important to know which tracks are included with a clip before editing it into
a sequence. You will begin editing and working with the Source Track buttons
later. For now, it is just good to see that all three windows of the editing interface
are working together as you load your clips.

Working with the Source Monitor

The Source monitor is where you can play, cue, and mark your clips before editing them to a sequence. Let's take a quick tour of the Source monitor, shown in
Figure 1.36, to help you understand the different tools for playing your clips.

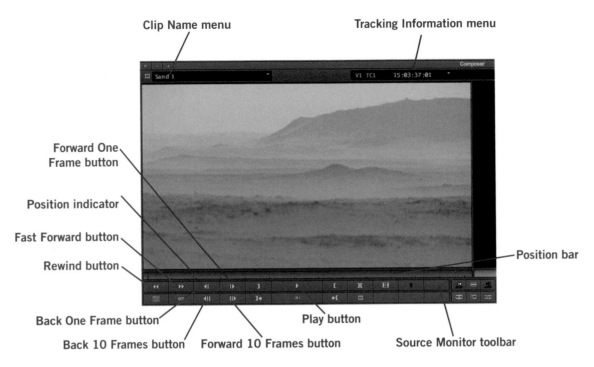

Clip Name menu

Tracking Information menu

Forward One Frame button

Position indicator

Fast Forward button

Rewind button

Position bar

Back One Frame button

Play button

Back 10 Frames button   Forward 10 Frames button

Source Monitor toolbar

Figure 1.36
The Composer window's Source monitor.

The top of the Source monitor includes two menus that display information about the current clip: the Clip Name menu on the left and the Tracking Information menu on the right. You can use the Tracking Information menu to view a clip's timecode. The bottom of the Source monitor includes the Source Monitor toolbar. Here, the position indicator shows which frame you are viewing as it moves along the Position bar. There are also buttons for navigation, as shown in Figure 1.36.

To explore the Source monitor:

1. Drag the position indicator right or left in the Position bar to scrub through your clip frames.

2. Click anywhere on the POSITION bar to move the position indicator to that frame.

3. Press the HOME KEY to go to the beginning (head) of the clip.

4. Press the SPACE BAR or click the PLAY button to play the clip. When the clip finishes playing, it stops on the last full frame of the clip.

Note: The arrow keys can also be used for easy navigation. The Right Arrow and Left Arrow keys step one frame forward or back, and the Down Arrow and Up Arrow keys rewind and fast forward to the head and tail of the clip, respectively. The Home and End keys can be used to move the position indicator to the beginning and end of the clip.

As you can see, loading and playing clips in the Source monitor is easy. You'll work with the Record monitor and Timeline in the next lesson. For now, let's get back to the Running the Sahara bin and get to know the footage. Trouble is, with so many clips in one bin, it makes familiarizing yourself with the footage more difficult. In the real world, with a project like this, you would organize the clips before editing (or perhaps an assistant editor would do that for you). Either way, this is the perfect time to learn how to organize your clips into bins to prepare for editing in Lesson 2, "Editing a Basic Story."

Organizing Clips and Bins

Earlier you learned that clips are organized within bins and bins within a project. Project organization evolves throughout the post-production workflow. You can begin organizing your clips and bins even before capturing, during the logging process. As you proceed through each stage of the project, the organization continues to change as needed from working on your first rough cut to getting ready to finish your program.

Each type of project requires different organization. For example, a feature film may organize clips in bins for each scene or reel. Documentary projects may have different bins for each reel, location, or subject. Music videos may have bins that organize by location, artist, song section, or content.

Note: Whatever form of organization you choose for a project, it can be modified any time. As you've seen, it is easy to create new bins, move bins into folders, and even delete bins.

Creating New Bins

Viewing and sorting clips are important aspects of organizing your project. Real organization, however, involves creating more bins. In this section, you'll create five new bins: Audio, Interviews, Culture, Runners, and Scenery. (Other common bins for a project like this one might be B-roll, Locations, People, Places, and so on.)

Note: *B-roll* is an industry term for footage that you use to supplement an interview or news story.

To create new bins:

1 Click the **NEW BIN** button five times to create five new bins.

2. Name the new bins **AUDIO**, **INTERVIEWS**, **SCENERY**, **CULTURE**, and **RUNNERS**.

3. You could place the bins anywhere on your screen. For now, reposition and resize the new bins over the right side of the Timeline so that you can see each bin, as shown in Figure 1.37. It is okay to overlap some of the Record monitor as well.

Note: **Why cover the Record monitor and right side of the Timeline? Because you only need the Record monitor when you are looking at a sequence. Since you are previewing and sorting clips, that part of the screen won't be used. As for the Timeline, in a few minutes you may expand the Running the Sahara bin and cover the left side of the Timeline window. The right side, on the other hand, will remain as is.**

Figure 1.37
Creating and positioning five new bins.

Note: **If at any time you can't find an open bin, it is likely hiding behind another window. Simply double-click the bin icon in the Bins pane or open the Windows menu and choose the bin name.**

Copying and Duplicating Clips

Before moving clips into separate bins, it's a good idea to copy or duplicate them. That way, if you are looking for a clip but don't remember its name or which bin you put it in, you can always look in the original bin with all the clips. Copying or duplicating clips is also useful if you delete a clip but decide later that you want to use it after all. (Remember, *clip* refers not to an actual piece of media, but to the reference to that piece of media.)

Although *copy* and *duplicate* sound similar, they are actually two distinct things. A *copy* is a clone of the original master clip. Any changes you make to the master —say, changing the name—will be passed on to the copy. A *duplicate*, on the other hand—marked by the text Copy.01, which is appended to its filename—has a life of its own. Duplicates can be modified completely independently of the original file and vice versa. You'll get a chance to duplicate a sequence in the next lesson. For now, you'll only "clone" the master clips.

> Note: The rule of thumb is, clone your master clips, but duplicate your sequences. By duplicating sequences, you will have independent versions—for example, before and after for a new creative idea. Conversely, if you clone your clips, the changes ripple through, and you're assured that any changes you make to a copy of that clip will always be visible, no matter where you look at it—for example, comments added to an interview, copies of which are located in three different bins based on content.

To copy a clip:

1. Select the clip(s) you want to copy.

2. Hold down the **ALT** (Windows) or **OPTION** (Mac) **KEY** as you drag the selected clip(s) to a different bin window.

To duplicate a clip:

1. Select the clip(s) you want to duplicate.

2. Right-click a selected clip icon and choose **DUPLICATE** from the menu that appears. Alternatively, press **CTRL+D** (Windows) or **COMMAND+D** (Mac).

For this project, you will copy all the clips in the Running the Sahara bin, placing them in a new bin.

1. Create a new bin and name it **RTS SELECTS**.

2. Place the new bin next to the **RUNNING THE SAHARA** bin.

3. In the Running the Sahara bin, click any clip icon to select it, and choose **Edit > Select All** or press **Ctrl+A** (Windows) or **Command+A** (Mac) to select all the clips in the bin.

4. Hold down the **Alt** (Windows) or **Option** (Mac) **key** as you drag the selected clip(s) to the **RTS Selects** bin. A green circle with a **+** (+) appears to show that you are adding copies to the bin. If you release the Alt/Option key before you release the mouse, you will move the original clips and not make copies. If this happens, Alt-drag/Option-drag the clips that you moved from the RTS Selects bin to the Running the Sahara bin. Clones are clones, regardless of how many copies you make. Figure 1.38 shows the files copied to the RTS Selects bin.

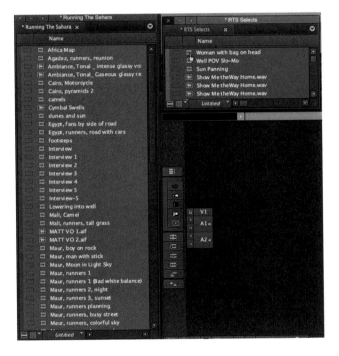

Figure 1.38
Copies in the RTS Selects bin.

Note: If you accidentally deselected the clips before Alt-dragging/Option-dragging them, select the first clip, and then Shift-click the last one in the list to select them all. Shift-clicking automatically selects all clips between the initial selected clip and the clip you Shift-clicked. You can then Alt-drag/Option-drag them to the RTS Selects bin.

5. Close the **RTS Selects** bin.

Mission accomplished. The original master clips have been duplicated. You're now free to sort and move clips to their corresponding bins.

Moving Clips Between Bins

Moving clips between bins is as easy as selecting the clips and dragging them to the appropriate bin. In this section, you'll start with the Running the Sahara bin in Text view, with the audio clips visible. Then, you'll switch to Frame view and resize and redistribute the clips so that you can see all of the clips in the bin. Finally, you'll move several of your clips to new bins to keep them organized.

To move clips between bins:

1. Drag the right edge of the Running the Sahara bin until you can see the Tracks column. This column shows which tracks are included with a clip. (see Figure 1.39.)

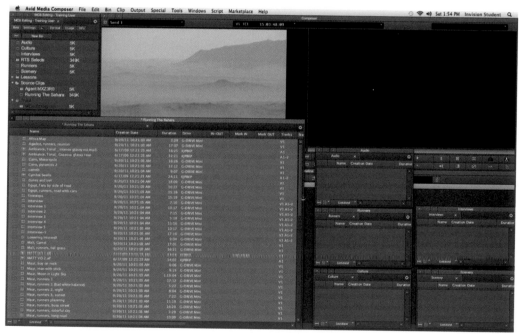

Figure 1.39
Resized bin with Tracks column showing.

2. Double-click the **Tracks** header at the top of the Tracks column to sort tracks and move the audio-only clips to the top of the list. (See Figure 1.40.) You can also right-click the **Tracks** column header and choose **Sort Column > Ascending Order**.

3. In the Running the Sahara bin, select the first audio clip at the top of the list. Then Shift-click the last audio clip in the list. All your audio clips will be selected, as shown in Figure 1.41.

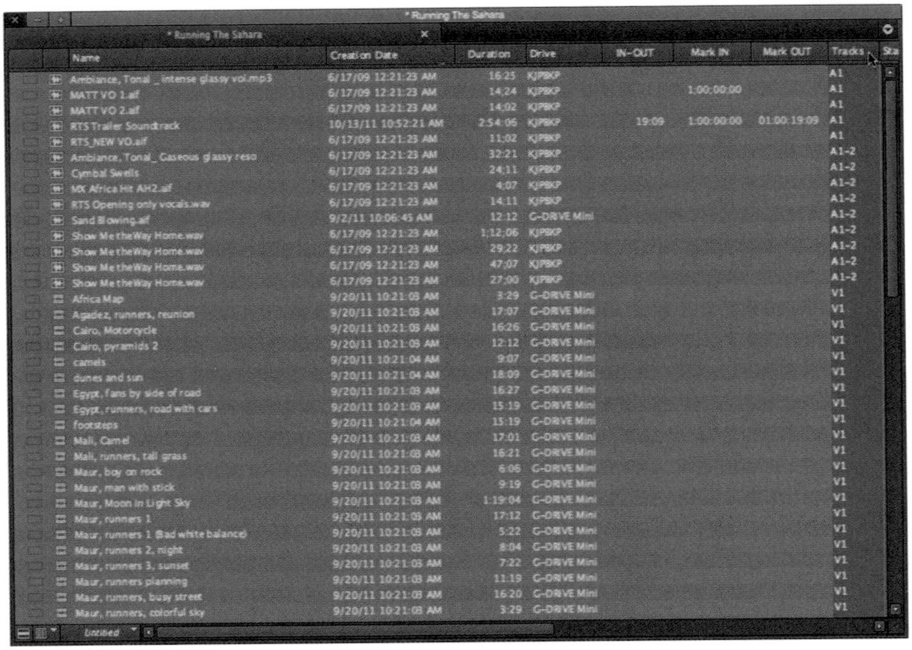

Figure 1.40
Resized bin with Tracks column showing.

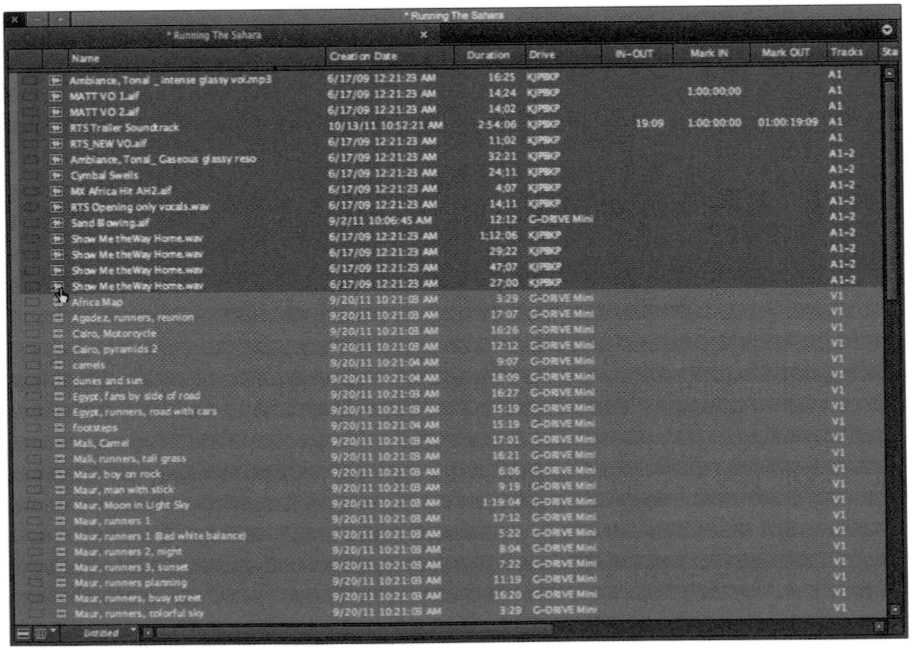

Figure 1.41
Selecting the audio clips in the Running the Sahara bin.

4. Drag the selected audio clips to the **Audio** bin, as shown in Figure 1.42.

Figure 1.42
Moving the audio clips to the Audio bin.

5. Switch the **Running the Sahara** bin to Frame view, as shown in Figure 1.43.

Figure 1.43
Switching to Frame view.

Note: To increase the size of the frames, choose Edit > Enlarge Frame or press Ctrl+L (Windows) or Command+L (Mac). To reduce the size of the frames, choose Edit > Reduce Frame or press Ctrl+K (Windows) or Command+K (Mac).

6. Click the **Fast Menu** button in the lower-left corner of the Running the Sahara bin window and choose **Fill Window** from the menu that appears (see Figure 1.44). If needed, the clips neatly fill the expanded bin window, making it easy to move clips to their appropriate bins.

Figure 1.44
Choosing Fill Window from the Fast menu.

7. Let's start with the Interview clips (talking heads) because they are the easiest to identify. In the bin, locate all interview clips with the man (endurance runner Charlie Engle) in the grey shirt. The clips are all named Interview, so they are easy to identify. Click below and to the left of the first **INTERVIEW** clip and drag a lasso around the other six clips, as shown in Figure 1.45. (If you can't get them all in one lasso, grab what you can. You can repeat this step to lasso the rest.) When you release the mouse button, the clips within the lasso will be selected, as shown in Figure 1.46.

Figure 1.45
Lassoing clips
to select them.

Figure 1.46
The lassoed
clips are selected.

Lassoing a Selection

For anyone who hasn't lassoed items in other applications, it's easy. Simply click in the empty space near an item that you want to select to create the lasso. Then, holding down the mouse button, drag the pointer to expand the lasso, which will be rectangular in shape. Anything inside the lasso will be selected. The larger the lasso, the more items you will select. You can lasso-select sequences, bins, or clips in any of the bin views.

---

8. Drag the **Interview** clips to the **Interviews** bin to move them.

9. To select multiple clips that are not located next to each other, you can Ctrl-click (Windows) or Command-click (Mac) them. To start, click any clip that shows the three runners in action. Then Ctrl-click (Windows) or Command-click (Mac) three additional clips that show the runners. The clips are selected, as shown in Figure 1.47.

Figure 1.47
Selecting multiple non-adjacent clips.

10. Drag the selected clips to the **Runners** bin.

Tip: Giving your clips descriptive names can be helpful not only for identifying clip content, but also for searching and sorting clips with Media Composer's Find feature. You'll learn how to search for clips in Lesson 4.

Changing a Clip's Representative Frame

By default, the representative frame—that is, the frame that represents a clip in a bin—is the first frame of the clip. If a clip starts with color bars or a black screen, or is panned away from the subject, you won't see a very good representation of the clip. No problem! You can change the representative frame.

There are several ways to choose a clip's representative frame. One is to play through the clip frames with the space bar; another is to use keyboard shortcuts to move forward or backward through the frames. In this section, you'll try both methods, starting with the first one.

To play through clips with the space bar:

1. Select the MAUR, RUNNERS 3, SUNSET clip. As shown in Figure 1.48, this clip's representative frame shows a sunset behind some brush. There is no sign of runners, so at first glance this looks like a scenery clip.

Figure 1.48
A representative first frame without runners showing.

2. Press the SPACE BAR to play the clip frames. When you see the three runners in the middle of the frame (see Figure 1.49), press the SPACE BAR again to stop. Next time you glance at this clip in Frame view, you will know exactly what the contents are.

Figure 1.49
Stop when you see three runners in the middle of the frame.

Note: Of course, you can always open a clip in the Composer window and play it in the Source monitor to see the full clip and its details. However, playing through clips in Frame view and setting the representative frame can be a real time saver when simply sorting clips into bins.

3. Drag the MAUR, RUNNERS 3, SUNSET clip to the RUNNERS bin.

To play through clips using keyboard shortcuts:

1. Select the SUN PANNING clip (see Figure 1.50). This clip is a panning shot of the sun that moves from frame left to frame right, and then the other direction. Your goal here is to advance enough frames that the sun (and flare) can clearly be seen in the representative frame.

Figure 1.50
Selecting the Sun Panning clip.

2. Press the **2 KEY** on your keyboard as many times as needed until the sun is near the center of the frame. (See Figure 1.51.) Note that holding the key down advances the clip continually 10 frames at a time.

Figure 1.51
Stepping through clip until the sun is in the middle of the frame.

3. Drag the **SUN PANNING** clip to the **SCENERY** bin.

Note: **The contents of a clip may not always be an exact match for the bin names, but they will be close enough if you understand your reasoning for naming them in the first place. For this project, the Scenery bin will contain any clip that doesn't include people of the region or the three runners who are the stars of the documentary. Clips containing the runners—even if they are in a well or in front of breathtaking scenery—go to the Runners bin. Clips containing footage of people from the region belong in the Culture bin.**

Keyboard Shortcuts for Navigating Clips

Media Composer groups shortcuts together, like instruments in an orchestra. This makes it both easy and intuitive to access features and control the interface. In this section, you'll work with the number keys 1 through 5 (see Figure 1.52), plus the Home and End keys. You'll notice that these keyboard shortcuts correspond with the buttons in the Source monitor that you learned about earlier. These keys do the following:

■ **1.** Step backward 10 frames.

■ **2.** Step forward 10 frames.

■ **3.** Step back one frame.

■ **4.** Step forward one frame.

■ **5.** Play (same as space bar).

■ **Home.** Go to the beginning of the clip.

■ **End.** Go to the end of the clip.

Figure 1.52
The number keys on the keyboard.

Learning the Media Composer keyboard shortcuts is like learning a musical instrument. The more you practice using these shortcuts, the faster your fingers will build muscle memory, enabling you to use them without looking or thinking about them. As you work, try placing your left hand so that each finger is over a different number key from 1 to 5.

4. Select the **Night Camera Inside well** clip, as shown in Figure 1.53. This shot's description is clear, but it is difficult to visually make out what is going on and who is involved. There is audio, but that isn't much help either.

5. Press **Ctrl+L** (Windows) or **Command+L** (Mac) to enlarge the frames. Now you should be able to see the selected clip better.

Figure 1.53
Larger frame in bin. Still difficult to make out contents of video.

Note: Feel free to use the Fast menu at any time to fit the frames to the window as needed.

Loading and Playing Clips as You Sort

Sorting clips from a bin in Frame view is a fast way to organize your footage. But when you need to see a larger version of the clip, it's time to open it in the Source monitor, located in the left half of the Composer window.

To open clips:

1. Double-click the **Night Camera Inside well** clip. As shown in Figure 1.54, the Composer window moves in front of the Running the Sahara bin, with the Night Camera Inside well.mov clip loaded and ready to play in the Source monitor.

2. Press the **space bar** or click the **Play** button to play back the clip. Alternatively, you use the aforementioned numeric keyboard shortcuts. Now you can make out what the shot is: one of the runners on a rope in a well, videotaping himself with his camera's night-vision setting. That means it belongs in the Runners bin.

3. Click anywhere on the **Running the Sahara** bin to move it in front of the Composer window.

4. Drag the **Night Camera Inside well** clip from the Running the Sahara bin to the **Runners** bin.

That's it. You have all the skills you need to finish sorting the clips on your own. Now let's take a moment to learn how to save your work.

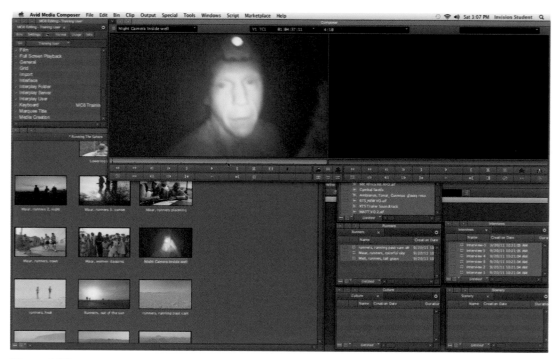

Figure 1.54
The clip opens in the Source monitor.

Saving Your Work

You should always save and back up your work as you go. In fact, keeping multiple backups on different drives is a good plan. That way, if anything were to happen to your computer or the drive that stores your projects, you will still have the project and bins that reference all your work for that job. For this book, the standard saving and auto-save features will suffice. However, on your own projects, it's a good idea to save and back up your work to a different drive. You'll learn how to back up your projects in Lesson 10, "Exporting a Program File."

So far, you haven't been directed to save your work during this project. The good news is, Media Composer has been saving your project for you automatically, and will continue to do so without interrupting your workflow. Not only does Media Composer automatically save your work, but it also waits for periods of inactivity to do it. Let's take a look at the auto-save options in the Bin Settings dialog box, and then manually save the project.

To view the auto-save settings:

1. Click the **SETTINGS** button in the Project window. The Settings pane appears.

2. Double-click the **Bin** entry in the Settings pane. The Bin Settings dialog box opens. The auto-save settings, shown in Figure 1.55, are fairly self-explanatory:

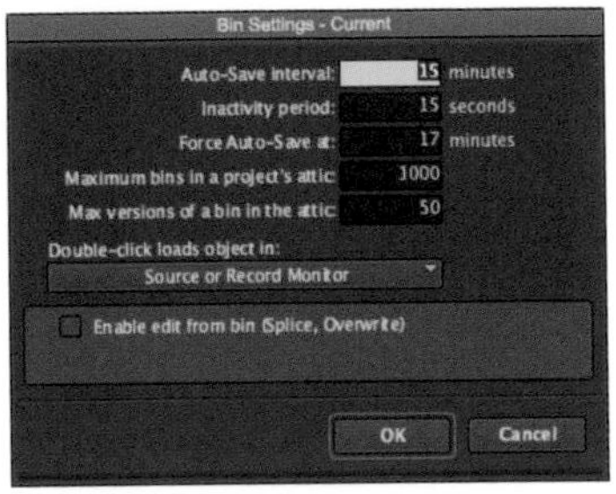

Figure 1.55
The auto-save settings in the Bin Settings dialog box.

- **Auto-Save Interval.** This setting establishes how often Media Composer automatically saves your work.

- **Inactivity period.** This setting establishes how many seconds of inactivity Media Composer waits for to perform the auto-save.

- **Force Auto-Save At.** If it is time for an auto-save, but you are working so fast and furiously that there hasn't been an adequate period of inactivity, Media Composer will auto-save anyway. (This is much nicer than it sounds; if you are working that fast and accomplishing that much, you should be grateful that your work will be saved automatically!)

- **Maximum Bins in a Project's Attic.** Auto-saved projects are stored in an Attic folder. This number (usually set to 1,000) indicates the number of bins that can be stored for that project.

- **Max Versions of a Bin in the Attic.** This is how many versions of the same bin can be stored. Each time the same bin is backed up, its name appended with a number.

3. Close the Bin Settings dialog box.

Now that you've reviewed the auto-save settings, it's time to manually save a project:

1. In the Project window, click the **Bins** button. The Bins pane opens.

2. If there have been changes made to an open bin that have not yet been saved, the bin name includes an asterisk (*). See Figure 1.56. To manually save any open bin with an asterisk, choose **File** > **Save Bin**.

3. To save all the bins at once, including the project organization in the Bins pane, first select the **Bins** pane in the Project window.

Figure 1.56
A bin with unsaved changes (*).

4. Choose **FILE > SAVE ALL**, a shown in Figure 1.57. All of your bins for this project are saved inside the project's folder.

Figure 1.57
Saving all the bins at once.

Note: Closing a project automatically saves all unsaved bins in your project.

Review/Discussion Questions

1. Which windows are showing by default in the Source/Record Editing workspace? (Check all that apply.)

    a. Composer window

    b. Timeline window

    c. Project window

    d. Media window

2. Where are clips stored in the Media Composer interface?

    a. In folders in the Project window's Bins pane

    b. In the Root level of the Project window's Bins pane

    c. In the Project window's Clips pane

    d. In bins in the Project window's Bins pane

3. What are the three different bin views?

    a. Text, Frame, Summary

    b. Text, Frame, Script

    c. Icon, Script, Frame

    d. Folder, Bin, Text

4. True or false: A clip can only be played in the Source monitor.

5. What keyboard shortcut is the space bar?

    a. Play/Stop

    b. Fast Forward

    c. Open Selected Bin

    d. Open clip in Source monitor

6. What does it mean if an open bin has an asterisk next to the bin name?

    a. The bin was imported from another project.

    b. The bin is in Frame view.

    c. The bin contains sequences and clips.

    d. The bin has unsaved changes.

7. Which of the Project window's panes allows you to change user, site, or project settings within Media Composer?

    a. Format

    b. Preferences

    c. Settings

    d. System

8. How do you change the representative frame of a clip in Frame view?

    a. Play the clip in the bin and stop at the frame you want to use.

    b. Press R to set the new representative frame.

    c. Play the clip in the Source monitor; whatever frame you pause on will automatically update the representative frame.

    d. Ctrl-click (Windows) or Command-click (Mac) the clip in the bin when you play to the frame you want to use.

Lesson 1 Keyboard Shortcuts

Key	Shortcut
1	Step backward 10 frames
2	Step forward 10 frames
3	Step back 1 frame
4	Step forward 1 frame
5	Play (same as space bar)
Home	Go to the beginning
End	Go to the end
Ctrl+9 (Windows)/Command+9 (Mac)	Select the Project window
Ctrl+W (Windows)/Command+W (Mac)	Close the Active window
Ctrl+A (Windows)/Command+A (Mac)	Select all of the contents of the bin
Ctrl+D (Windows)/Command+D (Mac)	Duplicate selected items in a bin
Ctrl+L (Windows)/Command+L (Mac)	Enlarge
Ctrl+K (Windows)/Command+K (Mac)	Reduce

Sorting Clips and Saving Projects

You now have all the skills you need to finish sorting the clips. Take a few minutes and finish the job. In this exercise, you will create a folder, move it into the Source Clips bin, then move all the *Running the Sahara* bins into that folder. Then you will save the project.

Media Used:
Running the Sahara

Duration:
20 minutes

GOALS

- Preview and sort clips into bins
- Change representative frames as needed
- Create a new bin
- Finish sorting the clips
- Close the bins
- Create and name a folder
- Move the bins into the folder
- Save the project

Sorting Clips

You now have all the skills you need to finish sorting the clips. Take a few minutes and finish the job.

To finish sorting clips:

1. Create a new bin named GRAPHICS AND STILLS.

2. Drag the AFRICA MAP clip into the new bin.

3. Close the GRAPHICS AND STILLS bin.

4. Sort the remaining clips into bins.

5. Play the clip frames in the bin or Source monitor as needed to identify the clip content.

6. When the Running the Sahara bin is empty, delete the bin.

7. Close all the open bins. A quick way to do this is to select all the bins for the Running the Sahara project in the Project window's Bins pane; then right-click a selected bin and choose CLOSE SELECTED BINS.

Organizing and Saving the Project

In this exercise, you will create a folder, move it into the Source Clips bin, then move all the Running the Sahara bins into that folder. Then you will save the project.

1. In the Project window's Bins pane, click the FAST MENU button and choose NEW FOLDER. An untitled folder appears at the root level of the Bins pane.

2. Name the new folder RUNNING THE SAHARA.

3. Select all the bins that contain clips for *Running the Sahara* and drag them to the new RUNNING THE SAHARA folder. The results are shown in Figure 1.58.

4. With the Bins pane selected, choose FILE > SAVE ALL to save the project.

5. Close the project. To do so, choose FILE > CLOSE PROJECT or simply click the Project window's × (CLOSE) button. The project closes, and the Select Project dialog box appears.

6. If you are finished using Media Composer, click the QUIT button. Otherwise, if you are continuing on to the next project, you're ready to go!

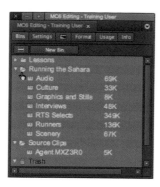

Figure 1.58
Bins moved into Running the Sahara folder.

That's it! You've organized the clips for this project. You are ready to start editing in the next project—almost.

Assembling a Basic Sequence

Assembling a rough cut is a necessary part of the editing process. Finessing and refining the edit comes later. In Lesson 1, "Exploring the Interface and Preparing to Edit," you learned how to organize your master clips and sequences in the Project window. Now it's time to mark the portions that you want to use and add them to the Timeline to build a sequence.

Media Used: Running the Sahara

Duration: 75 minutes

GOALS

- Explore the Record monitor and Timeline
- Play master clips and sequences
- Mark IN and OUT points
- Create a new sequence
- Splice and overwrite shots in a sequence
- Remove shots from a sequence

Opening the Project

For this section, you will continue working with the main project that you organized in Lesson 1: MC6 Editing.

To open the project:

1. Launch Avid Media Composer, if it isn't already open.

2. In the Select Project dialog box, click the **EXTERNAL** button.

3. Select **MC6 EDITING** from the project list.

Note: If you didn't complete all of the exercises in Lesson 1, feel free to select the project L2 RTS roughcut to catch up.

4. Make sure **USER PROFILE** is set to **TRAINING USER**, then click **OK**. The project opens with the Bins tab active in the Project window. You should see the Running the Sahara folder and all of the related bins in the Media folder.

Understanding the Record Monitor

In Lesson 1, you worked with the Source monitor in the Composer window to open and play clips. The Composer window also includes a Record monitor that lets you open and play sequences. Open sequences are displayed visually in the Record monitor and graphically in the Timeline at the same time. In this exercise, you'll use the Record monitor to load and play a teaser (short) version of the finished theatrical trailer for the documentary film *Running the Sahara*.

To load and play the teaser:

1. In the Bins tab, open the **2 FINISHED SEQUENCES** bin shown in Figure 2.1. It's in the Lessons folder.

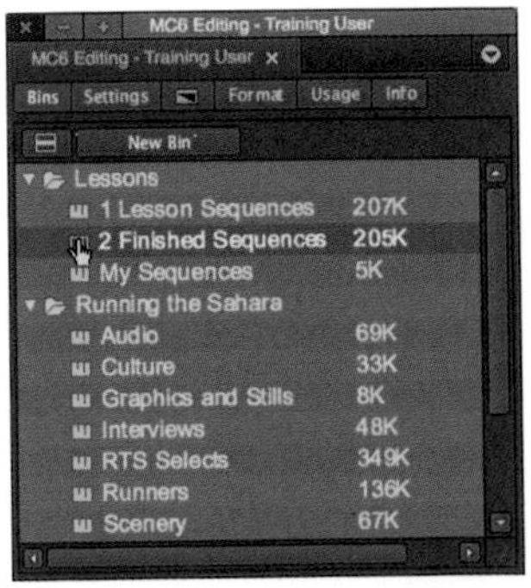

Figure 2.1
The 2 Finished Sequences bin in the Lessons folder.

Note: A bin containing an open sequence must remain open while you are actively working on that sequence. Closing the bin that has an open sequence will also close the sequence. The sequence remains intact, but you can't see it until you reopen the bin and reload the sequence.

2. Take a moment to drag the open bin out of the way so that it isn't in front of any of the editing interface windows. Consider placing it below the Scenery bin. Feel free to resize the bin as needed.

3. Loading a sequence in the Record monitor is very similar to loading master clips in the Source monitor. You can either double-click the sequence icon or drag the sequence to the Record monitor. See Figure 2.2. In the **2 Finished Sequences** bin, double-click the **Lesson 2 RTS Teaser Roughcut** sequence icon, or drag the sequence icon to the Record monitor. See Figure 2.3.

Figure 2.2
Double-click the sequence icon to load a sequence into the Record monitor.

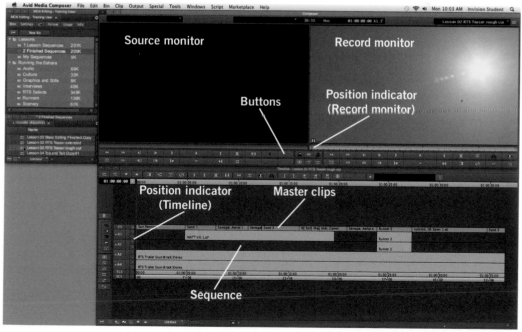

Figure 2.3
The Record monitor shows the frame where the position indicator is parked in the Timeline and vice versa. The Timeline window shows the sequence graphically.

4. In the Record monitor, drag the position indicator forward and back in the position bar. As you drag the position indicator in the Record monitor, the Timeline position indicator moves with it. That's because they are the same thing represented two different ways. Navigation in the Record monitor works the same as it does in the Source monitor, so you can try any of the keyboard shortcuts or buttons for navigation that you have learned so far.

5. In the Record monitor, press the **HOME KEY** to move the position indicator to the head of the sequence. Before you play the sequence, you might want to see how long it is.

Tip: To see the duration of a master clip or sequence, look at the Center Duration display at the top of the Composer window. The Center Duration display is multifunctional. Right now, the Center Duration display is showing the full duration of the sequence. As you go, you'll learn other ways to use this window to measure media durations.

6. Look for the Center Duration display at the top of the Composer window. Most full theatrical trailers are between two and three minutes. This sequence is 36:15 (36 seconds, 15 frames), as shown in Figure 2.4.

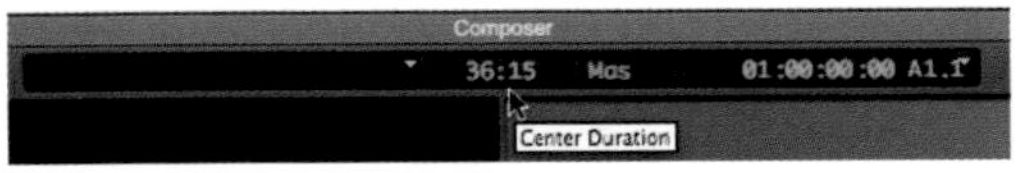

Figure 2.4
The Center Duration display shows the length (duration) of the sequence.

7. Click the **PLAY** button or press the **SPACE BAR** to play the sequence. You will edit this sequence later in the lesson.

You can see the full HD theatrical trailer at
On the Web   **www.youtube.com/watch?v=DhyVDqRQsd8&feature=related.**

Understanding the Timeline

The best way to get to know the Timeline is while you are editing your first sequence. While you have a finished sequence open, I will point out a few of the Timeline's basic elements. See Figure 2.5.

You saw the source track selectors when you were loading clips earlier. Timeline track selectors exist too: one for each track in the Timeline. These buttons assign (*patch*) the Timeline tracks where you want to edit your source tracks. The segments are organized in tracks.

Smart Tool   Timeline track selectors   Timeline ruler

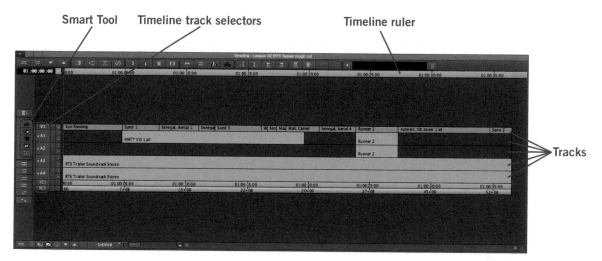

Tracks

Figure 2.5
The Timeline window with an open sequence.

To move the position indicator:

1. Click anywhere on the Timeline ruler to move the position indicator to that frame. See Figure 2.6.

Figure 2.6
Click in the Timeline ruler to move the position indicator.

Note: In the Timeline window, you can move the position indicator anytime by clicking the Timeline ruler or the Timecode track (TC1) located below the audio tracks. The Smart tool (located in the middle of the left edge of the Timeline window) determines whether clicking over the clip segments in the Timeline selects the segment or moves the position indicator. When the Smart tool is turned off, you can click anywhere in the Timeline window to move the position indicator. If it is turned on, clicking a segment selects that segment. The shortcut to toggle the Smart tool on and off is the Tab key. You'll work more with the Smart tool in Lesson 4, "Manual Timeline Editing," and Lesson 5, "Refining the Edit."

2. Drag the playhead back and forth along the Timeline ruler to manually scrub the position indicator. The View menu and scale bar are good tools to start working with right away. The View menu changes the Timeline view to other presets included with your current user settings. The scale bar zooms in and out of the Timeline. See Figure 2.7.

View menu   Scale Bar

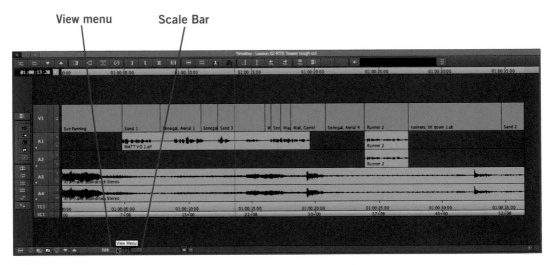

Figure 2.7
The Edit Timeline view preset.

3. At the bottom of the Timeline window, click the **View** menu (it currently is labeled "Untitled") and choose the **Edit** preset. The Edit preset is part of the Training User settings. As you can see, the video and audio tracks are enlarged and have been colored so you can see them more easily. The video segments in the Edit Timeline preset are green, and the audio segments are blue with the audio waveforms showing. You can modify audio data and clip colors in the Timeline Fast menu. You'll learn more about customizing settings in Lesson 7, "Customizing Media Composer."

4. Drag the scale bar toward the right to zoom in to the sequence at the current frame (position indicator); see Figure 2.8. Drag the scale bar to the left to zoom out; see Figure 2.9. The full left position in the scale bar fits all of the sequence segments into view.

5. Close the **2 Finished Sequences** bin. The Timeline window and Record monitor are now empty. Although clearing the Record monitor isn't necessary in normal workflow, for the those of you learning Media Composer for the first time, it will be easier to focus on marking clips in the Source monitor if the Record monitor and Timeline windows are empty.

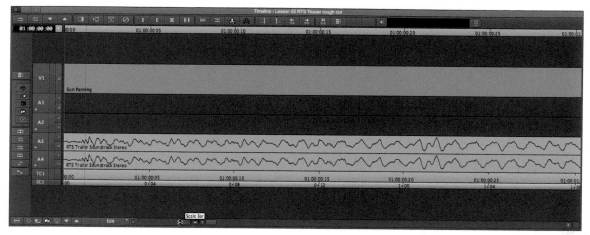

Figure 2.8
Zoomed in on the Timeline.

Figure 2.9
Zoom out to fit the Timeline window.

Note: When you are finished with a sequence, you can choose one of three ways
to clear it from the Record monitor and Timeline window:

- Open another sequence.

- Choose Clear from the Record monitor clip name menu.

- Close the bin containing the open sequence.

Creating a New Sequence

There are several options to make a new sequence for your teaser rough cut. You can create a new sequence automatically when you edit a clip into the empty Timeline, or you can create a sequence first. For this exercise, you will create and name a sequence prior to editing. When you create a new sequence, it automatically appears in the active bin.

To create a new sequence in the My Sequences bin that you made in Lesson 1:

1. In the **LESSONS** folder in the Bins pane, open the **MY SEQUENCES** bin. Move the open **SEQUENCES** bin below the Project window. Feel free to resize the bin as needed so that it fits your workspace.

2. Right-click the empty space inside the **MY SEQUENCES** bin and choose **NEW SEQUENCE** from the menu, as seen in Figure 2.10. A new, untitled sequence appears in the bin and is automatically opened in the Timeline and Record monitor. See Figure 2.11.

Figure 2.10
Choose New Sequence from the menu.

Figure 2.11
The new sequence automatically loads into the Record monitor and Timeline.

3. Name the sequence **RTS TEASER ROUGH CUT**. The new name appears in the bin, Timeline window, and Record monitor.

Note: **If you close the Timeline window, you can reopen it by pressing Ctrl+O (Windows) or Command+O (Mac) or choosing Tools > Timeline. You can also go to the Windows menu and choose Workspaces > Source/Record Editing. The workspaces method may require you to readjust your windows to your liking. Opening another sequence doesn't automatically open the Timeline window.**

Combining Bin Tabs

Now it is time to open the bins that contain the master clips you'll be marking and editing. In Lesson 1, you moved the clips to separate bins to organize them. Now that you will be using all of the editing interface windows to assemble a sequence, having a lot of open bins may not work as well—especially if your editing system has only one computer monitor. Fortunately, Media Composer has a handy feature to allow you to combine multiple open bins into one bin window. How? Open bins are not only separate windows, but they are also tabbed. For this exercise, you'll combine the tabs of three different bins so that you can easily move back and forth between tabs rather than clutter your workspace with three open bins.

To combine bin tabs:

1. In the Bins pane of the Project window, open the **RUNNING THE SAHARA** folder (if it is not already open). Next, open the **SCENERY** bin. Notice the Scenery tab in the upper-left corner of the open bin, as shown in Figure 2.12.

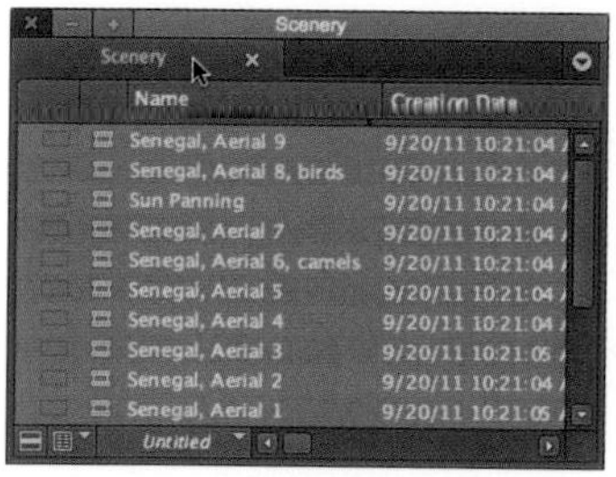

Figure 2.12
The open Scenery bin with the Scenery tab.

2. Drag the **SCENERY** tab (not the top of the tab window) to the open **MY SEQUENCES** bin and drop it next to the **MY SEQUENCES** tab, as shown in Figure 2.13. Although both bin tabs are in the same window, you can set them to different bin views. In this case, seeing the clip frame view may remind you of the footage and help you select which clips to use with the narration.

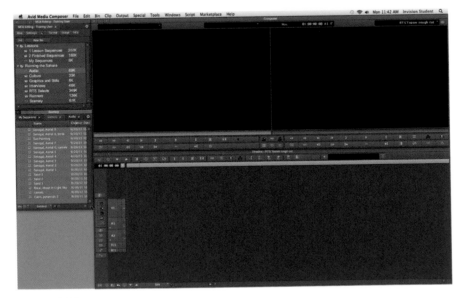

Figure 2.13

Dragging a bin tab to another open bin's tabbed area to combine bins.

Note: You can close a tab (bin) by clicking the × on the right side of the tab. You can also drag tabs left or right to change their order. Dragging a tab off the open bin window separates that bin window.

3. Open the **Audio** bin. Then drag the **Audio** bin tab next to the **Scenery** tab to combine the open bin windows.

4. Click the **Scenery** tab to make that bin active. Resize the open bin so you can see all the Scenery bin's clips listed in Text view. (See Figure 2.14.)

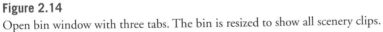

Figure 2.14

Open bin window with three tabs. The bin is resized to show all scenery clips.

That's it. Your bins are in place, the new sequence is open, and you're ready to preview and mark your clips.

Marking Edit Points

Before starting any editing job, it is crucial to know your footage. The best way to do that is to preview it in the Source monitor. From there you can determine which portion of a clip you wish to use. That process is called marking your edit points, including an *IN point* for the first frame of material and an *OUT point* for the last frame of material. You still have access to the remaining frames (*handles*) after marking a clip, and can change your IN and OUT points at any time. Media Composer has buttons and keyboard shortcuts for marking IN and OUT points. See Figure 2.15.

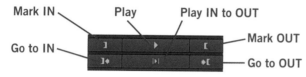

Figure 2.15
Use these Mark IN and Mark OUT buttons.

The Mark IN and Mark OUT buttons are on either side of the Play button under the Source monitor.

- Press I for mark IN.
- Press O for mark OUT.

In the next series of exercises, you will mark some of the master clips in the Scenery bin. Along the way, you'll also work with different methods of marking clips.

To mark clips:

1. Load the master clip **SAND 1** if it isn't already in your Source monitor.

2. Click the **REWIND** button or press **HOME** to move to the first frame.

3. Check the Center Duration display (13:05).

Note: The Center Duration display shows the duration for either the Source or Record monitor, whichever side of the Composer window is currently active.

4. Play the beginning of the clip. What words come to mind with this moving picture? It doesn't take more than a few seconds to make a lasting impression: vast, hot, desert, with hostile winds and blowing sand. Because a little bit goes a long way in most scenic shots, it's time to narrow the selection.

5. Move the position indicator about a third of the way into the clip, where you can really see the sand blowing heavily across the middle of the frame. Click the **MARK IN** button. An IN point appears in the position bar at the current position, and a jagged vertical overlay on the left edge of the Source monitor shows the clip's IN point. Notice that the Center Duration display shows 0:01. Interesting. When there is only one mark in the track—in this case an IN point—Center Duration displays the duration between the mark and the playhead; see Figure 2.16. This feature is incredibly useful for marking clips based on their duration.

IN point overlay   IN point   Center Duration display

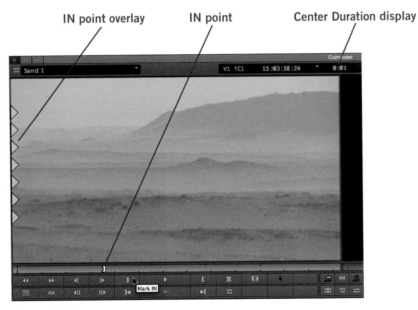

Figure 2.16
IN point in the position bar and IN point jagged overlay on the left edge of the frame.

6. Drag the position indicator toward the right until the Center Duration display shows three seconds (3:00).

7. Click the **MARK OUT** button. This time, an OUT point is in the position bar at the current position, and a jagged vertical overlay appears on the right edge of the Source monitor. These jagged overlays, shown in Figure 2.16 and Figure 2.17, are often called *teeth marks*.

OUT point   OUT point overlay   Center Duration display

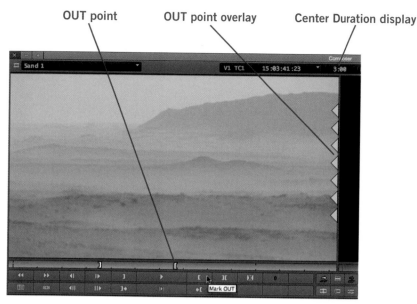

Figure 2.17
IN and OUT points in the position bar. The Center Duration display shows 3:00.

8. Click the **PLAY IN TO OUT** button or press **6** to play the clip from the IN point to the OUT point. For the next clip, you will use a number to move the playhead a specific duration.

9. Load the master clip **SAND 2** and play the first part of the clip to get a feel for the footage. More sand. But this time, the camera is moving over the sand, rather than just the sand blowing past the camera. Both shots have merits and support the narration.

10. Move the position indicator to the middle of the clip and press **I** to add an IN point. It doesn't need to be an exact frame.

11. If you have a numeric keypad on your keyboard, type **+300**. If you don't have a numeric keypad on your keyboard, press the **CTRL** (**CONTROL**) key twice; the same overlay will appear in the Source monitor. Then, using the number keys at the top of your keyboard, type **+300**. Media Composer automatically adds a colon between the seconds and frames; see Figure 2.18.

12. Press **ENTER** (Windows) or **RETURN** (Mac). (From this point, if you see instructions to "press Enter/Return," that means to press whichever is appropriate for your computer platform.)

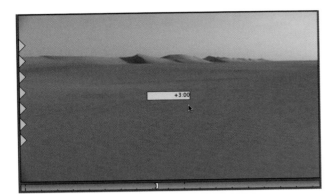

Figure 2.18
Numeric entry overlay over
the Source monitor.

13. Click the **MARK OUT** button or press **O**. Play the clip from IN to OUT. The marked section is okay, but what if the producer asks you to add a second to the tail of the clip? You'll need to change your OUT point.

Note: Typing timecode values is similar to entering cooking time on a microwave oven. The value grows by the number of digits that you type, always building from the right. You don't have to type a full timecode number with hours:minutes:seconds:frames (00:00:03:00) except when you are moving to a specific frame. Also, when you're typing timecode numbers in Media Composer, typing a period (.) automatically enters two zeros. This is a huge time saver when you're typing a lot of timecode numbers. For example, you can simply type 3. and press Enter/Return instead of typing 300.

14. If your position indicator is not already on the OUT point, click the **GO TO OUT** button. Then type **+100** and press **ENTER/RETURN**. The position indicator moves one second forward. Press **O** to set a new OUT point.

Changing Edit Marks

You can change edit marks by re-marking, dragging, or clearing. The easiest way to change marks is to simply move the position indicator and set new marks. To drag an edit point, hold down Ctrl (Windows) or Command (Mac) while dragging. Keyboard shortcuts for clearing marks are the D, F, G keys.

Key	Shortcut
D	Clears the IN point.
F	Clears the OUT point.
G	Clears both the IN and OUT points.

15. Play the clip from IN to OUT. Can you see the difference? In this case, the extra second adds more visual impact.

Finding an Audio Edit Cue

Because your sequence will be based on narration, the narration should be the first clip edited to the sequence to be used as a guide. Let's go ahead and load and mark the audio master clip with the narrator Matt Damon's voice. (He was also the documentary's executive producer.) The difference between audio master clips and video master clips is that you can't see a visual representation of audio (waveforms) in the Source monitor. If you need to see the audio waveforms to mark your audio, you can show it in the Timeline.

To see audio waveforms for a master clip in the Source monitor:

1. Click the **AUDIO** bin tab to make it active. Load the master clip **MATT VO 1**. The Source monitor looks empty; see Figure 2.19. However, the clip name and Center Duration display indicate something has been loaded. To see the audio clip in the Timeline, you can click the Toggle Source/Record in Timeline button located in the lower-left corner of the Timeline; see Figure 2.20. The button's icon resembles the Composer window over the Timeline window.

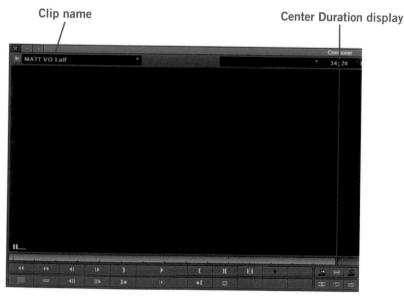

Figure 2.19
Audio master clip open in Source Monitor

Toggle Source/Record in Timeline button

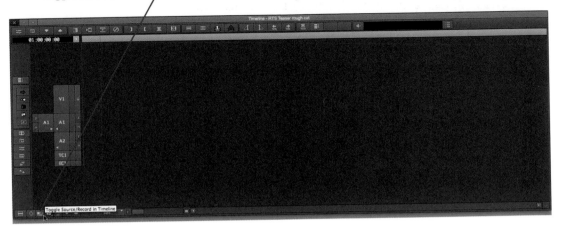

Figure 2.20
Toggle Source/Record in Timeline button turned off. Source audio does not show in Timeline.

2. Click the TOGGLE SOURCE/RECORD IN TIMELINE button. Both the button and the position indicator turn bright green to indicate the Source monitor is showing in the Timeline. The Matt VO 1 master clip segment is visible in the Timeline window. See Figure 2.21. Even though the clip is showing in the Timeline window, the timecode information, Center Duration display, and edit marks are displayed in the Composer window, just as they would be for any clip in the Source monitor.

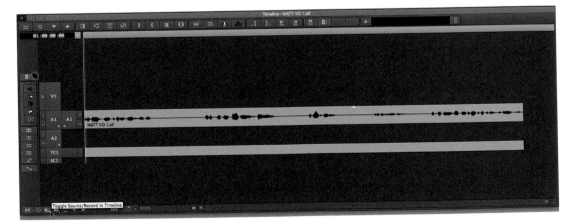

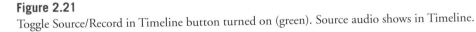

Figure 2.21
Toggle Source/Record in Timeline button turned on (green). Source audio shows in Timeline.

3. You'll use the entire clip, so rather than set separate IN and OUT points, you can simply mark the whole clip. Press **T** to mark the clip. IN and OUT points appear at the head and tail of the position bar in the Source monitor. See Figure 2.22.

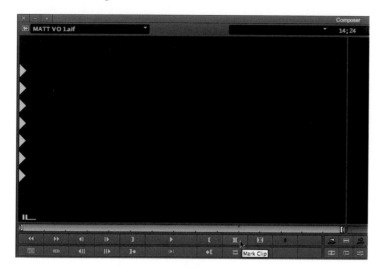

Figure 2.22
Marked audio clip
in Source monitor.

4. Click the **Toggle Source/Record in Timeline** button. The Timeline window toggles back to showing the Record monitor instead of the Source monitor. This is the first clip that you edit into your new sequence.

Performing Basic Editing

The marked portion of a clip that you edit into a sequence is called a *segment*. These segments are graphically represented over time in the Timeline. The position indicator determines where in the Timeline a new clip segment is edited. As you can see in Figure 2.23, the sequence example has two equal-length segments. The blue position indicator is currently at the edit point between the two clips. This edit point where the segments touch consists of the tail frame of the outgoing (first) clip and the head frame of the incoming (second) clip. The default setting for the position indicator is to snap to the first frame of a clip.

Splice-in and *overwrite* are the two methods for editing footage into a sequence. Splice-in edits always extend the duration of the active tracks when new material is added. Overwrites can also add material at the end of a sequence, or write over material already in the sequence. See Figure 2.24 for a comparison. These functions are similar to the editing tools used in word processing to insert text or to overwrite selected text.

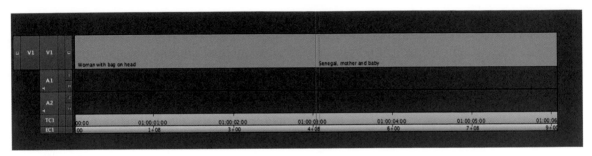

Figure 2.23
Sequence with two video segments. The position indicator is on the edit point between clips.

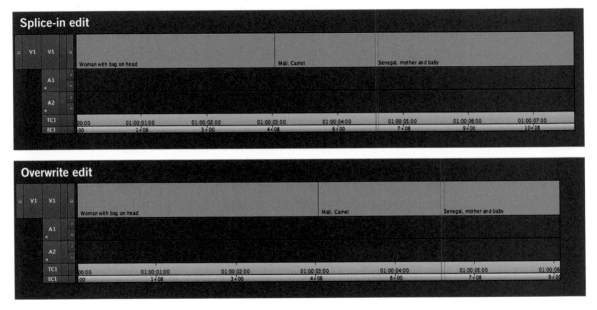

Figure 2.24
Compare a splice-in edit to an overwrite edit.

When you edit a clip into a sequence, the track selectors in the Timeline determine which source tracks are included and where they go in the sequence. The position indicator marks where a clip will be edited. See Figure 2.25.

You can edit clips into a sequence by dragging or by using edit buttons and shortcuts. This section focuses on the buttons and shortcuts. You will manually drag clips to assemble a sequence in Lesson 4.

Source track selector

Record track selectors

Figure 2.25
Track selectors all turned on (blue). A1 (source), V1, A1, and A2 (record).

Splicing Clips into the Timeline

To splice a clip into the Timeline, either click the Splice-In button or press the V key. For this exercise, you can use either method to edit the first few shots into the Timeline. The Splice-In button looks like a yellow arrow pointing toward the right over the top of two segments (as if it just spliced one segment in front of the other.) The Splice-In and Overwrite buttons are located in the middle of the Composer window's toolbar between the Source monitor and Record monitor buttons (see Figure 2.26).

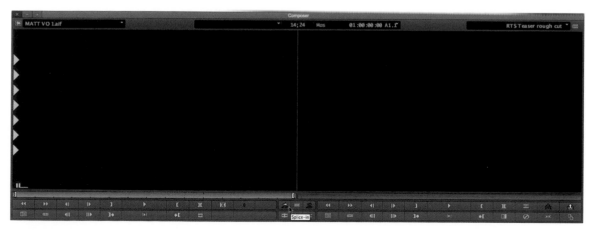

Figure 2.26
Edit buttons in Composer window.

To splice a clip into the Timeline:

1. The source track selector A1 is available and turned on, indicating that the clip in the Source monitor includes that track. (See Figure 2.27.) As long as the record track selector A1 is also on, it will be the destination track for the incoming clip. Click the **SPLICE-IN** button or press **V** to edit the **MATT VO 1** clip into the sequence.

Figure 2.27
The A1 source and A1 record track selectors are both turned on (blue).

2. Drag the Timeline scale bar to the full left position if needed to see the full Matt VO1 segment in the Timeline. After performing an edit, the position indicator automatically moves to the edge of the new clip. That way, it is on the first empty frame for the next edit, which is handy when editing shots one after another, as you can see in Figure 2.28.

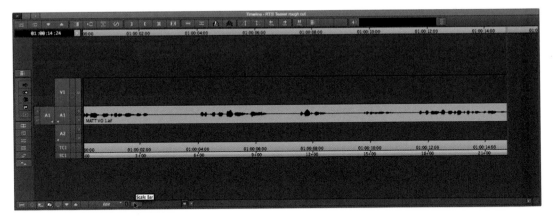

Figure 2.28
The Matt VO segment in the Timeline, with the position indicator at edge of segment. The scale bar in the full left position shows the entire sequence (in this case, one segment).

3. Play the beginning of the sequence to hear the first sentence: "It's the most unforgiving place on earth." Now it's time to find a video clip that supports that statement and edit it above the voiceover segment. No problem. You already marked several shots that would be perfect.

Note: **Feel free to adjust the scale bar in the Timeline window as needed while you edit your sequence.**

4. Click the **SCENERY** tab to see the Scenery bin's clips. Load the **SAND 1** master clip into the Source monitor. Move the playhead to the beginning of the sequence.

5. Click **SPLICE-IN** or press **V** to add the clip to the beginning of the Timeline. Oops. Since we neglected to change the track selectors, the entire clip (video and audio tracks) spliced in front of the VO clip, as shown in Figure 2.29. You can undo the edit and learn from the mistake.

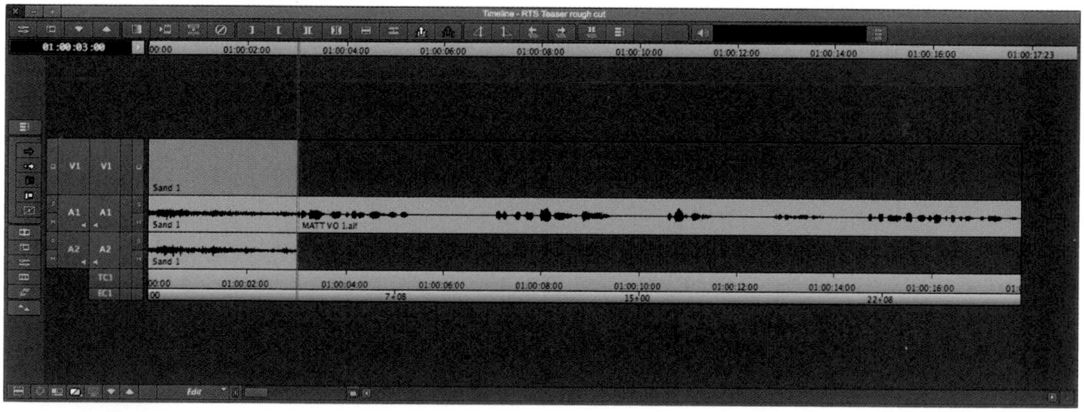

Figure 2.29
The Sand 1 clip spliced *in front* of Matt VO 1 instead of *above* on V1 only.

Tip: **It is crucial that you check your track selectors and position indicator before each edit. Very quickly, it will become second nature.**

6. Choose **EDIT** > **UNDO SPLICE-IN** or press **CTRL+Z** (Windows) or **COMMAND+Z** (Mac).

7. Click the **A1** and **A2** record track selectors to turn them off (as shown in Figure 2.30). Now material can only be edited to the active Timeline V1 track. Turned-off record track selectors remain off until you change them.

8. Click **SPLICE-IN** or press **V** to insert only the video track of the source clip. The position indicator should already be on the first empty frame after the **SAND 1** clip in the sequence. If you moved the position indicator, Ctrl-click (Windows) or Command-click (Mac) the Timeline ruler above the end of the **SAND 1** clip. The position indicator will automatically snap to the nearest edit point for the active track—in this case, the edge of the Sand 1 segment. See Figure 2.31.

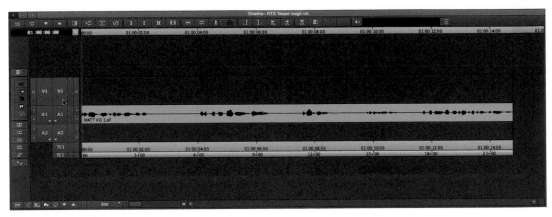

Figure 2.30
Turn on V1 track selectors only.

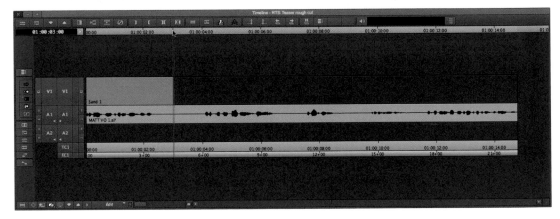

Figure 2.31
Ctrl-click/Command-click the ruler to snap the position indicator to the edit point. Here, the Sand 1 segment on the V1 track is above the voiceover segment.

Excellent! The first two segments have been edited into the Timeline. The next two segments will be aerial shots from the Scenery bin. Let's load all the aerial shots at once to make it easier to mark the ones you'll need for this sequence.

Loading Multiple Clips in the Source Monitor

You'll mark and edit some of the aerial shots next. Rather than load them one at a time, load all the aerial clips at once. Then you can load and preview them sequentially from within the Source monitor. You can load as many master clips into the Source monitor as you'd like. Whether you pre-load or load them one at a time, Media Composer keeps track of the 20 most recently loaded clips.

Position Overlays in the Record Monitor

You may see four different overlays in the Record monitor that show the first and last frame of a sequence, and the first and last frame of a clip segment. These are similar to the overlays in the Source monitor. (See Figure 2.32.)

First frame of sequence   Last frame of sequence   First frame of segment   Last frame of segment

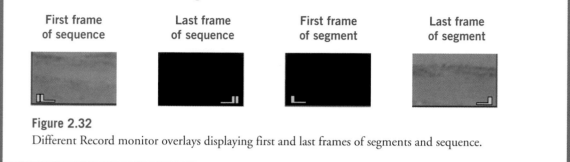

Figure 2.32
Different Record monitor overlays displaying first and last frames of segments and sequence.

To load multiple clips at once:

1. In the Scenery bin, select all the **SENEGAL, AERIAL** clips and drag them to the Source monitor. See Figure 2.33. This is easier if you have sorted the Scenery bin by the Name column. If the Senegal, Aerial clips are not sequential, double-click the **SCENERY** name header to sort by name.

Figure 2.33
Senegal, Aerial 9 (the last clip alphabetically) is loaded in the Source monitor.

2. Click the **Clip Name** menu to see the entire list of clips that have been loaded in the Source monitor. See Figure 2.34. The menu includes a variety of options. The bottom of the menu is a list of the most recent clips that were loaded into the monitor. The checked name is the one currently loaded in the monitor.

Figure 2.34
The Clip Name menu lists everything loaded in the Source monitor.

3. Using the **Clip Name** menu in the Source monitor, preview each of the **aerial** clips from 1–9. Some better represent deserts than others. It isn't that a flock of sea birds (Senegal, Aerial 8 birds) or a lush green wetland (Senegal, Aerial 7) aren't good shots; they just don't have the inhospitable Sahara desert feel you're going for in this teaser. Now that you have seen the aerial shots, let's mark three of them to edit into the sequence.

4. Load **Senegal, Aerial 1**. Mark an IN point midway through the clip, when the sun flare is less distracting. Mark the OUT point so that the marked duration is around three seconds.

5. Load **Senegal, Aerial 3**. Set IN and OUT points so that the marked duration is around three seconds.

6. Load **Senegal, Aerial 4**. Play the clip from the beginning. Notice that the clip changes speed as it plays. Mark IN and OUT points that isolate the portion of the clip that plays forward in fast motion (around 45:15:15–45:18:15).

Note: Don't worry about getting your marks perfect prior to editing. Embrace the idea of a rough cut. Refining or trimming your edits usually happen after you've completed your rough cut.

7. Load the **Senegal, Aerial 3** clip. Splice it into the sequence after the **Sand 1** clip. (See Figure 2.35.)

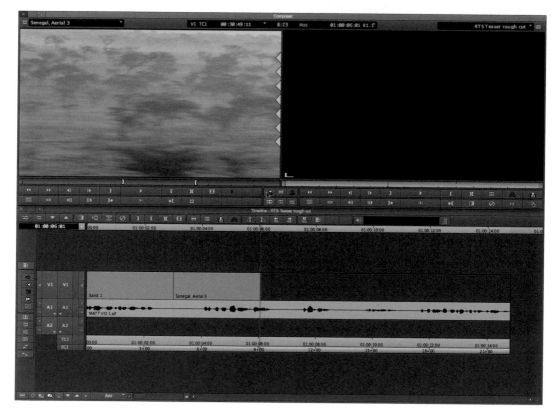

Figure 2.35
The Senegal, Aerial 3 segment spliced into the sequence after Sand 1.

8. Play the beginning of the sequence to see the first two video clips with the audio. The first clip works great. The second might be better if it came in a few seconds later. Now splice in a clip between the first two.

9. Ctrl-click (Windows) or Command-click (Mac) the Timeline ruler between the first two video segments. The position indicator snaps to the edit point between the two segments so that the current frame is the first frame of the Senegal, Aerial 1 segment, as shown in Figure 2.36. (From this point forward, when you see the instructions "Ctrl-click/Command-click," simply choose the modifier that is appropriate for your computer platform.)

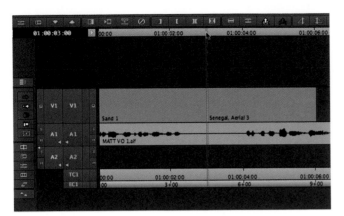

Figure 2.36
Snapping the position indicator to the edit point (first frame of Senegal Aerial 3).

10. Load **SENEGAL, AERIAL 1**. Then splice it into the sequence. Play the beginning of the sequence to see the first three video clips. This time, the video clips work much better with the voiceover. However, the voiceover starts a little abruptly. Since this is a teaser, it would be nice to have it lead in with music and another shot before the voiceover begins. No problem. That is one of the great things about the Splice-In function. You can simply splice in a video clip to move all of the other clips over, then add the music on new tracks below. First, let's mark the next few clips that you'll need. Along the way, you'll learn some more advanced marking techniques.

Marking on-the-Fly

Many editors prefer to mark by feel (visual timing) rather than duration. This method is called *marking on-the-fly*.

For this exercise, use the keyboard shortcuts I and O to mark the IN and OUT points while the clip plays:

1. Load and play the master clip **SAND 3**. The shot begins static (non-moving camera), then the camera pulls out to reveal more dunes in the foreground and background. Use the foreground sand dune as a visual guide for your marks. The marked duration will be around three and a half seconds (3:15).

2. Play the clip from the beginning. Watch the foreground sand dune.

3. Press **I** when the foreground dune passes the center of the frame, as shown in Figure 2.37.

4. Press **O** when the foreground dune is fully across the bottom of the frame, as shown in Figure 2.38. Press **5** or the **SPACE BAR** to stop playback.

Figure 2.37
The foreground dune is passing the center of the frame.

Figure 2.38
The foreground dune is all the way across the bottom of the frame.

5. Play the clip from IN to OUT. Feel free to change the edit marks to your liking. As you can see, marking on-the-fly works well for marking shots based on feel.

Tip: When you are working with non-dialogue clips, it is crucial to narrow the footage to the most interesting parts. (Unless, of course, your goal is to make something look boring and uninteresting.) Movement is a key element to look for when choosing IN and OUT points. If the camera is moving for the shot, mark your IN point after the move starts and is at speed, and mark your OUT point before the movement ends, if possible. If the shot is static, look for something moving within the frame.

Shuttling with J, K, and L

Until now, you have been previewing clips using the space bar or the Play/Stop buttons in the Composer window. Sometimes, being able to move through footage faster or slower than the normal frame rate is an invaluable way to preview and mark clips. The process of skimming though footage while watching it is referred to as *shuttling*. One of the most powerful and flexible tools in Media Composer is J-K-L shuttling. Once you know how to work J-K-L shuttling, you may never use your mouse to preview or mark clips again. See Figure 2.39.

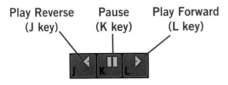

Figure 2.39
J, K, and L keys and their icons (from the Keyboard Settings window).

Rather than tell you all of the intuitive shuttling options with J-K-L, I'll have you use them to play and mark the next clip. To take advantage of these shortcut keys, place the three middle fingers of your right hand are over the J, K, and L keys. The I and O keys are conveniently located directly just above them, so you can easily mark IN and OUT points on-the-fly while you shuttle.

To shuttle a clip:

1. Load master clip **SUN PANNING** into the Source monitor. Press **HOME** to go to the head of the clip, if needed.

2. Press **L** once to play forward at normal speed. Press **L** again to play at 2× speed.

3. When the sun reaches the middle of the frame, press **K** to stop playback.

4. Press **J** to play in reverse at normal speed. When the sun reaches the upper-left corner of the frame, press **K** to stop playback.

5. Press and hold **K** and **J**. When the sun is no longer visible in the upper-left corner release both **K** and **J**. It is okay to see the sun flare, just not the sun itself. Instead of the sun moving frame left to frame right, let's find where it moves the other direction and remains in frame the entire time.

Note: Holding K in combination with either J or L plays the footage in slow motion (at about one-quarter speed). Holding K while tapping either J or L shuttles the footage one frame at a time, either forward or backward. Pressing J or L multiple times increases shuttle speed 2×, 3×, 5×, and 8×.

6. Shuttle forward at whatever speed you want until you see the sun pause in the upper right of the frame (around 13:19:11:21 in the Tracking Information menu). Press **K** to stop. Play forward in slow motion (press **J+K**) until the sun begins to move toward the left. Press **I** to mark an IN point; see Figure 2.40. Play forward (press **L**); when the sun crosses the center of the frame (around 13:19:16:15), press **O** to mark an OUT point. See Figure 2.41.

Figure 2.40
(Mark IN) Sun just beginning to move from the upper-right corner toward the left.

Figure 2.41
(Mark OUT) Sun crosses the center of the frame.

Nothing amplifies someone's mental image of a scorching hot desert more than a shot of the sun looming above in the sky. This will be the perfect shot to splice in to the beginning of your sequence.

7. Move the position indicator to the beginning of the sequence, if it is not already there. Turn on the **V1**, **A1**, and **A2** Timeline track selectors (so that all tracks will be affected by the edit).

8. Click **SPLICE-IN** or press **V**. As you can see, the Sun Panning segment moves the other video and audio segments forward in the Timeline without disrupting their alignment with one another. (See Figure 2.42.) This is a great example of using the Splice-In editing function to insert material. In the next section, you work with the Overwrite function to add music and additional clips to the sequence.

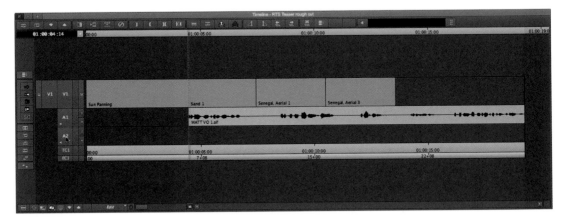

Figure 2.42
Splicing in the Sun Panning segment moves segments on all active tracks.

Now that you have added the new video clip and moved over the rest of the sequence clips, it's time to add the music.

Adding Tracks to a Sequence

The number of video and audio tracks you need depends on the project. You can have up to 24 video tracks and 24 audio tracks. For this sequence, you need to add two audio tracks for the music. You can either right-click and choose to make a new track from the Timeline menu, or use the keyboard shortcut Ctrl+U (Windows) or Command+U (Mac) to create a new audio track.

Before you create a new tracks, it's a good idea to load the media you plan to use into the Source monitor:

1. Click the **AUDIO** bin tab. Load the **RTS TRAILER SOUNDTRACK STEREO** audio clip. The clip has already been marked with IN and OUT points.

2. Press **6** to play the clip from IN to OUT. Notice the source control buttons include two audio tracks (A1 and A2). Therefore, the source clips have two separate audio tracks. You need to create two new audio tracks for the music.

3. Press **CTRL+U** twice (Windows) or press **COMMAND+U** twice (Mac) to create two new audio tracks. Two new audio tracks (A3 and A4) appear in the Timeline. The track selectors for A3 and A4 are already turned on and ready for the music segment.

4. Turn off the **V1**, **A1**, and **A2** Timeline track selectors (if they are on). The source track selectors A1 and A2 move down to A3 and A4. See Figure 2.43.

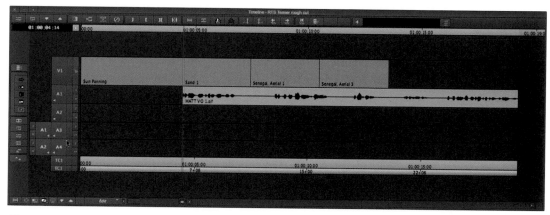

Figure 2.43
The track selectors for A3 and A4 are already turned on and ready for the music segment.

Overwriting Clips into the Timeline

Overwrite edits are great for placing clips above or below other segments in the Timeline, as well as for editing a clip into a track without altering the placement of other clips on the same track. The keyboard shortcut for Overwrite is B, which is right next to the shortcut for Splice-In (V). There is also a handy Overwrite button in the center of the Composer window, near the Splice-In button. It looks like a red arrow pointing right. (See Figure 2.44.)

Figure 2.44
The Overwrite button, in the middle of the Composer window toolbar.

In this exercise, you'll overwrite the music clip to tracks A3 and A4, and then use Overwrite to add a new clip to the Timeline while changing the duration of an existing segment at the same time.

To use Overwrite:

1. Move the position indicator to the beginning of the sequence. Make sure that the RUNNING THE SAHARA RUNNERS MUSIC clip is still loaded in the Source monitor.

2. Click the OVERWRITE button in the Composer window or press **B**. The music segment appears in tracks A3 and A4. You may only see the tail of the clip in the Timeline window after the edit.

3. Play the beginning of the sequence to hear the music with the clips and voiceover. (See Figure 2.45.)

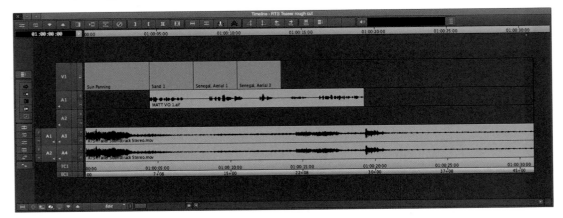

Figure 2.45
The music and Sun Panning clip add some nice drama to the beginning of the piece.

4. Play the last video clip in the Timeline and listen to the narrator. The Senegal, Aerial 3 clip works fine for the end of the narration ("over 3.5 million square miles"). However, since it is a clip of trees, and a little goes a long way, lets start the Sand 3 shot earlier because it is a more powerful image and portrays both "vast" and "The Sahara desert." Move the position indicator right before the narrator says "a vast wilderness" (around 01:00:12:00). This will be the position where a new video clip will be edited to the Timeline. Rather than splice in and split the existing clip in two, you will overwrite the new clip, covering up the unwanted portion of the existing clip.

5. Click the Timeline window if it is not already selected. Type **1200** and press **ENTER/RETURN** (or drag the position indicator in the Timecode ruler to the position in front of "a vast wilderness"). Use the Ruler Timecode display as a guide. See Figure 2.46.

6. Load the clip **SAND 3**. (You marked this clip on-the-fly earlier.)

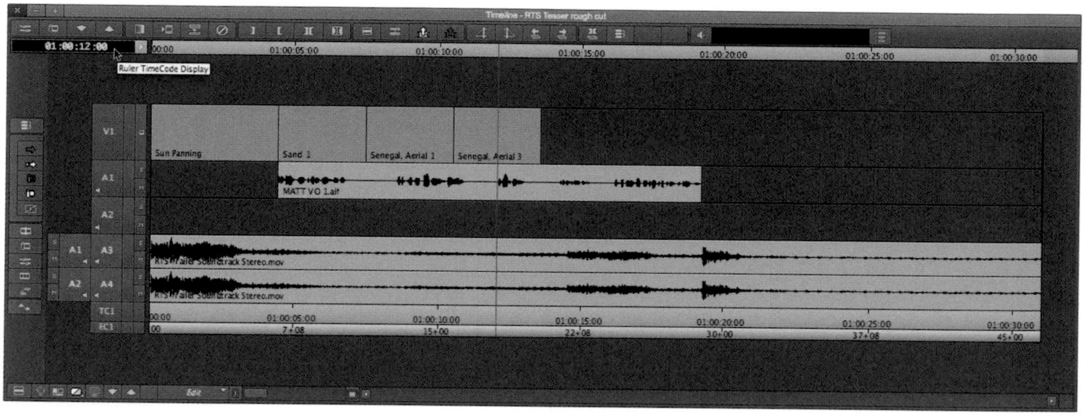

Figure 2.46
Move the position indicator to 01:00:12:00. Use the audio waveform and Timecode display as a guide.

7. Turn on the **V1** Timeline track button. Turn off the **A3** and **A4** Timeline
   track selectors.

8. Press **B** or click the **OVERWRITE** button. As shown in Figure 2.47, the Sand 3
   clip overwrites the second half of the Senegal, Aerial 3 clip in the sequence.

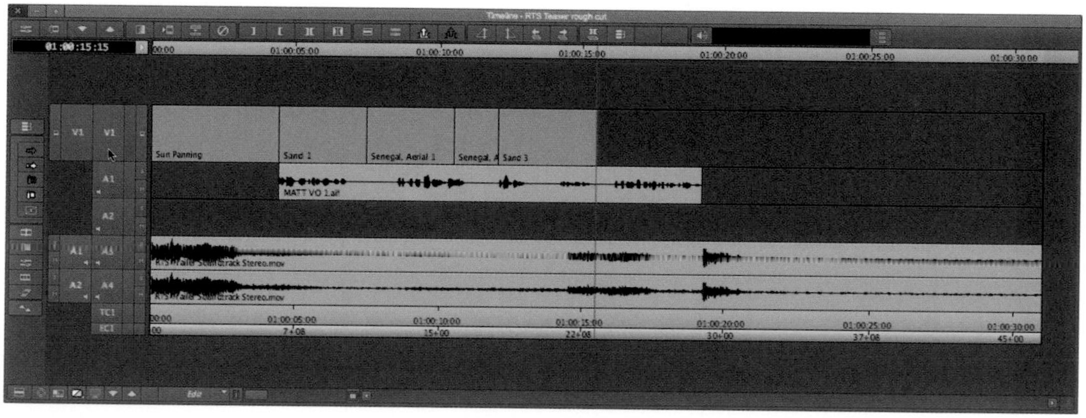

Figure 2.47
The Sand 3 clip overwrites the second half of the Senegal, Aerial 3 clip in the sequence.

9. Press the **DOWN ARROW KEY** three times to move the position indicator
   three clips earlier in the sequence. Play the last three video clips to see and
   hear how they work. The new clip works great, and really goes well with
   the fourth section of narration: "It's the Sahara desert." Remember that
   this is a rough cut, so timing doesn't have to be perfect—just close enough
   to keep going. Finessing the edits comes later.

Marking Edits in the Timeline

All edits use three points to determine which frames from the source clip will be edited and where in the Timeline they will go. Until now in this project, your edits have used an IN point, an OUT point (both marked in the Source monitor), and the position indicator in the Timeline as the three points. Sometimes, the exact placement of a shot in the Timeline is more important than the exact head or tail frame included in a shot. In that case, you can set IN and OUT points in the Timeline and use either an IN point, an OUT point, or the position indicator in the Source monitor to determine the third edit point. In the next series of edits, you mark IN and OUT points in the Timeline based on narration.

To mark edits in the Timeline:

1. Play the remaining narration (approximately 01:00:15:10–01:00:19:08). The narrator says, "with people and cultures as unpredictable as the landscape." All of the clips in the Culture bin could be used with this narration. However, you have only about four seconds. You must narrow it down to three or four clips.

2. Use **J-K-L** to shuttle the position indicator and the visual audio waveform in the Timeline as a guide to locate the audio cue "as unpredictable as the landscape."

3. Press **I** to mark an IN point at the beginning of the statement, and press **O** to mark an OUT point after the statement. See Figure 2.48.

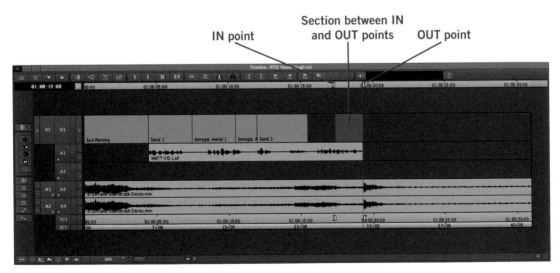

Figure 2.48
The highlighted section between the IN and OUT points shows where the next clip will be edited.

4. Open the **CULTURE** bin. Drag the **CULTURE** bin tab to the open bin tabs. Change the **CULTURE** bin to Frame view. Take a moment to resize the bin to use the empty space below the window. Press **CTRL+L** (Windows) or **COMMAND+L** (Mac) to enlarge the frames. Also use the bin's **FAST** menu to fit the frames to the window.

Note: If your open bin window contains more tabs than can be shown at once, you'll see two arrows pointing left and right on the far right side of the tabbed area. You can click these arrows to scroll left or right through the tabs.

5. Load the clip **MALI, CAMEL**. (See Figure 2.49.) Press **G** to clear the existing marks, and then play the clip. This clip demonstrates both people (hunkered down to avoid the blowing sand) and unpredictable landscape. The camel steals this shot as he dances back and forth to maintain his footing, then looks around.

Figure 2.49
Sequence with Mali, Camel edited into the Timeline.

6. Shuttle through the clip until the camel finishes moving his legs (approximately 08:56:05:11). The position indicator acts as the IN point for your edit. Now that all three edit points are marked (two in the Timeline and one in the Source monitor), you can perform an overwrite edit.

7. Press **B** to overwrite the clip from the Source monitor to the marked section of the sequence.

8. Play the sequence from the beginning to see how it is coming along. As far as rough cuts go, the sequence is working really well. Let's add a few more culture shots to complete the section of voiceover. Along the way, you can try some handy keyboard shortcuts.

9. Load the **SENEGAL, MAN WITH TREE** clip. Press **J-K-L** to shuttle through the clip from the beginning. Mark IN after you see a pair of legs walk past the foreground and the camera to shifts slightly.

10. Press **Esc** to toggle between the Source monitor and the Record monitor in the Composer window.

11. Press **J-K-L** to shuttle the position indicator over the empty gap (called *filler* in Media Composer) in the video track between the **SAND 3** and **MALI, CAMEL** segments.

12. Press **T** to mark the segment (in this case, the filler between clips) in the Timeline. Now that you marked three edit points, you can make your overwrite.

13. Press **B** or click the **OVERWRITE** button. (See Figure 2.50.) Play the end of the section in the Timeline to see how the new clip works with the voiceover. What did you think this time? The new shot is too long, and not as interesting as many other clips in the Culture bin. Perhaps adding another shot would make it better.

14. Drag the scale bar in the Timeline toward the right until you can read the full names of the clips in this section of the sequence.

15. In the Timeline, mark an IN point over the word **PEOPLE** (approximately 01:00:16:08). Mark an OUT point before the word **CULTURES** (approximately 1:00:16:26).

16. Load the clip **SENEGAL, MOTHER AND BABY**. Mark an IN point in the middle of the clip, when the baby looks at the camera (approximately 17:07:34:06). See Figure 2.51.

17. Overwrite the clip. There are now three clip segments instead of one long one. The first and third clips are still Senegal, Man with Tree. The middle clip segment is Senegal, Mother and Baby.

Figure 2.50
Overwriting Senegal, Man with Tree into the sequence.

Figure 2.51
Mark IN as shown when the baby looks at the camera.

18. Drag the scale bar in the Timeline toward the right until you can read the full names of the clips in this section of the sequence.

19. Move the position indicator over the second Senegal, Man with Tree segment. Press **T** to mark the clip. Up until now you have marked an IN point or used the position indicator in the Source monitor to determine the source IN point for the three-point overwrite edit.

Tip: Sometimes the end of an action in the frame is more important than the beginning. When that is the case, mark an OUT point, rather than an IN point, to use as the third edit point.

20. Load the Maur, Man with Stick clip. Mark an OUT point right after the man turns his back and you see his shepherd stick (12:04:13:28). See Figure 2.52.

21. Overwrite the clip.

22. Drag the scale bar to the far left to see the full sequence. Play the sequence.

Figure 2.52
Mark OUT when the man turns and you see the stick.

This first section of your rough cut is working pretty well. The music and narration have set up the Sahara portion of the documentary. Now it's time to see the endurance runners, who are the subject of the documentary.

Editing Audio and Video

Many of the scenery clips that you have worked with include both audio and video, even though you used only the video in the sequence. Clips showing people talking, often referred to as *talking head shots*, need both video and audio tracks.

In this exercise, you'll add an interview clip to the sequence:

Tip: When you are editing clips with both video and audio tracks, set the Timeline track selectors accordingly. You want to make sure not only that all tracks are included, but also that you don't accidentally overwrite existing audio in the Timeline.

1. Open the **INTERVIEWS** bin. Load the clip **RUNNER 2**. Play the clip from IN to OUT. Runner 2 says, "Actually, it's never been done. No one has ever run that far in that period." This is a good lead to the narrator's next section explaining the quest.

2. In the Timeline, mark an IN point at the end of the narration segment (approximately 01:00:19:08).

3. Check the Timeline track selectors. (They are currently set for a video-only edit.) Turn on the **A1** and **A2** Timeline track selectors. For this interview sound bite, you will also use the entire **RUNNER 2** clip. Instead of moving the position indicator and marking an IN point, you can simply mark the clip. To mark a full clip, press **T** in the Source monitor or click the **MARK CLIP** button; see Figure 2.53.

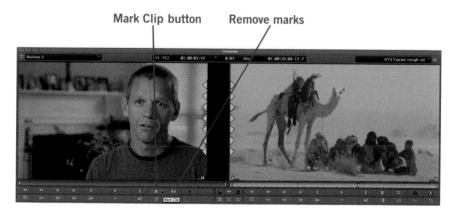

Figure 2.53
Mark a full clip with the button on the left.

4. Make sure the Source monitor is active, then press **T** to mark IN and OUT points on the head and tail frames. Overwrite the clip to the Timeline after the end of the narration. (See Figure 2.54.)

Figure 2.54
Runner 2 clip with both video and audio tracks in sequence.

5. Play the end of the sequence. You may notice a few things that you would like to tweak. The music levels may be too loud for the interview shot, for instance. That is a typical issue in a rough cut, and you can fix it in subsequent lessons. For now, review what you've learned so far so you can finish the rough cut.

Note: For the remaining shots, it is important to keep the V1, A1, and A2 Timeline track selectors turned on. That way, video and audio for the runner clips will stay intact. If you splice clips in the video tracks, the runner video is pushed away from its audio and gets out of sync.

6. Close the **INTERVIEWS** bin. Click the **SCENERY** tab to make it active. Load the **SAND 2** master clip. Use the **UP ARROW** and **DOWN ARROW KEYS** to move the position indicator in front of the **RUNNER 2** segments in the Timeline. Press **V** or click the **SPLICE-IN** button. See Figure 2.55.

7. Load the **SENEGAL, AERIAL 4** clip. Splice it in front of the **SAND 2** clip.

8. Play the sequence.

Figure 2.55
Senegal, Aerial 4, Sand 2, and Runner 2 segments in the sequence.

It's coming along well. However, in the next section you will remove some of the scenery between the narration and the interview clip, and use a different clip instead of the man with the tree for the culture section.

Extracting and Lifting Segments from the Timeline

After you edit clips to the Timeline, they are referred to as *segments*. You can remove these segments much the same way that you added them. In fact, Media Composer color codes the tool icons to make it easier to identify the similar functions. (See Figure 2.56 and Figure 2.57.) When you extract a shot, the entire shot is removed and the remaining clips on those tracks in the Timeline move to the left. This rippling effect shortens the duration of the active tracks. Both Splice-In and Extract affect the clips to the right of an edit on the active tracks.

 Splice-In   Extract   Overwrite   Lift

Figure 2.56
Yellow Splice-In and Extract buttons.

Figure 2.57
Red Overwrite and Lift buttons.

Lifting a segment removes the segment from the active tracks and leaves a gap. The remaining segments in the sequence are unaffected. Lift is similar to Overwrite in that this type of edit adds material without affecting the clips beyond the edit.

In this section you'll use both Lift and Extract to remove unwanted clips in the sequence. The Lift and Extract buttons are at the top of the Timeline window.

To use Lift and Extract to remove unwanted clips:

1. Move the position indicator over the **Senegal, Man with Tree** segment in the Timeline. (It is the segment after Sand 3.)

2. Click the **Mark Clip** button at the top of the Timeline or press **T** to mark the clip. Why are so many clips included within the IN and OUT points in the Timeline? Take a look at the Timeline track selectors. Just like adding material to the Timeline, track selectors count when marking segments and removing materials. The Mark Clip function looks at all the segments on active tracks under the position indicator, and adds marks at the first common edit on all tracks. In this case, since V1, A1, and A2 are all turned on, the audio segments on A1, A2 are also marked. (See Figure 2.58.)

3. Press **G** to remove the Timeline marks. Click any empty space above the segments in the Timeline to de-select them. Turn off the **A1** and **A2** Timeline track selectors. Click the **Mark Clip** button or press **T**. This time, only the video segment under the position indicator is marked.

Figure 2.58
Audio track selectors are on, so everything including the filler on A2 is selected.

4. Click the red **LIFT** button or press **Z** to lift the selected clip. You can add a shot there at the end of this section. Next, you extract the **SAND 2** segment from the sequence. You may use it later in the sequence, but for now it is one shot too many before the runner's sound bite. See Figure 2.59.

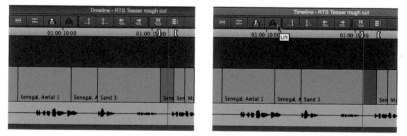

Figure 2.59
Senegal Man at Tree is lifted from sequence. This leaves a gap with filler in its place.

5. Move the position indicator over the **SAND 2** segment. Press **T** to mark the segment. After marking the segment, turn on the **A1** and **A2** track selectors. The filler on tracks A1 and A2 is now also selected below the Sand 2 segment. (See Figure 2.60.)

6. Click the **EXTRACT** button or press **X**. The Sand 2 clip and the filler below it on tracks A1 and A2 were extracted, and the Runner 2 clip ripples left to where the Sand 2 segment was earlier. See Figure 2.61. If you forgot to turn on the A1 and A2 track selectors before extracting the segment, you accidentally moved the Runner 2 video out of sync from the Runner 2 audio. Undo the extract edit, mark the **SAND 2** segment, then turn on the **A1** and **A2** track selectors to select the filler below the selected video clip. Finally, press **X** again.

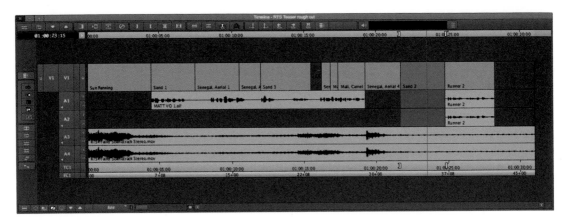

Figure 2.60
The Sand 2 clip plus the filler below on A1 and A2 selected.

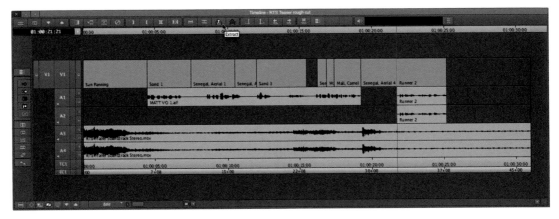

Figure 2.61
The Sand 2 segment was extracted without leaving a gap in the sequence.

Keep in mind, you can lift or extract any marked segment, as well as anything between IN and OUT points in the Timeline.

Now add a video segment in the gap over the culture section and a shot at the end:

1. From the Culture bin, load the clip **WOMAN WITH BAG ON HEAD**. Mark an IN point in the middle of the clip where the woman is smiling.

2. Turn off the **A1** and **A2** track selectors. Move the position indicator over the gap (filler) in the video track (approximately 01:00:15:26). Mark the gap. Overwrite the clip.

3. Load the **Sand 2** clip from the **Scenery** bin or the **Clip Name** menu in the Source monitor. Overwrite or splice it after the **Runner 2** segment in the Timeline. (See Figure 2.62.)

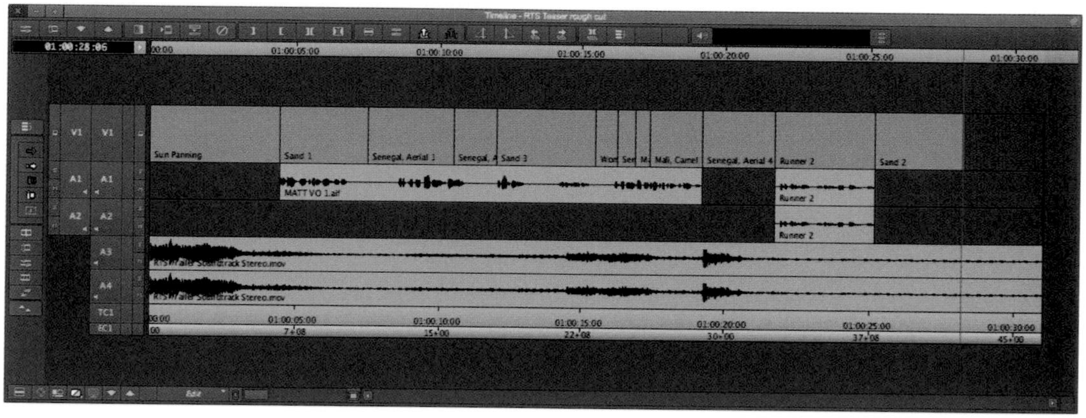

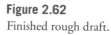

Figure 2.62
Finished rough draft.

4. Play the finished draft of your rough cut.

5. Click the **Bins** tab in the Project window.

6. Choose **File > Save All** to save your work.

Congratulations. You marked and edited a rough cut from scratch. In Lesson 5, you will read how to adjust the edit marks to fine-tune the timing and length of the segments within the sequence.

Review/Discussion Questions

1. What two monitors are included in the Composer window?

    a. Record monitor and Timeline monitor

    b. Project monitor and Source monitor

    c. Source monitor and Record monitor

    d. Timeline monitor and Source monitor

2. True or false: The G and T keys are the keyboard shortcuts used to mark IN and OUT points on a clip.

3. Which button is used to perform an overwrite edit?

    a.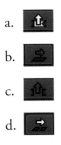

    b.

    c.

    d.

4. What is the maximum number of clips listed in the Clip Name menu?

5. True or false: The Toggle Source/Record in Timeline button needs to be on to see a source audio clip in the Timeline.

6. Why is the position indicator green in the image at the top of the next page?

    a. The Timeline is currently displaying the Source monitor clip.

    b. The position indicator is playing a clip.

    c. The position indicator is paused.

    d. Because of user settings.

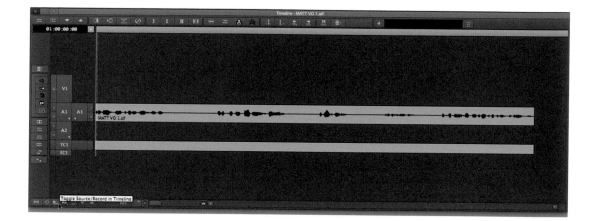

7. Which type of edit was performed to sequence A, shown in the first image, to make it look like sequence B, shown in the second image?

8. Which buttons are the Splice-In and Extract buttons?

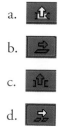

a.

b.

c.

d.

Lesson 2 Keyboard Shortcuts

Key	Shortcut
I	Mark IN
O	Mark OUT
T	Marks a clip
D	Clears the IN point
F	Clears the OUT point
G	Clears both IN and OUT points
6	Plays from IN point to OUT point
Esc	Toggles between Source and Record monitors
J	Plays backward
K	Pause/Stop
L	Plays forward
J+K	Plays one-quarter speed backward
L+K	Plays one-quarter speed forward
V	Splice-In edit
B	Overwrite edit
X	Extract edit
Z	Lift edit
Ctrl+O (Windows)/Command+O (Mac)	Opens the Timeline window
Ctrl+Z (Windows)/Command+Z (Mac)	Undo
Ctrl+U (Windows)/Command+U (Mac)	Creates a new mono audio track

Improving the Teaser

In this exercise, you will create an extended version of the teaser. You'll also build an interview sequence that includes six different interview shots of the same person.

Media Used:
Running the Sahara

Duration:
40 minutes

GOALS

- Duplicate and rename your sequence
- Add additional VO and music to extend the sequence
- Mark and edit video clips that go with the extended narration
- Save the finished rough draft

Creating an Extended Version of the Teaser

In this exercise, you will use the skills that you have already learned to create and finish an extended version of the teaser.

1. In the MY SEQUENCES bin, right-click the RTS TEASER ROUGH CUT sequence and choose DUPLICATE from the menu that appears. Name the duplicated sequence RTS TEASER ROUGH CUT EXTENDED. Open the new sequence.

2. Open the AUDIO bin (click the Audio bin tab) and load the MATT VO 2 clip into the Source monitor.

3. Click the TOGGLE SOURCE/RECORD IN TIMELINE button (the third button from the left in the bottom-left corner of the Timeline window) to see the narration waveforms in the Timeline window. Play the narration. Set an IN point at the beginning of the clip and an OUT point right after the narrator says, "an unprecedented personal challenge" (near the middle of the clip).

4. Click the TOGGLE SOURCE/RECORD IN TIMELINE button again to see the sequence in the Timeline. In the Timeline, move the position indicator to the middle of the SAND 2 segment (the last video clip in the sequence).

5. Make sure the track selectors are correct for editing A1 source audio to the A1 Timeline track. (Turn off all other tracks.)

6. Overwrite the entire MATT VO 2 AUDIO clip.

7. Load the RTS TRAILER SOUNDTRACK STEREO clip into the Source monitor.

8. Clear the OUT point and use the Center Duration display to set a new OUT point around 50:01. (Fifty seconds and one frame.) Due to the frame rate of the footage, you won't be able to make it exactly one minute.

9. Drag the A1 and A2 audio track selectors down to A3 and A4. Make sure the source A1 and A2 and Timeline A3 and A4 track selectors are turned on.

10. Move the position indicator to the beginning of the sequence and overwrite the extended music to tracks A3 and A4. The sequence is now extended to a 50-second version. All you need to do is add the video.

11. Turn off the track selectors for the A3 and A4 tracks.

12. Open the RUNNERS bin. Load the RUNNERS TILT DOWN 1 ALT clip. This clip has already been marked. Turn on the V1 track selector and splice in the clip before the SAND 2 clip. The video clips should work well with the first part of the Matt VO 2 segment.

13. Load the MATT VO 2 segment again. Your challenge for the remaining voiceover clip is to break up the sentences to add natural-sounding pauses and give you room to add dramatic video of the runners. Focus your attention on how the narration sounds. Mark each section of the narration as listed below and overwrite it to the Timeline on A1. You get to determine how much space to leave between statements. When you like the length of the pause between two segments, add the next segment. If you don't like the amount of pause that you added, undo the edit and try again in a different location until you are satisfied.

Note: If you would like to skip this part of the exercise, open the Finished Sequences bin, and Option-drag (Mac) or Alt-drag (Windows) a copy of the RTS Extended VO and Music sequence to the My Sequences bin. That version of the sequence already has the extended music and VO in place.

14. To make this process easier, toggle on the TOGGLE SOURCE/RECORD IN TIMELINE button so you can see the waveform as you set marks. It is also useful to clear marks as you go so that you can focus on the new marks for each section of the VO 2. Mark and edit the MATT VO2 sequence as follows:

- "Three ultra runners" (Overwrite this after the Sand 2 segment.)
- "Good friends"
- "Test physical strength, and mental toughness"
- "Running across the entire Sahara desert"

15. Find clips in the RUNNERS bin that go with the music and narration and edit them to the V1 track. Make sure that only the V1 track selector is on as you go.

16. When you are finished, select the BINS tab in the Project window and choose FILE > SAVE ALL. If you would like to see a version of the finished extended trailer, open the FINISHED SEQUENCES bin, and load the sequence RTS EXTENDED TRAILER FINISHED.

Building an Interview Sequence

In this exercise, you'll build an interview sequence that includes six different interview shots of the same person. You will first load them all into the Source monitor, then preview them and edit them into the Timeline in order. These shots all consist of video and audio tracks, so you'll also need to make sure that the V1, A1, and A2 track selectors are turned on. First, you'll need to make a new sequence.

1. In the **My Sequences** bin, create a new sequence and name it **RTS Interviews**. Open the new sequence.

2. Open the **Interviews** bin. Select all the clips with **Interview** in the name and drag them to the Source monitor.

3. Edit the interview clips in the following order into the Timeline. Do not worry about setting marks at this time. You are simply building a rough cut. You will fix this sequence and add supporting B-roll video clips in Lesson 5. For now, just edit these clips in this order:

   - Interview 1
   - Interview
   - Interview 2
   - Interview 3
   - Interview 5
   - Interview 4
   - Interview-5

4. Play the sequence to hear the interviews in order. You'll probably notice that the content in Interview 4 is also in Interview-5. Let's extract **Interview 4** from the sequence.

5. Move the position indicator over **Interview 4** and mark the clip. To extract the clip, click the **Extract** button or press **X**.

6. Save the finished sequence.

Bonus Exercise

If you have extra time, and want to try an experiment prior to learning Media Composer's powerful trimming tools, here is a challenging exercise for you to try. Duplicate your RTS Interviews sequence. Extract unwanted portions of the interview such as cutoff sentences by setting IN and OUT points in the sequence and using the Extract feature. You may want to zoom in (drag the scale bar) for a closer view of the waveform as you work. Good luck.

Ingesting File-Based Media

In Lesson 1, "Exploring the Interface and Preparing to Edit," and Lesson 2, "Assembling a Basic Sequence," you organized, marked, and edited master clips and built a sequence in a lesson that someone else created. In this lesson, you create a new project and look at importing or linking files into a project through Avid Media Access (AMA). First, you import two still images to the RTS project. Then you edit them into a new sequence. Next, you follow a real-world workflow to create a new project and add media by importing audio, opening a bin from another project, and linking through AMA. Finally, you add comments to the master clips in preparation for editing in Lesson 4, "Manual Timeline Editing."

Media Used: First Tracks Productions
Running the Sahara

Duration: 45 minutes

GOALS

- Import still images
- Create a new project
- Import audio
- Open a bin from another project
- Link QuickTime files
- Consolidate media
- Add comments in Script view

Opening the Project

For the first part of this project, you continue working with the main course project that you organized in Lesson 1 and edited a rough cut teaser in Lesson 2: MC6 Editing.

To open the project:

1. Launch Avid Media Composer, if it isn't already open.

2. In the Select Project dialog box, click the **EXTERNAL** button.

3. Select **MC6 EDITING** from the project list.

4. Make sure **USER PROFILE** is set to **TRAINING USER**, then click **OK**. The project opens with the Bins tab active in the Project window and the Composer window open. Feel free to close the Timeline window. You do not need the Timeline window for this exercise.

Understanding Importing and AMA Linking

Media Composer offers three options for bringing media into a project:

■ Capturing from tape

■ Importing

■ Linking with Avid Media Access (AMA)

For this lesson, you focus on importing and AMA linking.

 You can read about capturing footage from tape in Appendix B, "Capturing Tape-Based Media."

Importing a file into Media Composer converts the file to MXF format and places it in the Avid Media Files folder (in the MXF subfolder) on your selected media drive. AMA linking, on the other hand, gives you instant access.

Identifying Image Size

Whether you are importing video or still images into Media Composer, it is important to know the details about that media prior to importing it. Otherwise, you might inadvertently distort the image during the import process. To make sure you do it right the first time, check the frame size of the project and the frame size of the image you're going to import.

Previewing still images on your computer and looking at image properties is easy. If you're using Windows, open the image with Windows Photo Viewer. Then, when the photo opens, choose File > Properties or press Alt+Enter. If you're using a Macintosh, open the image with Preview and, when the photo opens, press Command+I. See Figure 3.1 and Figure 3.2. Once you ID the image size, you can quit the program.

Figure 3.1
The Image Properties window in Windows Photo Viewer.

Figure 3.2
The General Information pane in the Macintosh Preview window.

Tip: To save time, consider sorting your still images into subfolders by image size. For example, name one subfolder 1,338×1080 and another 720×486.

Looking at the Format Pane Before Importing

When importing image files (graphics, stills, or movies), make sure you adjust the image size in the Import window accordingly. To do that, you first need to know the current project's raster dimensions. You can find that information in the Format pane of the Project window.

To view the raster dimensions:

1. Click the **FORMAT** button at the top of the Project window. The Format pane has information about the project, including project type, aspect ratio, color space, stereoscopic format, and raster dimensions. As you can see in Figure 3.3, the raster dimension for the current project is 720×486. Compare this to the dimensions of the still images you want to import to ensure that you choose the right settings.

Figure 3.3
Format pane.

2. Click the **BINS** button to return the Project window to the Bins pane.

Importing Still Images

You've already worked with the video and audio master clips for the Running the Sahara project. The only things missing are the still images that may be used for the titles or transitions. To import a file, you first need to open a bin where the file will be placed. In this case, you open the Graphics and Stills bin.

To import a file:

1. In the Bins tab, open the **GRAPHICS AND STILLS** bin. Move the bin out of the way as needed. (See Figure 3.4.) For this exercise, you will import directly into the bin.

Figure 3.4
Open the Graphics and Stills bin.

To import a file, you can do one of the following:

- Choose File > Import.
- Right-click in the open bin and choose Import from the menu.

3. Right-click in the **GRAPHICS AND STILLS** bin and choose **IMPORT**.

4. In the Select Files to Import dialog box, click **DESKTOP**, and open the **MC6 EDITING BOOK FILES > ADDITIONAL PROJECT MEDIA** folder, as shown in Figure 3.5.

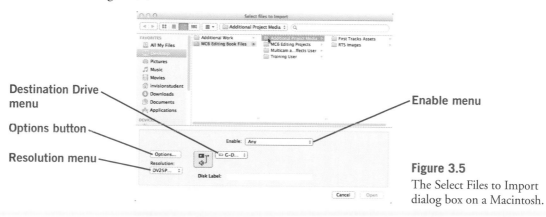

Destination Drive menu

Options button

Resolution menu

Enable menu

Figure 3.5
The Select Files to Import dialog box on a Macintosh.

5. Click the **Files of Type** menu (Windows). On a Mac, click the **Enable** menu. Then select an import file type. This feature is most useful to narrow down the list of files if you are working with a large number of files that are different types. Although this isn't the case for this particular exercise, it is always a good idea to learn the feature while you are here. For the files in this exercise that you will import, choose **Graphic**.

Read on to find out how to check your image settings before you import your files.

Working with the Image Settings Dialog Box

Before importing an image, check the Image Settings dialog box settings to make sure they are ideal for this project. To open the dialog box, click the Options button at the bottom of the Import Files window.

To check your settings:

1. Click the **Options** button in the Select Files to Import dialog box to open the Import Settings dialog box, shown in Figure 3.6.

Figure 3.6
Click Options to see the
Import Settings dialog box.

The Import Settings dialog box includes the following settings:

● **Image Size Adjustment.** This setting determines if the image will be resized or cropped on import.

● **File Pixel to Video Mapping.** This setting controls how Media Composer will treat the color in the image file. Set it to match the settings of the file you are importing, and Media Composer will respond accordingly. If the graphic has computer RGB levels, which is most common, Media Composer will clamp (limit) the colors to video black and video white levels. If the graphic was created specifically for video using video black and video white levels, select the third option (601 SD or 709 HD), and Media Composer will not clamp the colors.

- **Frame Import Duration.** This setting determines the duration of imported still images.

- **Alpha Channel.** This setting determines how Media Composer interprets transparency. If an image has transparency (alpha channel), and it was created in any application other than one from Avid, then choose Invert on Import (White = Opaque) If the image was created in Avid, choose Do Not Invert (Black = Opaque). If you don't want to include the alpha information, choose Ignore.

2. In the Image Size Adjustment section of the Import Settings dialog box, click the Resize Image to Fit Format Raster option button. This option will resize the image to the project settings, without stretching, cropping, or distorting the image. If you're unsure of the dimensions of the graphic you're importing, this is the best setting to choose. If an image is the same size as the project raster dimensions, choose the first option: Image Sized for Current Format. The middle options will crop the image or leave small images at their native size.

3. Click OK to close the Import Settings dialog box.

Completing the Import

Now that you have selected the import settings, you need to set the destination drive for the imported media in the Select Files to Import dialog box.

To complete the import:

1. Click the Destination Drive menu and select your media drive. This should be the same drive where you have the rest of the project media stored.

2. In the Select Files to Import dialog box, click the Video Resolution menu (Windows) or the Resolution menu (Mac). This menu allows you to choose the resolution of the MXF file to which you want to convert your image. The default setting will match the current video resolution of the project—in this case, DV 25 411. Be sure to keep the current setting, DV 25 411, before closing the menu.

Note: If you aren't sure of the resolution of your project, go to the Settings pane in the Project window and double-click the Video Display settings.

3. In the Select Files to Import dialog box, choose Desktop > MC6 Editing Book Files > Additional Project Media > RTS Images to open the RTS Images folder.

4. Click the file **Desert Mtn.jpg**, and then Ctrl-click (Windows) or Command-click (Mac) **Desert Plant.jpg**. Once both images are selected, click **Open**, as shown in Figure 3.7. Media Composer will convert the selected images to MXF video files and place them in the MXF folder on your media drive. You can now see the pointer files in the Graphics and Stills bin.

Figure 3.7
Images are selected to import.

5. Click the **Bin View** menu and change the Graphics and Stills bin to Text view. Notice in Figure 3.8 that the duration of both new image master clips is 30 seconds. The icon for still images is the same as the Video Master Clip icon. You can distinguish an image master clip by the file extension (in this case, .jpg).

Figure 3.8
Imported image files with 30-second durations are in the bin.

6. Load the **01 Desert Mtn.jpg** master clip into the Source monitor. Then load **02 Desert Plant.jpg**. Notice in Figure 3.9 that the first image fits the Source monitor horizontally, while the image in Figure 3.10 maintains its vertical proportions. In both cases, you can see the entire image in proper proportion without any cropping or stretching.

Figure 3.9
This horizontal image fits the Source monitor.

Figure 3.10
Media Composer adds black to this vertical image.

Creating a Sequence

Now that you have imported two image files, you can create a sequence and edit the stills into the video track.

To create a sequence and edit the stills into the video track:

1. Click the **OVERWRITE** button. The 02 Desert Plant.jpg image overwrites into the empty timeline. To accommodate this maneuver, Media Composer automatically creates a new untitled sequence and places it in the open/active bin.

2. Load the **01 DESERT MTN.JPG** image into the Source monitor. Move the position indicator to the beginning of the sequence. Splice-in the image. (See Figure 3.11.)

3. In the **GRAPHICS AND STILLS** bin, name the **UNTITLED** sequence **SCENIC IMAGES 60SEC**. This sequence is now available in the Graphics and Stills bin for the publicity team, Web design team, or anyone else working on

the Running the Sahara project to use. A sequence of high-quality stills is ideal as a background behind titles as well. In the real world, this sequence may be expanded periodically as more select still images become available.

Figure 3.11
An untitled sequence with two image segments in the V1 track.

4. Close the **GRAPHICS AND STILLS** bin. The Timeline and the Record monitor clear once the Graphics and Stills bin is closed. It is time to close this project for now and create a new project.

Creating a New Project

When you imported an image, you set the format and raster dimensions to match the project. Therefore, it should be no surprise that when you create a new project, you set the format, aspect ratio, color space (only on 1,080 projects), and raster dimension (only on 720 or 1,080 projects) based on the media that you'll be using. So it's a good idea to know what media format you are working with before you create your project. By creating a project that matches the format of your media, you'll get the best performance out of Media Composer.

Also, you aren't locked into one format for an entire project. Media Composer is so flexible that you can work with media of different frame sizes, aspect ratios, and pixel aspect ratios in the same sequence. For example, you can mix SD 4:3, HD 16:9, and film formats. In addition, in a project, you can work with master clips of any frame rate or field motion type (interlaced or progressive), regardless of the project's type.

 You can read more about different digital formats in Appendix A, "Technical Fundamentals."

Master clips that do not match the frame rate or field motion type of the project are known as *mixed rate master clips*. This project will consist of mixed formats of media that you will use to create a demo montage for First Tracks Productions in Lesson 4, "Manual Timeline Editing."

To create a new project:

1. Close the Project window. The Select Project dialog box opens, as shown in Figure 3.12.

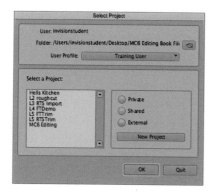

Figure 3.12
The Select Project dialog box shows Training User and External selected.

2. In the Select Project dialog box, make sure **USER PROFILE** is set to **TRAINING USER**. Also ensure **LOCATION** is **EXTERNAL** and the folder is **DESKTOP > MC6 EDITING BOOK FILES > MC6 EDITING PROJECTS**.

3. Click the **NEW PROJECT** button. The New Project dialog box opens.

4. Type **FIRST TRACKS DEMO** in the **PROJECT NAME** field.

Note: **The New Project dialog box includes all the possible format types and settings, while the Format pane of the Project window only displays the format types from a given "family" of frame rates.**

Now you need to set the format and aspect ratio for this project. Since most of the footage from First Tracks Productions is XD CAM HD 1080i/60, you'll make the new project accordingly.

5. Make the following changes to the New Project settings to match Figure 3.13:
    *   **Format:** 1080i/59.94
    *   **Aspect Ratio:** 16:9
    *   **Color Space:** YCbCr709
    *   **Raster Dimensions:** 1,920×1,080
    *   **Stereoscopic:** Off

Figure 3.13
Open the New Project dialog box.

6. Click **OK** to create the new project. First Tracks Demo appears in the project list. Once a project is in the list, you can open it.

7. Select the new **FIRST TRACKS DEMO** project and click **OPEN** in Windows. On a Mac, select the project and click **OK**. The new project opens with all of the editing interface windows in place, and one bin (named after the project) open and ready to use. See Figure 3.14.

8. Take a moment and arrange the windows to your liking.

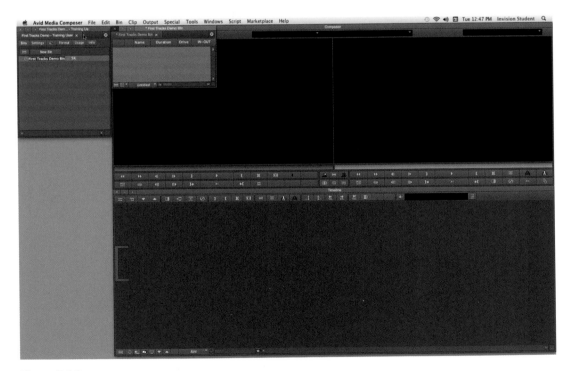

Figure 3.14
The First Tracks Demo project opens.

Importing Audio Files

The sequence that you will be editing in the next lesson consists of a series of action shots cut to music, also known as a *montage*. Since the music is the foundation for the edits, you will import some audio files.

Importing audio files is similar to importing image files. In both cases, Media Composer creates a new MXF version of the files according to settings that you choose and places them with the other project media in the MXF folder.

To import audio files:

1. In the Project window, change the name of the default bin to **AUDIO**.

2. Click inside the open **AUDIO** bin and choose **FILE** > **IMPORT**.

3. In the Select Files to Import dialog box, choose the **MC6 EDITING BOOK FILES** > **ADDITIONAL PROJECT MEDIA** folder on your desktop.

Note: Depending on the way you are viewing the window (in Icon view, List view, or Column view), your window may display items differently than seen in Figure 3.15. The screen shots show the window in List view. If you are using Column or Icon view, you will need to click or double-click the folders to view the contents within.

4. Click the disclosure triangle next to the **ADDITIONAL PROJECT MEDIA** folder. The **ADDITIONAL PROJECT MEDIA** folder contains two subfolders: **FIRST TRACKS ASSETS** and **RTS IMAGES**.

5. Click the disclosure triangle next to the **FIRST TRACKS ASSETS** subfolder. Then open the **MUSIC** folder to see the audio assets for the project. I made three different music files and exported them as .m4a files; see Figure 3.15. For this exercise, you will import all of the files at once.

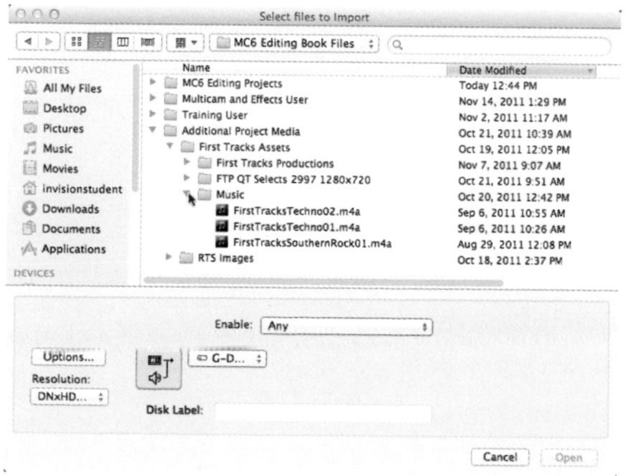

Figure 3.15

Get here via MC6 Editing Book Files > Additional Project Media > First Tracks Assets > Music.

6. In the Select Files to Import dialog box, make sure that your media drive is the destination drive. Select the first audio file, FIRSTTRACKSTECHNO01, then Shift-click the last file. This selects all three files.

7. Click OPEN. The files are converted to MXF and appear in the Audio bin. See Figure 3.16.

Figure 3.16
Imported files are in the Audio bin.

8. Load the song FIRSTTRACKSTECHNO01.M4A into the Source monitor. Play the song, which is the music that you will edit video to in the demo montage.

Opening a Bin from Another Project

Sometimes the same media is used in more than one project. If so, open a bin from another project into your existing project and copy the master clips to another bin. The original bin and media files remain intact. You'll also frequently open other bins on large projects with multiple editors working on shared media. For the First Tracks Productions demo, I had over 150 gigabytes of media from which to choose. Fortunately, some of the best master clips had already been organized into a Selects bin that I could repurpose for the demo. Repurposing is a real time saver when working against quick turnaround deadlines. You can identify bins by the file extension .avb (Avid bin).

Tip: To open a bin from another project, you need to be in the Bins pane of the Project window.

To open a bin from another project:

1. Right-click the empty space in the Bins pane and choose OPEN BIN from the menu; see Figure 3.17. An Open a Bin dialog box opens.

2. Let's open a bin from the First Tracks Assets folder. In the Open a Bin dialog box, go to the desktop and choose MC6 EDITING BOOK FILES > ADDITIONAL PROJECT MEDIA > FIRST TRACKS ASSETS > FIRST TRACKS PRODUCTIONS > FT_SELECTS.AVB. See Figure 3.18. Then click OPEN. The FT_Selects bin opens in Text view. The format in the Video column matches the project settings, XDCAM HD 1080i/60.

Figure 3.17
Choose Open Bin from the menu.

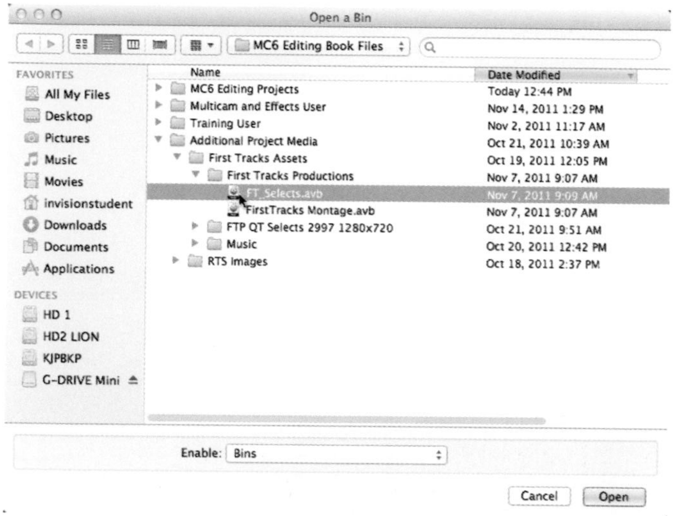

Figure 3.18
The bin file is in the
Open a Bin dialog box.

3. Drag the **FT_SELECTS** bin to the right (over the Composer window) so you can see the Bins tab in the Project window. An Other Bins folder is in the Bins tab. Bins opened from other projects remain in this folder within your project.

4. In the Bins tab, click the triangle to see the contents of the **OTHER BINS** folder.

5. Click the **BIN VIEW** menu at the bottom of the **FT_SELECTS** bin and change the bin to Frame view. As you can see in Figure 3.19, there are over 20 video master clips and one audio master clip.

6. Alt/Option-drag the **BRANDINGPOWER.AIF** audio master clip to the Audio bin, where a copy of the audio master clip appears. Why copy instead of simply dragging the master clip over to the Audio bin? Because if you remove a master clip from a bin and then close the project, the bin is saved without the audio master clip. The next time someone opens that bin and expects to find the stock music file, they will be disappointed.

Figure 3.19
The Other Bins folder and the opened FT_Selects bin.

7. Close the **FT_SELECTS** bin.

Tip: If you are working with a bin shared by other editors, such as a stock bin with a selection of master clips and graphics, duplicate the bin on your computer as a backup. You can save a copy from within Media Composer by selecting the open bin and choosing File > Save Bin Copy As. Rename the bin copy before you change the original bin.

Understanding AMA

Avid Media Access (AMA) is a plug-in architecture that allows you to link directly to master clips from a third-party volume. Media Composer uses the AMA plug-in to read those files in their native format. Once you link to the files, you can edit the media as you would any other master clip or sequence. Through AMA, you can also import or export master clips and sequences to and from third-party volumes.

AMA plug-ins are available for most popular file-based formats, including P2, XDCAM, GFCAM, Canon XF, QuickTime, RED, and AVCHD media.

Linking to Files Through Avid Media Access

For the First Tracks Productions demo project that you edit in the next lesson, you'll follow a fast turnaround workflow. That means the project needs to be edited and delivered very quickly, so you'll modify your editing workflow to expedite the process as much as possible. In the Additional Project Media folder, along with the music and FT_Selects bin, there is a subfolder containing QuickTime video clips. Rather than import the clips, use AMA to link to the files. You can edit a sequence and export the finished piece; you just won't take the time to import (and convert to MXF) each clip.

Working with AMA Settings

Before linking files through AMA, check the AMA settings. In the AMA Settings dialog box you can turn on or off AMA (it's on by default) to automatically mount your volumes and to customize your bin.

To check the AMA settings:

1. In the Project window, click the **SETTINGS** button to open the Settings pane.

2. In the Settings pane, double-click **AMA**. The AMA Settings dialog box appears.

3. Click the **VOLUME MOUNTING** button. The Enable AMA Volume Management option should already be selected, as shown in Figure 3.20. This is the default setting. If not, select it now.

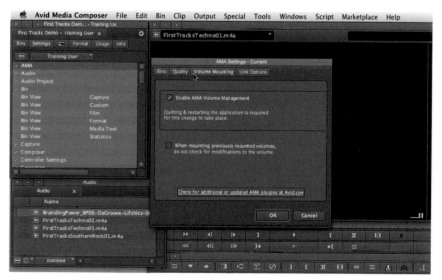

Figure 3.20
This is the Volume Mounting pane in the AMA Settings window.

4. If the Enable AMA Volume Management option was already selected, and you didn't change it, move on to step 5. If you just selected the Enable AMA Volume Management option, or deselected and reselected it, click **OK**. Then quit the application, relaunch Avid Media Composer, open the **FIRST TRACKS DEMO** project, and open the AMA settings. Welcome back.

5. Locate the **WHEN MOUNTING PREVIOUSLY MOUNTED VOLUMES, DO NOT CHECK FOR MODIFICATIONS TO THE VOLUME** check box. The default (unchecked) setting is preferred for most workflows. If Media Composer sees a change to the volume—e.g., new clips on an SxS card—it will automatically update the media in the bin to match the changes on the card. But, since this volume is being used for training, we want Media Composer to always mount it as if it were the first time (checked). Select (check) the **WHEN MOUNTING PREVIOUSLY MOUNTED VOLUMES, DO NOT CHECK FOR MODIFICATIONS TO THE VOLUME** check box.

6. Click the **BINS** button to see the Bins pane in the AMA Settings dialog box. By default, the system links your master clips into a new bin using the drive or volume as the bin name. If you want to change the bin name or use an existing bin, make these changes in the Bins tab.

7. Select **CREATE A NEW BIN** if it isn't already selected. In the Create a New Bin section, select **SPECIFY BIN NAME** and type **AMA QT MEDIA** in the name field. Finally, in the lowest section, select **DISPLAY EDITOR HEADFRAME**. See the settings in Figure 3.21.

Figure 3.21
The AMA Settings dialog box shows the Bins pane settings.

8. Click **OK**.

9. In the Project window, click the **BINS** button. The Bins pane is now showing in the Project window, and your AMA settings are ready to link to the additional QuickTime files.

Viewing Installed AMA Plug-ins

Since AMA is a plug-in based architecture, it is crucial that you have the current plug-in for the media format you are trying to use. Several plug-ins come with Media Composer, including QuickTime. If you followed the installation instructions in the "Getting Started" section of this book, then you should have the QuickTime plug-in installed. However, take a minute to view the plug-ins currently installed on your system.

To view the plug-ins on your system:

1. Select **Tools** > **Console**.

2. In the **Command Entry** text field, at the bottom of the Console window, type **AMA_ListPlugins**.

3. Press **Enter** (Windows) or **Return** (Mac). AMA_ListPlugins reveals the plug-ins installed on your system. See Figure 3.22.

Figure 3.22
The Console window, with the AMA plug-in list.

4. Look for the QuickTime plug-in in the list. If you do not see QuickTime, quit Media Composer and follow the directions in the "Getting Started" section to install the AMA plug-ins. After installation, launch Avid Media Composer and open the **First Tracks Demo** project.

5. Close the Console window.

Linking to a QuickTime Volume

Through AMA, you can link to any of these:

■ An individual file

■ A selected group of files

■ An entire volume

To link to a QuickTime volume, select the folder on your drive that contains the QuickTime files. You can use the same method to mount entire volumes of card-based media such as P2. QuickTime media is linked at the data rate at which it was recorded.

To link to a QuickTime volume:

1. Select the **BINS** pane in the Project window to make sure it is active.

2. Choose **FILE** > **LINK TO AMA VOLUME**. The Select the Root of the Virtual Volume dialog box opens.

3. Go to the desktop and choose the **MC6 EDITING BOOK FILES** > **ADDITIONAL PROJECT MEDIA** > **FIRST TRACKS ASSETS** > **FTP QT SELECTS 2997 1280×720** folder. *Selects* is an industry term that refers to a collection of the best footage. In this project, there are two sets of selects: the QT selects to which you are about to link, and those found in the FT_Selects bin you opened earlier. Each selects bin contains different footage. Notice in Figure 3.23 that the name of the folder includes the frame rate and frame size of the clips inside.

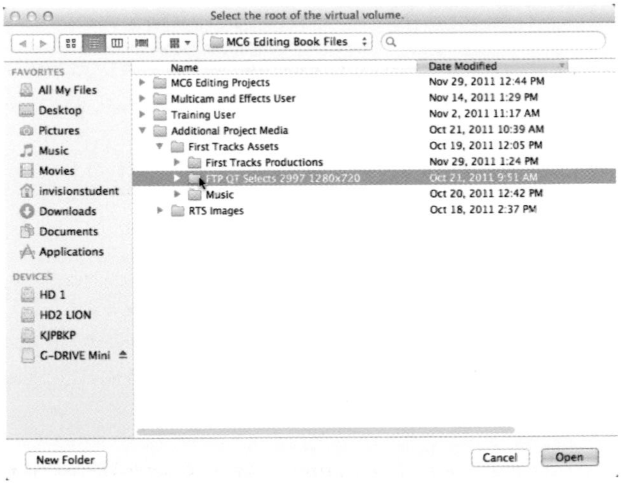

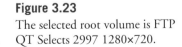

Figure 3.23
The selected root volume is FTP QT Selects 2997 1280×720.

4. Click the disclosure triangle to open the folder and see the contents. You can select the folder, but the clips inside are dimmed. That is because you are linking to a volume, rather than to individual clips. Do not select the Scenery and Timelapse folder. You'll link to that later in this lesson, in Exercise 3.

5. Select the **FTP QT SELECTS 2997 1280×720** folder. Click **OPEN**. A new bin named **AMA QT MEDIA** opens with the AMA-linked QuickTime files inside; see Figure 3.24. The .mov file extension has dropped from the linked filenames. Also, master clip icons are modified with a vertical link to indicate that they are linked AMA master clips rather than to master clips that were imported or captured from tape. You can now load, preview, mark, and edit the linked master clips just as you would any master clip in your project.

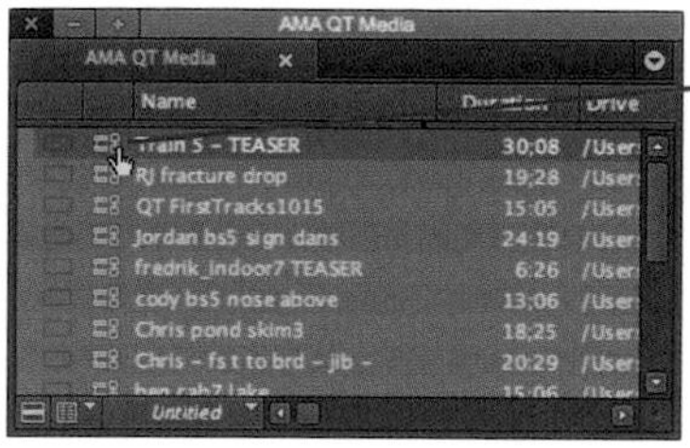

AMA-linked master clip icon

Figure 3.24
Linked master clips are in the new bin.

6. Change the name of the **AMA QT Media** bin to **QT AMA Selects**.

7. Load any **QT Selects** master clip into the Source monitor and play it. As you can see, the files look and play just as expected.

Importing Versus Linking to Media Files

Linking to files through AMA is an easy way to immediately see and start editing your digital media files right away. The advantage of linking to the media files directly on the camera or a portable hard drive is that you have immediate access to the media. This is a huge advantage for projects with a fast turnaround, such as news. It is also very useful in a production environment where the director of photography (DP) can quickly verify the footage before moving on to the next setup or location.

Linking directly to the media also has some notable disadvantages. Playback performance can be poor, depending on the devices you are using. For example, XDCAM discs were not designed for rapid random access and naturally aren't as fast as a solid-state card or hard drive. Another downside: Media management is now entirely dependent on the user. Finally, if the media isn't on permanent storage, your media goes away when you remove the card or disc.

Tip: Whether you convert files to MXF now, later, or never, it's always a good idea to copy the media from your camera or digital card to a media drive as a backup. The recommended AMA workflow is to link to digital media files for viewing and selection, then consolidate the media onto Avid-managed volumes as soon as possible.

Understanding Consolidate Versus Transcode

Although you are just starting a new project, this is a good time to learn about Media Composer's Consolidate and Transcode tools. Simply put, *consolidating* refers to copying media files, while *transcoding* not only consolidates the media (copies it) but also changes the resolution of the clips as it copies. You can also change the resolution by recapturing clips from tape, but transcoding is a lot faster and easier.

When working with AMA-linked media, it is always a good idea to consolidate the media to your primary media drive—especially if you have linked to files on a removable drive, card, or camera. This process could be done before you start editing or after you are finished with a sequence. The advantage of consolidating media after you finish editing a sequence or project is that you are only copying the media you used. On large projects with a lot of media files, this is invaluable for saving disk space.

In this section, you will take a look at the Consolidate/Transcode dialog box. Then, during the exercise at the end of the lesson, you will have the option to consolidate some of the project media. The Consolidate/Transcode tool is located in the Clip menu.

To explore the Consolidate/Transcode tool:

1. Select the **QT AMA SELECTS** bin. Then select the **TRAIN 5-TEASER** master clip. (You could select all the clips in the bin at once, but for this exercise one clip is enough.)

2. Choose **CLIP > CONSOLIDATE/TRANSCODE**. The Consolidate/Transcode dialog box opens, as shown in Figure 3.25.

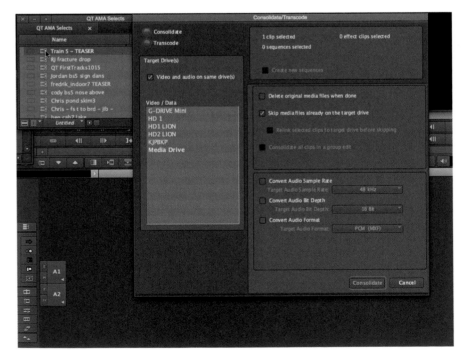

Figure 3.25
Train 5–TEASER selected, and the Consolidate/Transcode dialog box.

3. Select the **Consolidate** option in the upper-left corner.

4. Choose video and/or audio target drives. This determines the destination for your consolidated media. The **Video and Audio on Same Drive(s)** check box should be checked by default.

Note: Notice that the section in the top right of the dialog box shows 1 clip selected, 0 sequences selected, and 0 effect clips selected. If you had selected a sequence to consolidate, the number of clips in the sequence, as well as the sequence itself, would be accounted for here.

5. Look at the middle-right section. This is where you choose options for handling the media:

   • Check or uncheck the Delete Original Media Files When Done check box to delete or retain the original media files when you're finished, respectively. It's a good idea to leave this unchecked unless you are certain you are ready to delete the original clips.

   • You can choose to skip media files already on the drive by checking the Skip Media Files Already on the Target Drive check box. By default, this check box should be checked. That way, you don't accidentally overwrite or change media already on your drive.

6. Look at the lower-right section of the dialog box. It deals with options for converting the audio sample rate, bit depth, and format.

7. Click **Cancel** to close the Consolidate/Transcode dialog box.

Adding Comments to Master Clips in Script View

Getting to know footage based on the content or the clip name is fine. However, as you watch footage, you may have a particular thought or impression of the content that you want to add to the clip to help you locate it again later. In that case, you would add a comment to the clip.

For this project, you will add comments that can help you find and sort master clips based on their content. As you scan through the footage, you'll see that most shots show off the snowboarders' athletic talents. However, for the demo (and for fun), let's tag the shots that include wipeouts or falls, as well as shots that show boarding on something other than snow. For this exercise, you will add comments to several master clips in the QT Selects bin.

To add comments:

1. Move the open **QT AMA Selects** bin down so it's over the Timeline window.

2. Change the **QT AMA Selects** bin to Script view and resize the bin to your liking. Press **Ctrl+L** (Windows) or **Command+L** (Mac) to make the frame larger on the left column of the bin. See Figure 3.26.

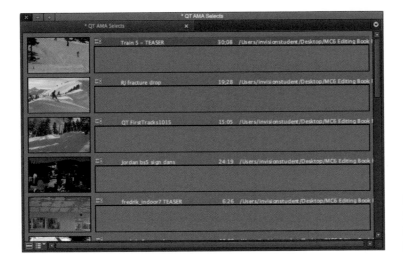

Figure 3.26
The QT AMA Selects bin has been moved and resized in Script view.

3. Load the master clip **Chris pond skim 3**. Press **Ctrl+4** (Windows) or **Command+4** (Mac) to select the Composer window. Use **J-K-L** to play through the master clip. (Read Lesson 2 for steps on how to do that.) Wow! The talent actually snowboards across a pond and lands safely on the other side. Okay, that counts as a surface other than snow.

4. In the **QT AMA Selects** bin, type **board on water** in the **Comments** field next to the frame. See Figure 3.27. Some master clips may already have descriptive names; others have numeric names based on the original camera metadata.

5. Load the master clip **0053KB** and play it. This time, the talent rides his board through a pipe. That's right. *Through* a pipe. Type **board through pipe** and press **Enter/Return**.

6. Load the master clip **00483D** and play it. This shot has a great jump through tree branches and a wipeout at the end of the landing. You may want to indicate all of those things to make it easier to search for in the next project. Type **great jump, board through branches, wipeout landing** and press **Enter/Return**.

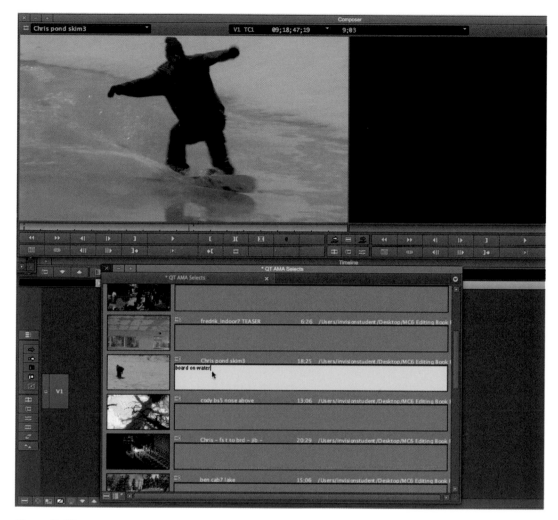

Figure 3.27
The Chris pond skim3 master clip with the "board on water" comment.

That's it. You've created a new project and filled it with the master clips and music that you need to edit an exciting demo montage. Along the way, you also learned some new shortcuts, discovered how to consolidate media, and added comments to a few clips.

Review/Discussion Questions

1. In which can you import media files?

   a. Composer, Source monitor

   b. Timeline

   c. Project window, Bins tab

   d. An open bin

2. Where can you find the raster dimensions of the current project?

   a. File menu

   b. Console

   c. Project window

   d. Timeline

3. What is AMA?

   a. Average Media Account

   b. Avid Media Access

   c. Access Media Aide

   d. Avid Media Aide

4. How does AMA work with Media Composer?

   a. Plug-in architecture

   b. Separate application

   c. Embedded media metadata

   d. It doesn't work with Media Composer

5. What is the difference between importing and linking through AMA?

   a. Importing converts files to MXF; AMA linking leaves files on a media drive in original format.

   b. AMA linking converts files to MXF; importing leaves files on a media drive in original format.

   c. Both methods convert files to MXF; linking lets you work with files while they convert.

   d. AMA linking does not let you change file size; importing lets you change file size.

6. Which icon shows a master clip linked through AMA?

   a.

   b.

   c.

   d.

7. If a bin from another project is opened in your current project, where will you find the bin in the Project window?

   a. Bins pane, Open Bins

   b. Bins pane, Trash

   c. Bins pane, any open bin

   d. Bins pane, Other Bins

8. What is the Media Composer feature used to copy media from the project to a specified location?

   a. Consolidate

   b. Comediate

   c. Copy

   d. Convert and Copy

9. In which default bin view can you see a frame and type comments at the same time?

   a. Frame view

   b. Text view

   c. Script view

   d. Comments view

Lesson 3 Keyboard Shortcuts

Key	Shortcut
Ctrl+U (Windows)/Command+U (Mac)	Creates a new mono audio track
Ctrl+6 (Windows)/Command+6 (Mac)	Opens the Console tool
Ctrl+4 (Windows)/Command+4 (Mac)	Selects the Composer window
Ctrl+W (Windows)/Command+W (Mac)	Closes the active window

Organizing and Consolidating Your Media

In this exercise, you'll familiarize yourself with other master clips and add comments to the ones containing wipeouts or surfaces other than snow. You'll also use AMA to link a volume of QuickTime time-lapse and scenery shots. Finally, you'll edit the sequence using skills you learned in Lesson 2.

Media Used:
First Tracks Productions

Duration:
30 minutes

GOALS

- Preview and add comments to master clips
- AMA volume link to a folder
- Rename the new bin
- Preview the new master clips
- Add comments to the new clips as needed
- Consolidate media

Adding More Comments

Familiarize yourself with other master clips and add comments to the ones containing wipeouts or surfaces other than snow.

1. Go through the master clips in the **QT AMA SELECTS** bin, feeling free to preview at 8× speed. Or, drag the position indicator through the master clips to skim the footage.

2. Add these comments to the following master clips:

   - Fredrik_indoor7 TEASER: board touches ceiling
   - Chris Fst to brd–jib: board on metal rail
   - Ben–sierra bc3–teaser.C: great jump, wipeout
   - Ab–rainbow–goggle cam.a: POV, board on bent tree
   - 0065OJ: board on bolder
   - 006P0: board up tree

3. Close the **QT SELECTS** bin.

4. In the Bins pane, open **OTHER BINS** > **FT_SELECTS**. Preview the master clips that have comments.

5. When you are finished, close the **FT_SELECTS** bin.

Linking Shots

In this exercise you link, through AMA, a volume of QuickTime time-lapse and scenery shots.

1. Make the Bins pane in the Project window active.

2. Link to the Scenery and Timelapse AMA volume. The location for the volume is on the desktop. Choose **ADDITIONAL PROJECT MEDIA** > **FIRST TRACKS ASSETS** > **FTP QT SELECTS 2997 1280×720** > **SCENERY AND TIMELAPSE**.

3. Name the new bin with AMA linked files **TIMELAPSE AND SCENERY**.

4. Preview the new master clips.

5. Optionally, if you have plenty of room on your media drive and you would like to try consolidating media, click the **TIMELAPSE AND SCENERY** bin, if it is not already active. Then select all the master clips in the bin.

6. Choose **CLIP** > **CONSOLIDATE/TRANSCODE**.

7. When the Consolidate/Transcode dialog box opens, select **Consolidate**, check the **Video and Audio on the Same Drives** check box, select the media drive where you want to copy the files (it should be the same drive as the Avid MediaFiles > MXF folder that you are using for the book media), make sure the **Delete Original Media Files When Done** check box is *not* checked, check the **Skip Media Files Already on the Target Drive** check box, and click the **Consolidate** button. A dialog box appears with two choices:

   - Keep Master Clips Linked to Media on the Original Drive
   - Relink Master Clips to Media on the Target Drive

8. Select **Relink Master Clips to Media on the Target Drive**. The original clips will be tagged with an .old extension and linked to the original media. The selected master clips will be linked to the new media on the target drive.

9. Click **OK** to consolidate the media. When the shots have finished consolidating, notice that there are two versions of each master clip in the Timelapse and Scenery bin. The original clips have .old 01 extensions and are still AMA linked.

10. Close the **Timelapse and Scenery** bin.

Editing a New Sequence

You have familiarized yourself with the new media and added comments. Now it's time to edit a new sequence using the skills that you learned in Lesson 2. Your challenge in this editing project is to not only edit together the rough cut, but also to make creative decisions to enhance the project. The producer wants a 30-second airborne sequence. That's right, airborne. What does it mean? Your job as the editor is to start and end the project with scenery. In between, you will show one jump and subsequent airborne shots of the snowboarding talent flying through or doing tricks in the air. There will be only one landing shot, at the end of the sequence right before the final shot of scenery. Which air shots and which scenery shots are used is up to you. Have fun.

1. Create a new bin called **My First Tracks Sequences**.

2. Inside the **My First Tracks Sequences** bin, create a new sequence called **30sec Airborne**.

3. Open the **30sec Airborne** sequence.

4. Open the **Audio** bin, if it is not already open. Listen to the different music. Choose one audio clip and mark a 30-second portion of the audio to use for your airborne montage.

5. Edit the 30-second music clip to the sequence.

6. Edit a scenery clip at the beginning of the sequence.

7. Edit a shot of someone jumping into the air on a snowboard.

8. Edit a series of airborne shots with people on snowboards.

9. For the last two video segments in the sequence, show a snowboard landing, followed by scenery. Make sure the entire duration does not exceed 30 seconds.

10. Play the finished sequence. When you are finished, close the open bins. Select the Project window; then choose **File** > **Save All**.

Manual Timeline Editing

Using interface buttons and keyboard shortcuts is an efficient way to edit a sequence. However, sometimes editors prefer a more hands-on approach. In this lesson you will create subclips. You'll locate clips in the Find window and drag clips to the Timeline to perform splice-in and overwrite edits. Along the way you'll also reposition segments using the Smart tool segment modes. Once you have a feel for the manual Timeline editing, you'll sort clips by comments, build a storyboard of clips, and edit the whole thing to the Timeline in one maneuver. Finally, you'll use Extend edit and Top and Tail trimming to extend or shorten the segments to finish the piece.

Media Used: First Tracks Productions

Duration: 90 minutes

GOALS

- Create subclips
- Drag and drop clips to the Timeline
- Use Find to search for clips
- Use Add Edit in the Timeline
- Rearrange clip segments in the Timeline
- Create a storyboard in a bin
- Edit a group of clips to the Timeline
- Use Top, Tail, and Extend to trim segments

Opening the Project

For this lesson, you will work with the First Tracks Demo project that you created in Lesson 3, "Ingesting File-Based Media."

To open the First Tracks Demo project:

1. Launch Avid Media Composer, if it is not already open.

2. In the Select Project dialog box, click the **EXTERNAL** button.

3. Make sure the **LOCATION** folder in the Select Project dialog box is set to **DESKTOP** > **MC6 EDITING BOOK FILES** > **MC6 EDITING PROJECTS**.

4. Click **FIRST TRACKS DEMO** in the project list.

5. Make sure **USER PROFILE** is set to **TRAINING USER**; then click **OK**. The project opens with the Bins pane active in the Project window and all of the editing interface windows open.

6. In the **BINS** tab, open the **TIMELAPSE AND SCENERY** bin.

7. Move the open bin under the Project window and resize it as needed. Change the bin to Text view if it is not already, as shown in Figure 4.1.

Figure 4.1
The Timelapse and Scenery bin is in Text view.

Note: If you consolidated the AMA clips in your Timelapse and Scenery bin at the end of Lesson 3, your master clip icons and subclip icons will not include the horizontal link indicating AMA media (seen in Figure 4.1 and subsequent screenshots).

Creating Subclips

Until now, you worked with whole master clips that included all the frames from the original media (which was either imported or linked through Avid Media Access, or AMA). Sometimes, master clips involve a series of different shots. In that case, you can break the clip into smaller portions called *subclips*. You can then rename the subclips and organize them based on their content. Best of all, once you edit a subclip to the Timeline, you can still access the handles of the entire master clip that it came from should you need to extend or trim the subclip in the sequence.

Tip: Subclips are handy for breaking up a long interview into individual question-and-answer segments.

To create a subclip, mark the portion of the footage that you want to include with IN and OUT marks. Then drag the master clip icon from the Source monitor to an open bin. In this exercise, you will create subclips from one of the time-lapse master clips.

To create a subclip, follow these steps:

1. In the TIMELAPSE AND SCENERY bin, load the **2007-08 TIMELAPSES 1** master clip.

2. Use **J-K-L** or drag the position indicator through the position bar to quickly preview the clip. This master clip is actually a series of different time-lapse shots. For this project, you are looking for scenic shots.

3. Drag the position indicator to the beginning of the clip, which shows the snowy mountain with the sun peaking behind it (about 00;01:23;12).

4. Mark an IN point at the beginning of that shot. You do not have to mark the first frame, just a frame near the beginning of that footage, as shown in Figure 4.2.

Figure 4.2
The snowy mountain has sun-peaking footage.

5. Play to the end of that footage, and mark an OUT point before the shot changes (about 00;01;36;22). Feel free to pass into the next footage and then back up to mark the OUT. Press **6** to play the marked portion of the clip.

6. In the Source monitor, click and drag the **CREATE SUBCLIP** icon (left of the clip name) shown in Figure 4.3 from the Source monitor to the **TIMELAPSE AND SCENERY** bin. A subclip that has been named after the original clip appears in the Timelapse and Scenery bin.

Figure 4.3
The Create Subclip icon is for creating subclips.

7. Name the subclip **SUN BEHIND MOUNTAIN**. Notice that the subclip icon is half the length of the master clip icon. See Figure 4.4.

Subclip icon ⸺

Master clip icon ⸺

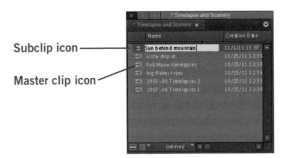

Figure 4.4
You renamed the subclip in the bin.

Note: Although a subclip represents a portion of a master clip, it still references the full master clip. That means it can be trimmed out to the full length of the master clip if you decide later you need more of the original shot. Also, because you're using AMA media for this subclip, if that media were removed/disconnected, the subclips would go offline too.

8. Double-click the subclip icon for the **Sun Behind Mountain** subclip. Play the subclip when it loads into the Source monitor. The head and tail frames (first and last frames) correspond to the IN and OUT marks that you set in the original clip.

9. Now create two more subclips from the same original clip. Open the **Clip Name** menu and choose **2007-08 Timelapses 1**, as shown in Figure 4.5.

Figure 4.5
Choose a previously loaded clip from the Clip Name menu.

10. Press **G** to clear the marks on the clip. Then step several frames ahead to the new shot: a different mountaintop with the clouds and a jet trail moving swiftly across the sky. Mark an IN point near the beginning of the shot (about 00;01;36;24). Play forward and mark an OUT point at the end of the shot (about 00;01;41;26).

Note: You can create a subclip by dragging the image from the Source monitor to an open bin.

11. Drag a subclip of the marked clip to the **Timelapse Scenery** bin. Rename the subclip **Sky over mountain**.

12. In the Source monitor, press **G** to clear the current marks. Step forward to the next shot: looking through the dashboard of a vehicle while driving along a snowy pass. Mark an IN after the camera is in position (about 00;01;42;01). Since this footage goes all the way to the tail frame of the clip, you don't need to mark an OUT point.

13. Create a subclip from the last portion of the clip. Name the subclip **Dashboard POV mtn highway**.

Excellent. You've created three new subclips from the same master clip. Now you are ready to start editing.

Preparing the Project for Editing

Prepare the project before you start editing your piece. In this section, you practice some of the skills that you learned in previous lessons.

To prepare for editing:

1. Change the TIMELAPSE AND SCENERY bin to Frame view. Then open the FAST menu and choose FILL WINDOW. Now you can see a visual representation of all the clips and subclips in the bin. Notice that the subclips look the same as the master clips in Frame view.

Tip: You can press Ctrl+L (Windows) or Command+L (Mac) to enlarge the thumbnails, and Ctrl+K (Windows) or Command+K (Mac) to reduce them as needed.

2. Open the AUDIO bin. Drag the AUDIO bin tab next to the TIMELAPSE AND SCENERY bin tab. Now both tabs are in the same tabbed bin window. Make sure that the AUDIO tab is active.

3. In the Project window, create a new bin and name it MY DEMO SEQUENCES. Open the MY DEMO SEQUENCES bin and place it below the other open bin window, as shown in Figure 4.6. Don't worry about creating a new sequence in the bin. That happens automatically during your first drag-and-drop maneuver.

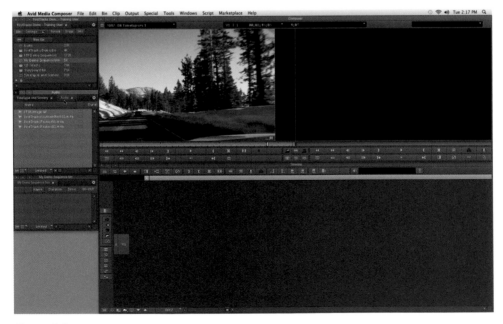

Figure 4.6
This project is ready for editing.

4. In the Timeline window, change the **View** menu to **Edit** if it is not already set. (The Edit view is a preset included in the Training User settings.)

Drag-and-Drop Editing in the Timeline

Dragging and releasing clips to the Timeline as either splice-in or overwrite edits is called *drag-and-drop editing*. Though this method may not always be as quick and precise as keyboard shortcuts, it offers a more tangible, hands-on way to compose a sequence. In this section, you drag and drop clips to the Timeline to build the beginning of a sequence. Along the way, you'll see how to differentiate between splice-in and overwrite edits, as well as how to use IN and OUT points in the Timeline to achieve your editing goals.

To drag and drop clips to the Timeline:

1. Drag and drop the **FirstTracksTechno01.m4a** audio clip from the **Audio** bin to the empty space in the Timeline window. Two things happen automatically: A new untitled sequence is created and the audio clip is edited to the new sequence. Why did the new sequence appear in the Audio bin instead of the My Demo Sequences bin? When you drag a clip from a bin to the Timeline, Media Composer will automatically create a new sequence in the same bin. This may not be where you're keeping the rest of your sequences. If the clip had been edited to an empty Timeline through the Source monitor, Media Composer would have asked you in a dialog box in which open bin you'd like to place the new sequence.

Note: If you're ever unsure of where a new sequence was created, or you need to do some cleanup, use the Find Bin button to quickly find the sequence in the bin. The Find Bin button is the first button on the second row of buttons under the Source monitor, and also in the same place under the Record monitor. You'll work with Find Bin later in this lesson.

2. Drag the untitled sequence from the **Audio** bin to the **My Demo Sequences** bin. Rename the sequence **FirstTracks Montage 01**, as shown in Figure 4.7.

Now that you have a clip in the Timeline, load the next clip and mark it for editing. Heads up: The bins that contain the selects clips are not open. Rather than open the bins and hunt for a specific clip, use the Find feature.

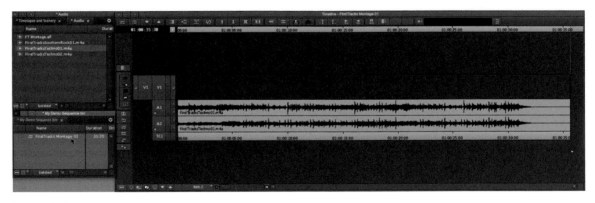

Figure 4.7
The audio clip segment is in the new sequence.

Finding Clips in the Bins Pane

When you first launch a project, the Find feature indexes all the bins in your project (even if they are closed) and creates a database of all of the metadata it finds. When you perform a search, Find accesses these databases to locate the information you are looking for. Re-indexing only occurs when a change is made to a bin.

Use the Edit menu's Find feature to look for a specific clip. Just as you might search for specific text in a document, Find searches through project text based on your criteria. Not only can you do a simple search for words, but you can customize in which bins or columns to search. Another advantage of using Find: Bins do not need to be open. In projects with a lot of bins and clips, this can be a huge time saver.

For this example, you will search for a specific clip based on the name of the talent, Ben. The clip is a shot of Ben snowboarding down a slope, up a steep ramp, and then, while airborne, doing a full horizontal revolution before landing. This shot is somewhere in one of the closed selects bins.

To look for a clip with the Find feature:

1. In the Project window, click in the empty space of the **Bins** pane. Or, press **Ctrl+9** (Windows) or **Command+9** (Mac) to activate the Project window.

2. Choose **Edit > Find** or press **Ctrl+F** (Windows) or **Command+F** (Mac) to open the Find window. The default Find settings are set to search any column and all the bins in a project.

3. In the **Find** text field, type **Ben**. Then click the **Find** button. Three clips appear in the results list, as shown in Figure 4.8. Notice that the bins that have the clips are still closed.

Find text field   Find button

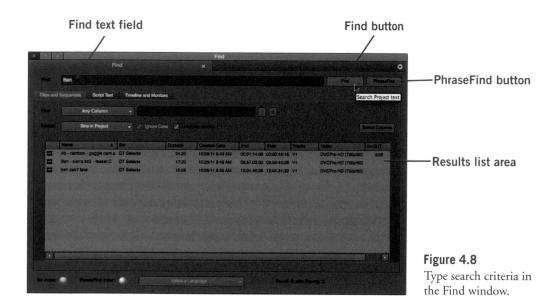

PhraseFind button

Results list area

Figure 4.8
Type search criteria in
the Find window.

Tip: **To load a clip from the Find window, double-click the clip icon in the results list.**

4. In the results list, double-click the **BEN-SIERRA BC3–TEASER.C** clip. The **QT AMA SELECTS** bin opens, and the selected clip loads into the Source monitor.

5. Click the × (**CLOSE**) button to close the Find window. Leave the **QT AMA SELECTS** bin open, and don't bother moving it out of the way.

6. Click anywhere in the Composer window or press **CTRL+4** (Windows) or **COMMAND+4** (Mac) to move the Composer window in front of the **QT AMA SELECTS** bin. Don't worry if you can't see your open bin. You will read about the Find Bin feature shortly.

7. Click the **PLAY** button to watch the clip in the Source monitor. The clip is fun, but way too long for a 32-second sequence. The Center Duration display shows that the clip is over 17 seconds, which makes it over half of the sequence. Narrow the clip down to the most interesting portion. Mark an IN point just after Ben passes the last tree on the left (around 09;56;48;23). Mark an OUT point at the moment he lands, but before the wipeout (around 9;56;57;18). You will be editing this clip later, and wipeouts aren't going to be part of that sequence.

To find out more about PhraseFind, watch a training video, or download a free trial, go to www.avid.com/US/products/phrasefind.

On the Web

Using PhraseFind in the Find Window

In addition to searching for text with Find, you can search for spoken words or phrases. This feature requires the award-winning Avid software add-on PhraseFind.

If you installed PhraseFind on your system, type a word or phrase in the Find text field and click the PhraseFind button. The system analyzes the audio in your footage to find all the times that particular word is said. You can even perform advanced searches for more than one word, spoken within a certain amount of time of each other. All results are presented in order of accuracy.

This tool is invaluable for news and documentary editors dealing with interviews, as well as feature and television editors looking for spoken dialogue—especially if there is improvisation beyond the script.

Dragging Clips to Splice-In or Overwrite the Timeline

When you drag clips to the Timeline, they are automatically edited as a splice-in edit unless you change your Timeline settings. As you learned in Lesson 2, "Assembling a Basic Sequence," a splice-in edit inserts a segment into the sequence, moving all segments to the right of the edit over to make room for the new segment. In this section, you drag a video clip to the Timeline and snap it to the beginning of the track. Remember, to snap a clip to the position indicator or an edit point, you press and hold Ctrl (Windows) or Command (Mac) as you drag.

To drag clips to the Timeline:

1. Click the **A1** and **A2** record track selector buttons in the Timeline window to turn them off.

2. Drag the clip from the Source monitor to the Timeline's video track. Do not release the clip yet. The white rectangular outline in the V1 track represents the clip that you are dragging to the Timeline. The yellow splice-in arrow indicates the type of edit you are performing. The Composer's four-frame editing display (see Figure 4.9) shows these things:

   - The clip's head and tail frames that you are adding to the Timeline (the middle two images in Figure 4.9)
   - The tail and head frames (the outer two images) on either side of the new clip. In this case, the frames are black filler.

Four-frame editing overlay

Tail and head frames of current
Timeline segments (1, 4)

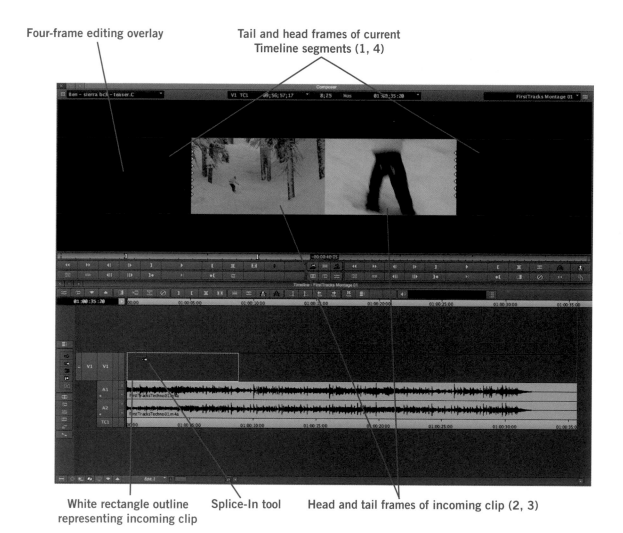

White rectangle outline
representing incoming clip

Splice-In tool

Head and tail frames of incoming clip (2, 3)

Figure 4.9
A four-frame display is shown when dragging segments.

3. Ctrl-drag (Windows) or Command-drag (Mac) the clip to the beginning of the **V1** track in the Timeline; then release the clip.

Tip: If you accidentally release a clip in the wrong position on the Timeline, press Ctrl+Z (Windows) or Command+Z (Mac) to undo the edit and perform the drag-and-drop edit again.

4. Click the **Play** button to see how the clip works with the music. The beginning is okay and the jump at the end is very cool, but the middle will lose the audience's interest because Ben disappears behind snowdrifts and a ramp. No problem. Add edits to split the clip into different segments, and then remove or overwrite the segments you don't want to keep.

Adding Edit Points in a Clip Segment

The Add Edit feature uses the position indicator as a guide so you can add an edit point to segments on active tracks. Add Edit splits an existing segment into separate segments in the sequence. In this section, you add two edit points to the video segment in the Timeline to separate the beginning, middle, and end of the shot. The Add Edit button is on the left of the Lift button in both the Composer and Timeline windows.

To add an edit point to a clip:

1. Drag the position indicator across the video clip segment in the Timeline to the frame when Ben's head and arm reappear behind the ramp (about 1;00:05:07 in the Record/Timeline timecode displays).

2. Click the **Add Edit** button in either the Timeline or Composer windows. An edit point is added to the clip segment at the current position. The tiny red equal sign between the two clip segments indicates that there are no frames missing between the two clips and that they will play continuously in the Timeline. This equal sign across the add edit in the sequence is the matched frames mark. (See Figure 4.10.)

3. Use **J-K-L** to find the last frame where the snowboard is fully visible, before Ben starts uphill toward the ramp (about 01:00:02:01).

4. Click the **Add Edit** button or press **Shift+C** to add an edit at the current position. The Shift+C shortcut is part of the handy Training User settings. After you have separated the original clip into three parts, you can mark and remove the middle portion or overwrite it with different footage.

5. Move the position indicator over the middle clip segment in the Timeline. Click the **Mark Clip** button or press **T** to select and highlight the middle video segment. (See Figure 4.11.)

6. Press **6** to play from the IN mark to the OUT mark in the Timeline. You probably agree this footage won't be missed.

7. Click the **Extract** button or press **X** to remove the middle clip segment from the sequence.

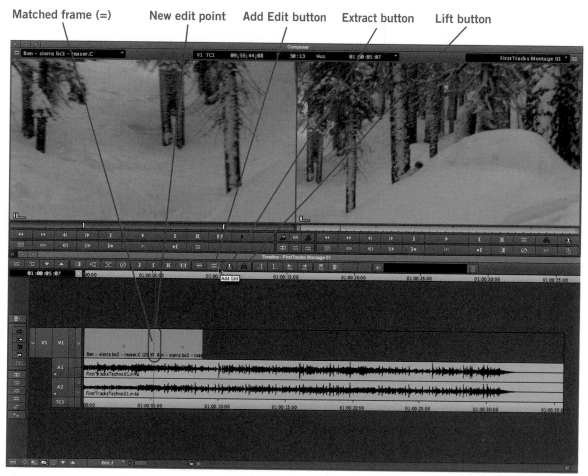

Figure 4.10
Use the Add Edit button in the Timeline to divide segments.

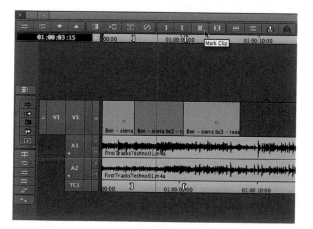

Figure 4.11
The middle clip segment is marked in the Timeline.

Note: Of course, you could have accomplished the same thing by just setting
        IN/OUT marks. However, adding edits can be very useful for splitting up
        a segment into parts so that you can quickly snap to specific parts when
        rearranging a segment or if you simply want to divide it into parts in
        case you decide to break up the action later to create parallel editing.
        (*Parallel editing* is when you cut back and forth between different pieces
        of action—for example, showing three different snowboarders approaching
        a ramp, then showing all three in succession making their jump, and then
        show all three in succession landing.)

8. Now that the boring middle segment is gone, you can insert another clip
    between the remaining segments. Something dramatic like a 360-degree
    vertical flip would be great. First, you need to find your QT AMA Selects
    bin. Under the Source monitor, click the **FIND BIN** button. The QT AMA
    Selects bin moves in front of the editing interface windows. (See Figure 4.12.)

Find Bin button

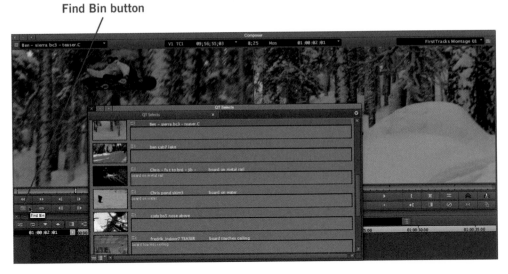

Figure 4.12
Clicking the Find Bin button puts the source bin in front of the interface windows.

9. In the **QT AMA SELECTS** bin, load the FREDRIK_INDOOR7 **TEASER** clip.
    Mark the shot so that you include the entire vertical flip from the frame
    before Fredrik's head appears in the bottom of the frame to the first frame
    after his back clears the frame (about 01:00:01:24 –01:00:04:17).

10. The shot will look cleaner if he is fully clear of the frame at the head and
    tail of the clip. Click the Timeline window and then click the Composer
    window to move the editing interface windows in front of the open bin.

Finding a Bin

When you are working with large open bins, they often end up hidden behind the other editing interface windows. Fortunately, Media Composer includes a handy Find Bin button for locating an open bin based on the current clip or sequence loaded in the Source monitor or Record monitor. The Find Bin button looks like an open bin in text view. There is one located under each monitor of the Composer window; in both cases, it is the first button on the second row of buttons. The Find Bin button under the Source monitor reveals the bin containing the current clip. Likewise, the Find Bin button under the Record monitor can be used to find the bin containing the current sequence.

11. Drag the FREDRICK_INDOOR7 TEASER clip from the Source monitor to the Timeline. Press CTRL (Windows) or COMMAND (Mac) to snap it into position between the first two clip segments in the Timeline. (See Figure 4.13.)

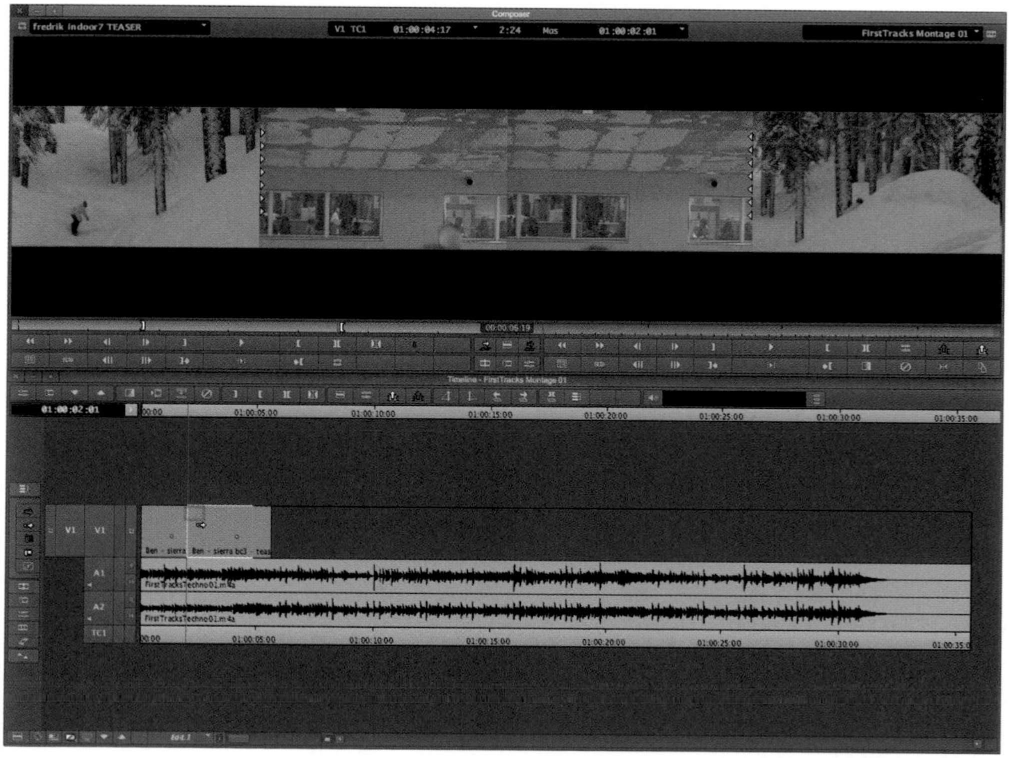

Figure 4.13
Use Extract/Splice-In mode to insert a clip between two segments.

As you can see, it is easy to drag clips to the Timeline and splice them in wherever you need them. But what if you want to overwrite a clip? In this sequence, the second and third shots work great with the techno music, but the first shot (Ben snowboarding downhill) doesn't seem to hold up in comparison. In fact, one of the time-lapse subclips that you created earlier might make a much more interesting opening shot.

Changing Segment Modes in the Timeline

To manually drag a clip as an overwrite, you first need to change which type of edit will occur during drag-and-drop editing. As you have seen, the default edit is splice-in. You can change the default in the Edit pane of the Timeline settings, but that isn't necessary. Instead, click the red Lift/Overwrite Segment Mode button in the Smart Tool palette. The Smart Tool palette, shown in Figure 4.14, is the vertical button set located on the left edge of the Timeline window. These five buttons are inside a larger button that resembles a left bracket. This button is actually the Smart Tool button. You work more with the Smart Tool button in Lesson 5, "Refining the Edit"; but for now, focus on the top two buttons within the Smart Tool palette: the Lift/Overwrite Segment Mode button and the Extract/Splice-In Segment Mode button. These two buttons control the type of edit that can be performed in the Timeline.

Smart Tool button
Lift/Overwrite Segment Mode button
Extract/Splice-In Segment Mode button

Figure 4.14
Choose from the Smart Tool palette.

Before you start, keep in mind that drag-and-drop editing uses the marked source duration and edits the clip into the sequence where you drop it, regardless of track selection or marks in the Timeline.

Tip: If you want a drag-and-drop edit to use the Timeline marks to define duration, you need to Ctrl-drag (Windows) or Command-drag (Mac) the segment to Timeline mark.

To use the segment mode buttons to change the edit type:

1. Click the red LIFT/OVERWRITE SEGMENT MODE button in the Smart Tool palette. The button is highlighted when activated.

2. Move the position indicator over the first clip segment in the Timeline and press **T** to mark the clip.

3. Load the **SUN BEHIND MOUNTAIN** subclip. You'll find the subclip in the **TIMELAPSE AND SCENERY** bin. Or, you can use the **CLIP NAME** menu in the Source monitor to find the subclip.

4. Press **G** to clear any marks on the clip, and move the position indicator to the middle of the clip. Mark an IN point when the sun rays first start to flare (about 00;01;28;05).

5. Drag the clip from the Source monitor to the Timeline. Do not release the clip. Notice two things (see Figure 4.15):

   ● The red Overwrite tool appears when you hover over the other clips in the Timeline.

   ● The incoming clip's white outline is much larger than the IN and OUT marks set in the Timeline. That is because the clip in the Source monitor is longer than the marked section of the Timeline.

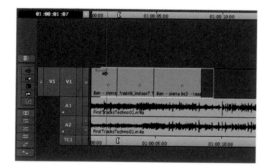

Figure 4.15
Dragging a clip uses source marks rather than Timeline marks.

6. Ctrl-drag (Windows) or Command-drag (Mac) the incoming clip to the beginning of the marked clip (to the IN mark) in the Timeline. When the white outline of the incoming clip fits the IN and OUT marks, release the clip. (See Figure 4.16.)

7. Press **G** to clear the Timeline marks. Play the video clips in the sequence. What do you think? Keep in mind that this type of montage editing is fairly organic in that editors are continually changing their minds or trying different things to improve the sequence.

When you are working with an unscripted montage, you just don't know how well something will work until you try it. These shots work okay together, although now that I look at it, I wish Ben's jump came *before* Fredrik's flip. No problem. Use the segment mode buttons to reposition clips in the Timeline.

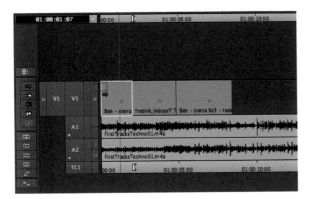

Figure 4.16
Use a modifier to edit the clip according to Timeline marks.

Moving Segments in the Timeline

To move a clip in the Timeline, first decide what type of segment mode you want to use: Lift/Overwrite or Extract/Splice-In. These segment modes work as a combination of two edits at once—the first to remove the clip from its original position, the second to edit it to the new position. Moving a clip in Lift/Overwrite segment mode means the space you move it from will remain empty—like a lift edit—and if you drop it over another segment, those frames are written over by the clip you moved (see Figure 4.17). On the other hand, moving a clip in Extract/Splice-In segment mode fills in the space where the clip was with the clips to the right (just like an Extract edit), and wherever you move the clip, it will splice in, moving the shots to the right to make room (see Figure 4.18).

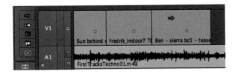

Figure 4.17
The Lift/Overwrite mode appears over the top part of a segment.

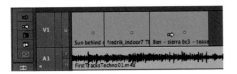

Figure 4.18
The Extract/Splice-In mode appears over the bottom part of a segment.

In this case, you are moving the third shot in front of the second shot. In essence, they switch places in the Timeline. You will experiment more with changing clip position after you finish the edit.

Note: This kind of swapping of segment positions only works if the shots are next to one another. Also, you can toggle the entire Smart tool on and off at any time with the Tab key (Training User settings) or click the Smart Tool button that frames the Smart Tool palette. When you toggle the Smart tool off, then back on, the button selections are retained.

To change clip positions:

1. In the Smart Tool palette, click the **Extract/Splice-In** button. Both segment mode buttons should be on. With both modes turned on (highlighted in the Smart Tool palette), choose a segment mode with the position of the pointer.

2. Move your pointer over the top half of the third segment in the Timeline. The pointer becomes the red Lift/Overwrite tool. Move the pointer to the lower half of the segment. The pointer changes to the Extract/ Splice-In tool. To fully appreciate both segment modes, try them both.

3. Move the pointer back up to the top half of the third clip. Drag the clip in Lift/Overwrite segment mode toward the left and press **Ctrl** (Windows) or **Command** (Mac) to snap it to the beginning of the second clip. Release the clip. As expected, the clip that you moved overwrote the preceding clip (see Figure 4.19 and Figure 4.20). Since that isn't the result you're looking for, undo and try again from the lower half of the clip.

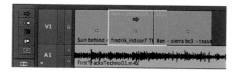

Figure 4.19
The Lift/Overwrite segment mode move.

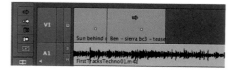

Figure 4.20
This is the finished Lift/Overwrite segment mode move.

4. Choose **Ctrl+Z** (Windows) or **Command+Z** (Mac) to undo the Lift/ Overwrite operation. Drag the third clip from the lower half in Extract/ Splice-In segment mode and press **Ctrl** (Windows) or **Command** (Mac) to snap it to the beginning of the second clip. See Figure 4.21 and Figure 4.22.

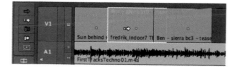

Figure 4.21
The Extract/Splice-In segment mode move.

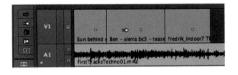

Figure 4.22
This is the finished Extract/Splice-In segment mode move.

5. *Voilà!* Click the **Play** button to watch the clips in the sequence. Mission accomplished.

Now that you know how to drag clips to the Timeline in Overwrite or Splice-In segment mode, and you can reposition the clips, you can edit in the remaining clips all at once. First, sift through your select clips and sort out the shots that involve talent snowboarding on surfaces other than snow.

Sorting and Sifting Clips

In Lesson 1, "Exploring the Interface and Preparing to Edit," you sorted clips into bins based on their overall content. Earlier in this lesson, you used the Find feature. You could use Find to look for clips with the word *board* in the comments. However, the Find window can load or move only one clip at a time. The most efficient way to see all the clips with *board* in the comments is to sort the bin using the Comments column as the sort criteria. Sift allows you to actually sift the contents of a bin to show only the clips that match the certain criteria. This can be extremely useful if you are working with a bin containing hundreds of clips. Let's first take a look at Sort, then use Sift to narrow the bin's contents.

To sort the clips based on the comments that you added in Lesson 3:

1. Click the **Find Bin** button under the Source monitor. The QT AMA Selects bin moves to the front of the interface. With the bin in Script view, you can scroll up and down to see which clips have comments, but you cannot sort the clips based on which clips have comments and which don't. You have to change the bin view to sort by the Comments column.

2. Change the **QT AMA Selects** bin to Text view. Change the Text view to the **Custom** preset, as shown in Figure 4.23. This is a great time to see how to add or hide columns in your bins.

Tip: Why use a custom bin view preset? Because the Comments column does not appear in the Text view presets.

Figure 4.23
The Text view allows for custom bin views.

3. Right-click the column header area and click **Choose Columns**, as shown in Figure 4.24. The Bin Column Selection dialog box opens and lists all the available columns, as shown in Figure 4.25.

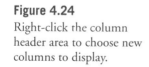

Figure 4.24
Right-click the column header area to choose new columns to display.

Figure 4.25
Choose the info you want to see from the Bin Column Selection dialog box.

4. You can select as many columns as you'd like. In this case, you'll choose to display the Duration and Comments columns. In the columns display, scroll to the bottom of the list and click **COMMENTS**. Then scroll toward the top of the list and click **DURATION**. Finally, click **OK**. Not only did both columns appear in your custom bin layout (see Figure 4.26), but the name Custom in the presets menu changed to Custom.1, indicating that you changed the original preset. Now that the Comments column is showing, you can sort by that column.

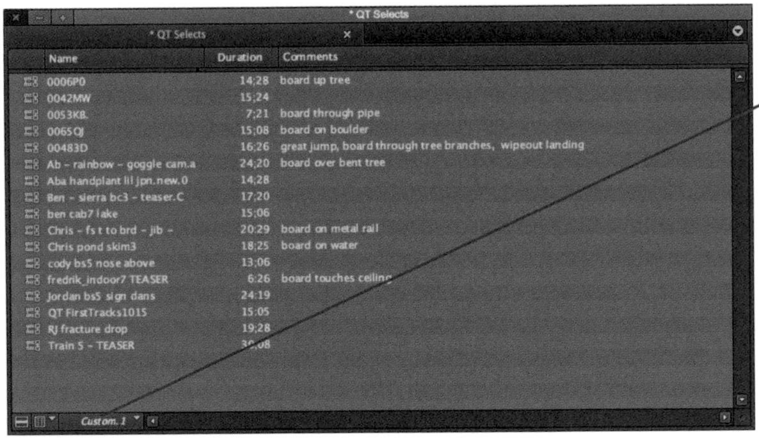

Modified Custom preset

Figure 4.26
You added Duration and
Comments columns.

Note: To save a bin preset, click the preset name and choose Save As from the
Bin View Preset menu. Once saved, the preset becomes part of your user
settings. You read more about saving presets and customizing Media
Composer in Lesson 7, "Customizing Media Composer."

5. Double-click the **COMMENTS** column header to sort in ascending order. The clips with comments are at the bottom of the list because when you sort alphanumerically, empty space precedes numbers and letters. Click the column header again to move the clips with comments to the top of the list (descending order). Now that you have access to all of the comment clips in the bin, you can copy them to another bin to build your storyboard.

First let's take a quick look at the Sift feature. Suppose that instead of looking at all the clips with comments, you want to see only master clips that include a comment with the word *wipeout*. Using Sort, you still have to visually scan through the comments to find the word you are looking for. Sift, on the other hand, will eliminate every clip from the list that does not meet the criteria.

To sift a bin:

1. Click the **QT AMA Selects** bin **Fast** menu and choose **Custom Sift**. The Custom Sift dialog box opens.

2. In the Custom Sift dialog box, type **WIPEOUT** in the first **Text to Find** field, as shown in Figure 4.27. Then click **OK**. All the clips that don't contain the text *wipeout* have been sifted out. Only a few master clips remain, as shown in Figure 4.28. If you had sifted the **FT_Selects** bin, you would have additional wipeout clips.

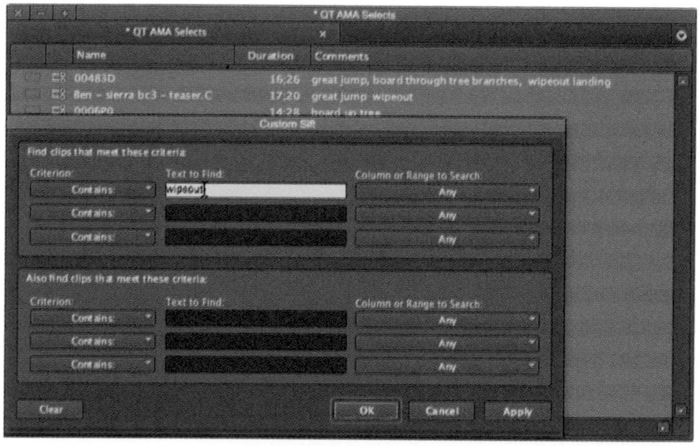

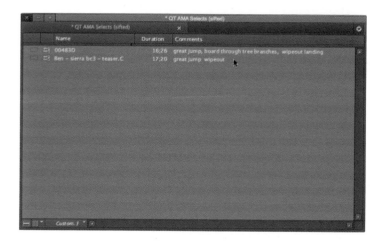

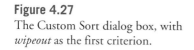

Figure 4.27
The Custom Sort dialog box, with *wipeout* as the first criterion.

Figure 4.28
The bin sifted to show only shots with *wipeout*.

3. Click the **Fast** menu and choose **Show Unsifted**. All the original clips are visible in the bin again. This time, let's sift the list for clips with the word *board*.

4. Click the **Fast** menu in the **QT AMA Selects** bin and choose **Custom Sift**.

5. In the first **Text to Find** field, type **board**; then click **OK**. Only the clips with the word *board* remain showing in the bin. Now you can select them all and create copies (clones) to move into a separate Storyboard bin.

To copy clips in a bin to another bin to build your storyboard:

1. In the Project window's **Bins** pane, create a new bin and name it **Storyboard**.

2. Move the **Storyboard** bin above or next to the **QT AMA Selects** bin. Resize it so you can Alt-drag (Windows) or Option-drag (Mac) the clips as a group to make cloned copies in the new bin.

3. Click the first clip in the **Comments** column. Then Shift-click the last clip that has a comment. Alt-drag (Windows) or Option-drag (Mac) the group of selected clips to the **Storyboard** bin. (See Figure 4.29.) You have one Selects bin down, and one to go. This time you sort the commented clips from the FT_Selects bin.

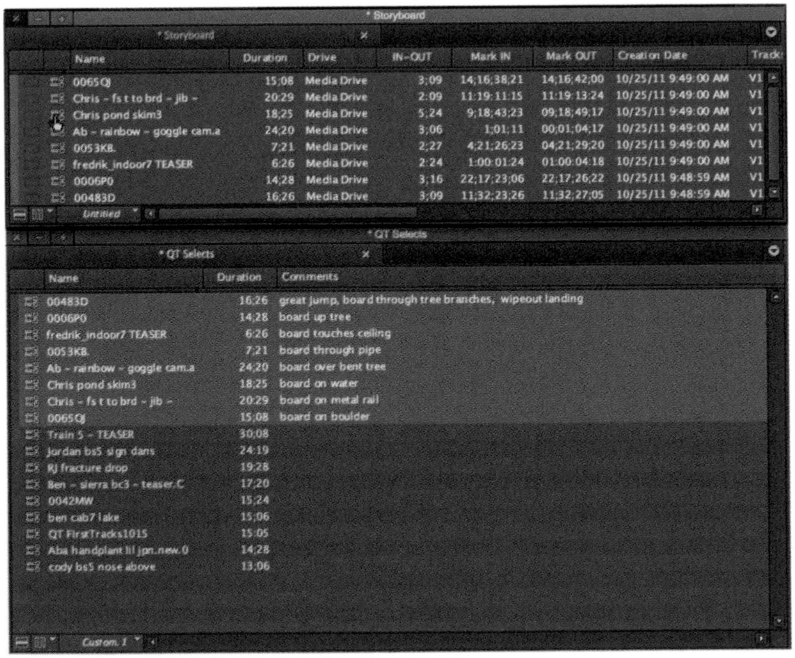

Figure 4.29
Clips with comments copied (cloned) to the Storyboard bin.

Note: One big advantage of Sort and Sift over Find is that you can select and drag multiple clips at a time from the sorted or sifted bin to other bins. Also, in the Custom Sift dialog box, you can use the drop-down menus on either side of the Text to Find field to perform more complex Sift procedures. These allow you to adjust criteria with the following settings: Contains, Begins With, or Matches Exactly. The drop-down menu on the right lets you choose the column or range to search, with the following options: None, Color, Name, Duration, Comments, and Any. You can also click the column header area and create a custom column header such as one for ratings to add stars. You can learn more about custom Sift operations on the Avid Web site and documentation.

4. Click the × (**Close**) button to close the **QT AMA Selects** bin. Open the **FT_Selects** bin, which is in the **Other Bins** folder.

5. Make sure the bin is in Text view, then go to the **Custom** preset.

6. Right-click the column header and click **Choose Columns**.

7. In the Bin Column Selection dialog box, click **Duration** and click **Comments**. Then click **OK**.

8. Double-click the column header to move clips with comments to the top of the column.

9. Alt-drag (Windows) or Option-drag (Mac) the commented clips to the **Storyboard** bin.

10. Click the × (**Close**) button to close the **FT_Selects** bin.

All the clips that you need have been moved to the Storyboard bin. You're ready to start building your storyboard.

Storyboard Editing Techniques for Creative Projects

Some projects, such as a video montage cut to music, leave a lot of room for creative exploration. For example, the shot choices are neither scripted nor planned and there is no voiceover track to use as a guide. Instead, you have infinite possibilities for assembling the footage to the music. When faced with so many choices, an editor's instincts and creative skills are often better served by handling the clips physically with the mouse, dragging them into position—similar to an artist creating a pictorial collage on paper. Often this creative process involves first building a storyboard of clips in Frame view, then editing a group of clips, based on the storyboard, to the Timeline.

Building a Storyboard

Artist storyboards have been used in professional film and television work since the advent of the industry. Originally, storyboards were hand-drawn sketches depicting a scene. These sketches are still used today. As technology has evolved, however, so have storyboards. Many modern productions use computer-rendered pictures or photos (or combinations of film frames with computer drawings) to depict a scene. Regardless of the medium, the result is the same: Storyboards map out your scene or sequence before you shoot or edit it. As an editor working on an unscripted piece, this invaluable technique helps you visualize how shots will look juxtaposed before you commit them to the Timeline. To build a storyboard, change the bin to Frame view, enlarge the clips, and arrange them to fit in the window.

To resize the Storyboard bin and mark the the clips in Frame view:

1. Move and resize the **STORYBOARD** bin so that it covers the lower half of the screen from edge to edge (without overlapping the Composer window).

2. Change the **STORYBOARD** bin to Frame view. Press **CTRL+L** (Windows) or **COMMAND+L** (Mac) to enlarge the frames to their largest. It is important that you clearly see the content of each frame as you work.

3. From the **STORYBOARD** bin, open the **FAST** menu and choose **FIT IN WINDOW**.

4. Now mark the clips. For this, a little basic math is helpful. The music for the sequence is only 33 seconds. You used eight seconds in your intro clips, so you have about 25 seconds of music left to fill. That means you should limit your storyboard to eight or nine clips (averaging two or three seconds). If the shots run a little long, no worries. You'll learn how to trim the head or tail of the clip after you edit your storyboard to the Timeline.

Note: You get a chance to create a storyboard from scratch at the end of this lesson. Let's do this one together. This demo sequence simply shows the outrageous talents of both the snowboarders and the First Tracks Productions' crew that shot the footage. You can accentuate these elements by editing together shots that show snowboarding on, over, or through surfaces other than snow. If you are familiar with the footage, several shots may come to mind right away.

5. Load the **GOALPOST FS SICK** clip. Mark an IN point when the talent is in frame, but before you see his board (about 02;08;36;21). Mark an OUT point after he clears the goalpost and his board touches snow (02;08;40;06). Figure 4.30 shows the results of steps 1 through 5.

Figure 4.30
The Storyboard bin looks like this after steps 1 through 5.

6. Load the following clips and mark them accordingly:

Clip	Mark IN	Mark OUT
0053KB	04;21;26;23	04;21;29;09
0065OJ	14;16;38;27	14;16;42;02
00483D	11;32;23;26	11;32;27;04
0006P0	22;17;23;27	22;17;26;17
Jordan–big wood-teaser	11;53;59;25	11;54;02;11
Chris fs3 Tail to splice2	13;21;39;29	13;21;43;26
Chris–fs t to brd–jib	11;19;09;29	11;19;13;19
Jordan fast plan hv rock	12;56;35;26	12;56;39;01
Chris pond skim3	09;18;44;06	09;18;49;02
Darian rock spray	10;03;00;21	10;03;03;11

Arranging a Storyboard

With clips marked, put them into the order you wish to edit them in the sequence. Media Composer will read a group of clips in Frame view just as you would read a document: from left to right, top to bottom. As long as your clips are in the right order, Media Composer will place them in that same order in the sequence.

The first shot that you choose will follow the last shot already in the sequence (Fredrik doing a flip indoors). It would be nice to start with something outrageous, but not the most outrageous. (I'm thinking the goalpost or pond clip for the top of the outrageous list.) Try the shot of Jordan boarding down the long wooden handrail.

You can arrange the storyboard in the empty space in the bottom half of the Storyboard bin. Feel free to move or resize your bin as needed to create more or less space to work.

To arrange the storyboard:

1. Drag the **JORDAN–BIG WOOD-TEASER** clip to the lower left of the empty space in the bin. If this were a text paragraph, the first clip would represent the first word.

2. With the clip still selected, use **J-K-L** to play through the clip frames and find a good representative frame for the clip.

Tip: When you're arranging a storyboard, change the representative frame in the bin to show the content of the clip. J-K-L is a fast way to play through the clip in the bin and set a new representative frame.

3. Place the clips in the following order (see Figure 4.31):
   - Jordan fast plan hv rock
   - 00483D
   - 0006P0
   - Chris fs3 Tail to Splice2
   - Chris pond skim3
   - Chris–fst to brd–jib
   - 0053KB
   - Goalpost fs sick

These clips were arranged so that the action in the footage alternates camera direction as well as the type of action. The night clips were grouped together at the end, with the climax clip at the goalpost. It seemed fitting at the time. The only way to know if they actually work together is to edit them to the Timeline.

Figure 4.31
Your arranged storyboard looks like this.

Editing a Storyboard into a Sequence

You can drag a group of clips to the Timeline and edit them just as you would an individual clip. Pay attention to the following:

- Which tracks are active

- Where you release the clips

- What type of edit you are performing

In this case, you overwrite the clips and snap them to the end of the three clips that you edited to the sequence earlier. When you release a group of clips in the Timeline, they automatically align to either an IN point or to your position indicator. In this case, you use the position indicator. The first step is to move the Storyboard bin and select the arranged clips.

To edit the storyboard into the current sequence:

1. Move the **STORYBOARD** bin to the top of the screen so that it overlaps the Composer and Project windows.

2. Check the track selector buttons to make sure that only the video tracks (**V1**) are active. Click the **EXTRACT/SPLICE-IN** button in the Smart Tool palette to turn it off. Only the Lift/Overwrite button should be active.

3. Move the position indicator to the end of the last video clip in the Timeline.

4. In the **STORYBOARD** bin, select the nine clips that you arranged into a storyboard.

5. Drag the selected storyboard clips to the Timeline window and release them anywhere in the empty space of the video track, as shown in Figure 4.32. Figure 4.33 shows an edited storyboard.

Figure 4.32
Drag storyboard clips to the video track.

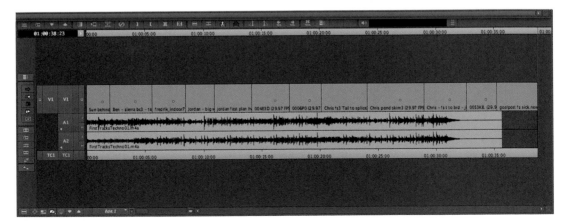

Figure 4.33
This is an edited storyboard.

6. Click the x (**Close**) button to close the **Storyboard** bin. Click the **Play** button to watch the edited sequence. Looks pretty good.

The clips work well together; they are just a little too long for this demo. To remedy that, you can either remove shots or trim them. But first, duplicate your sequence.

Note: When you drag a group of clips to the Timeline, Media Composer processes each clip in order as a separate edit. Therefore, if you want to undo the storyboard edit, undo once for each clip in the group, starting with the last one.

After you have edited the first draft of the demo, it's a good idea to create a duplicate version to work from. Seasoned editors back up their sequences to keep track of their progress. The copies also come in handy when you want to compare sequences. Sometimes during the trimming and refinement process, a scene loses some of its magic. When that happens, it's handy to be able to look back at earlier versions to figure out what might is missing.

To duplicate a sequence:

1. Load **FirstTracks Montage 01** into the Record monitor if it isn't there already.

2. From the **Clip Name** menu above the Record monitor, choose **Duplicate**; then select **My Demo Sequences** from the dialog box that opens and click **OK**.

3. In the **My Demo Sequences** bin, change the duplicate sequence name to **FirstTracks Montage 02**.

4. Change the name of the original sequence to **FirstTracks Storyboard 01**.

Trimming Segments with Top and Tail

Editing clips to the Timeline is only the beginning of the process. Trimming and fine-tuning an edit are crucial to making it look and feel professional. In this section, you fully explore Media Composer's different trimming tools. This section focuses on the Top and Tail tools because these are two of the easiest, most useful tools for quickly cleaning up a montage. Top and Tail tools use the position indicator to extract unwanted footage at the top (head) or tail of a clip. The best way to learn top and tail trimming is to use it. Start with the first clip in the Timeline.

Tip: By using the Top and Tail functions, you are essentially creating new IN and OUT points for a segment in the Timeline. The keyboard shortcuts on the Training User profile are Shift+I for Top and Shift+O for Tail.

To use the Top and Tail tools:

1. Click the **SMART TOOL** button, shown in Figure 4.34, to disable the Smart tool now that you're finished with it.

Figure 4.34
Click the Smart Tool button
to disable the Smart tool.

Note: When the Smart tool segment mode buttons are turned off, you can drag the pointer over a clip to move the position indicator. If any segment mode buttons are turned on, move the position indicator by clicking in the time-code track (below the audio tracks) or Timecode ruler.

2. Make sure **V1** is the only track enabled; then move the position indicator to the middle of the first video clip, as shown in Figure 4.35. Press **SHIFT+I** to extract the top half of the clip from the position indicator. The Timeline clips move to the left, filling in for the extracted portion of the clip, as shown in Figure 4.36.

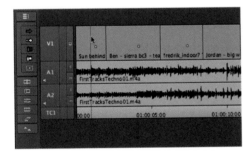

Figure 4.35
The position indicator is in the
middle of the first clip.

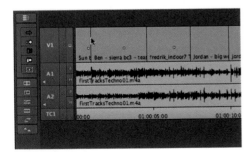

Figure 4.36
The first clip looks like this after a top trim.

3. Play the beginning of the sequence. Wow. That little top trim on the first clip made a huge difference in how the second and third clips fit with the music. It is as if you had planned it that way all along.

The first trim was obvious. What else can be trimmed without losing shots altogether? One strategy for this type of montage is to trim out the beginning or end of the clips and show one or the other. By the fifth clip, the audience will understand that these snowboarders are talented and assume that their take-offs and landings are good. So why not trim the head off of the pond skim shot? Showing someone skimming across the pond and landing is more unbelievable and awe inspiring. This is also a great opportunity to use the Find window to locate a clip in the sequence.

4. Press **CTRL+F** (Windows) or **COMMAND+F** (Mac) or choose **EDIT > FIND** to open the Find window.

5. Click the **TIMELINE AND MONITORS** tab in the Find window to search for text in the Timeline or the monitors.

6. Type **POND** in the **FIND** field. Click **FIND**. The position indicator jumps to the head of the Chris pond skim3 shot in the Timeline, as shown in Figure 4.37.

7. Close the Find window.

Figure 4.37
The Find window position indicator moves to a segment with the word *pond* in the title.

8. Move the position indicator just past the halfway point of the clip, before Chris raises his arms to steady himself. Press **SHIFT+I** to extract the top of the clip.

9. Move to the clip where Chris rides down the metal rail. The beginning is pretty cool, so just trim the tail. Put the position indicator at the end, right after the camera flash (where you see all of Chris, but he hasn't left the rail yet). Press **SHIFT+O** to extract the tail of the clip beyond the position indicator.

10. Trim the tail of the next shot so it ends just as he clears the pipe and spins.

11. Trim the tail of the last clip after the camera flash when he gets to the end of the goalpost. Don't have him jump back down. Use your music waveform in the audio tracks as a guide. Have the last clip end just as the music does.

12. Play the finished sequence. (See Figure 4.38.) Feel free to make other adjustments after the lesson.

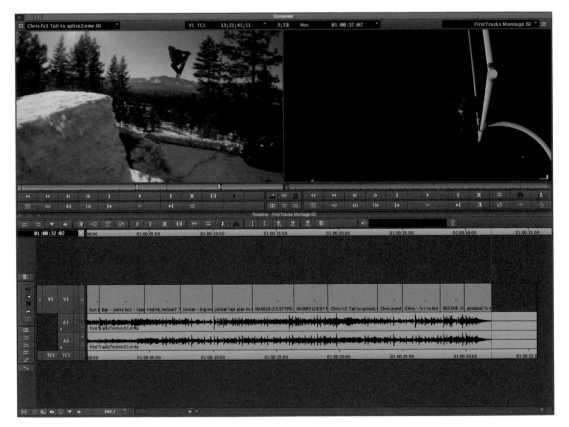

Figure 4.38
The montage is finished.

Top and Tail are just two of the many tools you can use to refine you sequence. There are many trim tools in Media Composer that add more flexibility. Let's take a look at another trim tool: Extend.

Trimming Segments with Extend

Similar to Top and Tail, Extend is another trimming function that helps to refine your sequence. The Extend tool uses an IN or OUT mark to move a cut point back or forward. Unlike Top and Tail, Extend can make a segment longer as well as shorter.

To use the Extend tool:

1. Make sure **V1** is the only track selected.

Tip: To extend multiple tracks, all the tracks must have the same edit point in the Timeline. Otherwise, you must extend the tracks separately.

2. Place the position indicator just before the end of the sequence and mark an IN point, as shown in Figure 4.39. The IN point indicates that the trim point is before the edit.

Figure 4.39
Mark an IN point just before the end of the sequence.

3. Click the **EXTEND** button below the Record monitor. The edit point on the V1 track moves backward to the location of the mark IN point, as shown in Figure 4.40.

Figure 4.40
After you click the Extend button, the edit point moves backward to the location of the mark IN point.

Note: **You can use Extend on transitions between two segments, not just at the end of a sequence. When extending an edit between two segments, the segment handles are used to extend one side of the cut as the other side gets shorter.**

4. You can also use an OUT point with Extend. Place the position indicator just after the end of the **V1** track where the audio tracks end.

5. Clear the IN point and then mark an OUT point, as shown in Figure 4.41. The OUT point indicates that the trim point is after the edit.

Figure 4.41
Mark an OUT at the end of the sequence.

6. Click the **EXTEND** button. The edit point on the V1 track moves forward to the location of the mark OUT point.

Excellent work. You not only learned how to manually edit clips to the Timeline, but you also created subclips, repositioned clips, created a storyboard edit, and trimmed the segments with Extend, Top, and Tail.

Review/Discussion Questions

1. How do you create a subclip (Select all the apply)?
   a. Press Alt+S (Windows) or Option+S (Mac).
   b. Ctrl-click the Source monitor and choose Make Subclip.
   c. Drag the clip icon from the Source monitor to a bin.
   d. Choose File > Make Subclip.

2. True or false: You can drag a clip to the Timeline and release it as either an overwrite or splice-in edit depending on where the pointer is when you release the clip in the Timeline.

3. True or false: If both segment mode buttons are turned on in the Smart Tool palette, you can reposition a segment with either Lift/Overwrite or Extract/Splice-In depending on the pointer position at the time of the maneuver.

4. If a clip is loaded in the Source monitor, how can you quickly open the bin that contains the master clip?

   a. Double-click the clip icon in the Source monitor.

   b. Open the Bin Settings dialog box.

   c. Click the Find Bin button.

   d. Click the Master Clip Bin button.

5. What features are available in the Find window? (Mark all that apply.)

   a. Find text in a project bin.

   b. Find text in project Timeline and monitors.

   c. Find clips based on spoken words.

   d. Select all clips in a results list and move them to an open bin.

6. In which dialog box can you add columns to a bin?

   a. Find dialog box

   b. Choose Column dialog box

   c. Custom preset dialog box

   d. Storyboard dialog box

7. What order does Media Composer use when you select a group of clips in Frame view and drag them to the Timeline?

   a. Lowest to highest, left to right

   b. Highest to lowest, right to left

   c. Left to right, highest to lowest

   d. Random order based on duration

8. What type of edit is most similar to top and tail trimming?

   a. Extract

   b. Lift

   c. Splice-In

   d. Overwrite

Keyboard Shortcuts

Key	Shortcut
Ctrl+9 (Windows)/Command+9 (Mac)	Select the Project window
Ctrl+F (Windows)/Command+F (Mac)	Open the Find window
Ctrl+4 (Windows)/Command+4 (Mac)	Select the Composer window
Shift+C	Add an edit
Shift+I	Trim the top of the clip
Shift+O	Trim the tail of the clip

Building a Storyboard and Montage

In this exercise, you create 12 subclips. You'll then drag a music clip to the Timeline and create a new sequence for which you will build a scenic storyboard. Finally, you'll build a montage.

Media Used:
First Tracks Productions

Duration:
60 minutes

GOALS

- Create subclips
- Create a new sequence
- Build a storyboard
- Edit a storyboard to the Timeline
- Practice repositioning clips in the Timeline
- Trim clips as needed with Top and Tail
- Duplicate a sequence to make a new version
- Drag and drop overwrite and splice-in edits
- Find specific clips
- Sort clips in a bin by comments
- Reposition clips to change the storyboard
- Use Top and Tail trim to clean up the sequence

Creating Subclips

This assignment may be more challenging than it seems. In this section, you create 12 subclips that you will edit with in the next section. Chances are you are pretty familiar with the exciting jumps, stunts, and wipeouts in the First Tracks Productions footage. In this exercise, you look for scenery footage *sans* snowboarders. There isn't enough footage in the Timelapse and Scenery bin, so look through some of the action shots and grab empty space before a stunt.

1. Create a new bin called SCENERY-ONLY SUBCLIPS.

2. Open the bin and place it in an easy-to-reach place on the left side of the interface.

3. This job requires fast turnaround, so work on it in Frame view to visualize the clip. Open the TIMELAPSE AND SCENERY bin and make the following subclips:

Clip	Footage
Icicle Drip	Anywhere—include one drip
Full Moon Timelapse	Moon moves from behind branch
big flakes trees	Do not include trees on left and right
2007-08 Timelapse 2	Shot of the mountain at the end

Remember to drag each new subclip to the SCENERY-ONLY SUBCLIPS bin. Try to keep the subclips between two and five seconds. Finally, don't worry about renaming all of the subclips.

4. Drag over all three subclips that you originally made in the Timelapse and Scenery bin. Add IN and OUT marks to these three subclips so they are around three seconds.

5. Make the following subclips from clips in the FTSELECTS bin.

Clip	Footage
Jordan fast plan hv rock	Beginning before Jordan appears
Chasefs7	Beginning with peeps and scenery

6. Open the QT AMA SELECTS bin. Create two more subclips from footage. Make sure they do not include snowboarders.

7. Resize the SCENERY-ONLY SUBCLIPS bin and enlarge the frames to make the clips fit the window.

8. Use J-K-L to play through each clip's frames and set a good representative scenic frame. Imagine that you have to build a storyboard based on the information shown in the bin in Frame view.

9. Close all open bins.

Creating a Storyboard

In this section, you drag a music clip to the Timeline and create a new sequence. Then you build a scenic storyboard to go with the music. After you have edited the storyboard, reposition at least three shots in the Timeline. Finally, you trim the clips as needed with Top and Tail.

1. Clear the Record monitor so there are no open sequences.

2. Open the **Audio** bin and load the **FirstTracksSouthernRock01.aif** song. Drag it to the Timeline to create a new sequence. The sequence will be in the Audio bin.

3. Drag the new sequence to the **My FirstTrack Sequences** bin and name it **FT ScenicMontage**.

4. Look at the Timecode ruler in the Timeline to determine the length of the music.

5. Calculate approximately how many shots you need, at an average of three or four seconds to fill the music. This depends on the duration of your subclips.

6. Open and resize the **Scenery-Only Subclips** bin. Arrange the subclips based on the content to create a storyboard. Don't worry about setting IN and OUT marks; you can trim the clips after they are in the Timeline.

7. In the Timeline, turn off the audio track buttons so you are editing only video.

8. Move your position indicator to the beginning of the Timeline; then drag and drop the entire storyboard to the Timeline.

9. Watch your storyboard with the music. (Feel free to laugh.)

10. If your storyboard is short, add shots.

11. Turn on both of the segment mode buttons in the Smart Tool palette.

12. Reposition at least three segments.

13. Use top and tail trimming (**Shift+I** and **Shift+O**, respectively) to trim the segments.

14. Play your sequence again.

Editing a Montage

The producer who thought up the scenic montage idea was fired. His replacement wants you to change the music and intersperse wild stunt and jump shots and wipeouts with the scenery. In this section, you duplicate the original storyboard and rename the copy. Then you drag and drop a more energetic piece of music to the Timeline to cover up the original song. Next, you use Find to locate several specific shots and drag them to the Timeline to splice in between scenic shots and to overwrite unwanted shots. Along the way, feel free to reposition clips and trim with Top and Tail as needed. Be creative and have fun. These kinds of exercises may seem simple, but they are like improvisation to actors: They challenge your mind as well as your knowledge of Media Composer. Besides, you never know what kind of project may be thrown at you. Being able to quickly turn out a creative piece is a skill that won't go unnoticed.

1. Duplicate the **FT ScenicMontage** sequence. Name the duplicate **FT WildScenicMashup**. Load the sequence.

2. Turn on the **A1** and **A2** track buttons and turn off the **V1** button.

3. Make sure that only the **Lift/Overwrite Segment Mode** button is active in the Smart Tool palette.

4. Drag and drop the **BrandingPower.aif** stock music clip from the **Audio** bin to the beginning of the audio tracks and overwrite the current song. This song is 20 seconds shorter than the original southern rock piece, so remove the remaining audio from the original song at the end of the Timeline. Mark that portion of the audio clip and extract or lift it out. Be sure to clear your Timeline marks.

5. Play the sequence with the new music.

6. Use **Find** to locate the **Full Moon timelapse** shot. Mark IN and OUT points where you think is best.

7. Drag the clip to the end of the sequence as the last shot.

8. Open the **QT AMA Selects** and **FT_Selects** bins. Change them to Text view and sort them by comments. Look for any clips with the word *wipeout* in the comments.

9. Mark IN and OUT points in any three of the wipeout clips. Splice or overwrite them to the Timeline.

10. Add as many other shots as you like to complete your mashup. If you are overwriting scenic shots, keep at least five scenery or time-lapse shots in the final edit. (They can be short, but they need to be in there.)

11. Reposition and trim the clips as needed to finish your mashup sequence.

12. Play the piece and savor the fact that you completed it by using new skills.

Refining the Edit

After you have created different rough-cut sequences, it is time learn how to use the powerful Media Composer tools that clean up your work. In this lesson, you trim and refine edit points in a sequence to finesse the timing. Then you learn different methods for adding cutaway shots to support dialogue, as well as tools to slide a clip's position and slip the footage within a clip itself. Sound intriguing? It should. Knowing how to enhance your edit from a rough cut to a professional-looking polished cut is what defines an editor's work and makes or breaks the finished project.

Media Used: Running the Sahara

Duration: 90 minutes

GOALS

- Learn about trimming
- Work with various trim functions to finesse timing
- Use ripple trimming to reduce or add dialogue frames
- Work with a second video track and cutaway shots
- Slide and slip segments in a sequence

Opening and Preparing the Project

For this lesson, you work with the main course project that you organized in Lesson 1, "Exploring the Interface and Preparing to Edit," and edited a rough cut teaser for in Lesson 2, "Assembling a Basic Sequence."

To open the project:

1. Launch Avid Media Composer, if it isn't already open.

2. If you have a project open, select the Project window then choose FILE > CLOSE PROJECT.

3. In the Select Project dialog box, click the EXTERNAL button.

4. Select MC6 EDITING from the project list.

Note: If you didn't complete all of the exercises in Lesson 3, "Ingesting File-Based Media," and Lesson 4, "Manual Timeline Editing," feel free to select the project L5 RTSTrim to catch up.

5. Make sure USER PROFILE is set to TRAINING USER, then click OK. The project opens with the Bins tab active in the Project window, and the Timeline and Composer windows open.

6. Close any open Running the Sahara footage bins.

7. In the Project window BINS pane, open the 1 LESSON SEQUENCES bin. Then open the MY SEQUENCES bin. You will use both bins throughout this lesson.

8. In the 1 LESSON SEQUENCES bin, duplicate the LESSON 05 OVERWRITE TRIM sequence. Drag the duplicate to your MY SEQUENCES bin. See Figure 5.1.

Figure 5.1
The My Sequences bin showing the duplicate sequence, Lesson 05 Overwrite trim.Copy.01.

9. Open the LESSON 05 OVERWRITE TRIM COPY.01 sequence.

Understanding Your Trimming Options

The term *trimming* originally came from the act of removing film frames with a razor blade to improve an edit. These types of changes could be drastic or subtle, similar to a trip to the barber. Nowadays, the term is more widely associated with the process of cleaning up edits to improve the sequence's overall feel and timing. That's easily said, but what does it mean?

Start with the rough cut, which isn't difficult to put together in Media Composer. Creating a rough cut is a carefree experience because you know you can later tweak and fix the things that you didn't worry about during the initial assembly. Like in writing, it is much easier to create a draft and fix it later than it is to create a perfect document from the start. Frankly, what seems perfect one day will need improvement the next.

As an editor, the rough cut is your starting point. Once you assemble the rough cut, you can examine each edit to determine if it is what you really want. Is the shot too long or too short? Does the footage seem to have missed the action, or is it coming in too early? Is the dialogue clearly spoken, with sentences starting and ending where you want, when you want? Are the visuals in the video track supporting what is said? How are the cuts working with the music? And so on....

In this lesson, you work with the five fundamental elements of trimming:

- Moving edit points earlier or later with dual-roller trim
- Adding or reducing a segment's footage with ripple trim
- Introducing cutaway shots to support dialogue and enhance the scene
- Nudging clips one direction or another, as needed, with Slide
- Tweaking which segment frame can be seen in the sequence without changing the duration with Slip

The Anatomy of a Basic Sequence

Before learning the specific trimming tools, this is a good time to clarify the terms and building blocks that make up your sequence. Most of these things you have already learned throughout the previous lessons. Now it is time to put it all together. See Figure 5.2.

- A sequence is comprised of segments.
- Segments represent the marked portions of a master clip.
- Each segment contains video and/or audio tracks.
- A segment's video and/or audio tracks reside in video and audio tracks in the Timeline.

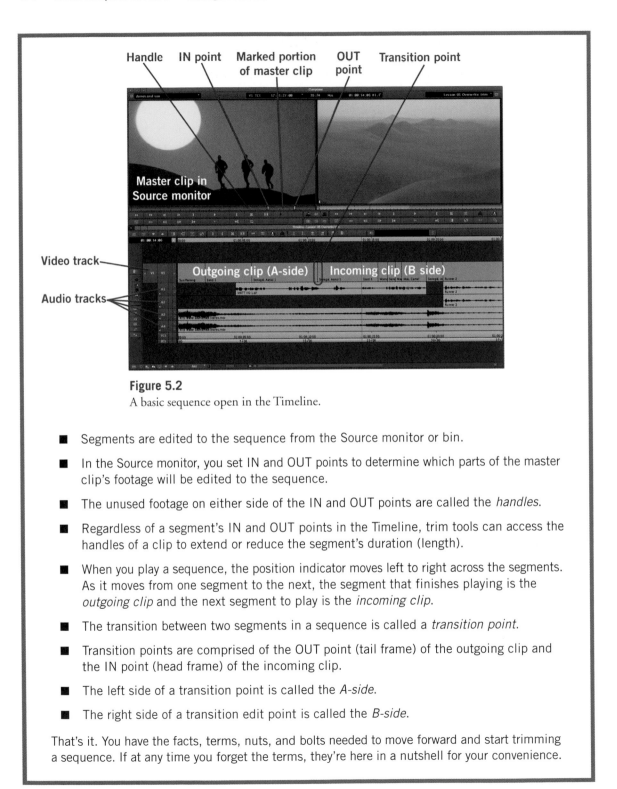

Figure 5.2
A basic sequence open in the Timeline.

- Segments are edited to the sequence from the Source monitor or bin.

- In the Source monitor, you set IN and OUT points to determine which parts of the master clip's footage will be edited to the sequence.

- The unused footage on either side of the IN and OUT points are called the *handles*.

- Regardless of a segment's IN and OUT points in the Timeline, trim tools can access the handles of a clip to extend or reduce the segment's duration (length).

- When you play a sequence, the position indicator moves left to right across the segments. As it moves from one segment to the next, the segment that finishes playing is the *outgoing clip* and the next segment to play is the *incoming clip*.

- The transition between two segments in a sequence is called a *transition point*.

- Transition points are comprised of the OUT point (tail frame) of the outgoing clip and the IN point (head frame) of the incoming clip.

- The left side of a transition point is called the *A-side*.

- The right side of a transition edit point is called the *B-side*.

That's it. You have the facts, terms, nuts, and bolts needed to move forward and start trimming a sequence. If at any time you forget the terms, they're here in a nutshell for your convenience.

Overwrite Trimming with the Smart Tool

In Lesson 4, you worked with the Top and Tail tools. These forms of trimming extract or extend segment frames based on the position indicator. For this lesson, you take a more hands-on approach—manually dragging an edit point to a new position using the Overwrite Trim button in the Smart tool. Overwrite Trim physically moves an edit point earlier or later, simultaneously changing the duration of the incoming and outgoing clips. See Figure 5.3.

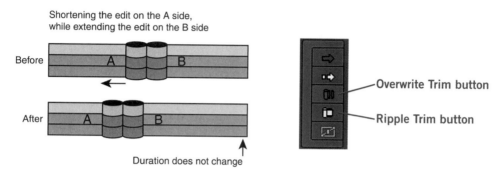

Figure 5.3

Selecting the Overwrite Trim button in the Smart Tool palette trims an edit point but does not change the overall duration of a sequence.

As you can see in Figure 5.3, the Overwrite Trim button in the Smart Tool palette is red. Just like the Overwrite button, the Lift button, and the Lift/Overwrite Segment Mode button in the Smart Tool palette. Rather than explain the Overwrite Trim tool first, see the results for yourself.

To use the Smart tool:

1. In the Smart Tool palette, click the **OVERWRITE TRIM** button to enable it. Turn off any other active buttons in the palette.

2. Click the **PLAY** button and watch the beginning of the sequence. The Sun Panning segment is a bit short, while the Sand 1 segment hangs there a long time before the narrator begins. The timing of the edit from one shot to the next is way off. No problem: With the Overwrite Trim tool, you can grab and move the transition point earlier or later. In this case, you drag the transition point later so that the Sand 1 shot starts just as the narrator begins talking. You can use the audio segment and waveform in track A1 as a guide.

3. In the Timeline's **V1** track, click the transition point between the **Sun Panning** and **Sand 1** segments at the beginning of the sequence. The pointer becomes an Overwrite Trim tool, and both sides of the transition point are selected (and appear pink). The A-side of the transition is the OUT point of the Sun Panning clip; the B-side of the transition is the IN point of the Sand 1 segment. See Figure 5.4.

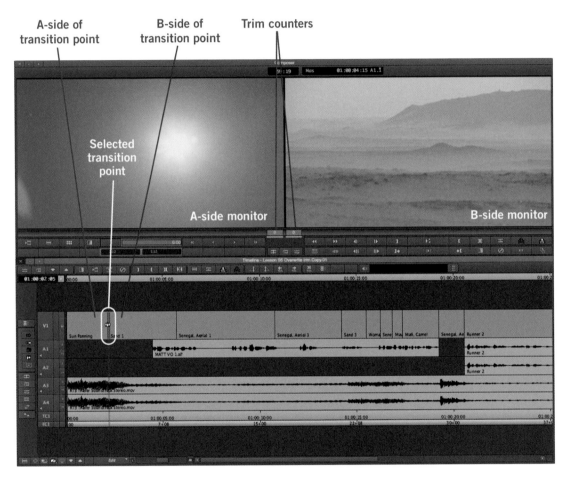

Figure 5.4
The transition point is selected with the Overwrite Trim tool. Both sides of the edit are selected (pink). The Composer window is in Trim mode.

Note: Selecting a transition point in the Timeline automatically shifts Media Composer from Edit mode to Trim mode. This change is most evident in the Composer window, where the Source and Record monitors display the A-side and B-side, respectively, of the active transition point. You work more with trimming in the Composer window shortly. For now, focus on dragging the transition point in the Timeline. Make sure that both sides of the transition are selected (pink). If only one side of the transition point was selected, that side will be selected red. (See Figure 5.5.) Be sure to click the center of the transition point to select both sides.

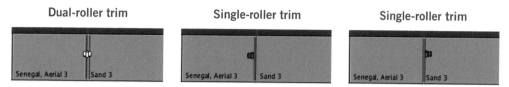

Figure 5.5
Dual-roller trim: Both sides of the transition point are selected (pink). Single-roller trim: The A-side of the transition is selected (red). Single-roller trim: The B-side of the transition is selected (red).

4. Click and drag the selected transition point to the right until it is even with the beginning of the **MATT VO 1** AUDIO segment on track **A1**. A Hand tool points to a vertical line over the Timeline segments to indicate where the new transition point will be as you drag. (See Figure 5.6.) Release the mouse button when the pointer is in the right position. The edit point appears where you released it (within the boundaries of the two segments). See Figure 5.7.

Nice Overwrite trim. As you can see, the Sun Panning segment just got longer, and the Sand 1 segment got shorter. How? The Sun Panning master clip had enough handle material in the original master clip to extend it in the Timeline. As you trimmed out Sun Panning, you also trimmed back Sand 1 by the same amount. You'll explore handles further in a few minutes. For now, drag another transition point to improve the timing.

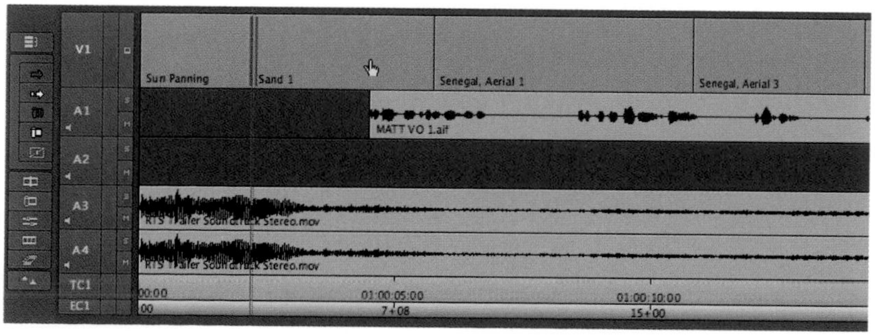

Figure 5.6
A pointer and vertical line show the transition point as you drag.

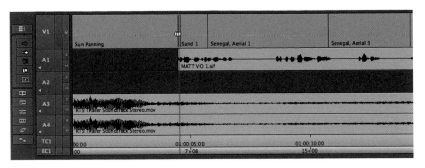

Figure 5.7
The transition point is in a new spot: at the beginning of the MATT VO 1 segment.

Note: Selecting one side of the transition point will perform a single-roller overwrite trim, where only one side of your cut changes. A single-roller overwrite trim still maintains the overall sync relationships of the tracks as well as the overall duration of the sequence. It does this by either adding a black segment or overwriting frames to fill the duration of trimmed frames.

Note: Holding Ctrl (Windows) or Command (Mac) while you drag a transition point allows you to snap to other segments or to IN and OUT points in the sequence.

5. In the Timeline window, click the Timecode ruler to switch from Trim mode to Edit mode. Click the **PLAY** button and watch the first five clips in the sequence, from Sun Panning through Sand 3. The first segment's timing works pretty well, but the others don't fit the voiceover. For example, the narrator says, "It is the most unforgiving place on Earth" while the video shows trees. Trees don't feel nearly as unforgiving as sand. Fix that by moving the transition point to extend the **SAND 1** segment. This fixes another problem: The Senegal, Aerial 1 segment feels too long.

6. Click and drag the transition point between the **SAND 1** and **SENEGAL, AERIAL 1** segments to the right. Release it just before the narrator's second statement: "over 3.5 million square miles" (about 01:00:08:13).

Tip: It may be easier to find the correct location for step 6 if you enable Digital Audio Scrub and listen for the narration.

7. Click and drag the transition point between **SENEGAL, AERIAL 3** and **SAND 3** to the left. Release it after the narrator says, "A vast wilderness." See Figure 5.8.

8. Click the Timecode ruler or press **U** to switch back to Edit mode.

Figure 5.8
The second transition point precedes the second narration (in A1 waveform). The fourth transition point moved follows the third narration (in A1 waveform).

Tip: Generally, the editor's work on a documentary scene with video over narration should help tell the story without calling attention to the edits. Make subtle edits that flow and feel less literal by trimming the transition points so they are not aligned exactly with the start or end of a phrase. A transition between two shots that happens a beat or two (8–20 frames) *before* or *during* a statement will feel more natural. An exception to making subtle edits: You are cutting a commercial and want to dramatically accentuate a statement. To see and hear an example of cutting too close to a phrase, play the first two shots in the sequence. You'll fix that timing with a shortcut in the next exercise.

Using the Trim Keyboard Shortcuts

Dragging transition points with the Overwrite Trim tool is an easy maneuver. Like most Media Composer editing features, you can use handy keyboard shortcuts. In this case, four trimming shortcuts are in the lower-right corner of the keyboard. See Figure 5.9. Don't confuse these with the Step Frame keyboard shortcuts in the upper-left corner of the keyboard (keys 1–4). The difference between shortcut sets is this: The Step Frame shortcuts move the position indicator, but the Trim mode shortcuts move the selected transition point. Just like the Step Frame shortcuts and buttons, the multiple frame trim is 10 frames or eight frames in 24p projects.

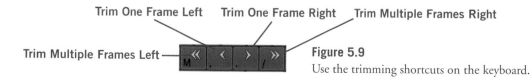

Figure 5.9
Use the trimming shortcuts on the keyboard.

To use the trim keyboard shortcuts:

1. Click the **PLAY** button. Watch the beginning of the sequence and listen to the narration. You may notice (especially if you read the preceding tip) that the second segment, Sand 1, abruptly cuts in at the beginning of the narrator's statement. You could drag the transition a few frames, but it is much easier to use the shortcut.

2. Select the transition point between the **SUN PANNING** and **SAND 1** segments. Press **M**. The selected transition point moves left eight frames.

3. In Trim mode, press the **SPACE BAR** to preview the transition point in the Composer window. One monitor plays in the center of the Composer window as you preview the transition point. See Figure 5.10. The playback automatically loops so you can evaluate the edit. Watch the transition point at least twice and press the **SPACE BAR** again to pause playback.

Figure 5.10
Composer window during looped Trim mode playback.

What do you think of the trim? The edit feels smoother than before, but it could use another eight frames so the audience has an extra moment to comprehend the desolate image prior to the narrator's words. So far you trimmed the transition point –8 frames. If you aren't sure how far you've trimmed, take a look at the pink highlighted numbers in the Composer window's trim counters. The number on the left is the A-side trim counter; the number on the right is the B-side trim counter. The counters currently show that both sides moved eight frames to the left (–8). See Figure 5.11.

Figure 5.11
The trim amount is indicated for the transition point's A-side and B-side (–8).

4. Press **M** to move the transition point eight more frames to the left. The trim counters in the Composer update to show –16 frames total. Press the **SPACE BAR** to see the looped playback. When you preview the transition in looped playback, press the **SPACE BAR** again to stop playback.

5. While the first transition point is still selected (select it if you exited Trim mode), press the **UP ARROW KEY** to fast forward to the next transition point. This shortcut is part of the Training User settings.

6. Press the **SPACE BAR** to see looped playback of the second transition point. Press the **SPACE BAR** again to pause playback. Use the trim shortcuts to move the transition point so it is at least eight frames before the beginning of the second narrative statement ("over 3.5 million square miles").

7. Press **U** to exit Trim mode.

Note: You can change the duration of the Trim mode play loop: Adjust Preroll and Postroll Duration in the fields under the A-side of the Trim mode Composer window. *Preroll* is how early the loop starts before the transition point; *postroll* is how late the loop plays after the transition point.

8. Play the beginning of the sequence to see the improvements that you have made.

You'll get a chance to trim the remaining transition points later. For now, excellent trimming. As you gain experience, trimming transition points will become second nature.

Note: **Dual-roller overwrite trimming is often used to create split edits in dialogue scenes to smooth either the video or audio. You will learn more of this technique if you continue on to the advanced editing course, *Media Composer 6: Professional Picture and Sound Editing*. An example of split edits is included in the exercise at the end of this lesson.**

Preparing the Project

Before you dive into the next trim tool, duplicate and open the next sequence that you will be using.

To prepare the project:

1. In the **My Sequences** bin, select the **RTS Interviews** sequence that you created at the end of Lesson 2. If you don't have an RTS Interviews sequence, open the **1 Lesson Sequences** bin and select the **Lesson 05 Ripple trim** sequence.

2. Right-click the sequence and choose **Duplicate**. Rename the duplicate sequence **RTS Interviews Trimmed.**

3. Move the **RTS Interviews Trimmed** sequence to the **My Sequences** bin if it is not already there.

Tip: **If you combined your open bins into one tabbed bin window, you can drag items from the open bin to the tab of the bin where you'd like the item to be.**

4. Open the **RTS Interviews Trimmed** sequence.

Using Ripple Trim to Fix Dialogue

Now focus on a new trimming tool called Ripple Trim. The Ripple Trim button in the Smart tool is yellow, which indicates it is similar to the Extract/Splice-In segment mode, and the Splice-In tool. All three of these yellow tools affect a sequence's overall duration. In the case of the Ripple Trim tool, as you add or remove frames from either the A-side or B-side of a transition point, the remaining segments *to the right* of the transition also move accordingly. (See Figure 5.12.) This rippling effect is similar to what happens when you splice-in or extract a segment from the sequence. The yellow Ripple Trim button is below the Overwrite Trim button in the Smart Tool palette.

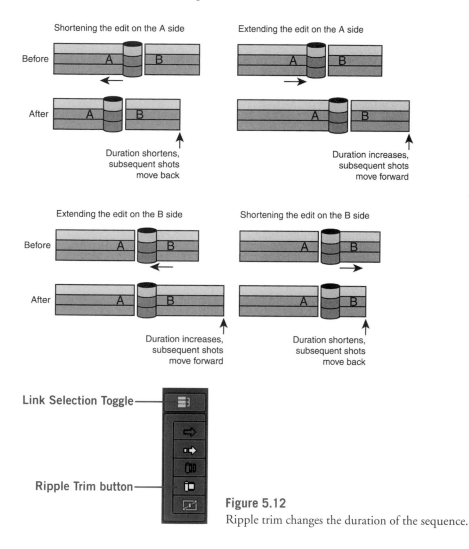

Figure 5.12
Ripple trim changes the duration of the sequence.

In this exercise you work with the first four segments, starting with the A-side of each transition point. Then you fix the B-side.

To use the Ripple Trim tool:

1. In the Smart Tool palette, turn off the **OVERWRITE TRIM** button.

2. Turn on the yellow **RIPPLE TRIM** button. Also, make sure that the **LINK SELECTION TOGGLE** button (above the Smart Tool palette) is highlighted.

3. Play the first four segments in the sequence, paying attention to how each segment starts and ends and how they transition. This sequence needs a lot of work. Fortunately, the Ripple Trim tool makes it easy.

Note: **The important thing to do as an editor is listen to the sequence, figure out what is wrong, and fix it. When fixing dialogue, you only worry about the audio at this point. Doing an *audio-driven pass* (cleaning up a sequence while focusing only on audio) is often referred to as a *radio edit*. When you are finished, the sequence sound (both context and pacing) plays well enough for radio. It is a given (especially when all segments show the same person) that the jump cuts from segment to segment need smoothing.**

4. With the Ripple Trim tool, move the pointer over the first transition point. The tool changes depending on the position over the left, right, or middle of the transition point. (See Figure 5.13.) Click the tail of **INTERVIEW 1**, the outgoing shot at the first edit point on V1. This selects the A-side at this transition point.

Figure 5.13
A: Both sides of the transition point are selected (pink). B: The A-side of the transition is selected (yellow). C: The B-side of the transition is selected (yellow).

5. See how many tracks were selected in the transition point. (See Figure 5.14.) If only the video transition point is selected, and you ripple trim only the video, you will inadvertently move the rest of the video segments out of sync.

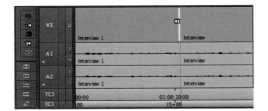

Figure 5.14
Because V1 is the only track selector button enabled, only the transition point on V1 gets selected.

6. Trimming is still editing, so be vigilant about which track selector buttons are turned on. These interview segments contain one video and two audio tracks. Therefore, you'll need to be sure you have all three track selector buttons selected as you work. To make this easier, you can enable the **LINK SELECTION TOGGLE** button at the top of the Smart Tool so it is highlighted

7. Turn on the track selector buttons for **A1** and **A2** (if they are not already selected). All three edit points should be selected. See Figure 5.15. The yellow selection shows that only the A-side (the last frame of the outgoing segment) is selected and that is the only part of the transition point that will be trimmed.

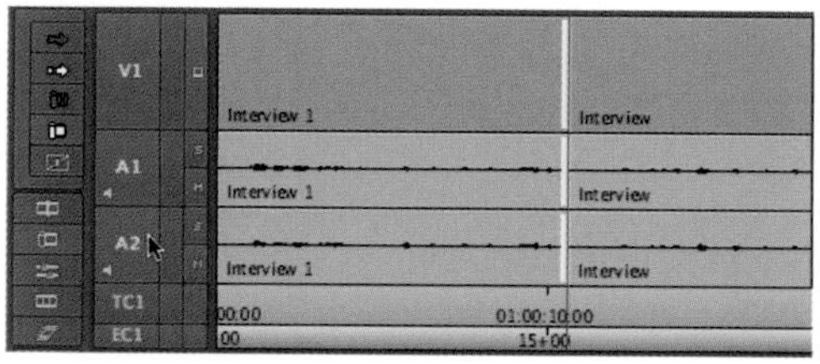

Figure 5.15
All three tracks (V1, A1, and A2) are selected.

8. Press the **SPACE BAR** to play the selected transition point. There isn't enough preroll in the play loop to determine the gist of what the talent is saying and how much A-side dialogue should be trimmed.

9. In the Composer window, below the A-side (left) monitor, click the **PREROLL FOR PLAY LOOP** field. See Figure 5.16.

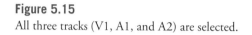

Figure 5.16
The Preroll for Play Loop field is in the A-side of the Composer window.

10. Type **400** and press **ENTER/RETURN**. The preroll changes to 4:00 (four seconds).

11. Press the **SPACE BAR** to play the loop again. This time you can hear where the talent finishes the sentence ("…then to go down in it myself"). Then he begins a tangent with, "And I have this twisted…." As you listen to the loop, ignore the B-side (second segment) at this point. Ignoring large sections takes practice, but you'll learn to focus on the part you need to hear. Stop the play loop. It should be obvious that the A-side of the transition point needs to be trimmed all the way back to where he finishes saying "…go down in there myself." The trouble is that this is tricky to see in the waveform at the moment. Enlarge the audio tracks to make it easier to see the waveforms.

12. Turn off the **V1** track selector button. Press **CTRL+L** (Windows) or **COMMAND+L** (Mac) to enlarge the audio tracks until you can see the waveform well. (See Figure 5.17.) Turn on the **V1** track selector button.

Tip: It may be helpful to also enlarge the audio waveforms. To enlarge the waveforms, press Ctrl+Alt+L (Windows) or Command+Option+L (Mac).

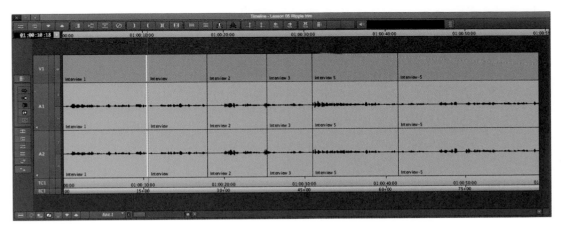

Figure 5.17
Enlarged audio tracks help you see dialogue.

13. At the bottom of the Timeline window, click the **Focus** button to scale
    the Timeline. Now focus is on the selected transition point. See Figure 5.18.

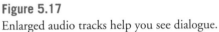

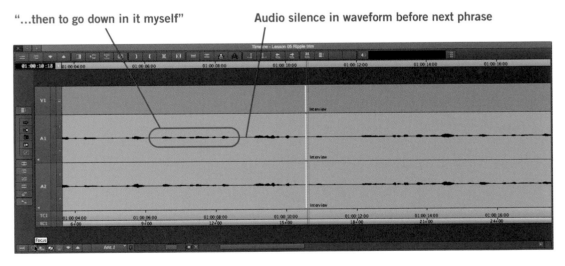

Figure 5.18
The Timeline focused on the selected transition point.

That's much better. Now that you can really see the audio waveforms and
the transition point, you can see where you need to ripple trim the A-side
of the outgoing segment.

14. Press the **SPACE BAR** to play the loop. Watch the waveform in the audio tracks
    to see where the talent ends the statement ("…then to go down in it
    myself"). Stop playback when you locate that portion of the waveform.

15. Drag the selected (yellow) transition point to the left until you reach the middle of the silent section (flat horizontal line) in the waveform; it is between the dialogue statements (about 01:00:08:21). A Hand tool points to a vertical line over the Timeline segments to indicate where the new A-side transition point will be as you drag. (See Figure 5.19.) Release the mouse button when the pointer is in the right position. The A-side of the transition point appears wherever you release it. See Figure 5.20. Because you trimmed frames and reduced the outgoing segment's duration, you just performed a reductive trim.

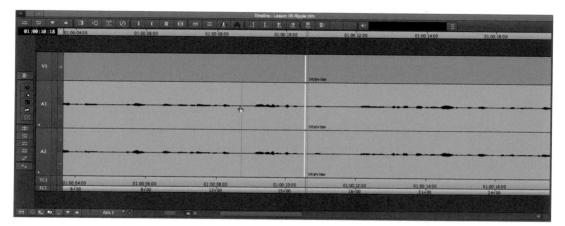

Figure 5.19
The pointer and vertical line show the new transition point as you drag.

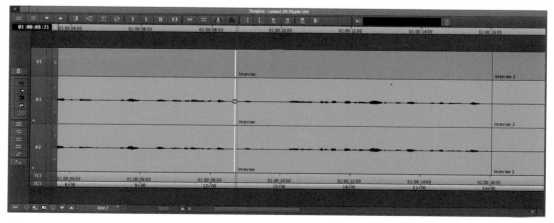

Figure 5.20
The transition point is in a new location.

16. Press the **SPACE BAR** to loop playback. The A-side sounds great, so you can focus on the B-side. Feel free to adjust the preroll and postroll for the play loop. Can you find where to trim the B-side (the beginning of the incoming segment)? On the transition point's B-side, the talent starts abruptly in the middle of a statement as he says, "…for weeks. Uh and we did in fact…." You want to remove everything prior to where he says, "We did in fact…." This is a reductive trim.

17. Move and click the pointer over the transition point's B-side select it. See Figure 5.21.

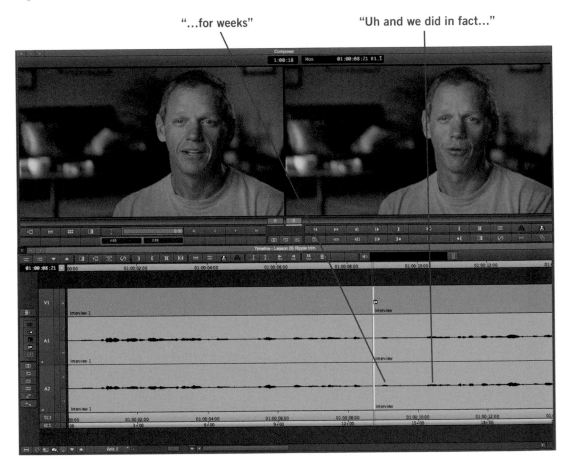

"…for weeks"   "Uh and we did in fact…"

Figure 5.21
The B-side is selected with the Ripple Trim tool.

Tip: You can lasso a transition point to quickly enter Trim mode, set up for dual-roller trim. Then, use these keyboard shortcuts to change which side of the transition point is selected:

- P trims the A-side.

- [trims the AB-side.

-] trims the B-side.

18. Drag the yellow B-side of the transition point to the right and release it before the part in the waveform where he says, "Uh and we did in fact…." (See Figure 5.22 and Figure 5.23.) Why stop before the statement, instead of exactly where you want it? In this case, it is too hard to visually determine the exact spot. You will get it close and then fix the B-side with keyboard shortcuts.

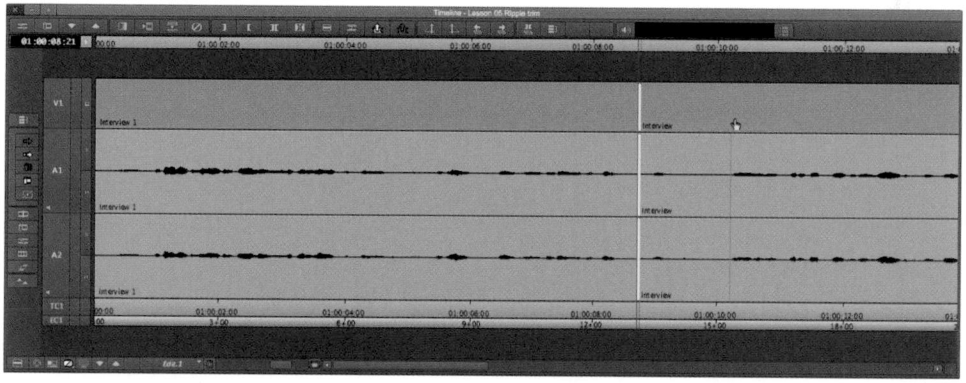

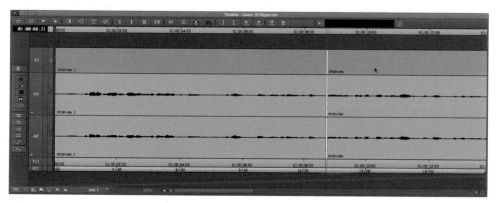

Figure 5.22
The pointer and vertical lines show the new transition point as you drag.

Figure 5.23
This reductive trim reduces frames from the B-side.

19. Play the transition to get a feel for the trimmed transition point. Stop playback. Press the / (SLASH) KEY once to trim eight frames to the right. Play the transition. Close, but not quite. Continue playback and press the . (PERIOD) KEY several times. The change will update in time for the next pass in the play loop.

20. Press the . (PERIOD) and , (COMMA) KEYS to trim the B-side one frame at a time (right or left) until it sounds good to you. Try to cut off the "uh" and smooth the "and we did in fact go to one well…." You can try to remove "and" altogether and lead with the "we," or you can split the difference and keep the "and." Close your eyes as you listen to the transition between the segments. When it sounds good enough for radio, stop playback. Notice that the amount you trimmed the B-side shows in pink in the B-side trim counter in the Composer window. See Figure 5.24.

Figure 5.24
The finished B-side trim shows pink.

Good work finessing the first transition point. By now, you have figured out that there is no exact formula for trimming. In some instances (like when you trimmed the A-side here), it was obvious. For the B-side, on the other hand, you had to get it close and then finesse it one frame at a time. Media Composer offers myriad ways to trim your sequence. You get to figure out which method to use in each instance.

Trimming on-the-Fly

If you liked trimming one frame at a time while listening to the play loop, you are going to love this section. In fact, many editors prefer to trim dialogue by ear (on-the-fly, as they listen) rather stopping, starting, and staring at waveforms. In this section, you incorporate I and O, as well as J-K-L, playback to edit the next few transition points on-the-fly. Along the way you also work more with Trim mode shortcuts.

To trim on-the-fly:

1. In the Timeline window, press **Ctrl+/** (**slash**) (Windows) or **Command+/** (**slash**) (Mac) to see the entire sequence in the Timeline.

2. Select the second transition point in the sequence (between **Interview** and **Interview 2**).

Note: If your selection only includes one video or audio track, make sure that the Toggle Link Selection button is turned on (above the Smart tool). Also make sure that the track control buttons for all three tracks are turned on.

3. Press **P** to select the transition point's A-side, if it is not already selected.

4. Press the **space bar** and listen to the play loop a few times. You want to trim the A-side so it ends after he says, "We did, in fact, find one well that was being dug." Rather than dragging the transition point to the left, use a shortcut to jump to the precise moment that you want make the cut.

5. Continue listening to the play loop while the A-side of the transition point is selected. Press **O** precisely when the talent finishes saying, "We did, in fact, find one well that was being dug." The A-side updates, the play loop restarts, and you can hear the new OUT point on the next loop. Don't worry if you are off a few frames. Use the period and comma shortcuts to trim the A-side a frame or two. Stop playback when you are finished. See Figure 5.25.

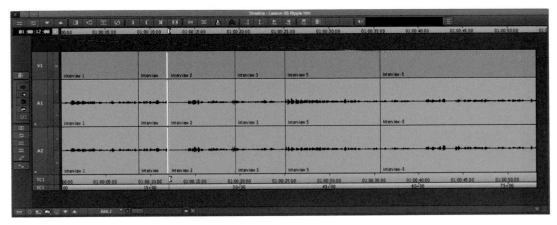

Figure 5.25
Set a new OUT point for the A-side of the transition point.

6. Press **G** to clear the OUT point in the Timeline. Press **]** (RIGHT BRACKET) to select the transition point's B-side. Press the SPACE BAR to start the play loop.

7. Press **I** to mark a B-side IN point just after the talent says "uh" and before he says, "So they put me on this bar…." If you trimmed too tightly, mark an IN point on the next pass while the position indicator is over the out-going clip on the A-side. Then you can set another IN point on the next pass. (Or you could stop playback and use the period and comma shortcuts to finesse the transition as needed.) When finished, stop playback and clear the IN and OUT points in the Timeline.

Tip: **Trimming is more than just getting the right words. If you cut it too tightly, it will feel unnatural. You can always try to add frames to either the A-side or the B-side to give a pause between phrases. Later, when you add supporting video shots, you can splice-in some filler between segments.**

For the next transition, you will try J-K-L to trim on-the-fly. This may be more difficult at first, but with practice can become one of the most effi-cient, powerful trim methods for you in Media Composer. Whether you are playing at regular speed or are slowed to one-quarter speed, trimming with J-K-L is real time and happens the instant you release any of the keys. For your first J-K-L trim, you trim an "uh" from the beginning of the sequence.

8. If the transition point is still selected in the sequence, press the **Down Arrow key** twice to move the position indicator to the beginning of the sequence. (Otherwise, select the transition point at the beginning of the sequence.) See Figure 5.26. The B-side of the first segment is automatically selected because there is no A-side.

Figure 5.26
B-side transition into first segment selected.

Note: The Up Arrow and Down Arrow keys work for fast forward and rewind (moving from transition to transition in Trim mode) because of the Training User settings.

9. Press the **SPACE BAR** to loop the sequence beginning. You can clearly hear the "uh." Press the **SPACE BAR** again to stop playback.

10. Press and hold **K+L** to play forward at one-quarter speed. You can hear the audio in slooooow motion, which helps you hear the "uh" much more precisely. Release **K+L** the instant the "uh" completes. For this maneuver, you may want to watch the talent's lips move in the Source monitor. You can see his lips move for "uh," then purse to say the next word. See Figure 5.27.

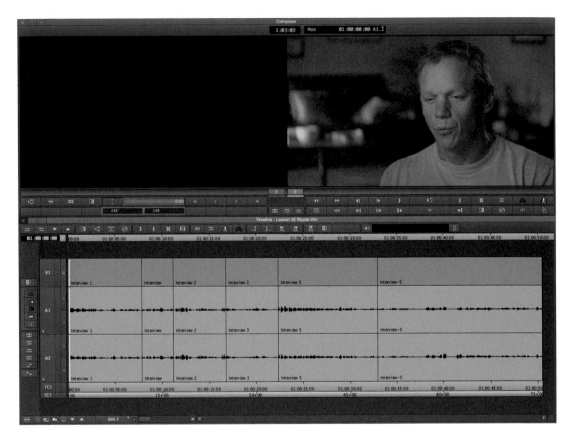

Figure 5.27
"Uh" is trimmed from the beginning of the first segment.

11. Press the **SPACE BAR** to loop play the transition. If you overshot the point and cut off a bit of the first line ("We were getting ready to leave…"), no worries. Just use the shortcut keys to move the transition point to the left as needed (or try **J-K-L** to fix the transition at the head of the sequence).

12. Press **U** to exit Trim mode and play the first three segments in the sequence. What a difference a little trimming makes. Of course, there is still plenty to do, but you are armed with different methods for using the Ripple Trim tool. The last method that you will explore is the Composer window in Trim mode.

Trimming in the Composer Window

You have used the Composer window in Trim mode to preview transition points, change the preroll, and check the trim counters. Two primary features that you haven't used include:

■ Trim buttons, which correspond with the trim shortcuts you have been using already

■ Physically clicking the A-side or B-side monitors to change the transition selection

To trim in the Composer window:

1. In Edit mode, move the position indicator to the transition point between the **INTERVIEW 2** and **INTERVIEW 3** segments in the Timeline.

2. Press **U** to select the transition point and switch to Trim mode. Both sides of the transition point in the Timeline as well as both of the trim counters in the Composer window are highlighted pink. See Figure 5.28.

Figure 5.28
Select the transition; the Composer and Timeline windows are in Trim mode.

The Trim Frame buttons are on the right side of the toolbar below the A-side monitor. The Step Frame buttons are under the B-side monitor, just as they are in Edit mode.

3. In the Composer window, below the B-side monitor (the right monitor), click the **PLAY LOOP** button. It looks like the Play button with revolving arrows.

4. Listen to the transition between the two segments. Stop the play loop. In Interview 2 and Interview 3, the talent is talking about being rigged onto a bar. The challenge is to trim the segments in such a way that they flow together and sound like a complete thought. As always, start with the A-side.

5. Click the image in the A-side monitor (the left monitor). The B-side trim counter turned off, but the A-side trim counter remained active (pink) in the Composer window, as shown in Figure 5.29. You can always tell which part of the transition point is selected by looking at the trim counters.

Figure 5.29
The transition is selected. The Composer and Timeline windows are in Trim mode.

6. To make this a little easier on the ears, extend the preroll (A-side) and eliminate the B-side of the transition from the play loop. In the Composer window, click the **Preroll** field and type **500**. Press **Enter/Return**. See Figure 5.30.

Figure 5.30
Preroll is set to 5:00.

7. Click the **Play Loop** button in the Composer window to play the transition again and press the **Q** key to only play the A-side. With the B-side out of the loop (literally and figuratively), you can focus on the A-side's dialogue. Trim the A-side of the transition toward the left so that it ends right after he says, "They put me on this crossbar."

8. Press **H** to focus the Timeline on the selected transition. Now you can use the waveform as well as the audio as guides for trimming.

9. Use whatever method you like to trim the A-side so it ends after the talent says "crossbar." This is a great opportunity to practice J-K-L trimming; or, use the step trim shortcuts or Trim Frame buttons in the Composer window to perform the A-side trim. Because where you need to trim to is easy to see, you can also drag the A-side of the transition to do a manual ripple trim. The finished trim should be somewhere around 01:00:13:11, which is about –81 frames. See Figure 5.31. Now you are ready to trim the B-side.

10. Change **Postroll** to **4:00**.

11. Loop play the transition and press the **W** key to only listen to the B-side dialogue. The talent says, "…get onto this bar they get me sort of rigged up and they start to lower me down."

12. Trim the B-side so that the trimmed dialogue is "they get me sort of rigged up and they start to lower me down…." Use the method you want to try. Feel free to combine methods to accomplish your goal. When you are finished, the dialogue from the A-side and B-side combined should be, "So they put me on this crossbar; they get me sort of rigged up and start to lower me down."

13. Press **U** to switch to Edit mode. Play the first four segments to hear how they work.

Nice job. You get a chance to finish trimming the sequence in an exercise at the end of this lesson.

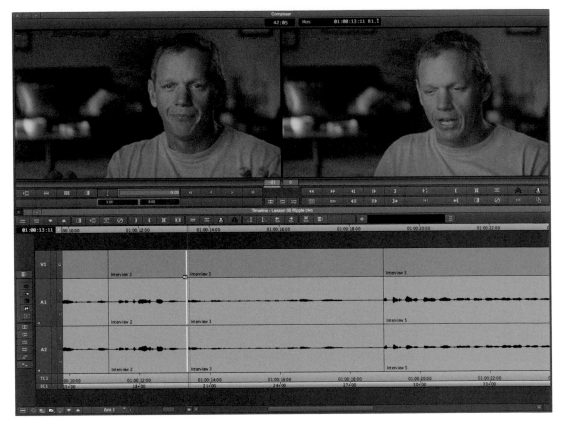

Figure 5.31
The A-side is trimmed around –81 frames.

Preparing the Project

Before you add a second video track, duplicate and open the next sequence that you will be using. Making backup sequences as your project progresses is a great way to study the evolution of your sequence. It is also a good way to keep track of your project in case you need to back up a level and try something different.

To make a duplicate and open the sequence:

1. In the **1 Lesson Sequences** bin, select and duplicate the **Lesson 05 Add Cutaways** sequence.

2. Name the duplicate sequence **RTS Interviews with Cutaways**.

3. Move the **RTS Interviews with Cutaways** sequence to the **My Sequences** bin.

4. Open the **RTS INTERVIEWS WITH CUTAWAYS** sequence. The remaining interview segments have already been trimmed in this version of the sequence.

5. Open the **RUNNERS** bin.

6. Load four master clips from the **RUNNERS** bin into the Source monitor:
   - Well POV Slo-Mo
   - Lowering into Well
   - Night Camera Inside Well
   - Maur, with Camera

   Feel free to play the clips to remind you what footage you have available.

7. Resize and move the **RUNNERS** bin out of the way.

8. In the Smart Tool palette, turn off the **RIPPLE TRIM** button. No buttons in the Smart Tool palette should be active.

Using Additional Video to Enhance a Sequence

The audio portion of the Interviews sequence is coming along nicely, thanks to your expert trimming. The video, on the other hand, has a lot of issues. First, it is all talking-head footage (medium close-up shots of someone talking). Second, all the shots are of the same person, so there is a visual jump (*jump cut*) between every segment. Finally, no matter how fascinating your subject is, talking-head shots alone will never hold an audience's interest. Adding cutaway shots that show what the person is talking about solves all three issues at once. During the next few sections, you will learn two methods for adding video cutaways. For the first method, you will create a second track of video and edit cutaway shots to the V2 track. For the second method, you will edit the cutaway video directly into the V1 track. Both methods have advantages that you will explore along the way.

Editing Video to a Second Video Track

In this section, you create a new video track, edit a segment to the track, move it, and then trim the segment.

To edit video to another video:

1. Press **CTRL+Y** (Windows) or **COMMAND+Y** (Mac) or right-click anywhere over the sequence in the Timeline window and choose **NEW VIDEO TRACK**. A new video track appears above V1 in the Timeline. See Figure 5.32.

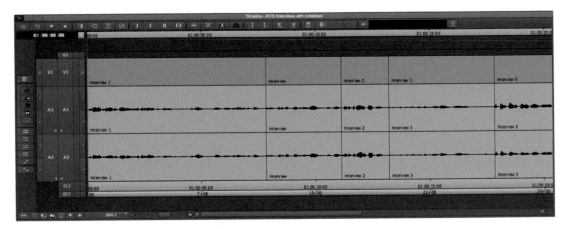

Figure 5.32
A new video track (V2) appears in the Timeline.

You probably noticed that the new video track is fairly diminutive in height compared to V1. To fix that, deselect the other tracks and enlarge the track. While you are at it, you can reduce the other tracks' sizes. Go ahead and reduce the others before enlarging the V2 track.

2. Click the **V2** track selector button to deselect the track.

3. Press **CTRL+K** (Windows) or **COMMAND+K** (Mac) several times to make room in the Timeline window to enlarge the V2 track.

4. Deselect the **V1**, **A1**, and **A2** track selector buttons. Turn on the **V2** track selector button and press **CTRL+L** (Windows) or **COMMAND+L** (Mac) until the track is as big as V1. See Figure 5.33.

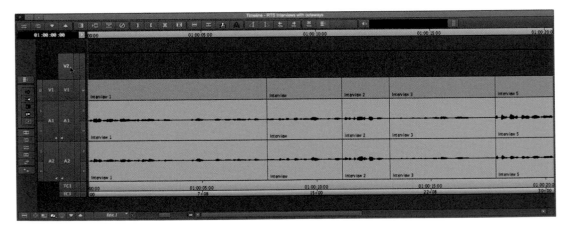

Figure 5.33
The V2 track is the same height as the V1 track.

Editing cutaway shots to a second video track is an easy way to add supporting video clips, especially for new editors. It seems to be the "safe" way to add video. However, it also limits your workflow speed and trimming options. You can decide for yourself which is more important. Keep in mind, your goal here is to use cutaway shots to patch over the cuts between interview segments and offer visual reinforcement. There is a lot riding on these four shots. Make them count.

5. Play the first two segments, focusing on what the talent says. In the first segment, he says he had the idea to go down into a well. In the second segment, he says he went to a well that was being dug. Given your limited footage, this is a good place for the Well POV Slo-Mo shot.

6. Use the Source monitor's **CLIP NAME** menu to load the **WELL POV SLO-MO** master clip, which should have IN and OUT points. If not, mark the portion of the clip that looks down into the well (01:03:19:05–01:03:20:19). Press **6** to play the clip from IN to OUT. Since it is easy to move the segment once you place it on V2, overwrite it at the beginning of the second segment.

7. Ctrl-click (Windows) or Command-click (Mac) the first transition point between the **INTERVIEW 1** and **INTERVIEW** segments. The position indicator moves to that position. See Figure 5.34.

8. Make sure the **V2** track is selected; then make sure the **A1** and **A2** Timeline track selector buttons are off.

9. Overwrite the clip. The Well POV Slo-Mo segment appears on the V2 track. See Figure 5.35.

10. Play the beginning of the sequence to see how the cutaway shot on V2 works with the audio. Well? (Pun intended.) The shot is fine, but it feels late. It might work better if it ended at the transition instead of starting there. Also, rather than have it end at the transition, overlap the transition slightly. It's better to overlap the transition by a few frames than to be short and reveal a jump cut in the video—especially since that is one of the reasons for using the cutaway in the first place.

Note: There are two advantages to editing cutaway shots (or *B-roll*) to a second video track. First, there's lots of flexibility in terms of where you can place the shot (because you can easily move it after it's in the Timeline; use Lift/Overwrite segment mode). The second advantage is that you can trim the segment's head and tail with Extend, Top, and Tail, or the Overwrite Trim tool without affecting any other edits on V1.

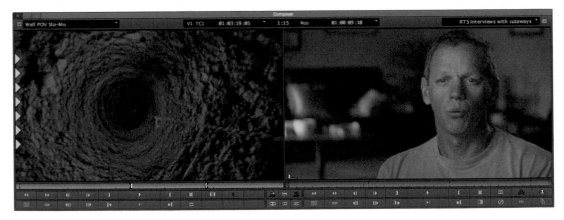

Figure 5.34
The position indicator is between the first two segments. The V2 track selector button is turned on.

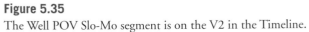

Figure 5.35
The Well POV Slo-Mo segment is on the V2 in the Timeline.

11. Turn on the LIFT/OVERWRITE SEGMENT MODE button in the Smart Tool palette.

12. Drag the segment on **V2** to the left so that the segment ends just past the transition. See Figure 5.36.

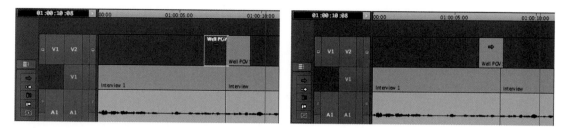

Figure 5.36
Drag the segment so that it ends just over the transition.

> **Tip:** In segment mode, you can *nudge* (precisely move with keyboard shortcuts) a selected segment using the trim keys. In essence, you are trimming the position of a selected segment rather than the segment's frames or duration.

13. Play that sequence section to see how it works with the cutaway shot ending just after the transition. Much better. Now use a cutaway shot to completely cover the INTERVIEW video for INTERVIEW 2 and INTERVIEW 3. Once again, you edit the video to the **V2** track.

14. Load the LOWERING INTO WELL master clip, which has an IN point at its head (first frame).

15. In the Timeline, press **I** to mark an IN point at the beginning of the INTERVIEW 2 segment; press **O** to mark an OUT point at the beginning of the INTERVIEW 5 segment. Turn off all Timeline track selector buttons except **V2**. See Figure 5.37.

16. Press **B** to overwrite the clip into the marked portion of the sequence. See Figure 5.38.

17. Play the sequence from the beginning. Nicely done. The Lowering into Well segment covers three different transition points and visually takes the audience into the well as he describes it.

Watch the sequence again. Notice that the POV shot inside the well is a little short? It works okay, but it would be even better if it were a bit longer. See if the shot has any handles before the IN point. If so, you can extend the shot left by performing an Overwrite trim.

Figure 5.37
V2 is marked between from Interview 2 to the beginning of Interview 5.

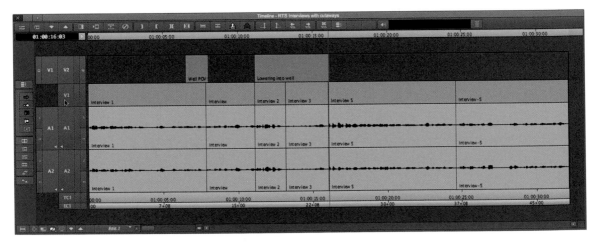

Figure 5.38
The Lowering into Well segment in the V2 track is above Interview 2 and Interview 3.

Using Match Frame to Determine Handles

Handles are portions of a master clip that are not included between the IN and OUT points. Reductive trimming shortens a segment's duration in a sequence, extending the unused portion (handle). Additive trimming lengthens a segment's duration in a sequence, reducing the handles. The amount you can add to the duration is contingent on the master clip's handles. See Figure 5.39.

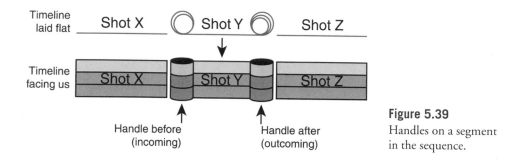

Timeline laid flat — Shot X — Shot Y — Shot Z

Timeline facing us — Shot X — Shot Y — Shot Z

Handle before (incoming)   Handle after (outcoming)

Figure 5.39
Handles on a segment in the sequence.

Match Frame is a handy feature that you'll use here to load a master clip into the Source monitor based on the position indicator in the Timeline. Not only will Match Frame load the clip into the Source monitor, but it will automatically match the position indicator in the Source monitor to the exact frame that the position indicator is over in the Timeline. How will that help you determine a clip's handles? Because if you use Match Frame at the head of a segment in the Timeline, you will see the handles before the master clip's IN point in the Source monitor. Keep in mind that Match Frame uses the position indicator and the selected track to determine which master clip to load into the Source monitor.

To use Match Frame:

1. Make sure that only the **V2** Timeline track selector button is turned on. Ctrl-click (Windows) or Command-click (Mac) the Timeline ruler above the head of the **WELL POV SLO-MO** segment to snap to the first frame of that segment. See Figure 5.40.

2. Press **N** to load the **WELL POV SLO-MO** master clip into the Source monitor; the current frame matches the current frame in the Timeline. An IN point is there in case you move the position indicator to preview the rest of the clip. (See Figure 5.41.) The current frames in both the Source and Record monitors are identical.

Figure 5.40
Snap to the beginning of the Well POV Slo-Mo segment in V2.

3. In the Source monitor, drag the position indictor left to see the footage in the incoming handle. Use the **J-K-L** or **STEP FRAME** buttons if you prefer. How much of the handles is usable? That depends on your criteria for adding footage in the first place. For this shot, you extend the point of view (POV) without including any portion of the man in the well. If you see him, it spoils the illusion that the audience (camera) is being lowered into the well. The last usable frame is around 01:03:18:18.

As you can see, using Match Frame is a fast, simple way to see a segment's handles prior to trimming. You can also use Match Frame to get back to a clip in order to use another portion of it or see an alternate take.

Handles at head of clip
before IN point

Matched frame IN point

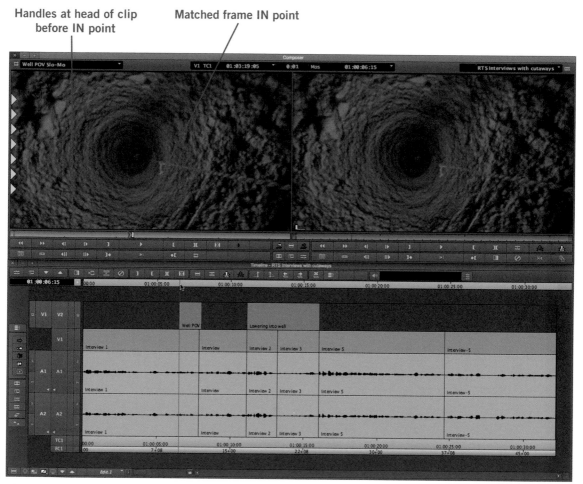

Figure 5.41
The matched frame in the master clip is identified with an IN point.

Trimming Cutaways on V2

There are several ways to extend this shot using trim tools. In this section, you'll work with the Overwrite and Ripple Trim tools.

To trim cutaways:

1. In the Smart tool, select the **OVERWRITE TRIM** button and **RIPPLE TRIM** button. Why both tools? Because you can choose the type of trim you want to do based on where you click the transition. This is similar to choosing either Lift/Overwrite or Extract/Splice-In segment modes to move segments based on where you select them.

2. Move the pointer over the transition point between the filler and the beginning of the **Well POV Slow-Mo** segment. The Single-Roller Overwrite tool is over the top half of the A-side or B-side. The Single-Roller Ripple tool is over the lower half of the A-side or B-side. The Dual-Roller Overwrite tool is anywhere over the center of the transition between the A- and B-sides. Now you know why it is called the Smart tool. See Figure 5-42.

The Single-Roller Ripple tool is over the lower half of the A-side or B-side

The Single-Roller Overwrite tool is over the top half of the A-side or B-side

The Dual-Roller Overwrite tool is anywhere over the center of the transition between the A and B sides

Figure 5.42
The Smart tool changes based on the pointer position.

3. Click the center of the edit point to select both A- and B-sides for a dual-roller overwrite trim. Drag the transition point left and watch the Composer window to see when to release the transition. What's this? There is no visual clue as you drag a transition point on the V2 track. That is a distinct disadvantage to manually dragging your transition point. Choose **Edit > Undo trim** to undo the trim.

4. With the transition still selected, use the trim shortcuts or click the **Trim Frame** buttons in the Composer to move the transition point left. Do so until you see a piece of the runner's harness dangling in the frame. This time, a live update in the B-side of the Composer window shows you exactly what you are doing as you trim. When you see a part of the harness, trim a few frames right until the harness is gone. The entire amount should be around −11 in the trim counters. See Figure 5.43.

5. Press the **SPACE BAR** to play the beginning of the sequence. See how the extended version of the cutaway shot works with the talking-head dialogue.

Figure 5.43
This is the finished −11 frame dual-roller overwrite trim.

Editing Cutaways into the V1 Track

New editors are sometimes hesitant to edit cutaway video directly into their primary video track. It seems destructive to overwrite the subject's video with another shot. There's nothing scary about it. In fact, you'll discover that keeping all the video on one track gives you more options and makes it easier to trim and finesse the video segments.

In this sequence, you have two video cutaway shots left to use, and only one remaining transition to cover. This time, you edit the cutaways directly into the V1 track based on the content rather than as a bandage to cover a transition. When you're finished, you'll learn some new tools to trim the segments and enhance the sequence.

To edit cutaways:

1. Load the **MAUR, WITH CAMERA** clip. This master clip has been marked to include the close-up of the runner's camera and a fast pull-out to reveal him holding the camera. If you used this shot in another sequence and changed the IN and OUT points, re-mark IN and OUT points at 08:20:18:07 and 08:20:19:11, respectively.

2. In the Timeline, select the **V1** Timeline track selector button; turn off the **V2** selector. Press the **SPACE BAR** to play the Interview 5 segment. Press **I** to mark an IN point after he says, "My favorite part of the experience was...." See Figure 5.44.

Figure 5.44
The V1 track selector button is active; the V2 track selector button is inactive. An IN point shows on the Timeline.

3. Press the **B** key to overwrite the marked master clip into the **V1** track of the sequence, as shown in Figure 5.45. Press **H** to focus the Timeline on the position indicator (at the end of the edited segment).

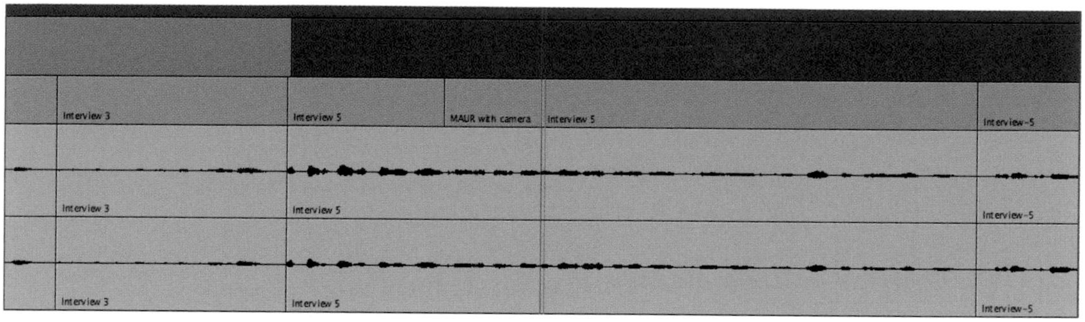

Figure 5.45
A focused view of the MAUR, with Camera segment in V1 is between Interview 5 video segments.

4. Load the **Night Camera Inside Well** segment into the Source monitor.
    Then, in the Timeline, press **I** to mark an IN point just before the talent
    says, "It was dark" (around 01:00:22:15). Press **B** to overwrite the master
    clip to the Timeline. The Night Camera Inside Well segment overlaps the
    transition between the Interview 5 and Interview-5 segments.

5. Play the **Interview 5** and **Interview-5** segments to see how the talking-
    head footage works with the cutaways in V1. Honestly, they make the
    piece more interesting. However, the first cutaway is too short and not in
    the right position. The night-camera cutaway is interesting, but would
    work better if it came in sooner and ended earlier (so he lands just as he
    says he makes it to the bottom).

    Extending the camera shot is a matter of using the dual roller. However, to
    physically slide a shot earlier or later, you need to learn a new tool: Slide.
    First, extend the shot.

6. In the **V1** track of the Timeline, click the transition point between the
    Interview 5 and **MAUR, with Camera** segments. (See Figure 5.46.)
    An audio transition point was selected as well.

    When you edit into your Timeline a master clip that has video and audio,
    the tracks are treated as linked (because they share the same timecode from
    the same camera source). For example, the audio is automatically selected
    if you select the video track. In the case of the transition point you just
    selected, the transition point's A-side belongs to the Interview 5 segment,
    which has linked audio. You can select linked clips for both segment and
    trim editing, or disable the Link Selection Toggle button to select a single
    track of a linked clip. For this exercise, you disable the Link Selection
    Toggle button.

Selected transition points

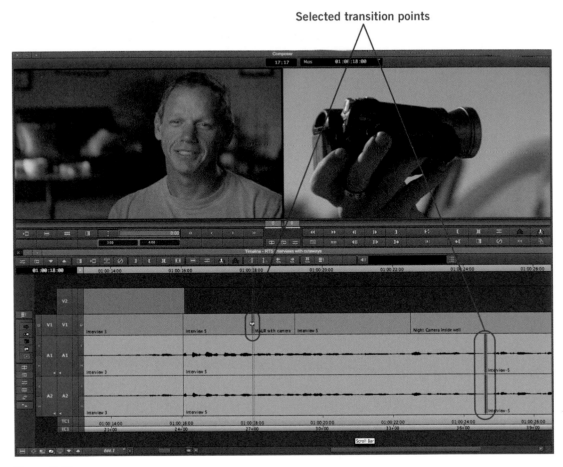

Figure 5.46
Video transition and audio transition points are selected because of linked audio.

7. Click the empty space above the **V2** track to deselect the transition point.

8. Click the **LINK SELECTION TOGGLE** button above the Smart tool to toggle it off. See Figure 5.47.

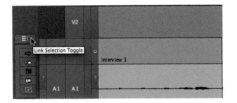

Figure 5.47
Turn off the Link Selection Toggle button.

9. Select the transition point at the head of the **MAUR, WITH CAMERA** segment in the **V1** track. This time, only the V1 transition point is selected.

10. Click the **Step Trim frame** buttons (or use the shortcuts) twice to trim –20 frames to the left (extending the clip by 20 frames). Or, type **–20** and press **Enter/Return**. See Figure 5.48.

Figure 5.48
The transition point is trimmed –20 frames (left) to extend a cutaway shot.

11. Press the **space bar** to play the extended cutaway shot. You solved the first problem by extending the shot. Now slide it to the right a bit to fix the timing with the spoken dialogue. To accomplish that, use Slide.

Slipping or Sliding Segments

Slipping and sliding segments are unique trimming techniques that let you make frame-accurate adjustments to a selected segment. Neither technique affects a sequence's overall duration, and as long as you select all the linked tracks simultaneously (with Link Selection Toggle on), the sync relationship between multiple tracks is unaffected. *Slipping* allows you to slip frames left or right within a segment without changing the segment's duration or position. (See Figure 5.49.) *Sliding*, on the other hand, moves a segment left or right between its neighboring segments without changing its content or duration. See Figure 5.50.

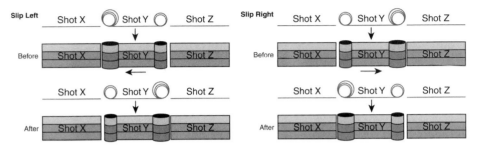

Figure 5.49
Slipping changes the content of a shot, but not its duration or position.

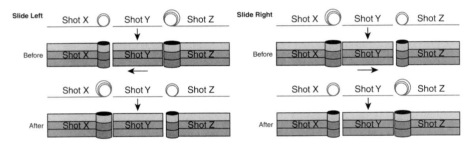

Figure 5.50
Sliding only changes a shot's position, not its content or duration.

The best way to get your head around these techniques is to use them. Start with the MAUR, with Camera segment. The tactical difference between slipping or sliding segments is double-clicking the transition point of a segment. Media Composer toggles through the Trim, Slip, and Slide modes as you double-click. You'll know you've succeeded when both of a segment's transition points are selected (showing pink) and the Composer window shows four images. First, make sure you know what you are trying to accomplish with the trim.

To use Slip or Slide:

1. Play the **INTERVIEW 5** segment in the sequence and listen to what the talent says about the camera. As is, you see the cutaway shot of the camera before he says he carried a camera. Your goal is to slide the segment to the right so that the cutaway begins as he talks about the camera and holds up his hand as if he had one in it. Use the visuals in the Composer window as a guide.

2. In the Timeline, double-click the B-side of the transition point at the beginning of the **MAUR, WITH CAMERA** segment. If the B-side at the head of the segment and the A-side at the tail of the segment are selected, you are ready to slip the frames. See Figure 5.51.

Figure 5.51
A slip selection slips footage within the segment.

3. Double-click just inside of the same transition point again to switch to Slide mode. This time, the outgoing segment's A-side and incoming segment's B-side are selected (pink). That means the segment can freely move left or right, making one longer and the other shorter as it goes. (See Figure 5.52.) Keep in mind that the amount you can trim depends on the length of the available handles.

Figure 5.52
A slide selection slides a segment between its neighbors.

4. Press the **SPACE BAR** to preview the segment in a Trim mode play loop. The preroll and postroll determine how much of the neighboring clips will play before and after the selected segment.

5. Make sure the segment is selected for a slide. (It should show a single-roller pink selection on neighboring segment transition points.) If the single-roller pink selected transition points are on the segment, double-click the segment again to change to Slide mode. (See Figure 5.53.) When a segment is selected for the right trim method, you can use the trim shortcuts or Trim Frame buttons in the Composer window to slide the segment. For this exercise, use the trim shortcuts: Press the , (COMMA) KEY to move one frame to the left and press the . (PERIOD) KEY to move one frame to the right. Press and hold the . (PERIOD) KEY to slide the segment right one frame at a time. As it moves, watch the outer two frames of the four-up display in the Composer window. The first and last of the four displays are the frames on either side of the segment as it moves. When you see the talent hold up his fingers (as if he is holding a camera in the first frame), you are there. (See Figure 5.54.) The total amount trimmed should be around 52 frames; check the trim counters.

Tip: If you know by how many frames you want to slide a segment, type the number and press Enter/Return. Keep in mind that positive numbers move to the right and negative numbers move to the left.

Figure 5.53
The MAUR, with Camera segment is selected for sliding and ready to move.

6. Press **U** to deselect the clip and switch back to Edit mode. Play the full **INTERVIEW 5** segment to see the improvement in the first cutaway shot. The visual play—matching his hand position between the interview and the cutaway —is a classic editor's trick. Nicely done. But see the quick pan and pull-out from the camera close-up to him holding the camera? It is a bit distracting. Slip the footage within the **MAUR, WITH CAMERA** segment so you can see only the camera.

7. Double-click inside (B-side) the transition at the beginning of the **MAUR, WITH CAMERA** segment. If the segment is selected for slipping, the first and last frames are pink. See Figure 5.55.

Imagine your segment in the Source monitor. It already has IN and OUT points that represent the head and tail frames. Slipping maintains the duration, but slips the marks in unison to the left or right, including different footage from the handles. Now you try it.

Figure 5.54
The segment has been slid to the right.

Figure 5.55
The MAUR, with Camera segment is selected for Slip in the Timeline.

Tip: You can use the lasso to go directly into Slip or Slide mode, without entering Trim mode first. To enter Slip mode, lasso the shot you want to slip from *right to left*. Be sure to encompass the whole segment side to side and top to bottom. To enter Slide mode, press and hold Ctrl+Shift (Windows) or Command+Shift (Mac); then lasso the segment right to left.

8. Press the **,** (COMMA) KEY and watch the two inside monitors in the Composer window. Those windows show the head and tail frames as they slip over the available footage. Release the **,** (COMMA) KEY when both center displays in the Composer show only the camera. The second and third display show the selected segment's new head and tail frames. The total amount that you'll slip is around –22 frames. See Figure 5.56.

Figure 5.56
The two inside monitors show the head and tail frames as they are slipped.

9. Press the **SPACE BAR** and see how the slipped cutaway works with the rest of the interview. Your work here is done.

10. Press **U** or click an **Edit Mode** button. Press **Ctrl+/** (slash) (Windows) or **Command+/** (slash) (Mac) to view the entire the sequence if it is focused on the edit point. Play the entire sequence to see how it works with the cutaways.

Note: To move a segment from the V2 track to the V1 track, select the segment in Lift/Overwrite segment mode and drag it down to the V1 track. If you press the Shift (Windows) or Command (Mac) key while dragging the segment to the lower track, your mouse movement is constrained to maintain the segment's position as you move.

Review/Discussion Questions

1. Which two Trim mode buttons are in the Smart Tool palette?
   a. Lift Trim and Overwrite Trim
   b. Extract Trim and Ripple Trim
   c. Overwrite Trim and Ripple Trim
   d. Top Trim and Tail Trim

2. Which side of the transition point is the B-side?
   a. Left
   b. Right
   c. Center
   d. Left and right

3. Assume Media Composer is in Edit mode and the Timeline window is active. You press U. What happens? (Select all that apply.)
   a. Media Composer switches to Trim mode.
   b. The transition point nearest to the position indicator is selected.
   c. The Composer window shows the A-side and B-side of the selected transition.
   d. The outgoing and incoming clips on either side of the active transition point are selected.

4. What determines the duration of the play loop in Trim mode?

   a. Preroll and postroll

   b. Trim counters

   c. Smart tool

   d. The play loop is a set duration that cannot be changed.

5. What are the keyboard shortcuts to change which side of a transition point is selected?

   a. J   K   L

   b. I   O

   c. M ,   .   /

   d. P   [   ]

6. If you are using J-K-L to trim on-the-fly, when does the trim occur?

   a. When you release J or L.

   b. When you release the K.

   c. When you release J, K, or L.

   d. When you press the space bar.

7. What type of trim moves an entire segment between its neighboring segments but doesn't change the footage or duration of the moving segment?

   a. Overwrite

   b. Ripple

   c. Slip

   d. Slide

8. What type of trim creates split edits on the video track without changing the transition points on the audio tracks?

   a. Dual-roller overwrite

   b. Single-roller overwrite

   c. Ripple

   d. Slide

Lesson 5 Keyboard Shortcuts

Key	Shortcut
M	In Trim mode, trims left multiple frames
, (comma)	In Trim mode, trims left one frame
. (period)	In Trim mode, trims right one frame
/ (slash)	In Trim mode, trims right multiple frames
Space bar	In Trim mode, starts and stops play loop
U	Selects closest transition point; toggles on/off Trim mode
P	Selects A-side of transition
[	Selects A-side and B-side of transition
]	Selects B-side of transition
H	Toggles on/off Timeline Focus
N	Matches frame
Up Arrow (in Training User settings)	Fast forwards to next transition point
Down Arrow (in Training User settings)	Rewinds to previous transition point
Ctrl+L (Windows)/Command+L (Mac)	Enlarges active tracks in Timeline
Ctrl+K (Windows)/Command+K (Mac)	Reduces active tracks in Timeline
Ctrl+Y (Windows)/Command+Y (Mac)	Creates a new video track
Ctrl+/ (Windows)/Command+/ (Mac)	Show entire sequence

Making Further Refinements

In this exercise, you'll further refine the sequences you've been working on using some of the techniques you've learned in this chapter.

Media Used:
Running the Sahara
First Tracks Productions

Duration:
60 minutes

GOALS

- Practice dual-roller overwrite trims
- Trim interview dialogue with the Ripple Trim tool
- Add cutaway segments to an interview sequence
- Use Slip and Slide to fix a montage

Finishing the Sequence

You worked with dual-roller overwrite trimming. Use that tool to finish the sequence Lesson 05 Overwrite trim.Copy.01.

1. In the MY SEQUENCES bin, duplicate the LESSON 05 OVERWRITE TRIM. COPY.01 sequence. Name the new copy RTS OVERWRITE TRIM. Open the sequence.

2. Make sure the Smart tool has only the red OVERWRITE TRIM button turned on.

3. Move the position indicator to the four short video segments over the end of the first narration segment. Press H to focus the Timeline on that area of the sequence.

4. Select the transition point between the MAUR, MAN WITH STICK and MALI, CAMEL segments. Make sure the selection is dual-roller (pink with both sides selected). Trim the transition point left −23 frames so the shot ends right as the narrator says "As unpredictable…" and the man with the stick dips down his head.

5. For the next trim, work with only the video portion of the RUNNER 2 segment. This clip has linked audio, so override the link and work with video only; turn off the LINK SELECTION TOGGLE button above the Smart tool. Your goal is to create a split edit to smooth the transition into the RUNNER 2 segment. Do this by rolling the video transition point to the right between the SENEGAL, AERIAL 4 segment and the RUNNER 2 segment so the aerial shot overlaps the beginning of the RUNNER 2 audio. This smoothes the edit. Select the V1 transition point. Use the shortcut keys or the TRIM FRAME buttons to move it right 16 frames (around a half second). Play the transition to notice the difference.

6. Each of the remaining transitions is video only and trimmed by dual-roller overwrite. Trim these remaining transitions accordingly:

   - Trim the transition between Runners, Tilt Down 1 and Sand 2 to the right. Use the Composer window to determine when the trim is finished. Trim with shortcuts or Trim Frame buttons in the Composer window so you can watch the trim update. Watch for at least two footfalls of the running shoe on the sand (around 44 frames). The movement matches well with the sand on the incoming segment. Feel free to use your own criteria to finesse the transition point.

   - Move the transition point between Runners, Focus on Runner 1 and Mali, Runners, Tall Grass to the right until you reach the end of the segment's handles. Your goal is to see them chatting as a narrator says, "good friends" and you see a bit of the third runner in the background. You'll know you've reached the end of the outgoing clip's handles because you won't be able to trim any further. Also, a red end-of-clip overlay appears on the A-side of the edit.

- Use J-K-L to trim the next transition point around 35 frames to the right, so it ends about halfway over the gap between the last two voiceover segments. Use the runner in the back. He crosses behind the other two runners and they are evenly spaced as they run through the tall grass.

- Trim the transition at the end of the Runners, Out of the Sun segment toward the left so that it extends the duration of the Maur, Runners 2, Night segment. Use the music as a guide to place the transition point.

7. Play the entire sequence to see how it works. Finesse the edit points as you like. You can find a finished version of the sequence in the **2 FINISHED SEQUENCES** bin.

Using Ripple Trimming

In this exercise, you'll finish ripple trimming the interview sequence to clean up the dialogue. When you are finished, add cutaway shots to hide the jump cuts and add interest to the sequence.

1. In the **MY SEQUENCES** bin, open the sequence called **RTS INTERVIEWS TRIMMED**.

2. Turn on the **LINK SELECTION TOGGLE** button.

3. In the Smart tool, turn on the **RIPPLE TRIM** tool. Turn off all other Smart tools.

4. Go through the different transition points, starting with the A-side, to remove unwanted dialogue. Adjust the preroll and postroll for the play loop. Try different trim methods, including keyboard shortcuts, pressing **I** and **O** on-the-fly and using **J-K-L** trimming.

5. Load the following master clips into the Source monitor:
    - Night Camera Inside well
    - Well POV Slo-Mo
    - MAUR, with Camera
    - Lowering into Well

6. Use as cutaways the four master clips that you just loaded to finish the sequence. Edit them directly into the **V1** track.

7. Use dual-roller overwrite trim to extend or reduce the cutaways' duration. Slide to move the cutaway left or right. Slip to adjust the frames within the cutaway.

8. When you are finished, play the full interview sequence.

Improving the Montage

In this exercise, you use your own editing instincts to improve the First Tracks Demo montage. Five segments need timing adjustments; slide them earlier or later to better match the music. Another five segments would greatly benefit if you slip the footage within the segment. Slide the even segments, starting at the beginning (2nd, 4th, 6th, 8th, and 10th). Slip the last five segments. Along the way, make adjustments to polish the sequence.

Refining and Mixing Audio

Audio refining is often overlooked, but it's an important part of putting together a sequence. This lesson starts with ways to set up Media Composer's interface so it can better assist with the audio tasks that follow. Then you'll add audio elements to your program and learn how to mix the relative audio levels between these elements. For this lesson, as well as the majority of the remaining lessons in this book, you'll use the popular reality TV competition show *Hell's Kitchen*.

Media Used: Hell's Kitchen

Duration: One hour

GOALS

- Tailor the interface for audio editing
- Add markers
- Add and patch new tracks
- Solo and mute tracks
- Use the link selection toggle
- Record voiceover narration
- Monitor the Audio tool
- Adjust levels and pan in the Audio Mixer
- Change levels within a segment
- Create audio crossfades

Tailoring the Interface for Audio Editing

When focusing on the audio portion of your sequence, it helps tremendously if you also focus Media Composer's interface on audio. You can do a few things in the Timeline to make it easier to edit, mix, and output the audio for a sequence. One of the first Timeline modifications you can do is shrink the video tracks and enlarge the audio tracks.

Open the Hell's Kitchen project and make some interface modifications:

1. Launch Media Composer and select TRAINING USER. Select the HELLS KITCHEN project in the Open Project dialog box, and then click the OPEN button.

2. In the Project window, double-click the HELLS KITCHEN SEQUENCES bin to open it.

3. In the HELLS KITCHEN SEQUENCES bin, double-click the HK AUDIO-START sequence to load it into the Record monitor (see Figure 6.1). This sequence's video and dialogue are already complete. The dialogue is on A1 and A2.

Figure 6.1
Load the HK Audio-START sequence into the Record monitor.

4. Place the position indicator at the start of the sequence and then press the SPACE BAR to watch the sequence in the Record monitor. This dramatic exchange is between Chef Gordon Ramsay and a contestant. Although the exchange is a bit heated, it lacks a lot of drama because it has no music or sound effects. Let's set up Media Composer to make those changes.

5. Highlight the **V1** record track selector and press and hold the **CTRL KEY** (Windows) or the **OPTION KEY** (Mac). Place the cursor at the bottom boundary of the V1 track in the Track Selector panel until the cursor changes to a double-sided arrow.

6. Drag up the bottom boundary of the track selector to shrink the track, as shown in Figure 6.2.

Figure 6.2
Drag the track selector's bottom boundary to change its size.

7. In the Timeline, select the **A1** and **A2** tracks.

Tip: Why do you need the audio tracks to be so large? It lets you see data in the tracks—most importantly audio waveforms. An *audio waveform* is a graphical display of the track's amplitude or loudness. It can help you visually locate points in an audio track for editing, trimming, or alignment. You can display waveforms for all audio tracks in the Timeline or you can select individual tracks for waveform display.

- To shrink or enlarge more than one track, select the tracks you want to modify.

- To enlarge the audio tracks, repeatedly press Ctrl+L (Windows) or Command+L (Mac).

- To reduce the audio tracks in the Timeline, repeatedly press Ctrl+K (Windows) or Command+K (Mac).

- To enlarge the size of the waveform without enlarging its track, select the track and press Ctrl+Alt+L (Windows) or Command+Option+L (Mac).

- To reduce the size of the waveform without reducing its track, select the track and press Ctrl+Alt+K (Windows) or Command+Option+K (Mac).

8. To display audio waveforms for selected tracks, click the Timeline **FAST** menu and make sure **AUDIO DATA > ALLOW PER TRACK SETTINGS** is selected, as shown in Figure 6.3. (This setting is enabled by default. If disabled, the options in this menu are applied to all tracks.)

9. Click the Timeline **FAST** menu and choose **TRACK CONTROL PANEL** to display each audio track's control panel. The panel is where you enable and disable waveforms on a given track.

Figure 6.3
Choose Audio Data > Allow Per Track Settings from the Timeline Fast menu.

10. For A1 and A2, click the **WAVEFORM** button in the Track Control panel (see Figure 6.4). The waveform appears in the two enabled tracks.

Figure 6.4
Use the Track Control panel to enable the waveform on a specific track.

11. Place the position indicator at the start of the sequence and press the **SPACE BAR** to play the sequence. Watch how the waveform display matches the dialogue as each person talks on screen. You can save this as a view that you can recall in the Timeline. In this case, there is already an Audio Timeline view included with the Training User setting. Open the **VIEW** menu and choose **AUDIO** at the bottom of the Timeline, as shown in Figure 6.5. This saved view has reduced video tracks, enlarged audio tracks, and the waveforms displayed. With the view set in the Timeline, you can find locations that need audio improvement.

Figure 6.5
Choose Audio from the View menu at the bottom of the Timeline.

Working with Markers

Markers are electronic bookmarks that identify specific frames; you can enter comments to markers during editing. Though you can add markers to master clips in the Source monitor, many editors find more uses for them in sequences. With the help of markers, for instance, you can more easily find and remember all the places additional audio elements are needed.

A few markers are set for you in this sequence, but you'll find other locations for music cues and sound effects. All the markers in this sequence are on the Timecode track, but you can add markers to a segment as well. When you add a marker, it is always placed on the highest enabled track.

To add markers to a segment:

1. Click the last marker in the Timeline ruler, located on 01;29;39;00 to go directly to a marker. When you land on a marker, an oval appears at the bottom of the frame in the monitor. Any text associated with that marker also appears. This marker's text indicates that this spot needs a short piece of music that will emphasize the dramatic ending of the scene. First, listen to a few seconds at the end of the sequence to understand the comment better.

2. Place the position indicator just before the last marker, at around 01;29;36;00, and then press the **SPACE BAR** to play until the end of the sequence. This marker, shown in Figure 6.6, identifies a place that seems a bit too early to add emphasis. It would be better if the emphasis came right after the contestant says, "Chef, yes."

Add dramatic musical hit here

Figure 6.6
The emphasis would work better if placed elsewhere.

3. Click the last marker at 01;29;39;00 in the Timeline ruler. Now you can see the marker and its text at the bottom of the monitor. Press the **DELETE KEY**. The marker is removed from the Timeline ruler and is no longer displayed in the Record monitor.

4. Using the waveforms on the last audio segment, place the position indicator just after the contestant says, "Chef, yes." That spot is around 01;29;39;24. (See Figure 6.7.)

Figure 6.7
Place the position indicator just after the contestant says, "Chef, yes."

5. Make sure all tracks are disabled in the Track Selector panel and then select the **TC1** track. Selecting a track in the Track Selector panel places the marker on that track. If you want an audio or video segment to get the locator, enable an audio or video track.

6. Though it's more efficient to map the Add Marker button to the keyboard, you can easily use the Tool palette to access the Add Marker button. Click the **FAST** menu in the Composer dialog box, then click the **ADD MARKER** button, as shown in Figure 6.8. The Marker dialog box opens.

Figure 6.8
Click the Add Marker button in the Fast menu in the Composer window.

7. In the **COLOR** drop-down list, choose **BLUE**. This adds a blue marker to the TC1 track. Use blue markers for sound effects that you need to add. In the **COMMENTS** box, type **ADD DRAMATIC MUSICAL HIT HERE**, as shown in Figure 6.9. Then click **OK** in the Marker dialog box. The sequence has many other markers already added.

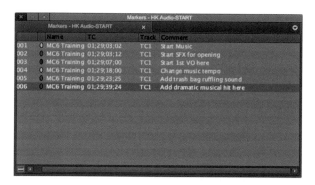

Figure 6.9
Change the marker color to blue and type text in the Comments box.

8. Choose **Tools** > **Markers** to display the list of markers in a loaded sequence or source clip, as shown in Figure 6.10. The Markers window displays the markers for the master clip or sequence in the selected monitor. This sequence has six markers. Green markers identify where music needs to be added. Blue markers represent locations for sound effects. Red markers are places where narration is needed.

Figure 6.10
Choose Tools > Markers to display the list of markers.

Tip: To delete several markers, choose Tools > Markers. Then Ctrl-click (Windows) or Shift-click (Mac) the markers you want to delete. Press the Delete key and respond to the prompt.

9. Starting with **0001**, double-click each marker to view the location and comment for each. Play the sequence a few seconds before and after each marker to get an understanding of some of the tasks that you will do later in this chapter. When you're done, click the × (**Close**) button to close the Markers window.

Tip: You can play a sequence and add markers on-the-fly. Map one or more marker buttons in the Command palette's More tab to keys on the keyboard. Play the sequence and press marker keys at any time. When you stop playback, all markers appear in the Markers window.

Identifying audio cues is just one of the many ways you can use markers. Other common instances for markers include the following:

■ Identifying the location of good sound bites in an interview

■ Providing the correct spelling for titles

■ Including notes for a producer, colorist, or audio engineer

You will find other valuable uses for markers as you create your own projects, but now you'll make the audio additions to the current sequence.

Adding and Patching Tracks

Your sequence has two audio tracks, but needs more for sound effects and music. You'll add new audio tracks and patch the source tracks to the target Timeline tracks to place the material where you want it, just like you did in Lesson 2, "Assembling a Basic Sequence."

To patch source video or audio tracks to different record tracks:

1. In the Project window, double-click the **HK AUDIO SOURCE CLIPS** bin to open it. Then double-click the **MX POUNDING HEARTS FULL** master clip to load it into the Source monitor. The MX Pounding Hearts Full master clip has A1 and A2 tracks. A marker notes where the music begins.

2. Drag the position indicator in the Source monitor to the marker. Mark an IN point. (You don't need an OUT point because you'll edit the music into the end of the clip.)

3. In the Timeline, place the position indicator at the start of the sequence. Press **G** to clear any marks. Let's set positions for the edit and add audio tracks to edit onto.

4. Make sure the **HK AUDIO-START** sequence is in the Timeline. Choose **CLIP > NEW AUDIO TRACK MONO** twice. Two new audio tracks are added, as shown in Figure 6.11.

Figure 6.11
To add two mono audio tracks, choose
Clip > New Audio Track Mono—twice!

Tip: To add a specific track, press Ctrl+Alt+U (Windows) or Option+Command+U (Mac). The Add Track dialog box opens and lets you specify which track is added and choose whether it is mono or stereo. For instance, if it's common practice in your facility or school to have music on tracks A5 and A6, you may need to add those tracks specifically if you haven't edited on to A3 and A4 previously.

5. Click and drag the **A1** source track to the **A3** record track. A connection arrow appears as you drag, as shown in Figure 6.12. When you release the mouse, the A1 track jumps next to the A3 record track and becomes highlighted.

Figure 6.12
Click the A1 source track and drag it to the A3 record track.

6. Click and drag the **A2** source track to the **A4** record track.

7. Make sure only **A3** and **A4** tracks are enabled on the record side of the Track Selector panel. Make sure **A1** and **A2** are enabled on the source side. Then click the **OVERWRITE** button or press **B**. The two music tracks are edited into the sequence, as shown in Figure 6.13.

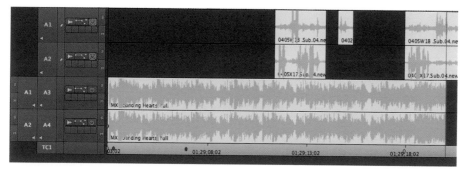

Figure 6.13
Click Overwrite to edit the music into A3 and A4.

8. Place the record-side position indicator at the start of the sequence. Press the **SPACE BAR** to play it back and hear your new edit. Now you find the next audio task to do by going back to the Markers window and reviewing the list.

9. Choose **Tools** > **Markers** to open the Markers window if it's not already open.

10. Double-click the **005** green marker (for music tracks), shown in Figure 6.14. Now the music should change to a slower tempo to match the investigation in the video.

Figure 6.14
Green marker 005 identifies where you need slower tempo music.

11. Mark an IN point on the sequence at marker 005. In the **HK Audio Source Clips** bin, double-click the **MX pounding Hearts Drum Bass** master clip to load it into the Source monitor. Press the **space bar** to play the clip. This is a big musical drum hit that will create a dramatic impact before you change the music.

12. Make sure **A1** and **A2** on the source clip Track Selector panel are enabled and still patched to **A3** and **A4** of the sequence. (The IN point is already marked on the source clip.) Then click the **Overwrite** button or press **B** on the keyboard to edit in the source clip. See Figure 6.15.

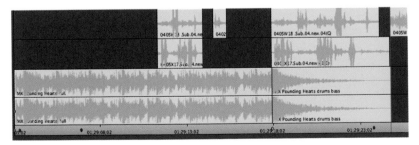

Figure 6.15
Edit in a musical hit.

13. With the edit completed, place the position indicator in the sequence a few seconds before the new edit. Then press the SPACE BAR to listen to the addition. The hit works perfectly to create a dramatic impact, so now you can change the music's tempo without it being so jarring. You first need to add two new tracks for the new tempo music.

14. Press CTRL+U (Windows) or COMMAND+U (Mac) twice. Two new audio tracks are added below the existing music tracks. The new audio tracks in the sequence are labeled A5 and A6.

15. Load MX TICK TOCK FULL 09 in the HK AUDIO SOURCE CLIPS bin into the Source monitor.

16. Patch the A1 and A2 tracks of the source music to tracks A5 and A6, respectively, in the sequence (as you did for tracks A3 and A4). See Figure 6.16.

Figure 6.16
Patch A1 and A2 to newly added A5 and A6 in the sequence.

17. Place the position indicator just before the musical hit you just added on tracks A3 and A4. Press the SPACE BAR to listen to the dialogue; stop playback after Chef Ramsay says, "Show me." Here's a good location to start the new music: just after Chef Ramsay says, "You didn't start a fresh one" and before the contestant obviously lies and says, "Yes I did, Chef."

18. Using the waveforms to guide you, mark an IN point between these two lines of dialogue, as shown in Figure 6.17.

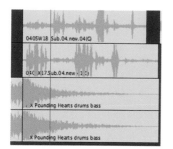

Figure 6.17
Use the waveforms on A1 to find where Chef Ramsay says, "You didn't start a fresh one."

19. Make sure only the A5 and A6 tracks are enabled on the record side Track Selector panel and that A1 and A2 are enabled on the source side. Then click the OVERWRITE button or press B on the keyboard.

20. Place the position indicator at the start of the sequence and then press the **SPACE BAR** to play it back and listen to the entire sequence's music.

Now the sequence has some great layered sounds on different tracks. With all these new audio tracks, you need ways to help manage what you hear and when you hear it. That's what the next section will help you achieve.

Monitoring, Soloing, and Muting a Track

With the music and dialogue in place, you can think about sound effects. They can be subtle, so you will use Media Composer's Mute and Solo features to isolate the tracks you want to hear and nothing more.

To find the locations where sound effects are needed, you'll use the Markers tool:

1. Choose **TOOLS** > **MARKERS** to open the Markers window, if it's not already open.

2. Double-click the second blue **006** marker. The position indicator on the sequence moves to where the sound effects should be added. As shown in Figure 6.18, the text indicates that you need to add a trash bag ruffling sound.

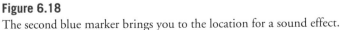

Figure 6.18
The second blue marker brings you to the location for a sound effect.

3. In the **HK Audio Source Clips** bin, double-click the **0405W18** master clip to load it into the Source monitor. Press the **SPACE BAR** to play the clip. This sound is from one of the cameras. It includes the trash bag as well as well as the contestant's voice. You need just one part of this clip: where the IN and OUT points are already set. Next, you add a track to place this sound effect.

4. Press **CTRL+U** (Windows) or **COMMAND+U** (Mac) to add the A7 audio track.

Tip: **Professional editors are not only creative, but also need to be highly organized. A good professional habit to develop is to organize all similar audio content onto tracks within a range—for instance, all dialogue on tracks 1–4, all music on tracks 5–8, and all sound effects on tracks 9–10. This not only makes it easier to find the type of tracks you are looking for, but maintains consistency when you export to other applications.**

5. Patch **A1** to **A7** of the sequence. Click the **OVERWRITE** button or press **B** to edit in the sound effect. (See Figure 6.19.)

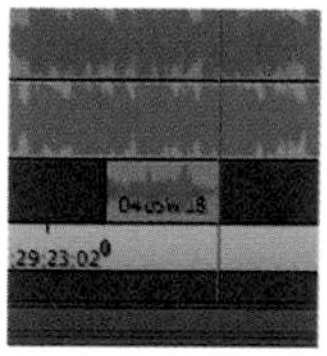

Figure 6.19
Edit the sound effect onto track A7.

6. With the edit completed, place the position indicator in the sequence a few seconds before the new edit; then press the **SPACE BAR** to listen to the addition. It's a little difficult to hear if it works in the current location; one solution is to solo the track so it is the only sound you hear.

7. Click the **SOLO** button (**S**) in the Track Control panel for A7. As shown in Figure 6.20, the Solo button turns green. In addition, Mute buttons on all other audio tracks turn orange. This means that no matter which track monitors are turned on, you will only hear the ones with green speaker icons.

Figure 6.20
Click the Solo button to solo track A7.

Tip: **To mute an individual audio track, click the Mute button in the Track Control panel for the track you want to mute.**

8. Place the position indicator in the sequence a few seconds before the sound effect and press the **SPACE BAR** to listen to it. You can solo as many tracks as you want. In this case, you add the dialogue tracks so you can hear it and the effects.

9. Click the **SOLO** button in the Track Control panel for A1 and A2. The Solo button turns green. See Figure 6.21.

Figure 6.21
Solo tracks A1 and A2 to hear them with the previously soloed A7 track.

10. Place the position indicator in the sequence a few seconds before the sound effect and then press the **SPACE BAR** to listen to it.

Soloing tracks helps you edit and refine the subtle sounds that louder tracks can overwhelm. Even though the final mix will contain all your tracks, take the time to solo or mute tracks. It helps you understand how even the smallest sounds affect the feel of a sequence.

Recording a Voiceover

In previous sections, you edited audio into sequences from captured clips, but editors commonly have to record a temporary narration as a placeholder until professional voiceover talent can be recorded. This temporary narration is sometimes called *temp VO* or a *scratch track*. In these circumstances, you can use Media Composer's Audio Punch-In tool along with a microphone to record narration directly into the Timeline. A couple of locations in your sequence need some narration to better describe the situation in the kitchen. The Markers window lists the two narration locations.

Note: It may not be possible for all readers to complete this section—for example, if you are working on a desktop system without a built-in microphone or any other mic on hand.

Note: Typically, microphones are connected to a hardware I/O device, such as an Avid MBox, Mojo DX, or third-party device, but could also be a simple USB microphone. For more information on I/O options for both audio and video, go to www.avid.com/products/Media-Composer and click on Hardware Options.

To record a voiceover:

1. Choose TOOLS > MARKERS to open the Markers window, if it's not already open.

2. Double-click the first red **003** marker. The position indicator on the sequence moves to where the narration should be added. The text shows the narration you need to read. (See Figure 6.22.)

Figure 6.22
Double-click the first red marker (003) to locate the start of the narration.

3. Choose TOOLS > AUDIO PUNCH-IN to open the Audio Punch-In tool.

4. Before you begin recording, select what source you will use for the recording. The input source in this case is the built-in microphone on your computer. Click the INPUT SOURCE drop-down list and choose BUILT-IN MICROPHONE (see Figure 6.23).

Note: You may have to select a different input source if your microphone is connected to a hardware I/O device such as an Avid MBox, Mojo DX, or third-party device

Figure 6.23
Make sure Input Source matches the microphone
in use and Channel is set to CH1.

5. Make sure the **CH 1** button is highlighted to select the input channel (see
Figure 6.24). In this case, the built-in microphone has only one channel;
the input channel may be different if you are using other audio hardware.

Figure 6.24
The Audio Punch-In tool can record
narration directly to the Timeline.

6. Make sure the Timeline **TRACK** menu next to **CH1** is set to **NEW TRACK**.
You can record to an existing track in the Timeline by selecting it from the
New Track menu or can have Media Composer create a new track as it
records the narration.

**Note: You can only use mono audio tracks for punch-in. You cannot select stereo
or locked tracks.**

7. In the Timeline, drag the position indicator to about 1;29;06;00, just
before the current marker position; then mark an IN point. Next, place
the position indicator around 1;29;11;00 and mark an OUT point in the
Timeline. These marks specify the part of the sequence that play back
when you click Play in the Audio Punch-In tool. You can begin recording
anywhere within the IN and OUT points. (See Figure 6.25.)

Figure 6.25
Mark IN and OUT points to define the
playback range for the Audio Punch-In tool.

8. Click the **PLAY IN/OUT** button or select the Audio Punch-In dialog box and press **V**. Loop play begins from the IN point.

9. Practice the narration line a few times to make sure you can fit it easily within the playback range. "It's an hour into dinner service and the blue team is just delivering their first entrée."

10. When you are ready to start the voiceover, wait for the loop playback to start and then click the **RECORD** button (see Figure 6.26) or press **B**. The button blinks bright red while you are recording.

Figure 6.26
Click the Record button to begin recording.

Tip: You can use the Pre/Post Roll settings in the Audio Punch-In tool to help improve the timing of the voiceover to other elements in the sequence.

11. Click the **STOP** button or press the **SPACE BAR** to stop play and recording. Media Composer places the narration in the Timeline and names it with a voiceover tag (see Figure 6.27). A new master clip of the narration is also created in the selected bin.

Figure 6.27
After you record, the clip is added to a new track in the Timeline.

Even though the Audio Punch-In tool is primarily meant for recording temporary audio tracks, try to get the best possible recording from it. With that in mind, the next section introduces another tool that helps you achieve the best recording by monitoring your input source volume.

Using the Audio Tool

Although you used the Audio Punch-In tool exactly as directed, I skipped over one critical step: setting the levels of the incoming audio you are about to record. The Audio tool is an audio meter that helps you calibrate, set the level, and monitor your incoming audio signal. By default, the Audio tool monitors your outgoing signal, but in this case you want to monitor the incoming sound over the internal microphone.

To calibrate, set the level, and monitor your incoming audio signal:

1. Choose **Tools** > **Audio Tool** or press **Ctrl**+**1** (Windows) or **Command**+**1** (Mac) to open the Audio tool.

Tip: You can open the Audio tool by clicking the Audio Tool (speaker) icon in the Audio Punch-In tool.

2. Click the **In/Out Toggle** button on each of the two channels until they show an I (see Figure 6.28). That means you have switched the meter displays from monitoring output levels to monitoring input levels from a source device. You can use the Audio tool to check the audio input levels as you speak. If Media Composer's input levels are too high or too low, adjust the source's output. In this case, try speaking louder.

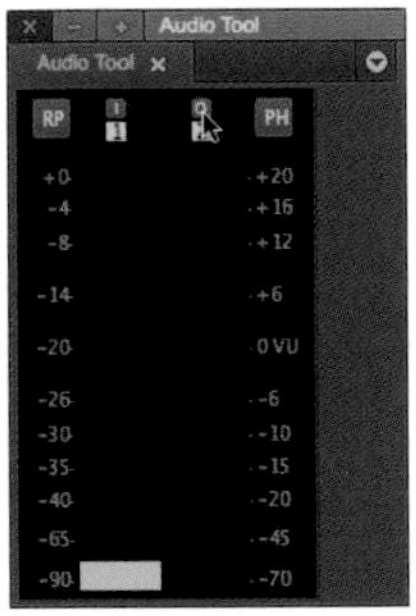

Figure 6.28
Switch the meter displays by clicking the In/Out Toggle button.

3. Start speaking. Adjust your speaking volume and distance to the microphone so your voice is consistently around –20db or 0 VU. The meters are green while the audio is below the target reference level of –20dB, as shown in Figure 6.29. The meters are yellow while the audio is above the target; audio is still acceptable to about –3dB. Above –3dB, audio is distorted and the meters are red.

Figure 6.29
Meters are green below –20dB.

Note: Most professional edit bays are set up with a small audio mixing board. This allows the editor to quickly adjust the incoming or outgoing audio levels. If you are on a software-only system, you can use the computer's audio settings to adjust the incoming audio level. On a Mac, choose System Preferences > Sound > Input. On Windows, choose Control Panel > Hardware and Sound > Sound > Recording.

4. Choose **TOOLS** > **MARKERS** to open the Markers window, if it's not already open. Use the marker list to pinpoint where the second line of narration should go.

5. Double-click the **004** second red marker. The position indicator on the sequence moves to where the second narration should be added. The text shows the narration you need to read: "But Chef Ramsay is a little suspicious." See Figure 6.30.

Figure 6.30
Move to the marker where the second narration should be added.

6. Set a mark IN point just prior to the second narration marker and mark an OUT point just before the dialogue comes back in on tracks A1 and A2. When you can read the narration line consistently and remain around −20dB without ever entering the red levels above −3dB, you can set up the Audio Punch-In tool to record.

7. In the Audio Punch-In tool, make sure **CH1** is enabled. Record on track A8, as shown in Figure 6.31, since it has the narration you recorded earlier.

8. Click the **PLAY IN/OUT** button to start playing from the IN point to the OUT point.

Figure 6.31
Make sure CH1 is enabled and choose to record on track A8.

9. Practice the narration line a few times to make sure it fits easily within the mark IN and mark OUT points and that the audio levels are still within the acceptable range.

10. When you are ready to start narrating, click the **RECORD** button or press **B** just after the loop play begins. Then click the **STOP** button or press the **SPACE BAR** to stop play and recording.

11. Click the **IN/OUT TOGGLE** button on each of the two channels until they show an O (see Figure 6.32). The Audio tool returns to monitoring the outgoing signal.

Figure 6.32
Have the Audio tool monitor output levels by clicking the In/Out Toggle button.

12. Close the Audio Punch-In tool. Play back the new recording to make sure it sounds perfect. If not, don't worry. In the next section, you'll learn how to adjust the levels if they're not quite right. To get the best possible recording from the beginning, make sure the Audio tool meters always remain in the green or yellow range below –3dB.

The Audio tool plays a more fundamental role when you're adjusting audio track levels. When setting levels, you need some way to ensure that the entire mix is not being raised too much and causing distortion. The Audio tool handles this job when you use it in conjunction with the Audio Mixer.

Setting Levels and Pan in the Audio Mixer

While you have been editing audio, you may have noticed problems with the audio levels; maybe a segment was too quiet or too loud. It is not uncommon to find inconsistencies in the audio levels while putting together a sequence. To keep these inconsistencies from distracting the viewer, you need to *balance*, or *mix*, the audio levels from shot to shot. The goal of mixing is twofold:

- To set a consistent audio level

- To balance the audio elements to focus the viewer's attention on the appropriate character or element within the scene

The Audio Mixer is the tool that facilitates the mix process. The Audio Mixer is designed like a real, hardware audio mixer. You can display four, eight, or 16 mixer panes in multiple groups. Each pane maps to a track in your sequence and contains controls for pan, level, gang, track, solo, and mute. A Level slider in the Audio Mixer is only displayed for tracks that contain audio.

Each pane also includes its own audio meter, which shows you the level of the individual tracks. The Audio tool is still helpful because it shows you the levels of the overall mix in the sequence.

To use the Audio Mixer:

1. Choose **TOOLS** > **AUDIO MIXER** to open the Audio Mixer, shown in Figure 6.33.

Figure 6.33
To open the Audio Mixer, choose Tools > Audio Mixer.

2. Move the position indicator to the start of the sequence and press the SPACE BAR to play. Listen carefully to the levels of the music, narration, and dialogue. The music is too loud and drowns out the dialogue—and probably your narration as well. The Audio Mixer makes it easy to set the level for a clip, sequence, or multiple clips within a sequence. Changes you make in the Audio Mixer affect the entire segment on which your blue position indicator is parked in the sequence.

Tip: **Professional audio mixing suites are carefully calibrated to provide a consistent listening experience for making judgments about a program's audio mix. Similarly, when mixing audio in Media Composer, it is ideal to work in a calibrated listening environment. If you cannot, at the very least minimize ambient noises and listen through high-quality headphones. If editing on location, consider using noise-isolating headphones.**

3. In the Timeline, place the position indicator anywhere within the first music segments on tracks A3 and A4, as shown in Figure 6.34.

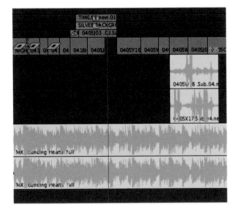

Figure 6.34
The position indicator goes over the first music segments on A3 and A4.

Tip: **You can perform level adjustments on source clips by loading a clip in the Source monitor and adjusting the Audio Mixer. If you know that an entire clip is too loud or soft, it is more efficient to adjust the clip before editing it into the sequence, especially if you know you will edit repeatedly from the clip.**

4. To adjust the music level, move the slider for track pane A3 down to **–15**. Then do the same for the track pane A4. See Figure 6.35.

5. Move the position indicator to the start of the sequence and press the SPACE BAR to play. Listen to the change in the first music segment's level. That music sounds good, so start working on the next music segment.

Figure 6.35
Move the slider for track panes
A3 and A4 to adjust their level.

The levels of the second music segment (on tracks A5 and A6) sound okay compared to the dialogue, but the music hit that you edited at the end of the first music track is a bit too loud. This time, you'll change both tracks simultaneously as you play the tracks back.

6. Place the position indicator at 01;29;16;00 and mark an IN point. Then mark an OUT point at 01;29;25;00. See Figure 6.36.

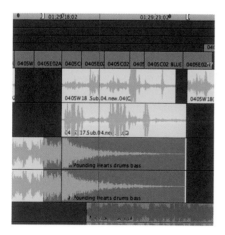

Figure 6.36
Mark IN point and OUT points
around the area you want to adjust.

7. In the Audio Mixer, click the **Group** buttons for both A3 and A4, as shown in Figure 6.37.

Figure 6.37
Click the Group button for both A3 and A4.

8. Click the **PLAY LOOP** button, shown in Figure 6.38. The system repeatedly loops through the marked area.

Figure 6.38
Click the Play Loop button in the Audio Mixer.

9. Since the IN point is within the first musical segment (MX Pounding Hearts full), do not adjust the Level slider during that segment's playback. Adjust the **A3** slider down to **–20** when the musical hit MX Pounding Hearts drum bass is playing. (See Figure 6.39.) Because A3 and A4 are grouped, both tracks are adjusted. After you adjust the level while playing, the new level goes into effect in the next loop around.

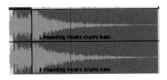

Figure 6.39
Adjust the A3 slider while the blue bar is over MX Pounding Hearts drums bass.

Tip: **To quickly reset to unity (0), Alt-click (Windows) or Option-click (Mac) the Level slider.**

10. When you are satisfied with the mix, press the SPACE BAR to stop the loop playback and click the **GROUP** buttons for both A3 and A4 to ungroup them.

11. The Audio Mixer tool can also pan audio to the left or right speaker. In these next steps, you'll adjust the pan across the entire A3 and A4 music tracks. First, click the Record monitor to activate it and press **G** to clear any IN and OUT marks in the sequence.

12. At the top of the Audio Mixer tool for track A3, drag the **PAN** control left until it reaches **L30**, and then drag the A4 **PAN** control right until it reaches **R30**, as shown in Figure 6.40.

13. From the Audio Mixer **FAST** menu, choose **SET PAN ON TRACK–GLOBAL**, as shown in Figure 6.41. All the segments on the enabled tracks A3 and A4 now have the same pan settings.

Tip: **To quickly reset the pan to mid, Alt-click (Windows) or Option-click (Mac) the Pan knob for a given track.**

The Audio Mixer is your primary tool for changing your audio track levels, but you can adjust audio directly in the Timeline, as you'll see in the next section.

Figure 6.40
Drag the A3 Pan knob to L30 and
the A4 Pan knob to R30.

Figure 6.41
Choose Set Pan on Track–Global to apply
the pan settings to the entire track.

Changing Levels Within a Segment

Adjusting levels on a segment is the most common way to even out a mix, but
sometimes setting multiple audio levels within a single segment comes in handy.
Audio gain automation (also called *audio rubberbanding*) allows you to change the
volume over time, within segments, using audio keyframes in the Timeline. Audio
keyframes are points on the Timeline at which you can set the volume level or pan.
This comes in handy for this sequence's first music track. You lowered the volume
to hear the dialogue better, but louder music should come in at the beginning of
the sequence, where there is no dialogue.

To set different levels within a clip, you need at least two keyframes:

■ The first keyframe identifies the start of the transition to the new audio level.

■ The second keyframe identifies where the transition ends.

To set different levels:

1. In the Timeline, select tracks **A3** and **A4**. These tracks include the music
   that you need to adjust.

2. Open the Timeline **FAST** menu and choose **TRACK CONTROL PANEL** if it is
   not already displayed.

3. In the Track Control panel for track A3, click the **Clip Volume/Pan** button and choose **Volume** from the menu, as shown in Figure 6.42. Then do the same for track A4. Choosing the volume for each track lets you set volume keyframes for audio in the Timeline.

Figure 6.42
Click the Clip Volume/Pan button and choose Volume from the menu.

Note: If a clip already has volume automation or pan data, and you do not select Volume or Pan from the Clip Volume/Pan menu, Media Composer displays a pink triangle on the clip to indicate that automation data is present but not displayed.

4. To make it easier to set keyframes, press **Ctrl+L** (Windows) or **Command+L** (Mac) four or five times to expand the tracks.

5. To set the first keyframe, place the position indicator at 01;29;06;00 and press ' or click the **Add Keyframe** button on the Tool palette. Media Composer adds a keyframe at the position indicator's location to each enabled track; a straight line appears in the selected audio track (see Figure 6.43). The keyframe is set at 0dB because audio volume keyframes are additive. You are adding the audio volume keyframe's value to the existing clip gain values set earlier in the Audio Mixer tool.

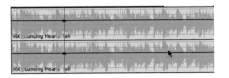

Figure 6.43
Place the position indicator at 01;29;06;00 and then press '.

6. To add the second keyframe, place the position indicator one second later, at 01;29;07;00. This should be just before the narration on track A8. Press ' or click the **Add Keyframe** button on the Tool palette. Keep in mind that the volume adjustment is additive to the mixer's gain level. That being the case, you do not want to change the second keyframe; that would change the volume of the music under the dialogue and narration. You do, however, want to raise the first keyframe, which raises the volume from the start of the clip.

7. On track A3, click the first keyframe and drag it up to **6DB**. Since A4 is also enabled and there is a point at the same position, it moves also, as shown in Figure 6.44.

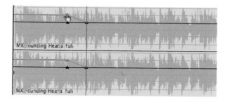

Figure 6.44
Click a first keyframe and drag it up to increase the volume.

8. Place the position indicator at the start of the sequence and press the **SPACE BAR** to begin playback. Click the **STOP** button when you hear the music become quieter.

9. To cause the music to get quieter more quickly, place the pointer over the first keyframe on the A3 track. When the pointer changes to a hand, press **ALT** (Windows) or **OPTION** (Mac), click the keyframe, and drag it to the right until you are at 01;29;06;10. The keyframe is moved in time but remains at the same volume level. (See Figure 6.45.)

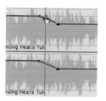

Figure 6.45
Press Alt (Windows) or Option (Mac), click the keyframe, and drag it horizontally.

10. Place the position indicator at the start of the sequence and press the **SPACE BAR** to begin playback. Click the **STOP** button when you hear the music become quieter.

Tip: **Move several keyframes vertically on a track at the same time by placing IN and OUT points to select an area. When you move one keyframe up or down within the marked area, all keyframes within the marked area move in relation to each other. This is useful for a region of music that has been keyframed around dialogue, but now needs to change overall to be louder or softer.**

Add as many keyframes and level changes to a segment as you need. Raising the music track works best during extended periods without dialogue or narration. Raising the music can enhance the mood of a montage. It can also be helpful to quickly duck a small segment down and back up to obscure an unwanted cough or mic bump, but be careful not to overuse it. It can easily become a distraction.

Audio Crossfades

In Media Composer, an *audio crossfade* is used between two audio segments to blend the sound from one segment to another. Use audio crossfades to eliminate unwanted pops at cut points or to smooth out level changes. In general, a short crossfade (between two and 10 frames) can smooth audio transitions. This sequence has a gap between the trash bag sound effect and the continuation of the trash bag sound on track A1. You can soften how the A1 trash bag starts in the sequence by adding a quick crossfade.

To add a crossfade, follow these steps:

1. Place the position indicator on or near the start of the trash bag clip on track A1, around 01;29;25;11. (See Figure 6.46.)

Figure 6.46
Place the position indicator on or near the start of the trash bag clip on A1.

2. Deselect all the tracks in the Timeline except the A1 track, which is where you want to add the dissolve.

3. Click the **Quick Transition** button in the Tool palette (see Figure 6.47) or press \ (**backslash**). The position indicator jumps to the closest transition on the selected track. The Quick Transition dialog box appears. You'll probably use Quick Transition tool more than any other method of adding effects in Media Composer because it applies both to audio crossfades and video dissolves.

Figure 6.47
Click the Quick Transition button in the Tool palette.

4. Type **10** in the **Duration** field (see Figure 6.48) and click **Add** to add a 10-frame crossfade to the start of the segment. An icon for a crossfade appears in the Timeline over the cut point. Instead of transitioning from one segment to another, this crossfade acts as a fade up, going from silence to the music.

Figure 6.48
Enter 10 in the Duration field to create a 10-frame crossfade.

Tip: **To remove a crossfade, enable the track that the crossfade is on. Then place the position indicator over it in the Timeline. In the Tool palette, click the Remove Effect button.**

5. Place the position indicator at the start of the sequence and press the SPACE BAR to hear all of your audio adjustments.

You now have some great fundamental skills for fine-tuning audio. Sound plays a critical part in every project. From making the dialogue clear and concise to enhancing the mood with the right music, project audio requires the same effort as the picture requires.

Review/Discussion Questions

1. Where can you find the Quick Transition button and what is its default keyboard shortcut?

2. Two audio keyframes are on different tracks but at the same location in the Timeline. How do you ensure that when you drag one, the other will move as well?

3. How many audio keyframes does a segment need so you can lower the volume in the middle of the segment and then return it to a louder starting level?

4. What is the difference between moving an Audio Mixer slider up to 3dB and moving a volume keyframe up to 3dB on the Timeline?

5. True or false: If the meter in the Audio tool shows yellow, you have to lower the volume so the audio does not distort.

6. True or false: Setting an IN point with the Audio Punch-In tool determines where the audio will begin recording.

7. How do you select an existing track onto which you can record using the Audio Punch-In tool?

8. On a sequence with six audio tracks, how do you solo three tracks and mute the remaining three?

9. True or false: When patching tracks, press Ctrl (Windows) or Option (Mac) to get the connection arrow.

10. How do you add a marker to the Timeline ruler?

Lesson 6 Keyboard Shortcuts

Key	Shortcut
\ (backslash)	Open the Quick Transition dialog box
' (apostrophe)	Add a keyframe
Shift+L	Toggle the Link Selection button
Ctrl+Alt+L (Windows)/Command+Option+L (Mac)	Enlarge audio waveforms
Ctrl+Alt+K (Windows)/Command+Option+K (Mac)	Reduce audio waveforms
Ctrl+L (Windows)/Command+L (Mac)	Enlarge selected tracks
Ctrl+K (Windows)/Command+K (Mac)	Reduce selected tracks
Ctrl+U (Windows)/Command+U (Mac)	Create a new audio track
Ctrl+1 (Windows)/Command+1 (Mac)	Open the Audio tool

Setting Levels

In this exercise, you'll go through the sequence to identify any distorted segments. Then you'll adjust the level to correct the problem. Finally, you'll edit in new sound effects on new tracks and use the Audio Mixer tool to set levels for the new segments.

Media Used:
Hell's Kitchen

Duration:
20 minutes

GOALS

- Set the level for any distorting segments
- Set levels for new tracks

Correcting the Distorted Segment

1. Continue with the **HK AUDIO-START** sequence that you have been working on.

2. Play through the sequence and use the Audio tool to find the one distorted segment.

3. Open the Audio Mixer and adjust the segment's level to correct the distortion.

Adding and Editing Sound Effects

1. Continue with the **HK AUDIO-START** sequence that you have been working on.

2. Open the Markers window and add two remaining sound effects: blue markers 002 and 007.

3. For marker 002, add two new tracks. Edit in the **SX30-IMPACT** master clip from the **HK AUDIO SOURCE CLIPS** bin.

4. For marker 007, use the same newly added tracks and edit in **MX TICK TOCK FULL 10** clip from the **HK AUDIO SOURCE CLIPS** bin.

5. Trim A5 and A6 music tracks to end when **MX TICK TOCK FULL 10** begins.

6. Open the Audio Mixer and adjust the level of the newly added segments to best match the sequence.

Customizing Media Composer

The ability to customize your work environment is another powerful Media Composer feature. This lesson walks you through many of the interface settings that you can change, including the interface, buttons, keyboard shortcuts, and Timeline view. You will also read about saving your settings. You will create a new user profile and explore the Media Composer default settings, and then customize settings of your own.

Media Used: Running the Sahara

Duration: 40 minutes

GOALS

- Create a new user profile
- Customize the interface settings
- Work with the Command palette
- Save your workspace and interface settings
- Adjust font sizes
- Change Timeline settings

Creating a New User Profile

User settings are stored in the Avid Media Composer folder on your hard drive in the Avid Users folder. You can change them anytime from within a project, in the Project window's Settings pane. You can also change users or create a new user profile in the Select Project dialog box when you first launch Media Composer. For this lesson, you will create a new user as you open the main course project MC6 Editing.

To create a new user:

1. Launch Avid Media Composer, select the Project window, and choose FILE > CLOSE PROJECT.

2. In the Select Project dialog box, click the EXTERNAL button.

3. Select MC6 EDITING from the project list.

4. Choose USER PROFILE > CREATE USER PROFILE, as shown in Figure 7.1.

Figure 7.1
Choose Create User Profile in the User Profile menu.

Note: You can also choose Import User or User Profile to import a user from an external drive or other location on the computer.

5. When the Create User Profile dialog box opens, type your first name in the PROFILE NAME field and click OK. (See Figure 7.2.) The new user name appears as the user profile in the Select Project dialog box, as shown in Figure 7.3.

Figure 7.2
Name the user profile.

Figure 7.3
The new profile is in the User Profile menu.

6. Make sure that your new user profile is selected, then click **OK**. The MC6 Editing project opens with all the windows light gray and the text black, as shown in Figure 7.4. The last project you worked with had a darker gray interface with white text. Welcome to Media Composer customization. All of the settings within Media Composer have been reset to the default configuration.

Figure 7.4
The default interface looks like this.

Tip: It is recommended to create new user settings each time you upgrade the Media Composer software.

Viewing and Changing User Settings

All of your Media Composer settings are located together in the Project window's Settings pane. The settings are in alphabetical order, enabling you to easily find a specific setting. Each setting has a unique window with options specific to that setting. Take a look.

To see and change user settings:

1. In the Project window, click the **SETTINGS** button. The Project window shows the Settings pane, as shown in Figure 7.5.

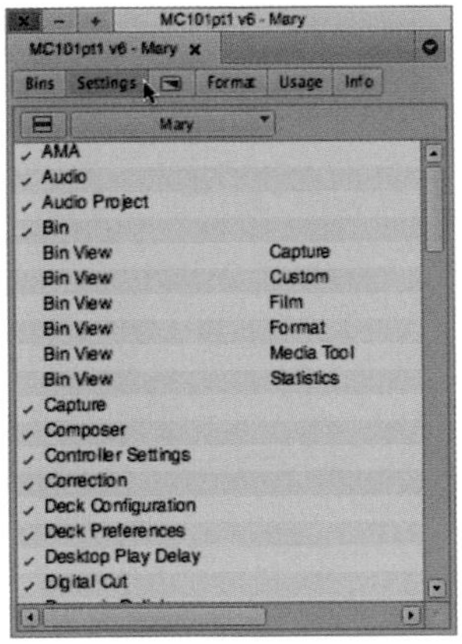

Figure 7.5
The Project window's Settings pane.

2. Resize the Project window to see a more complete list, and to view the categories for each setting. Click and drag the lower-right corner of the Project window to the bottom of the screen. It should be wide enough to display each setting's category and type. (See Figure 7.6.) Setting types include the following:

   ● **Site settings.** These are based on the computer workstation and include hardware settings such as deck and server configurations.

   ● **User settings.** These follow the user to any project on this computer (or another computer, if you bring them with you on a portable drive and import them). These are personal preference settings, like customized keyboard and workspace settings.

   ● **Project settings.** These are specific to the current project. These are based on such things as the project's media-creation and video-display settings.

3. In the **SETTINGS** pane of the Project window, double-click **INTERFACE**. The Interface–Current dialog box opens, as shown in Figure 7.7. As the name suggests, it contains settings for adjusting Media Composer's interface.

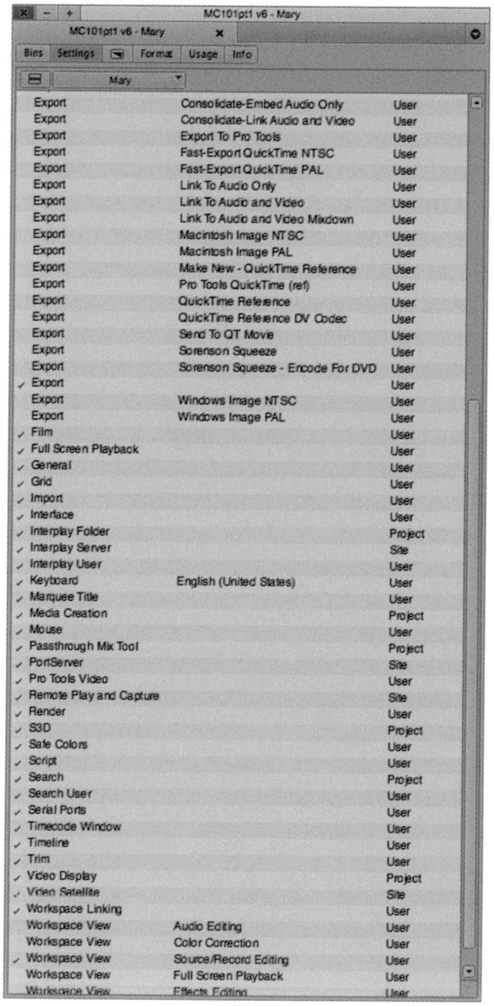

Figure 7.6
Expand the Project window.

Figure 7.7
The Interface–Current dialog box opens.

4. At the top of the Interface–Current dialog box, drag the **INTERFACE BRIGHTNESS** slider all the way to the left (darker). Then click the **APPLY** button. The interface darkens considerably, as shown in Figure 7.8.

5. Adjust the **INTERFACE BRIGHTNESS** setting to your own liking and click the **APPLY** button. Click **OK** to close the Interface–Current dialog box. For the rest of this lesson, your interface brightness may not match what you see in the book. Now you understand why.

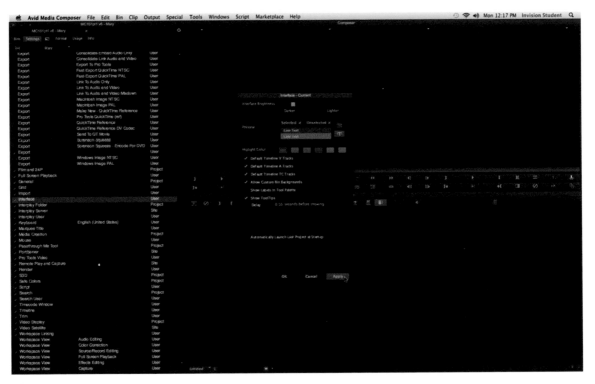

Figure 7.8
This interface is darker.

Working with Sets of Preconfigured Settings

You may have waded through quite a few settings to find what you were looking for. Sometimes, it is easier to narrow the settings to a preconfigured set. The Fast menu narrows lists. In this exercise, you use the Bin Views setting to find the Custom bin view settings. Then you'll modify the Custom bin view settings.

To modify Custom bin view settings:

1. In the **SETTINGS** pane in the Project window, open the **FAST** menu and choose **BIN VIEWS**, as shown in Figure 7.9. When the list narrows to the six available bin views (see Figure 7.10), double-click the **BIN VIEW CUSTOM** option. The Bin View–Custom settings dialog box opens. This looks like the Choose Column settings dialog box from Lesson 4, "Manual Timeline Editing." The difference is that the columns you add or remove here are saved to this user profile. Also, the Comments column is not available.

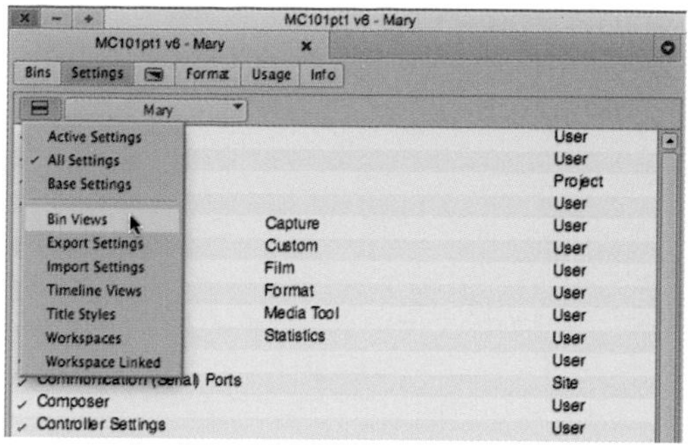

Figure 7.9
The Fast menu has preconfigured sets.

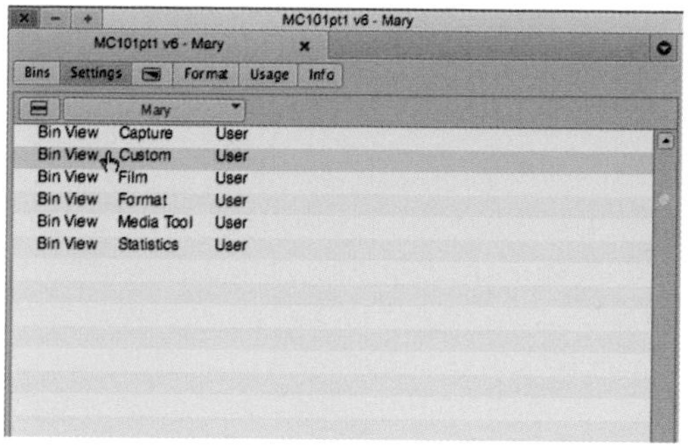

Figure 7.10
Check out the Bin View set.

2. In the Bin View–Custom dialog box, shown in Figure 7.11., choose **DURATION** and **TRACKS**. Then click **OK**. The custom bin view for this user now includes both the Duration and Tracks columns. After customizing any setting, it's best to name it so you have some idea how it has been customized. File that tip under "Do As I Say, Not As I Do," because we'll skip the naming part and now look at the Timeline settings. First, change which settings appear in the Settings pane.

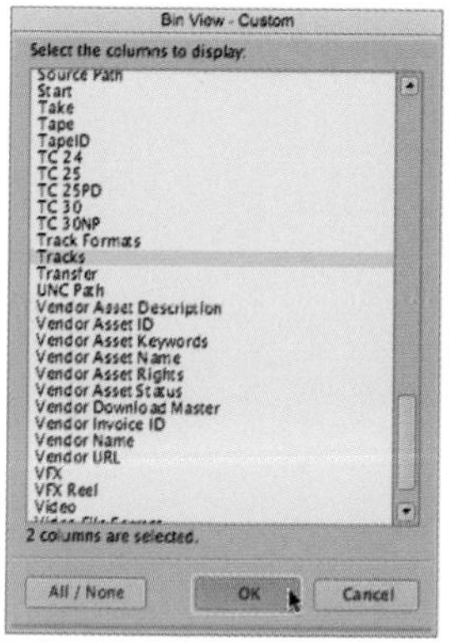

Figure 7.11
The Bin View–Custom dialog box.

3. In the Project window, open the **FAST** menu and choose **BASE SETTINGS**. This narrowed list includes the base Media Composer settings, but not the additional customized presets. The next settings that you customize are Timeline settings. For these, it is helpful to have a sequence open to see the changes.

4. In the Project window, click the **BINS** button to show the Bins pane. In the **LESSONS** folder, open the **2 FINISHED SEQUENCES** bin. Then load the sequence **RTS TEASER ROUGH CUT**. Move the open bin out of the way or minimize it.

5. Change the Project window back to the Settings pane. Resize the right edge of the Project window so you can see the entire Timeline window.

Exploring the Timeline Settings

The Timeline's default view has the video track fairly small—about half the height of the audio tracks. You may also notice that there is no audio waveform showing in the audio tracks. Finally, notice that all of the Smart Tool buttons are active. Make some changes to the Timeline settings so you can learn how to adjust them on your own later.

To change the Timeline settings:

1. In the **SETTINGS** pane of the Project window, double-click **TIMELINE** to open the Timeline Settings–Current dialog box, shown in Figure 7.12. This dialog box features two panes of settings: Display and Edit. Start with the Timeline Display settings.

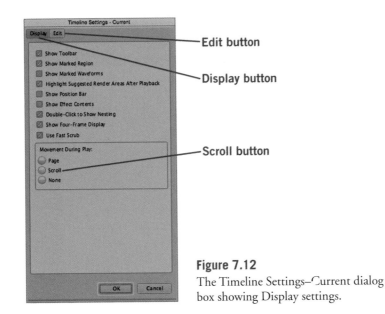

Figure 7.12
The Timeline Settings–Current dialog box showing Display settings.

2. Uncheck the **SHOW TOOLBAR** setting. Then, in the **MOVEMENT DURING PLAY** section, click the **SCROLL** button. Click **OK** to apply the changes. The toolbar at the top of the Timeline no longer shows. Some editors who are very adept at keyboard shortcuts and prefer a sparser interface use this. To see how the scroll playback works, you'll first need to expand the sequence. Why? For this feature to work, the sequence must be longer than the Timeline window.

3. Drag the Timeline scale bar toward the right, or press **CTRL+]** (Windows) or **COMMAND+]** (Mac) to zoom into the sequence. Play the sequence from the beginning. Instead of moving across the Timeline, in Scroll mode the position indicator stays motionless and the sequence scrolls underneath. Move the position indicator to another position and continue playback. The position indicator moves back to the middle of the Timeline window for scrolled playback, as shown in Figure 7.13.

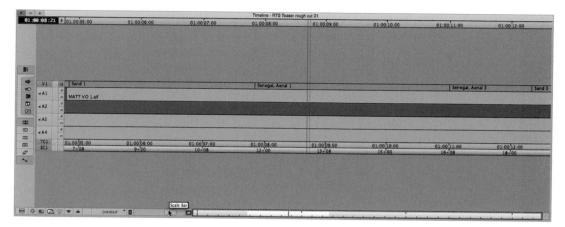

Figure 7.13
The toolbar is hidden. The Timeline is scrolling beneath the position indicator.

4. With the Timeline window selected, press **CTRL+=** (Windows) or **COMMAND+=** (Mac) to open the Timeline settings.

Note: **You can open the settings for any selected window by pressing Ctrl+= (Windows) or Command+= (Mac).**

5. In the Timeline Settings–Current dialog box, click the **EDIT** button to open the Edit pane (see Figure 7.14). This contains the default settings for edit-related functions in the Timeline. For example, you can change the default segment mode to Overwrite instead of Insert. Notice the **ONLY ONE SEGMENT TOOL CAN BE ENABLED AT A TIME** option in the middle of the dialog box. When enabled, it allows an editor to use a single keyboard stroke to toggle the Smart tool functions (i.e., if you enable the yellow, the red goes off). Take a look at the bottom of the Edit settings. Here you can set the number and type of tracks automatically included in new sequences.

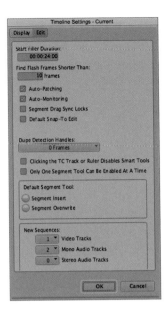

Figure 7.14
The Timeline Settings–Current dialog box's Edit pane is shown.

6. Click **OK** to close the Timeline Settings–Current dialog box. Now that you have explored the Timeline settings, restore them to the defaults.

7. In the **SETTINGS** pane, select the **TIMELINE** entry. Then right-click the selected entry and click **RESTORE TO DEFAULT**, as shown in Figure 7.15.

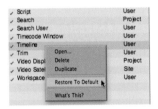

Figure 7.15
Choose Restore to Default.

8. If you see the warning shown in Figure 7.16, click the **RESTORE** button.

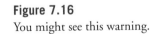

Figure 7.16
You might see this warning.

9. Play the sequence. The position indicator moves across the sequence, instead of vice versa. Also, the handy toolbar has reappeared at the top of the Timeline window.

Creating a Timeline View Preset

You can also make changes to the appearance and functionality of the Timeline using the settings in the Timeline Fast menu. You can save these changes as a Timeline view that's added to your current user profile. In this section, you will make and save changes in the Timeline as a new Timeline view. Timeline views are user settings, so they will automatically be included with your user profile if you move it to another system.

To save Timeline changes to a user profile:

1. Click the Timeline **FAST** menu and choose **SHOW ENTIRE SEQUENCE**, as shown in Figure 7.17. Alternatively, press **CTRL+/ (SLASH)** (Windows) or **COMMAND+/ (SLASH)** (Mac) to fit the entire sequence into the Timeline window.

Timeline Fast menu

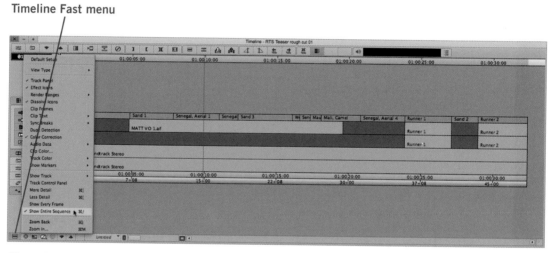

Figure 7.17
The Timeline Fast menu provides quick access to common Timeline appearance options.

2. Click the Timeline **FAST** menu and choose **VIEW TYPE > HEADS TAILS**. The Timeline changes from showing clip segments (time) to the head and tail frames of each segment, as shown in Figure 7.18.

3. Reset the Timeline view type by clicking the **FAST** menu and choosing **VIEW TYPE > TIME**. Now go to the audio data and turn on the waveform.

4. Click the Timeline **FAST** menu and choose **AUDIO DATA > WAVEFORM**. That might look more familiar. The audio track sizes are okay, but the video track is pretty small. Enlarge it.

Figure 7.18
Click the Timeline Fast menu and choose View Type > Heads Tails.

5. Click the **TC1** (timecode) and **EC1** (edge code numbers) track control buttons to turn them off. Then make sure that only the **V1** track control button is highlighted.

6. Press and hold **CTRL+L** (Windows) or **COMMAND+L** (Mac) to enlarge the V1 track. Keep holding until the video track is the same height or taller than the audio tracks.

Note: If you wind up enlarging the V1 track too much, you can reduce it with Ctrl+K (Windows) or Command+K (Mac).

7. Click the Timeline **FAST** menu and choose **CLIP FRAMES**. A representative frame, large enough to show the frame, appears for each clip, as shown in Figure 7.19.

Tip: Using tails, head tail frames, or clip frames in the Timeline can be useful if you need to quickly evaluate the pacing of shots, such as in a narrative scene. At a glance, you can see the cutting flow from wide shot, to medium shots, to back-and-forth close-ups, and so on. It is also great for action pieces like chase sequences. You can see the cross cutting and different shots that are building momentum.

8. Click the Timeline **FAST** menu and choose **CLIP COLOR**. The Clip Color dialog box opens. Here you can assign a vibrant red clip color for segments in the timeline that have offline media.

9. Click the **OFFLINE** check box and then click **OK** to close the Clip Color dialog box.

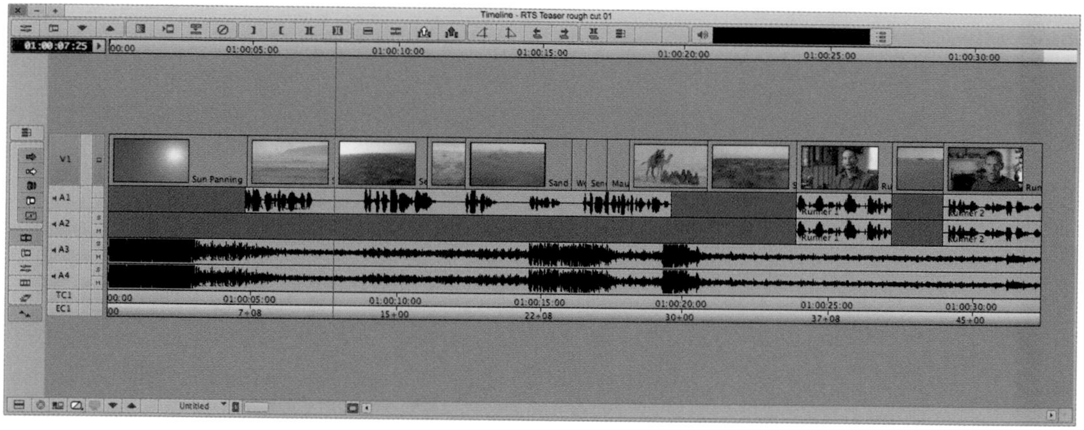

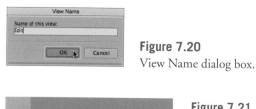

Figure 7.19
The enlarged video track shows clip frames.

10. Again in the **Fast** menu, turn off **Clip Frames**. The Timeline is perfectly set up for an editing preset. Save the current settings.

11. At the bottom of the Timeline, click the **Timeline View** menu. The default Timeline view is named Untitled. Click **Save As**.

12. When the View Name dialog box shown in Figure 7.20 opens, type **Edit** in the Name of This View field. Then click **OK**. As shown in Figure 7.21, the name of the selected preset in the Timeline Preset menu changes to Edit. That's it. Your Timeline View preset has been saved.

Figure 7.20
View Name dialog box.

Figure 7.21
The Edit preset name shows as the selected preset.

Changing the Font Size

Did you know that the higher your computer screen's resolution, the smaller some things (like text) can appear and still be clear? Interface brightness correlates with the brightness and contrast of the text within the interface. This leads to the next customizable feature, which can greatly improve your overall comfort when you are working long hours: font size. Start with the font size of text in the Project window. Then change the font in the Timeline window.

To change font and brightness:

1. Select the Project window, if it is not already selected.

2. Choose **EDIT > SET FONT** to open the Set Font dialog box.

3. Choose **FONT > ARIAL**. Then type **14** in the **SIZE** field, as shown in Figure 7.22.

Figure 7.22
The Set Font dialog box.

4. Click **OK**. All of the text in the Project window changes to 14-point Arial.

5. Click the Timeline window. Choose **EDIT > SET FONT** and choose **FONT > ARIAL**. Type **14** in the **SIZE** field. Click **OK**. As shown in Figure 7.23, the Timeline and Project window now contain 14-point Arial text.

As you can see, changing the font and font size can make it much easier to read the text in your project. Feel free to adjust the font and size in the Timeline or even in your bins to whatever you like after this lesson.

Figure 7.23
The Timeline and Project window are shown with 14-point Arial text.

Working with the Command Palette

The last customizing tool that you'll work with in this lesson is the Command palette. This palette allows you to access and remap buttons, keyboard shortcuts, and menu commands within Media Composer. Any changes that you make are saved in your user settings. Rather than tell you how it works, I'll have you dive in and start customizing your interface, starting with the Composer window.

Tip: The Command palette is in the Tools menu. To use the shortcut, press Ctrl+3 (Windows) or Command+3 (Mac).

To customize with the Command palette:

1. Choose TOOLS > COMMAND PALETTE to open the Command palette, shown in Figure 7.24. All the interface buttons in the palette are organized by function, ranging from Move and Play to Smart Tools and Workspaces. You also can see the three different Command palette modes:

   ● Button to Button Reassignment
   ● Active Palette
   ● Menu to Button Reassignment

Figure 7.24
The Command palette.

2. Click the ACTIVE PALETTE button to change the mode to Active Palette. This means that all the buttons within the Command palette are active and will work just as they would anywhere on the interface.

3. On the Command palette's MOVE tab, click the REWIND button. The position indicator moves to the beginning of the sequence. Click the FAST FORWARD button. The position indicator moves to the end of the sequence. Now try reassigning several buttons to the Composer and Timeline windows. Although you can overwrite an existing button with a new one, for this exercise you'll keep the standard buttons in place. Instead, you'll assign functions to the empty interface buttons.

4. Click the BUTTON TO BUTTON REASSIGNMENT button on the Command palette.

5. Click the **EDIT** button at the top of the Command palette to reveal the edit buttons (see Figure 7.25). Your goal is to reassign the Top and Tail buttons to two of the empty buttons in the Composer window (below the Source monitor). (Refer to Lesson 4 for more information about the Top and Tail buttons.)

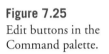

Figure 7.25
Edit buttons in the Command palette.

6. Click and drag the **TOP** button from the palette to the second empty button on the second row of Composer window buttons (below the Add Marker button). Click and drag the **TAIL** button to the empty button space to the right of the Top button that you just reassigned. See Figure 7.26. Excellent. Now you can use the buttons in the Composer window.

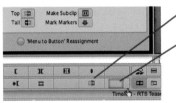

Reassign Top button

Reassign Tail button

Figure 7.26
The Top and Tail buttons are moving into their new positions.

Working with Menu to Button Reassignment

To assign menu functions to a button, select the button and then select the menu choice. For this part of the exercise, you reassign two workspace layouts to the first two buttons at the top of the Timeline.

To reassign workspace layouts to buttons:

1. Click the **MENU TO BUTTON REASSIGNMENT** button in the Command palette.

2. Click the **WORKSPACES** button at the top of the palette. You could just reassign the SE (Source/Record Editing) button from the Workspaces buttons on the palette. Instead, you will assign the menu from the top of the interface.

3. Click the **EFFECT MODE** button at the top of the Timeline window (see Figure 7.27). The mouse pointer changes to a menu icon.

Effect Mode button

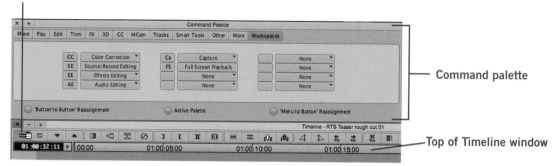

Command palette

Top of Timeline window

Figure 7.27
The pointer changes to a menu icon.

4. Choose **WINDOWS > WORKSPACES > SOURCE/RECORD EDITING**. The selected button in the Timeline window changes to SE.

5. Select the **TRIM MODE** (second) button at the top of the Timeline window. Choose **WINDOWS > WORKSPACES > AUDIO EDITING**. The selected button changes to AE, as shown in Figure 7.28.

Assigned Audio Editing button

Figure 7.28
Menu items are assigned to buttons.

Now that you have successfully reassigned buttons and menu items to the interface, take a look at reassigning keyboard shortcuts.

Customizing Keyboard Shortcuts

Keyboard shortcuts are in the Keyboard window. In this section, you use the Command palette to reassign buttons to several keys in that window. First, open the keyboard settings.

To customize keyboard settings:

1. In the **SETTINGS** pane of the Project window, open the **FAST** menu and choose **ALL SETTINGS**.

2. Double-click **KEYBOARD** in the **SETTINGS** list to open the keyboard settings. These are the default keyboard settings.

3. Press and hold the **SHIFT KEY**. As shown in Figure 7.29, the Keyboard window displays the shortcuts assigned with the Shift modifier key.

Shift+I, Shift+O, Shift+C, and Shift+B are empty. You might have used these shortcuts quite a bit for Top and Tail, Add Edit, and Replace Edit in previous lessons. Now map them to the keyboard settings.

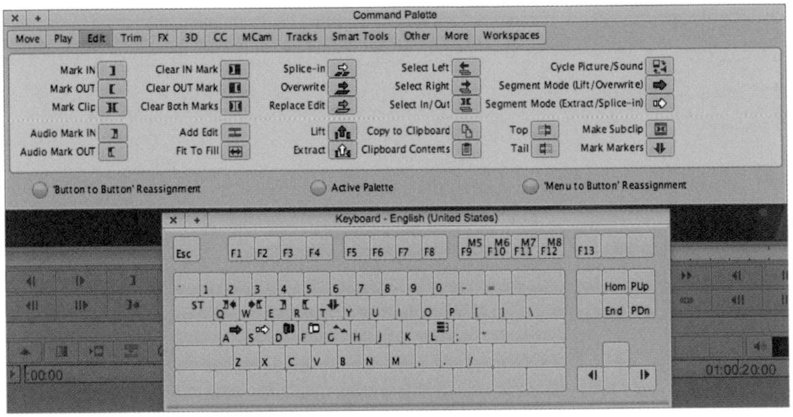

Figure 7.29
Shift-modifier keyboard settings appear.

4. Move the Command palette dialog box directly over the Keyboard window so you can easily drag buttons from one to the other.

5. Click the **BUTTON TO BUTTON REASSIGNMENT** button in the Command palette. Then click the **EDIT** button at the top of the Command palette.

6. Press and hold the **SHIFT KEY** while dragging the following buttons from the Command palette's Edit pane to the Shift-modifier Keyboard window. Figure 7.30 shows the result.

Button	Keyboard Key
Replace	Shift+B
Add Edit	Shift+C
Top	Shift+I
Tail	Shift+O

Figure 7.30
The shortcuts are finished.

7. Close the Keyboard window and the Command palette.

Customizing a Workspace

In Lesson 1, "Exploring the Interface and Preparing to Edit," you saw that you can resize the editing interface windows to fill your screen. In this lesson, you will adjust and save changes to the Source/Record Editing workspace. Keep in mind that you can always restore the workspace to the default settings if you change your screen resolution or monitor. Instead of using the Windows menu at the top of the screen, work with the button you created a few moments ago.

To customize a workspace:

1. Click the **SE** button at the top left of the Timeline window (see Figure 7.31). The windows change to the default Source/Record Editing workspace.

SE button

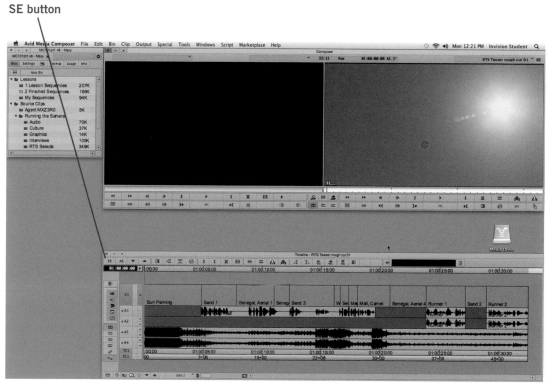

Figure 7.31
The default Source/Record Editing workspace layout looks like this.

2. Click and drag the top edge (not the header) of the Timeline window upward. It should touch the bottom of the Composer window, as shown in Figure 7.32.

Figure 7.32
The layout is modified.

3. Choose **WINDOWS > WORKSPACES > SAVE CURRENT**. The current layout represents the customized Source/Record Editing workspace for the current user settings. Test to see if it worked.

4. At the top of the Timeline window, click the **AE** button. The windows change to represent the default Audio Editing workspace.

5. Click the **SE** button. The windows return to the modified Source/Record Editing workspace.

Note: You can create and save a new workspace to reflect a unique window layout that best fits your workflow. This is especially useful if you are working with dual monitors or additional applications running in tandem with Media Composer.

Excellent customization. The settings that you have modified are saved as part of your current user settings the next time you quit Media Composer.

Review/Discussion Questions

1. What are the three types of settings? (Mark all that apply.)
   a. Composer
   b. User
   c. Site
   d. Project

2. Where do you change the interface brightness?
   a. Settings pane's Fast menu
   b. Interface settings
   c. Composer settings
   d. Brightness settings

3. How do you reset Media Composer to all default settings?
   a. Create a new user profile.
   b. Change the Settings pane to the default user profile.
   c. Create a new project.
   d. Right-click anywhere in the Settings pane and choose Reset to Default Settings.

4. In what window do you reassign buttons in the interface?
   a. Composer Settings window
   b. Buttons Settings window
   c. Interface Settings palette
   d. Command palette

5. Correctly order the steps to reassign a menu to a button.
   1. Click the Menu to Button Reassignment button in the Command palette.
   2. Choose the menu item in the interface that you want to reassign.
   3. Choose the button where you want to assign the menu item.
   a. 3, 2, 1
   b. 1, 3, 2
   c. 1, 2, 3
   d. 2, 1, 3

Lesson 7 Keyboard Shortcuts

Key	Shortcut
Ctrl+= (Windows)/Command+= (Mac)	Open settings for selected window
Ctrl+/ (Windows)/Command+/ (Mac)	Fit the entire sequence into Timeline window
Ctrl+3 (Windows)/Command+3 (Mac)	Open the Command palette

Customizing Your Media Composer Setup

In this exercise, you'll practice modifying keyboard shortcuts, creating a customized interface, and creating a new user profile.

Media Used:
Running the Sahara

Duration:
30 minutes

GOALS

- Create a new user
- Modify keyboard shortcuts
- Arrange and save a Source/Record Editing workspace
- Customize and save a Timeline view preset
- Export a user to the desktop
- Create a multicam and effects user profile
- Customize interface brightness settings
- Customize Composer settings

Modifying Keyboard Shortcuts

In this section, you'll re-create the keyboard shortcuts from the Training User settings. This is also a great way to learn the Training User shortcuts as you rebuild them.

1. Open the **SETTINGS** tab of the current project.

2. Create and name a new user profile with your first name and Training in the title (e.g., Mary's Training User).

3. Open the Command palette and the Keyboard window.

4. Reassign the following commands to the key suggested:

   - Smart tool toggle = Tab
   - Link Selection = Shift+Tab
   - Toggle Source/Record = Escape
   - Toggle Source/Record in Timeline = Tilde (~)
   - Replace = Shift+B
   - Match Frame = N
   - Find Bin = Shift+N
   - Add Edit = Shift+C
   - Top = Shift+I
   - Tail = Shift+O
   - Extend Edit = Semicolon (;)
   - Fast Forward = Up Arrow
   - Rewind = Down Arrow
   - Source/Record tool set = F9
   - Audio tool set = F10
   - Color Correction tool set = F12

Creating a Customized Interface

In this section, you will customize and save a preset in the Edit interface. For this exercise, you continue working with your new Training User setting that you created in the previous exercise.

1. Choose **WINDOWS > WORKSPACES > SOURCE/RECORD EDITING**.

2. Resize the windows to your liking and save the current workspace layout.

3. In the Timeline window, have only the audio tracks selected and enlarge their height until they are twice the height as the V1 track.

4. In the Timeline **Fast** menu, choose **Audio Data** > **Waveforms**.

5. Save the untitled timeline preset as **Audio Edit**.

6. In the Project window's **Settings** pane, click the **User Profile** menu and choose **Export User or User Profile**.

7. In the Export User Profile dialog box, select your desktop as the location. Set **Shared User Profile Type** to **Personal** (auto-load and auto-save). Click **OK**. You can move this profile to a flash drive and or to another system.

Creating a New User Setting

In this section, you will create a new user to use in Lesson 8, "Introduction to Multicamera Editing." Why? Because the default keyboard shortcuts and layout work great with multicamera and effects editing. Rather than call the user Default, name it after the types of editing that you'll use it with in this book. After you modify the interface brightness, change one item in the Composer settings to make it more multicam friendly.

1. Open the **Settings** tab of the current project.

2. Create a new user profile and name it **Multicam and Effects User**.

3. In the **Settings** tab, open the **Interface** settings. Change **Interface Brightness** setting to one shade lighter than the darkest setting. Click **Apply** and then click **OK**.

4. Open the **Composer** settings. Look at the **Window** pane of the Composer Settings–Current dialog box. The top settings are for data display. Select **Always Display Two Rows of Data**; then click **OK**.

Introduction to Multicamera Editing

Previous lessons focused on skills that you can use in just about any project. In this lesson, you read about a more specific feature set geared at editing multicamera projects. You start with master clips from the reality TV show *Hell's Kitchen*. You see how to sync the master clips, view them individually and together, and edit them using Media Composer's MultiCamera mode.

Media Used: Hell's Kitchen

Duration: 45 minutes

GOALS

- Create group clips
- Edit with multicamera displays
- Use multicamera editing techniques
- Revise a multicamera edit

Creating Group Clips

The MultiCamera feature set in Media Composer is primarily helpful for editing scenes simultaneously shot with two or more cameras. Projects that fit into this category can range from two-camera interviews, to four-camera sitcoms, to 12-camera reality TV shows. Those are the most typical uses for multicamera editing, but you'll also find it handy for the multiple takes of a single-camera music video.

When scenes are shot with multiple cameras simultaneously, each camera is captured as a master clip in Media Composer. *Grouping* is a way to gather those master clips into a single entity while you edit. You can efficiently edit those grouped clips with special multicamera editing features. Group clips are created out of two or more master clips that are synced together primarily based on one of the following:

- Source timecode

- IN points

The *Hell's Kitchen* reality program, a perfect example of a multicamera shoot, is what you will use to create a group clip in this section. Instead of using the Training User setting as you have throughout this book, you'll use the Multicam and Effects User setting you created in the previous lesson.

To create group clips:

1. Launch Media Composer. In the Select Project dialog box, choose **USER PROFILE** > **MULTICAM AND EFFECTS USER**, as shown in Figure 8.1.

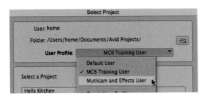

Figure 8.1
Load the Multicam and Effects User setting from the User Profile menu.

2. Select the **HELLS KITCHEN** project from the list and click the **OK** button.

3. In the Project window, double-click the **HK MULTICAM** bin. The bin opens with four clips that represent the four cameras used to record this scene.

4. Double-click the **0405Y** clip in the bin to load it into the Source monitor, as shown in Figure 8.2. Press the **SPACE BAR** to play until the end. The remaining clips are various angles of the same scene recorded at the same time.

Figure 8.2
Double-click the 0405Y clip into the Source monitor.

5. The remaining clips are various camera angles of the same scene recorded at the same time. Select all four clips and choose **BIN** > **GROUP CLIPS** or press **CTRL+SHIFT+G** (Windows) or **COMMAND+SHIFT+G** (Mac). The Group Clips dialog box opens to show the syncing options. In this production, all four cameras were recording with matching timecode, so the source timecode is identical.

6. Select **SOURCE TIMECODE** as shown in Figure 8.3 to align the clips based on the timecode.

Figure 8.3
Select Source Timecode in the Group Clips dialog box.

Note: When you're using clips without an identical source timecode, load the clips one by one into the Source monitor and mark an IN point at the same spot on each clip. You can use any visual or aural event recorded by all cameras simultaneously. Then, in the Group Clips dialog box, select In Points to group the clips by the marks you have added.

7. Click **OK**. A group clip appears in the bin with a square quad-split icon, as shown in Figure 8.14. The group clip is named after the first clip (0405Y), followed by the filename extension Grp.01.

Tip: The 01 is incremental. It represents the number of group clips with the same name in the same bin. If you are working with a number of group clips, you might want to rename them for easier identification.

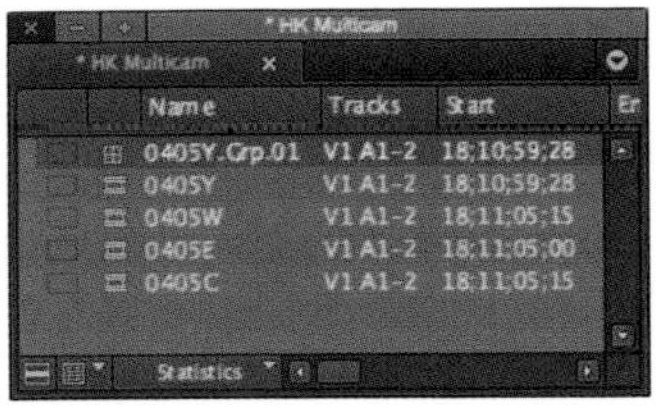

Figure 8.4
The group clip appears in the bin
with a square quad-split icon.

8. Double-click the **0405Y.GRP.01** group clip to load it into the Source
   monitor.

Nothing in the Source monitor visually distinguishes the group clip from any
other clip, although a Group Clip icon appears next to the clip's name above the
monitor. You can play and edit the group clip like any other clip you load from a
bin. However, the alternative displays for group clips can help significantly when
you begin editing. In the next section, you take a look at the multicamera displays
in the Source monitor.

Editing with Multicamera Displays

You could edit a group clip just like you would a regular master clip, but then you
would miss all the benefits of creating it in the first place. By grouping the clips
together, you can view what is happening at the same exact time in each camera
angle. You can view a group clip in the Source monitor in two main ways:

- **Full Monitor display.** In this case, each camera in the group is shown individually.

- **MultiCamera Mode view.** Here, multiple cameras are shown simultaneously.

To edit using multicamera displays:

1. Press the **UP ARROW** or **DOWN ARROW KEY** on the keyboard to cycle
   through the four cameras contained within the group clip. When you first
   load a group clip into the Source monitor, only one camera is displayed in
   Source/Record mode. This full-monitor view shows only one camera angle
   from the group at a time. When showing two rows of data above the Source
   and Record monitors, a Group Menu button is displayed. Clicking this
   opens the Group menu, which has an alternative way to select a new
   camera from the group.

2. With the two rows of data displayed above the Source and Record monitors,
   click the **GROUP MENU** button and choose **0405E** from the V1 section,
   as shown in Figure 8.5. The Source monitor switches to the new clip.

Press the SPACE BAR to play the new clip for a few seconds. The Group menu also has a way to independently select the audio or have the audio automatically selected with its matching video clip.

Figure 8.5
From the Group menu in the V1 section, choose the 0405E clip.

Note: **The 0405E, 0405W, and 0405C clips start with black filler because the cameras were not recording at the same starting point as the 0405Y camera.**

3. Click the GROUP MENU button. The selected video is 0405E, but the audio remains on 0405Y. If one microphone captured the best sound during the shoot, it is undesirable to have the audio switch every time video switches. The default setting works well in this situation.

4. Click the GROUP MENU button and choose AUDIO FOLLOW VIDEO, as shown in Figure 8.6. Now when you select a V1 clip in the Group menu, the audio from that video is also selected.

Figure 8.6
From the Group menu, choose Audio Follow Video.

5. Click the GROUP MENU button and choose **0405W**. The Source monitor shows the new camera. Click the GROUP MENU button again and notice the selected audio tracks. They have switched to 0405W (because you chose Audio Follow Video). Even though you are only viewing one camera at a time, the cameras are synced together.

6. Drag the position indicator to the center of the position bar under the Source monitor until it roughly matches the frame shown in Figure 8.7.

7. Click the GROUP MENU button and choose **0405C**. The Source monitor displays the new camera at the same timecode location as the 0405W clip. All cameras in the group move the exact same amount when you drag the position indicator.

Figure 8.7
Drag the position indicator to the center of the position bar under the Source monitor.

8. Click the **GROUP MENU** button and choose **0405Y.** You're returned to that camera in the Source monitor.

Note: When editing a multicamera program, the first edit is typically made using the group's longest camera recording. It should be the camera that provides the most coverage of the entire scene.

9. Mark the entire clip in the Source monitor and click **OVERWRITE** to edit it into the sequence, as shown in Figure 8.8. If more than one bin is open, the Select dialog box opens and asks you to select a bin in which to save the sequence and to give the sequence a name.

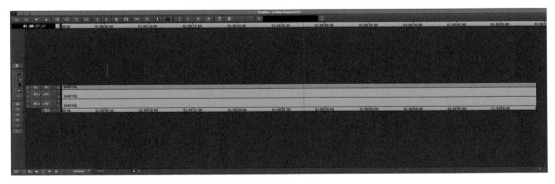

Figure 8.8
Mark the whole clip in the Source monitor; click Overwrite to edit it into the sequence.

10. Choose **HK MULTICAM** as the bin and name the sequence **HK MULTICAM EDIT** and click **OK.** A sequence appears in the Timeline. Although it appears you have edited in one clip, you've actually edited in the group clip.

Note: A (G) appended to the end of a segment name in the Timeline indicates that you've edited in a group clip, as shown in Figure 8.9.

Figure 8.9
A (G) is appended to the end of a group clip's name in the Timeline.

11. Although you can edit in full-monitor view by switching camera angles with the Group menu or the arrow keys, it's easier to cut a multicamera sequence if you can see all grouped cameras simultaneously. Choose SPECIAL > MULTICAMERA MODE. The MultiCamera Quad Split view appears in the Source monitor, as shown in Figure 8.10.

Figure 8.10
Choose Special > MultiCamera Mode to view a quad split in the Source monitor.

Note: If a group clip with more than four cameras is in the Source monitor, you can enter Nine Split Source view by clicking the Nine Split button. The button is in the Command palette in the MCam tab. The Source monitor is then divided into nine sections.

12. Press the SPACE BAR to play the sequence in MultiCamera mode. The mode synchronizes and continuously updates all the cameras in the group clip during playback and editing. The sequence controls all multicamera material so no controls are under the Source monitor. All of the playback and cueing occur in the sequence; the Source monitor follows along.

You can watch all four cameras simultaneously as you play back the sequence in MultiCamera mode. The camera with the green underline in the Source monitor is the currently active camera in the sequence. In the next section, you read about various ways to change the sequence's active camera so you can edit while in MultiCamera mode.

Exploring Multicamera Editing Techniques

Now you get to the benefit of editing in MultiCamera mode. With the four source cameras synced to the sequence, it becomes easy to see which camera is best to use at any given point in the sequence. Using either the mouse or the keyboard, you can switch to any camera from the group at any point in the sequence. While you're in MultiCamera mode, the easiest way to begin editing your sequence is via the mouse.

To edit your sequence:

1. Place the position indicator at the start of the sequence. The other three cameras were not yet recording at the start of this clip, as shown in Figure 8.11, so you have no choice but to keep 0405Y as the first shot because it is the only camera displayed.

Figure 8.11
The other three cameras were not yet recording at the start of the 0405Y clip.

2. In the Source monitor, when the camera in the upper-right corner comes onscreen (see Figure 8.12), press the **SPACE BAR** to stop playing. At this point you switch to a shot of Chef Ramsay's face.

Figure 8.12
Stop playing back when the camera in the right comes onscreen.

3. Click the camera in the upper-right corner of the Source monitor. The green line moves under that camera to show that it is active. In the sequence, an edit is made at the position indicator's location using the active camera, as shown in Figure 8.13.

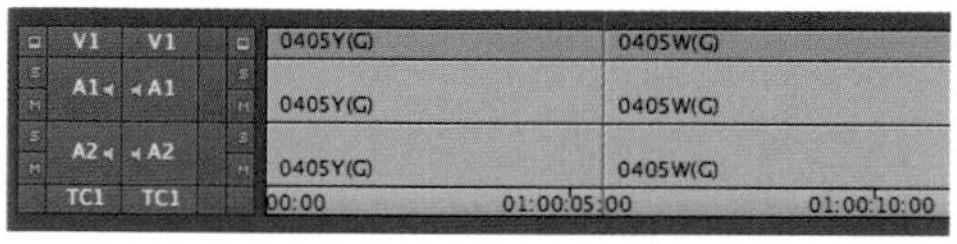

Figure 8.13
In the sequence, an edit is made when you click a camera in the Source monitor.

4. Drag the position indicator back to the start of the sequence and press the **SPACE BAR** to watch the new edit.

5. Stop playback immediately after Chef Ramsay says, "You didn't start a fresh one?"

6. Press and hold the **CTRL KEY** (Windows) or **COMMAND KEY** (Mac) to view the clip names in the Source monitor, as shown in Figure 8.14.

Figure 8.14
Press Ctrl (Windows) or Command (Mac) to view clip names in the Source monitor.

7. Release the modifier key and click the **0405E** clip to switch to that camera in the sequence. The green line moves under the 0405E clip and the edit is made in the sequence. As you continue editing the sequence in the next few steps, leave these three edits alone. You'll return to them later in this lesson.

8. In the **HK MULTICAM** bin, select **HK MULTICAM EDIT**. Choose **EDIT >**
   DUPLICATE to make a copy of the sequence. Trust me, you'll want to edit
   this sequence more than once.

9. Double-click **UNTITLED SEQUENCE 01 COPY 01** to load the copy into the
   Record monitor. Drag the position indicator in the Timeline to the start of
   the sequence and press the **SPACE BAR** to begin playing.

10. When the sequence plays past your last edit of 0405E, press the **F9**, **F10**,
    F11, and **F12** function keys to edit in the camera you want. See Figure 8.15.

Figure 8.15
For quad split display, use the F9, F10, F11, and F12 function keys to switch cameras as you
play the sequence.

Tip: You can speed up the entire process by playing the sequence and switching
     cameras without stopping. You can use the function keys to switch the display
     of camera angles on-the-fly.

Note: To use Media Composer's MultiCamera keyboard shortcuts on Mac OS X,
      disable the keyboard settings of the Mission Control shortcuts for F11
      and F12. Then change the Keyboard setting to Use All F1, F2, etc. Keys as
      Standard Function Keys. Both these settings are found in the Apple menu >
      System Preferences > Keyboard.

You won't get a perfect edit on the first try. That's why you made a duplicate. If you
want another crack at editing the sequence on-the-fly, load the original sequence into
the Record monitor. From the beginning of the sequence, press the space bar again.

When you are past the first three cuts, use the function keys to make your edits. Don't worry too much if you make mistakes. In the next section, you read how to make corrections to your edited multicamera sequence.

Revising a Multicamera Edit

Even when an on-the-fly multicamera edit is easy, there will be times when you want to go back and make changes. After editing your multicamera sequence, you can go back and swap out one camera for another using keyboard shortcuts or the Group menu.

To revise a multicamera edit:

1. Place the position indicator over a segment you would like to change. Press the **Up Arrow** and **Down Arrow keys** to cycle through the four camera angles and choose a different one for the segment. Find a segment toward the end of the sequence. Leave the first three cuts of the sequence alone. Instead of making a cut at the position indicator's location, using the Up Arrow and Down Arrow keys maintains the segment's duration in the sequence and cycles through the cameras. Or, use the Group menu to change a specific segment's camera. Regardless of track selection, using the Up Arrow and Down Arrow keys only changes the video track in a sequence. Audio remains as the original camera selection.

2. With the position indicator still over a segment toward the end of the sequence, open the **Group** menu and choose a different camera, as shown in Figure 8.16 .

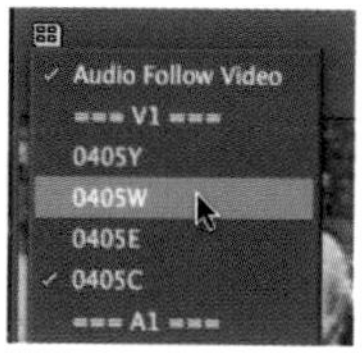

Figure 8.16
To replace a camera selection in a sequence, choose a different camera from the Group menu.

3. Click the **Group Menu** button and choose **Audio Follow Video**, as shown in Figure 8.17. Because Audio Follow Video is enabled in the Group menu, both audio and video tracks change to the newly selected camera, regardless of track selection in the sequence. However, using the Group menu does allow you to individually select audio tracks when Audio Follow Video is disabled, which is what you've done here.

4. Place the position indicator over the second segment in the Timeline (which should still be **0405W**). As shown in Figure 8.18, the 0405W camera has poor ambient sound on track 2 that needs replacement.

Figure 8.17
Choose the Audio Follow Video option
from the Group menu to disable it.

Figure 8.18
Place the position indicator
over the 0405W segment.

5. Click the **Group Menu** button and choose **0405E** from the A2 section, as
   shown in Figure 8.19. The video track and A1 track remain 0405W, but the
   A2 track in the Timeline has switched to 0405E. 0405E has good sound
   on A2.

Figure 8.19
Choose 0405E from the A2 section
of the Group menu.

6. Place the position indicator at the start of the sequence and play back your
   entire edit.

Once your basic multicamera cut is in place, you can continue editing using all
the techniques you used in previous lessons, including trimming, creating cutaways,
and adding sound effects and music.

Review/Discussion Questions

1. Where is the Group Clips command?

2. How can you identify a group clip in a bin?

3. How can you view a quad split screen view of a group clip in the Source monitor?

4. Why would MultiCamera mode be grayed out in the Special menu if a group clip is loaded into the Source monitor?

5. Name two ways you can change the camera that is shown when viewing a group clip in full-monitor view in the Source monitor.

6. What must you do to see the Group menu above the Source monitor after you load a group clip?

7. What does Audio Follow Video do in the Group menu?

8. True or false: Before you switch a sequence camera using the Up Arrow and Down Arrow keys on the keyboard (or by choosing a camera in the Group menu), you must first enable the tracks you want to switch.

Lesson 8 Keyboard Shortcuts

Key	Shortcut
Ctrl+Shift+G (Windows)/Command+Shift+G (Mac)	Group Clips
Up Arrow	Previous in Group
Down Arrow	Next in Group

Practicing Multicamera Editing

Using the same clips, go through the steps of creating a group clip and explore the different ways of editing a multicamera sequence.

Media Used:
Hell's Kitchen

Duration:
30 minutes

GOALS

- Re-create the group clip
- Practice multicamera editing

1. Delete your multicamera sequence and the group clip you created.

2. Try setting IN points on each camera angle and re-create the group clip using the IN points.

3. Edit the group clip into a sequence.

4. Edit the multicamera sequence using full-monitor view in MultiCamera mode.

Creating Quick Titles and Basic Transitions

As you move toward completion of your sequence, you will likely need to add titles and transitions. Titles are used in different ways, from opening and closing credits, to lower third-name banners, to a simple slate before the program start. When creating titles, it's important to understand their purpose and whether you are creating the final title design or temporary placeholders. Media Composer offers two distinct, integrated titling applications. Use the Avid Title tool for basic slates, lower thirds, credit rolls, or crawls. Use Marquee for 3D title design and animation. This lesson focuses on the Avid Title tool, how to edit titles into a sequence, and how to apply real-time fades and transitions.

Media Used: Hell's Kitchen

Duration: One hour

GOALS

- Make a new title
- Format and align text
- Select colors, shadows, and borders
- Save title styles
- Edit a title over video
- Work with shapes and gradients
- Apply a fade effect to titles
- Apply quick transitions

Making a New Title

The Avid Title tool is a separate application that you can open and close from within Media Composer. It has its own window and its own menu bar. In the Title Tool window you can create a page of text and graphics that can be saved over a color background or placed over video. Each title you create is saved into a bin and can be edited into a sequence using standard editing procedures.

To make a new title:

1. Launch Media Composer. From the **USER PROFILE** menu, choose **TRAINING USER**.

2. Select the **HELLS KITCHEN** project in the list of projects, and then click the **OK** button.

3. In the Project window, double-click the **HELLS KITCHEN** sequences bin to open it. The Hell's Kitchen sequences bin opens with three sequences.

4. Double-click the **HK TITLES AND TRANSITIONS** sequence in the bin to load it into the Record monitor (see Figure 9.1), then press the **SPACE BAR**. Play the video until you hear the first voiceover narration.

Figure 9.1
Double-click the HK Titles and Transitions sequence in the bin to load it into the Record monitor.

5. Choose **CLIP > NEW TITLE**. You can create titles using either the standard Avid Title tool or the Marquee 3D Title tool. This lesson covers the standard Avid Title tool.

6. A dialog box allows you to choose between the Avid Title tool or Marquee 3D Title tool. You create only standard titles for this book, so select **PERSIST** and then click **TITLE TOOL** to open the Avid Title Tool dialog box. For the rest of this editing session, Media Composer automatically opens the Avid Title tool and bypasses this dialog box. To switch to Marquee at a later time, you can go to the Marquee settings located in the Settings tab. The Avid Title tool opens with a dedicated menu bar, a toolbar at the bottom, and safe title/safe action lines surrounding the frame where you create your title, as shown in Figure 9.2. The frame displayed in the sequence is also visible in the Title tool as a reference.

Figure 9.2
The Avid Title tool shows the current frame as a reference with safe action and safe title guidelines.

Note: The outlined safe title/safe action boxes surrounding the Title tool frame are guidelines. The safe title area is the inner box. All text for television broadcast should remain within this inner box, which ensures that all television sets can view the titles. The safe action area is the outer box. These two guidelines have become slightly less important in the digital television age, but still help your titles stay a reasonable distance away from the edge of the screen.

7. Click the highlighted **VIDEO BACKGROUND** button in the Background Selection tools (see Figure 9.3). You will put this title over a color background.

Figure 9.3
Deselect the Video Background button
to create a title over a solid color.

8. The reference frame of video is replaced by a black background. To change the background color, click the **BACKGROUND COLOR (BG)** window. The Title tool Color Picker dialog box opens, as shown in Figure 9.4.

Figure 9.4
Click the Background Color (Bg) window
to change the background color.

9. In the Title tool Color Picker dialog box, click a medium deep crimson color. This kitchen is in hell, but you still want to be classy with colors. Close the dialog box, and the crimson color becomes the background.

The Avid Title Tool window is a straightforward and quick way to create titles. Although it does not have Marquee's 3D text or animation capabilities, it can provide a quick and easy way to generate great-looking titles.

Formatting and Aligning Text

Text-entering tools are structured very much like tools in a word processor. Begin by entering text that introduces the scene and then format the text to fit the program's style.

To format and align text:

1. Click the **TEXT** tool. The pointer changes to an I-beam.

2. Click in the frame's center and type **BLUE TEAM DINNER SERVICE,** as shown in Figure 9.5.

3. Click the **SELECTION** tool, and the pointer becomes an arrow. When you return to the Selection tool, selection handles appear around the text. Use the handles to resize the text box. They also determine how the text wraps. Words wrap when the text reaches the page's right border (or, in this case, the selection handles). For this example, the text should be on a single line. You need to increase the size of the text box.

Tip: To toggle back and forth between the Selection tool and the Text tool, press the Alt key (Windows) or the Option key (Mac) and click anywhere in the Title tool.

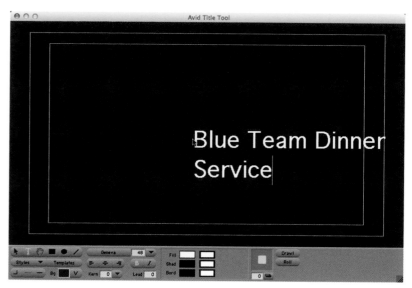

Figure 9.5
Select the Text tool and type Blue Team Dinner Service.

4. Click and drag the left selection handle toward the left safe title line, as shown in Figure 9.6. When you release the mouse button, the text should fit on a single line. Next, you select a font and font size for the text. Any font installed on your system is available through the **FONT** menu.

Figure 9.6
Drag the left selection handle toward the left safe title line.

Note: If you want to create titles with very large letters—larger than 128 pt.—make sure you use TrueType fonts. TrueType fonts still look good even at larger sizes.

5. Choose **Font > Trebuchet MS,** as shown in Figure 9.7.

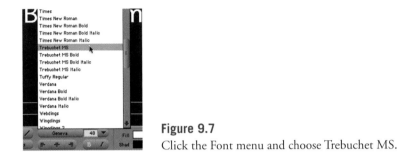

Figure 9.7
Click the Font menu and choose Trebuchet MS.

6. Type **55** in the **Font Size** field. because you are enlarging the text, you may need to resize again with the selection handles.

7. Click the **Center Alignment** button, shown in Figure 9.8, to center the text within the selection handles. Any chosen tool or formatting option in the toolbar is highlighted green.

Figure 9.8
Enter 55 in the Font Size field and then click the Center Alignment button.

8. Click the **Text** tool and type **7:04 PM** directly below the words Blue Team Dinner Service, as shown in Figure 9.9. Then click the **Selection** tool.

Figure 9.9
Type 7:04 PM just below the existing text.

9. Click the words BLUE TEAM DINNER SERVICE.

10. Choose ALIGNMENT > CENTER IN FRAME VERT to position the text vertically in the center of the screen. To center it horizontally, choose ALIGNMENT > CENTER IN FRAME HORIZ or press SHIFT+CTRL+C (Windows) or SHIFT+COMMAND+C (Mac).

11. Click the text 7:04 PM and choose ALIGNMENT > CENTER IN FRAME HORIZ or press SHIFT+CTRL+C (Windows) or SHIFT+COMMAND+C (Mac). If you center this text vertically, it will sit directly on top of the Blue Team Dinner Service text. You can, however, use an alignment grid to maintain the horizontal alignment as you drag the text into position vertically.

12. Choose ALIGNMENT > SHOW ALIGNMENT GRID and then choose ALIGNMENT > ALIGN TO GRID. The first menu item displays a grid over the frame; the second causes the text to snap to the grid.

13. Click and drag the 7:04 PM text down until it snaps to the safe title line at the bottom of the frame, as shown in Figure 9.10. As you drag, make sure the text does not snap vertically in either direction.

Figure 9.10
Drag 7:04 PM until it sits on the safe title line at the bottom of the frame.

Tip: If you accidentally move the text horizontally, use Undo in the Title tool to go back.

14. When you are done positioning the text, choose ALIGNMENT > SHOW ALIGNMENT GRID and then choose ALIGNMENT > ALIGN TO GRID to deselect both grid options.

The text is now in place for your title. It looks somewhat plain, but you have a number of options to enhance the look.

Selecting Colors, Shadows, and Borders

To make the text fit better within the fiery concept of the show, add some color to it. You can also make it stand out a bit more from the background by adding a shadow and outline. After that, you can save the entire look as a style. Then, in future episodes of the show, you can recall the settings and speed up title creation.

To select a new color, a shadow, and a border:

1. Select the **Blue Team Dinner Service** text in the Title tool.

2. Click the **Fill** box to open the Color Picker window, as shown in Figure 9.11.

Figure 9.11
Click the Fill box to open the Color Picker window.

3. Click the **Round Button** icon under the eyedropper (see Figure 9.12) to open the OS color picker. There you can select a more precise color.

Figure 9.12
Click the Round Button icon under the eyedropper to open the OS color picker.

4. In the Windows Color dialog box, shown in Figure 9.13, or the Mac Colors panel, shown in Figure 9.14, click a mustard yellow color for the fill. To apply the color, click **OK**. Finally, close the Title tool Color Picker.

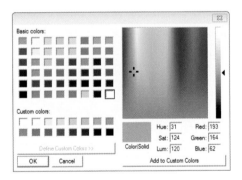

Figure 9.13
In the Windows Color dialog box, choose mustard yellow for the fill and click OK.

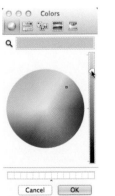

Figure 9.14
In the Mac Colors panel, choose a mustard yellow color for the fill and click OK.

5. Click and drag the shadow sample to the lower right until the **Shadow Depth** text box displays **5**, as shown in Figure 9.15. A drop shadow appears on the Blue Team Dinner Service text, making it stand out from the background.

Figure 9.15
Drag the shadow sample to the lower right until the Shadow Depth box displays 5.

Tip: **Shift-click the shadow in the Shadow Depth and Direction button and drag to restrict shadow placement to 45-degree angles around the title.**

Note: **As long as the Drop and Shadow Depth button is not enabled (not highlighted green), the shadow looks as if it is casted by a light. Enabling those shadows changes it to a depth shadow that extends from the text for a cheap 3D effect.**

6. To soften the shadow, choose **Object > Soften Shadow**. The Soft Shadow dialog box that opens allows you to create a beautiful soft-edged shadow.

7. Type **15** into the **Shadow Softness** text box and click **Apply**. The softness is applied to the drop shadow and the dialog box remains open. Try another value—15 is a bit too soft. Type **8** into the **Shadow Softness** text box as shown in Figure 9.16 and click **Apply**. That is much better. Click **OK** to close the Soft Shadow dialog box and return to the Title tool.

Figure 9.16
Type 8 into the Shadow Softness text box and click OK.

8. Click the **Border Width** button and choose the second width in the list, as shown in Figure 9.17. A thin border is placed around the text. Adding an outline is another way to ensure the text is clearly readable over the background.

Figure 9.17
Click the Border Width button and choose the second width in the list.

The text modifications are done and look great. The color and font fit the program and stand out from the background without being too garish. The next step is to format the 7:04 PM text; but you won't redo all the same formatting work you just did.

Saving Styles

After all the time it took to create the look of the Blue Team Dinner Service text, it would behoove you to save all the text attributes as a style. Title styles are saved as user settings, so the style is included anytime you create a new project with your user setting. In this exercise you save the style and then apply it to the 7:04 PM text.

To save a style:

1. Click the **Blue Team Dinner Service** text with the Selection tool.

2. Choose **Save Style Parameter > Save As,** as shown in Figure 9.18. The Title Style Sheet window shows all the text attributes that you can save in the style.

Figure 9.18
Click the Save Style Parameter menu and choose Save As.

3. Click the **Select All** button to ensure all the attributes of the selected text are included in the style.

Tip: You can enter the function key's number in the Function Key box to assign a shortcut. For example, typing 5 assigns the style to the F5 function key.

4. Type **Mustard Trebuchet** in the **Style Name** box, as shown in Figure 9.19. Click **Done** to exit the dialog box and save the style.

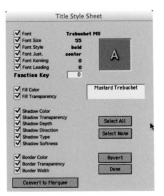

Figure 9.19
Type Mustard Trebuchet in the Style Name box.

5. Click the **STYLES** button, as shown in Figure 9.20, to display the Styles menu and see a thumbnail of each saved style.

Figure 9.20
Click the Styles button to display the Styles menu.

6. Select the **7:04 PM** text in the Title tool frame. Click the style in the menu to assign it to the selected text. You may have to resize and center the text box again if 7:04 PM wraps.

All the text in this title now has the same exact look. You can change a style's color or font any time, but using a style does help speed up things when you have a look repeated in a program. With the look in place and the style saved for future use, you are ready to edit the title into your sequence.

Editing a Title Over Video

You can save a title design into a bin and use it as you would any other clip. The title is rendered at a quality level that matches your sequence, but you can modify it any time if you have a content, style, or quality change.

To edit a title over video:

1. Choose **FILE > SAVE TITLE** or press **CTRL+S** (Windows) or **COMMAND+S** (Mac) to save the title you created in the previous exercise. The Save Title dialog box is where you can name the title, choose a bin, select a drive in which to save, and decide on media resolution.

2. In the **TITLE NAME** field, type **BLUE SERVICE 7PM** as shown in Figure 9.21. In the **BIN** drop-down list, choose **HELLS KITCHEN SEQUENCES**. In the **DRIVE** drop-down list, choose from the options. In the **RESOLUTION** drop-down list, select **2:1 MXF**.

Figure 9.21
Name it, choose a bin and a drive, and select the resolution.

3. Click **SAVE**; it loads into the Source monitor. The title is similar to a captured clip in that you can cut it anywhere in the sequence, including over
   video. Find a spot to edit in your title.

4. Click and drag the Timeline position indicator to the shot inside the dinner
   area, as shown in Figure 9.22. That segment is fifth in the Timeline, around
   01;00;03;00.

Figure 9.22
Drag the Timeline position indicator to the shot inside the dinner area.

5. Make sure **V1** is selected and make sure **A1** and **A2** are deselected on the
   record track pane.

6. Click **MARK CLIP** or type **T** to mark an IN point and OUT point around
   this segment in the Timeline. This is where your title will go.

7. Choose **CLIP > NEW VIDEO TRACK** or press **CTRL+Y** (Windows) or
   COMMAND+Y (Mac) to add a new video track, called V2, above the V1
   track, as shown in Figure 9.23. Just like you added multiple tracks of
   audio to layer sounds over each other, you can add tracks of video to layer.
   In this case you'll layer a title on top of a video track.

   Additional video tracks can host all the same media types and include all
   the same editing capabilities as the V1 track. To edit the title onto V2, you
   must patch the video tracks just as you did the audio tracks in a previous
   lesson.

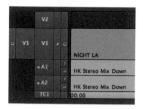

Figure 9.23
Choose Clip > New Video Track to add a new video track to a sequence.

8. To patch video tracks, click and drag the **V1** source track to the **V2** record track. As shown in Figure 9.24, a connection arrow appears as you begin to drag, to help you visualize the two tracks that are being connected. When you release the mouse, the V1 track jumps next to the V2 record track.

Figure 9.24
To patch video tracks, drag V1 to V2 on the record side.

9. Click the **OVERWRITE** button or press **B** to edit the title onto V2 above the V1 track. A Title icon makes it easily identifiable in the Timeline, as shown in Figure 9.25.

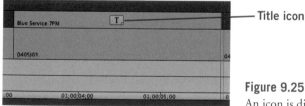 ── **Title icon**

Figure 9.25
An icon is displayed on the title that is edited on V2.

10. Click and drag the position indicator to the start of the sequence and press the **SPACE BAR** to play. Stop when you have played through the title. In the Record monitor, the title played with the background and obscured the clip. Although you may want a background on your title slate, in this case you want to see the underlying video. Also, since the narration mentions the Blue Team Dinner Service, that part of the title seems redundant. To correct these issues, you need to reopen and modify the title. You can edit the background and the text even though it has been edited into the sequence.

11. Click and drag the position indicator directly over the title in the Timeline.

12. To enter Effect mode, click and drag the position indicator over the effect. Make sure **V2** is the only selected track. Click the **EFFECT MODE** button (in the center of the Composer window's toolbar), as shown in Figure 9.26. Because Media Composer considers a title an effect, to edit a title you must enter Effect mode to edit effects.

Figure 9.26
Click the Effect Mode button located in the center of the Composer window's toolbar.

Note: When you enter Effect mode, the Record monitor becomes the Effect Preview monitor and the position bar under the Effect Preview monitor represents the selected segment (not the entire sequence). You'll read more about creating effects and Effect mode in *Media Composer 6: Part 2–Essential Effects*.

13. The Effect Editor window opens with the title controls. Click the **EDIT TITLE** button in the Effect Editor (see Figure 9.27) to open the Title tool. With the Avid Title tool open, you can make changes to the design.

Figure 9.27
Click the Edit Title button in the Effect Editor to open the Title tool.

Tip: To reopen a title, even if you haven't edited it into a sequence, Ctrl-double-click (Windows) or Command-double-click (Mac) the Title Effect icon in the bin.

14. Click the **SELECTION** tool in the Title tool's toolbar. Then select the text **BLUE TEAM DINNER SERVICE**. Press **DELETE** to remove the text.

15. Click the **VIDEO BACKGROUND** button (see Figure 9.28) to make the background of the title transparent, revealing the V1 track. You will use the V1 video track as the background; after clicking the button, you can see a reference frame of the V1 clip under the title.

Figure 9.28
Click the Video Background button to see the video on V1.

The two title issues are resolved: You replaced the background color with transparency so you can see the video under the title. You also removed the redundant part of the title. Unfortunately, you also introduced a problem. The 7:04 PM text is now difficult to read over the video background. You'll correct this problem in the next exercise.

Working with Shapes and Gradients

The Title tool has simple graphics capabilities that can improve your text's look and readability. Without a background color, the text is very likely to get lost. To make it easier to read, you can create a simple banner background. You start at the Avid Title tool toolbar, which has a group of drawing tools to help create graphics.

To create a banner background for text:

1. Click the **SQUARE AND RECTANGLE** tool, as shown in Figure 9.29. The pointer becomes a crosshair.

Figure 9.29
In the Title tool toolbar, click the Square and Rectangle tool to enable the tool.

2. Beginning at the left edge of the Title tool frame, click and drag a rectangle around the **7:04 PM** text (roughly two-thirds of the way across the frame), as shown in Figure 9.30. The drawn rectangle should cover the text completely.

Figure 9.30
Click and drag a rectangle around the 7:04 PM text.

3. Choose **OBJECT > SEND BACKWARD** to correctly position the rectangle behind the text. The rectangle is placed behind the text as shown in Figure 9.31.

Figure 9.31
Choose Object > Send Backward to place the rectangle behind the text.

Note: The same fill color you used for text can be used for any selected object.

4. With the rectangle selected, click the **FILL** box and choose a crimson red similar to the one you used for the background. Instead of filling the rectangle with a solid color, you can create a gradient that blends between two colors across an object. The fill color you select is the first color in the gradient blend.

5. Click the second **COLOR BLEND** box (to the right of the Fill box), as shown in Figure 9.32, to choose the second color.

Figure 9.32
Click the second Color Blend box.

6. In the Title tool Color Picker dialog box, choose a mustard color similar to the one applied to the text; then close the Color Picker dialog box. The gradient is added to the box, blending from left to right. You can change the direction of the blend using the Blend Direction box.

7. Click and drag in the **Blend Direction** box until crimson is at the bottom of the rectangle and yellow is at the top, as shown in Figure 9.33.

Figure 9.33
Drag in the Blend Direction box to change the direction of the gradient blend.

8. Select the text and click the **Fill** box to make the text stand out on the rectangle.

9. With the Title tool Color Picker dialog box open, select a plain white color; then close the Color Picker dialog box.

10. Choose **File > Save Title**. Then click **Save** in the Save dialog box that appears. The Title tool window closes and the title is updated both in the bin and in the sequence, as shown in Figure 9.34.

Figure 9.34
The title is updated in the bin and in the sequence.

This section covers the majority of the Avid Title tool's functionality. With the formatting and design tools you learned about in this lesson, you should be able to create titles for a large selection of program types.

Applying a Fade Effect to Titles

Once put into the context of your sequence, you may find that even your best designed titles lack something. It's not always the design itself, but their pacing within the sequence. If titles appear abruptly but need a softer touch, you can use the Fade Effect button to slowly fade titles on and off screen.

To add a fade effect:

1. The Hell's Kitchen project should be open, with the **HK TITLES** sequence loaded in the Record monitor. Before you begin, watch the new title in the sequence.

2. Press the **HOME KEY** (Windows) or **FUNCTION+LEFT ARROW** (Mac) to put the position indicator at the start of the sequence.

3. Press the **SPACE BAR** to play the sequence until you have viewed the entire title. The title pops on and off screen somewhat harshly. It might look nicer if there were a quick fade up and down of the title.

4. Park the position indicator over the title segment in the Timeline.

5. In the Composer window, click the Tool palette between the Source and Record monitors; then click the **FADE EFFECT** button as shown in Figure 9.35. The Fade Effect dialog box opens.

Figure 9.35
From the Tool palette, click the Fade Effect button.

6. You can enter the fade-up and fade-down duration in frames. Type **10** in the **FADE UP** and **FADE DOWN** fields. Then click **OK** to apply the fade effect and close the dialog box (see Figure 9.36).

Figure 9.36
In the Fade Effect dialog box, enter a 10-frame fade up and fade down.

Note: Fade is a real-time effect for titles, so you can play the result instantly without rendering or processing.

7. Press the **HOME KEY** (Windows) or **FUNCTION+LEFT ARROW** (Mac) to put the position indicator at the start of the sequence. Press the **SPACE BAR** to play the sequence and view the entire title.

Now your titles have nicer pacing. They come onscreen and go offscreen smoothly. The fade effect only works for titles and other effects. You cannot use the fade effect to smooth the transition between video cuts. Instead, like you do with audio, use the Quick Transition button to smooth the transition between video cuts.

Adding Quick Transitions

Media Composer uses the same basic method to create crossfade transitions for audio and dissolve transitions for video. Audio crossfades are covered in Lesson 6, "Refining and Mixing Audio." See it for creating an audio crossfade transition. Now add a dissolve transition to between video cuts in your sequence. You'll use the same HK Titles and Transitions sequence in the Record monitor.

To add a dissolve transition:

1. Press the **HOME KEY** (Windows) or **FUNCTION+LEFT ARROW** (Mac) to place the position indicator at the start of the sequence.

2. Press the **SPACE BAR** to play the sequence until you reach the title. The first two shots are similar, as shown in Figure 9.37, so the cut is a bit jarring. To smooth that transition, add a dissolve effect.

Figure 9.37
These two shots are similar and create a harsh cut.

3. Make sure **V1** is selected. Deselect **V2**, **A1**, and **A2**. You want the transition to be applied only to the V1 track.

4. Place the position indicator near the cut between the two nighttime city shots (around 01;00;01;00).

5. Click the **Quick Transition** button in the Timeline toolbar, as shown in Figure 9.38, or press **\ (backslash)** on the keyboard. The backslash is the same button you use to add the audio crossfade. The Quick Transition dialog box opens.

Figure 9.38
Click the Quick Transition button in the Timeline toolbar.

6. Type **15** in the **Duration** field in the Quick Transition dialog box, as shown in Figure 9.39.

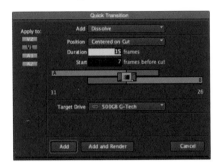

Figure 9.39
Enter 15 in the Duration field; then click Add.

7. Click **Add** or press **Enter/Return** to add the default dissolve transition and close the Quick Transition dialog box. (If you chose Add and Render, Media Composer would render the transition and create a new media file on your hard drive.) The transition is added to the sequence and indicated by a Dissolve icon in the Timeline, as shown in Figure 9.40. Now watch the transition to see if it improved your cut.

Dissolve icon

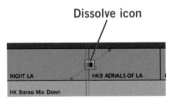

Figure 9.40
A Dissolve icon in the Timeline shows you where the transition was added.

Note: If you want to guarantee real-time playback on older systems, render quick transitions. In that case, you must also choose a storage location for the rendered media file. Target Drive in the Quick Transition dialog box is where you decide where to store the media for rendered transitions. Effect Source is the default drive, which is specified in the Media Creation settings' Render tab.

8. Press the **HOME KEY** (Windows) or **FUNCTION+LEFT ARROW** (Mac) to place the position indicator at the start of the sequence. Press the **SPACE BAR** to play through the dissolve transition; press the **SPACE BAR** again to stop playback after watching the transition.

The dissolve creates a much smoother transition between the two similar shots. In this lesson, you added a real-time transition between two video clips, quickly created a lower third title, added a second video track to a sequence, placed a title over video, applied title fades, and then played the entire sequence in real time without rendering. That's quite a few finishing touches. With all of the editing, audio mixing, transitions, and titling behind you, this book's next, and last, lesson helps you export a completed sequence for distribution and sharing.

Review/Discussion Questions

1. What must you do to ensure a quick transition is added only to a video cut point, not to an audio cut point?

2. In the Title tool, is the Send Backward command under the Object menu or the Alignment menu?

3. How do you assign a color to a rectangle shape?

4. How do you add a new video track?

5. True or false: After a title is edited onto V2 of a sequence, it always shows the video under it on V1.

6. If you edit a title into a sequence, how do you access the Edit Title button to re-open the title in the Title tool? Give specific steps.

7. True or false: To create a colored background for a title, first disable the Video Background button, and then click the Fill box.

8. Are the selection handles around a text object for resizing the text or resizing a text box?

9. How do you soften a text shadow in the Title tool?

10. How do you match a title's media resolution to the captured media resolution of the video clips?

Lesson 9 Keyboard Shortcuts

Key	Shortcut
Shift+Ctrl+C (Windows)/Shift+Command+C (Mac)	Title tool: Center Horizontal
Ctrl+Y (Windows)/Command+Y (Mac)	Create a new video track
\ (backslash)	Enter a quick transition effect

Creating a Title Credit Roll

In this exercise, you'll enter text, format it, and create a title credit roll that can be edited into a sequence.

Media Used:
Hell's Kitchen

Duration:
15 minutes

GOALS

- Create a title credit roll
- Edit the title roll

1. Choose CLIP > NEW TITLE.

2. In the Title tool, click the TEXT tool in the toolbar. Then click the ROLLING
   TITLE button to enter Rolling Title mode. The button changes to green,
   and a Page Number box appears in the lower-right corner of the Title tool.

3. Type at least 15 lines of text in the Title tool, pressing ENTER/RETURN to
   go to the next line.

4. When you are finished, click the SELECTION tool in the toolbar to select
   the new text object.

5. Center justify the text and set the font to TREBUCHET MS, size **36**.

6. Align the text to the frame top and then center it horizontally.

7. Add a drop shadow with a value of **5** to the lower left of the text.

8. Save the title and view it in the Source monitor.

Preparing for Output and Exporting a File

Your sequences won't do you much good if the only place people can watch them is when they are huddled around Media Composer. Conveniently, you can get sequences out of Media Composer by putting them out to videotape or converting them into other file types for distribution in a variety of ways. The viewing destination will determine how you choose to output your sequence. You can create a file for a Web site, create a DVD-ROM, or output to videotape, which is also called a *digital cut*. The method or combination of methods you choose depends on your situation. In this lesson, we'll cover some of the tasks you should do before you output to tape and also a few of the ways you can export a sequence.

Media Used: Hell's Kitchen

Duration: 45 minutes

GOALS

- Create a sequence report
- Add bars, tone, and filler
- Review work in full-screen playback mode
- Export a sequence for Web sharing
- Use Send To templates for DVD authoring
- Create your own Send To template

Creating a Sequence Report

Before you output to videotape, export your sequence as a file, or just pass on the sequence to someone else, you'll want to ensure everything is in order. The last thing you want to do is distribute your program with errors that could have been corrected had you done a few simple checks. Media Composer can output detailed sequence information in a report that can help you identify problem areas, like offline clips or unrendered effects. Sometimes, small details like these are easier to see in a report than by looking at a Timeline

To create a sequence report:

1. Launch Media Composer and select TRAINING USER. Then select the HELLS KITCHEN project and click the OPEN button.

2. In the Project window, double-click the HELLS KITCHEN SEQUENCES bin to open it.

3. In the HELLS KITCHEN SEQUENCES bin, double-click the HK EXPORT sequence to load it into the Record monitor. See Figure 10.1.

Figure 10.1
Load the HK Export sequence into the Record monitor.

4. Right-click (Windows) or Control-click (Mac) in the Record monitor and choose SEQUENCE REPORT, as shown in Figure 10.2. The Sequence Report dialog box appears.

5. The Sequence Report dialog box can be used to change the name and start timecode of the sequence. Type **HK OUTPUT** in the NAME field.

Figure 10.2
Right-click or Control-click in the Record monitor to open the Sequence Report dialog box.

6. If you are creating a tape for television broadcast in North America, Central America, Western South America, or Japan, the sequence should be set to drop-frame timecode. To indicate drop-frame timecode, you use semicolons between every two digits. As shown in Figure 10.3, type **01;00;00;00** in the **STARTING TC** field to change the start timecode of the sequence.

Figure 10.3
Type HK OUTPUT in the Name field and 01;00;00;00 in the Starting TC field.

Note: **Drop-frame and non-drop-frame timecode only exist if your video was recorded using the NTSC television standard. For all of Europe and most of Asia, the PAL standard is used and this issue does not exist.**

7. Click **APPLY CHANGES** to make the changes to the sequence. In the bin, the start timecode and the name are updated with the modified information.

8. The remainder of the Sequence Report dialog box provides options for the content included in the report. You'll use it here to generate a list of all the clips and sources that make up this sequence. First, make sure the **ENABLED TRACKS ONLY** and the **USE MARKS** check boxes are not enabled so you can create a list for all the tracks in the entire sequence.

9. The Summary Info Options section starts off with options for creating audio and video effect lists. These can be helpful for finding where the effects in your sequence are, what types are used, how many third-party plug-ins were used, and so on. For this lesson, you are only interested in the edited clips and sources, so make sure **CREATE EFFECT SUMMARY** and **CREATE EFFECT LOCATION LIST** are both unchecked.

10. Enable the **CREATE CLIP SUMMARY** check box. This option will generate a list of data about the clips in the sequence, including name, tracks, and maybe most importantly whether any of the clips are offline.

11. Enable the **CREATE SOURCE SUMMARY** check box, as shown in Figure 10.4. This will provide you with the tape names used in the sequence. It also lists all the imported files and the path from which they were last imported.

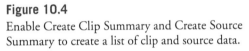

Figure 10.4
Enable Create Clip Summary and Create Source Summary to create a list of clip and source data.

12. To find all the clips that are currently offline and their associated source tapes, enable the **OFFLINE ONLY** check box.

13. Some of the clips are group clips from the multicamera shoot, so enable the **SKIP NON-SELECTED CLIPS IN GROUP CLIPS** check box. With this option, unused clips from the group will not appear in the list.

14. Choose **GENERATE REPORT** to create the text file. The Save Summary Output File As dialog box opens, with a name created based on the options selected.

15. Choose a location to save the file and click **SAVE**. The list is saved to your hard drive and is opened automatically for you to review.

You can read over the list and hopefully see that no clips are offline in the sequence. Reports can be very handy when your sequence becomes longer with multiple layers. Trying to find video plug-ins, audio plug-ins, or offline clips can be made much easier.

Adding Bars, Tone, and Filler

Most tapes that you deliver for broadcast television or plan to show in any public screening space should start with references for the color and sound, as well as 30 seconds of black just before the program begins. You should also include a slate that includes valuable program information like total running time and title. You can also include a 10-second countdown before the program. Both the slate and countdown can be created in the Title tool, so we'll skip those two items and go directly to the color bars, tone, and filler.

Using a color bar test pattern and audio tone ensures that when the show is broadcast, the sound is not distorted and the colors are reasonably accurate. The added black filler (just after the bars and tone and before the program) is padding to soften the transition between the bars and tone and the program. You can add black filler in Media Composer without importing or capturing a black clip.

To add bars, tone, and filler:

1. Make sure the **HK Output** sequence is loaded into the Record monitor.

2. Select **Clip > Add Filler at Start**. By default, Media Composer adds 30 seconds of filler to the head of the sequence. See Figure 10.5. (You can change this in the Timeline Settings > Edit tab.)

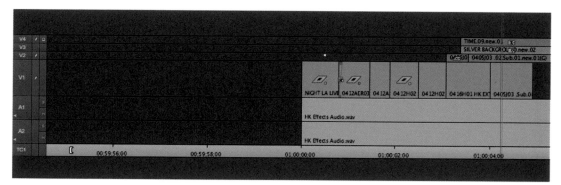

Figure 10.5
Choosing Clip > Add Filler at Start adds black at the start of the sequence.

Note: It is fairly standard practice to start a sequence on the hour. When you choose Add Filler at Start, the start of the sequence is back-timed so the program start time remains on the hour.

Tip: To edit in filler anywhere else in a sequence, choose Load Filler from the Clip Name menu above the Source monitor. Media Composer loads a two-minute clip of filler into the Source monitor that can be used like any other clip.

3. After black filler is added, a reference video test pattern and sound should be added as the first items in the sequence. A standardized pattern called *color bars* is used when calibrating the picture, and an audio tone is used when calibrating the sound. Media Composer can provide the color-bars graphic and tone signal for a digital cut. Choose **File > New Bin**. In the Project window, rename the bin **Test Patterns and Tone**.

4. Select the **TEST PATTERNS AND TONE** bin and choose **FILE > IMPORT** to open the Import dialog box.

5. Choose **FILES OF TYPE > GRAPHIC FILES** (Windows) or **ENABLE > GRAPHIC** (Mac) so only graphic files are displayed.

6. Choose **C:\PROGRAM FILES\AVID\AVID MEDIA COMPOSER\ SUPPORTINGFILES\TEST_PATTERNS\SD_NTSC** (Windows) or **MACINTOSH HD/APPLICATIONS/AVID MEDIA COMPOSER/ SUPPORTINGFILES/TEST_PATTERNS/SD_NTSC** (Mac).

7. Select **COLOR_BARS** in the Import dialog box. In the countries that use the NTSC standard, SMPTE bars are the standard pattern used, but we'll use the more internationally accepted full-frame color bars.

8. Click **OPTIONS** to open the Import Settings dialog box, shown in Figure 10.6.

Figure 10.6

Click Options to open Media Composer's Import Settings dialog box.

9. Click the **IMAGE** tab and select **IMAGE SIZED FOR CURRENT FORMAT** in the Image Size Adjustment area. This setting stretches the graphic file to fill the frame.

10. In the File Pixel to Video Mapping area, select **601 SD OR 709 HD (16-235)**. This sets the luminance and color space in the graphics file to broadcast standards (not to computer or print standards). Then click **OK** to close the Import Settings dialog box.

11. Click **OPEN** to import the file and create a master clip in the selected bin.

12. Double-click the **COLORBARS.TIF** master clip in the **TEST PATTERNS AND TONE** bin to load it into the Source monitor. See Figure 10.7.

Figure 10.7
Load the ColorBars.tif clip into the Source monitor.

13. Clear the marks from the Record monitor and drag the position indicator to the start of the sequence. Disable all the tracks in the Timeline except **V1**. Make sure the sync locks are on all the tracks as well.

14. Make sure the source-side position indicator is at the start of the clip and then click **SPLICE IN**. See Figure 10.8. It is fairly standard practice to edit in either 30 seconds or one minute of bars and tone before a program. This sequence uses 30 seconds, but you could edit the bars in twice or extend the imported graphic's duration in the Import Settings dialog box, just be sure to add enough filler. Now you can create tone. You create a tone master clip for editing directly into sequences within Media Composer.

Figure 10.8
Insert 30 seconds of the ColorBars.tif clip at the start of the sequence.

15. Select **TOOLS > AUDIO TOOL** to open the Audio tool.

16. Click the **PH (PEAK HOLD)** menu in the Audio tool and select **CREATE TONE MEDIA**, as shown in Figure 10.9. The Create Tone Media dialog box opens.

Tip: You can also generate tone using the Timeline Audio Meters menu.

Figure 10.9
From the PH menu, select Create Tone Media.

17. Set **Tone Media Level in dB** to **-20**. Set **Tone Media Length in Seconds** to **30**. The tone should represent the average level of your sequence's audio, which should be around −20db.

  To learn more about audio levels for broadcast and delivery, including how to conform your program to Commercial *In the Avid* Advertisement Loudness Mitigation (C.A.L.M.) Act standards, *Learning Series* see *Media Composer 6: Professional Picture and Sound Editing*.

18. Select **2** from the **Number of Tracks** menu.

Note: **You should create as many tracks of tone media as you have final output audio tracks. This is typically between two and four, but could be as high as eight.**

19. From the **Target Bin** menu, choose the **Test Patterns and Tone** bin. Then choose the appropriate target drive for the tone media file. See Figure 10.10.

Figure 10.10
Set the number of tracks to 2 and choose a target bin from the menu.

20. Click **OK** to close the Create Tone Media dialog box. Media Composer creates the media file and a master clip appears in the target bin. The default name reflects the options you selected.

21. Double-click the **TONE 1000Hz @ -20dB** clip in the **Test Patterns and Tone** bin to load the clip into the Source monitor.

22. From the Record monitor, drag the position bar to the start of the sequence. Disable all the tracks in the Timeline except A1 and A2, as shown in Figure 10.11.

Figure 10.11
Only enable tracks A1 and A2 in the Timeline.

23. With the source-side position indicator at the start of the clip, click **OVERWRITE** to match the 30 seconds of bars with 30 seconds of tone at the start of the sequence.

Tip: Most (if not all) of your digital cuts will require the bars and tone to start each program. To save time, think about keeping a Test Patterns and Tone bin to bring into every project.

You now have a digital cut–ready sequence with a test pattern and tone at the start, black padding just before the program, and the sequence correctly prepared.

Reviewing Work in Full-Screen Mode

When working on a program, no matter the genre, you probably have to work with other people. Yes, as bad as that sounds, it is a necessary evil. Even worse, they will inevitably have an opinion. To help brighten this painful process, Media Composer includes a few tools that can assist you when you and other members of the production come together to review edited sequences or raw unedited master clips.

In this section, you'll review an edited sequence using a full-screen playback mode. This mode enables you to view the content of either the Source or Record monitor full screen on your computer monitor.

To review a sequence in full-screen mode:

1. Place the position indicator at the start of the sequence.

2. Choose **SPECIAL > FULL SCREEN PLAYBACK** or press **SHIFT+CTRL+F** (Windows) or **SHIFT+COMMAND+F** (Mac). The Media Composer interface is replaced by a full-screen display of the current frame.

Note: Full-screen mode is not available on systems with Avid DX hardware. It is assumed that you will use the DX hardware to output to a client monitor instead. For this option to work with Avid Adrenaline, Avid Mojo, or Avid Mojo SDI input/output hardware, make sure to click the DNA/1394 button in the Timeline and set it to 1394 to disable the hardware.

3. Press the SPACE BAR to play the sequence in full-screen mode.

4. To return to Media Composer, press SHIFT+CTRL+F (Windows) or SHIFT+COMMAND+F (Mac).

Having a full-screen view of your sequence can help you notice a number of issues that may be difficult to detect in the smaller Source or Record monitor. You are better able to judge the audio and video sync and notice flaws in the picture or continuity problems.

Exporting a Sequence for Web Sharing

Media Composer offers two options for exporting your sequence as a digital file:

■ **Export.** This option offers format and compression settings for creating a file(s) that you can then bring to other applications or computers.

■ **Send To.** This option includes the same format and compression settings but uses templates, customized for a specific workflow, to send selected clips or sequences directly to other applications on your computer.

If your deliverables change with every job, then the Export option might be your best bet. If you have a consistent workflow on the same computer, then Send To is an easier option. You can create your own Send To templates that include all your personal export settings and even launch the application with which you plan to work.

A few video-sharing Web sites have become standard posting sites for producers, filmmakers, and artists. Independent film trailers, commercials and infomercials, PSAs, and even editor demo reels are just some of the content you'll find on these sites. Media Composer gives a broad range of options to export your sequence with great quality while keeping the file size small enough to upload to the Web.

To export a sequence for Web sharing:

1. Make sure the **HK OUTPUT** sequence is loaded in the Record monitor from the last exercise. The various enabled tracks, as well as IN and OUT points, do not matter when you export. No matter which V track you are viewing, all tracks are included when exporting, and non-real-time effects

get rendered. The enabled tracks and the IN/OUT marks are ignored by default, but you can change this in the Export Settings dialog box.

2. Choose **FILE** > **EXPORT** to open the Export As dialog box, shown in Figure 10.12 and Figure 10.13. This dialog box allows you to name the exported sequence, select a destination for the export file to be saved, and select export settings and options.

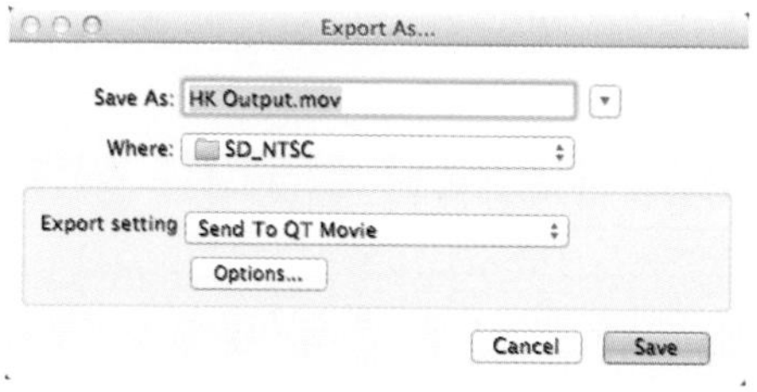

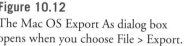

Figure 10.12
The Mac OS Export As dialog box opens when you choose File > Export.

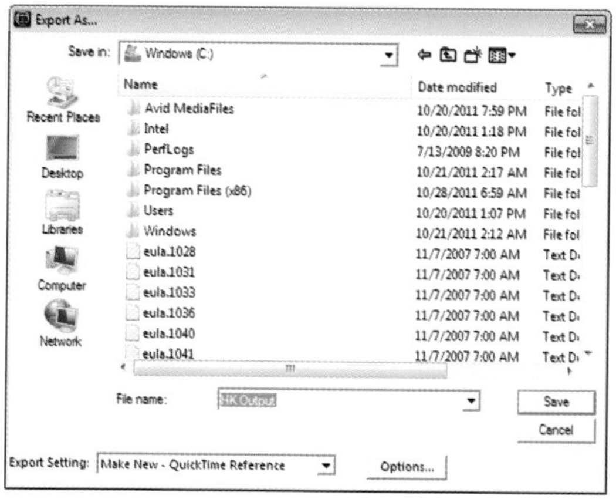

Figure 10.13
The Windows 7 Export As dialog box opens when you choose File > Export.

3. In Windows, type **HK WEB VERSION** in the **FILE NAME** field and click **LIBRARIES** in the column on the left. Then choose **VIDEOS** in the main window so the exported file is saved in the Videos directory on your PC. See Figure 10.14. On a Mac, type **HK WEB VERSION** in the **SAVE AS** field and click the disclosure triangle to expand the window; see Figure 10.15. Select **MOVIES** in the column on the left so the exported file saves into the Movies folder on your Mac.

4. From the **EXPORT** pop-up menu, choose **SEND TO QT MOVIE**. This creates a self-contained QuickTime movie that you'll further define in the Export Settings dialog box.

Note: You must have QuickTime installed on Mac and Windows to see the Send to QT Movie option in the list.

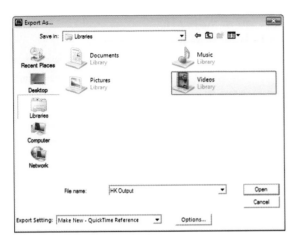

Figure 10.14
On the Windows, select Libraries > Videos.

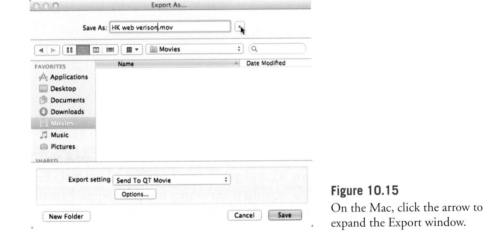

Figure 10.15
On the Mac, click the arrow to
expand the Export window.

5. Click **OPTIONS** to open the Export Settings dialog box; see Figure 10.16.
    The Export Settings dialog box includes options that change depending
    on the Export Setting field in the Export As dialog box. The setting at the
    top of the window, **EXPORT AS: QUICKTIME MOVIE**, lets you export a sub-
    section of the sequence by using edit marks and/or enabled tracks in the
    Timeline. For instance if your sequence is created with bars, a tone, and
    30 seconds of black filler per broadcast television requirements, you may
    want to use mark IN and mark OUT points to export the sequence for
    Web distribution without the broadcast requirements. Using marks saves
    you from duplicating the sequence just to export a Web version. Make
    sure **USE MARKS** and **USE ENABLED TRACKS** are not selected, so the entire
    sequence gets exported. You should set a few video and audio parameters
    before setting the compression format.

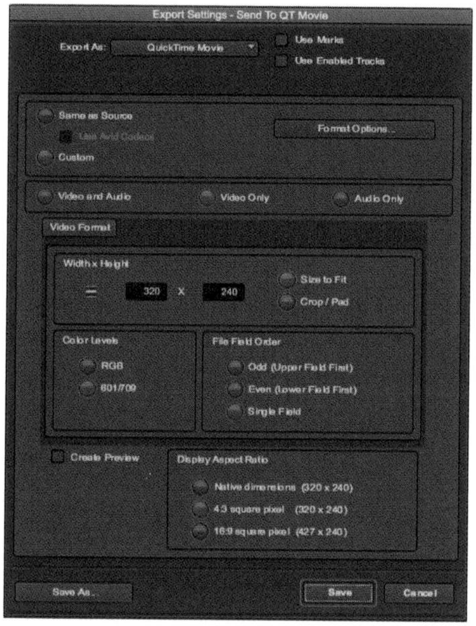

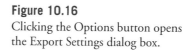

Figure 10.16
Clicking the Options button opens the Export Settings dialog box.

6. To ensure both audio and video are exported, click the **VIDEO AND AUDIO** button.

7. The Fast menu in the Video Format area predefines width and height options for the export. The options are divided into sections for full-frame output, more efficient Internet streaming sizes, and sizes optimized for disc-based media. Click the **FAST** menu in the Video Format area and choose **864×486 (16:9 SQUARE PIXEL),** which is the native size of the media in our sequence.

8. Click the **FORMAT OPTIONS** button to open the standard QuickTime Movie Settings dialog box. The Formatting setting is critical because it allows you to set the compression formats for video and audio.

9. In the QuickTime Movie Settings dialog box, click the **VIDEO SETTINGS** button. This opens the Compression Settings dialog box, where you can choose the compression format for the video.

10. Choose **H.264** for **COMPRESSION TYPE**, as shown in Figure 10.17. H.264 is a compression standard that creates high-quality movies with small file sizes.

Tip: If you installed additional QuickTime Export formats, also called codecs, they appear in the menu with tildes (~) before their names. This indicates they have not been qualified and are unsupported by Avid.

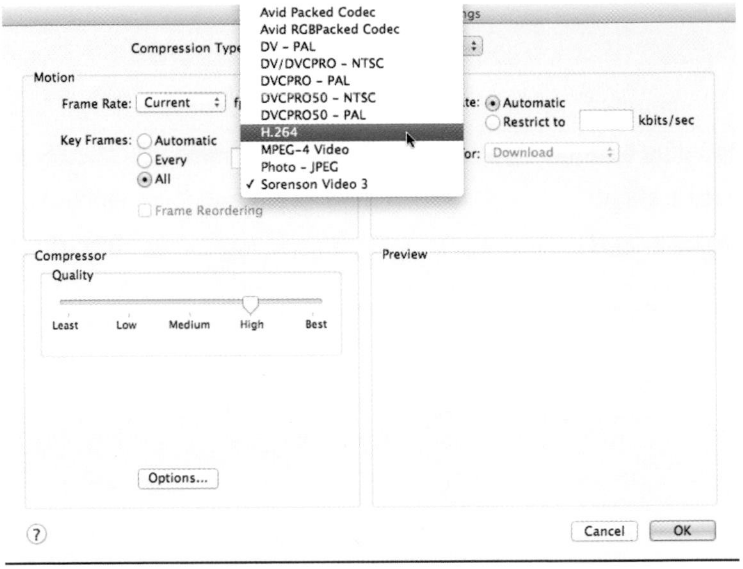

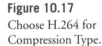

Figure 10.17

Choose H.264 for Compression Type.

11. Raise the compressor **Quality** slider to **Best** for a better-looking but bigger file. Since this sequence is pretty short, a larger file does not matter much. When your sequences are longer, you may have to lower the Quality slider. All the remaining default settings are suitable for uploading to the Web.

12. Click **OK** on the Compression Settings dialog box to return to the QuickTime Movie Settings dialog box.

Note: The Frame Reordering setting creates a more efficiently compressed movie file but it is more processor intensive to play back. Some smaller devices, like an iPod or a smart phone, cannot smoothly play back files with Frame Reordering enabled. You may want to disable this option if those devices are your final destination or if you are creating a movie with B-frames turned off.

13. Click the **Sound** check box. Click the **Settings** button to open the Sound Settings dialog box shown in Figure 10.18.

14. Choose **AAC** from the **Format** menu. AAC is a good choice with H.264 video because it is a high-quality audio-compression format.

15. Keep the **Channels** menu at **Stereo** (since this sequence is not mixed for surround sound). Choose **44.100** from the **Rate** menu shown in Figure 10.19. Rate sets the audio sample rate. This project uses the broadcast standard rate of 48kHz. Audio CDs (remember those?) use a 44.1kHz sample rate, which helps create a smaller file.

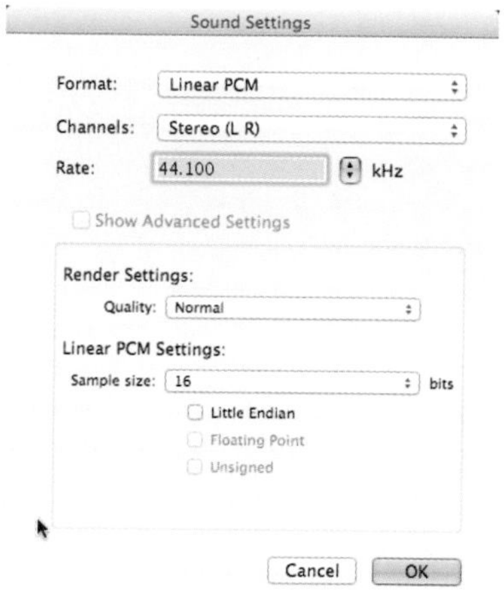

Figure 10.18
Clicking the Settings button opens the Sound Settings dialog box.

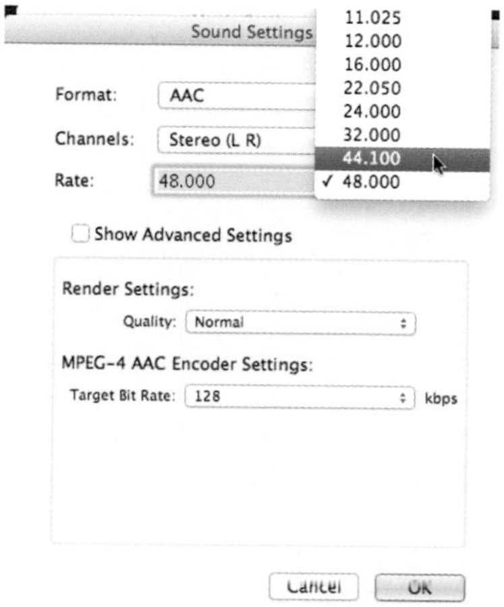

Figure 10.19
Choose 44.100 from the Rate menu.

16. If you are sensitive about audio quality, or it's important that your program have high fidelity reproduction, increase the RENDER SETTINGS and AAC ENCODER SETTINGS options. But for most programs with dialogue, background music, and sound effects, the defaults are fine. Click OK to close the Sound Settings dialog box and then click OK to close the Movie Settings dialog box.

17. In the Media Composer Export dialog box, choose the FILE FIELD ORDER setting. File field order deals with interlaced video for PAL or NTSC video formats. For uploading to video-sharing sites on the Web, deinterlaced or progressive files are required. To get a progressive file exported from an interlaced sequence, choose the Single Field option. See Figure 10.20.

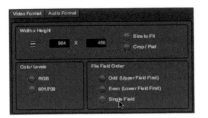

Figure 10.20
Choose the Single Field option
to export a progressive frame.

18. Choose **16:9 SQUARE PIXEL** for **DISPLAY ASPECT RATIO**. This is the sequence's aspect ratio.

19. To save these attributes as an Export user setting and recall these exact settings in any project, choose **SAVE AS** and then name the setting. Then you can retrieve that setting from the Project window's Settings tab. For this exercise, choose Save.

20. The Export As dialog box appears, since you have named the file for export and selected the Movie folder as the destination. Click **SAVE** to export the movie.

When the movie is exported, you can find it in the Movies folder. Double-click the folder to view it. If you want to make changes, return to Media Composer and export it again. If you're happy with the results, launch your Web browser and upload it to YouTube or Vimeo.

Export Templates

Media Composer ships with an assortment of preconfigured export templates for common export workflows. These templates are shown in the Export Setting menu in the Export As dialog box and in the Settings pane. You can create additional export templates by customizing the export settings and then using the Save As button. The active setting in the Media Composer Settings pane is what determines the default setting listed in the Export As dialog box.

Using Send To Templates for DVD Authoring

A Send To template can export sequences that are formatted for specific workflows. For instance, you can use a Send To template to export directly to Avid DVD by Sonic in Windows for DVD Authoring. On a Macintosh, the Send To template can launch your DVD authoring application of choice and auto-load the assets into that application. On a Windows system, the integration with Avid DVD by

Sonic allows you to load the encoded assets and automatically burn an autoplay DVD in one step. It is a very convenient feature if you just need a simple first-play or quick dailies DVD. This eliminates further authoring work and lets you create a DVD that plays without the encumbrance of graphics, menus, or other navigation devices. In either case, the Send To feature is the quickest, simplest way to perform these and other common export tasks. Let's use the DVD Send To templates. In Windows, you'll use the DVD One Step template and on a Macintosh you'll prepare the file for any DVD authoring application.

To use Send To templates for DVD authoring:

1. Select the **HK OUTPUT** sequence in the bin. In Windows, select **FILE > SEND TO > DVD > DVD ONE STEP**; see Figure 10.21. On a Mac, select **FILE > SEND TO > DVD > QUICKTIME REFERENCE**; see Figure 10.22. The Send To submenu offers pre-defined templates. These templates are set for the specific workflow so you need to do very little.

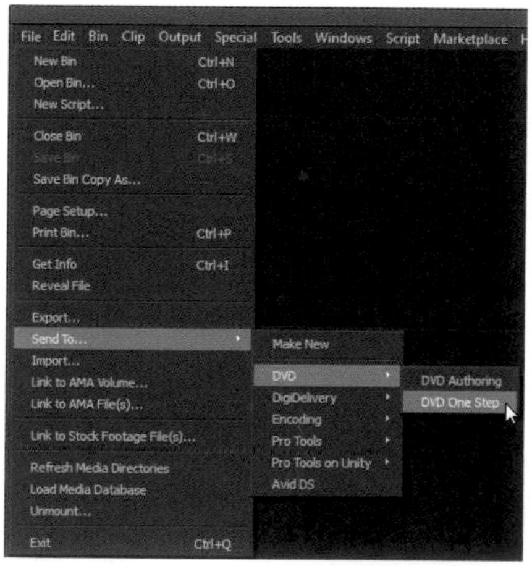

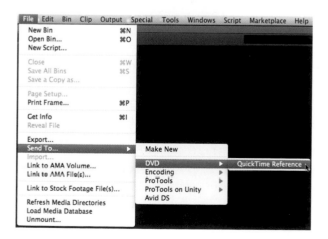

Figure 10.21
Choose Send To > DVD > DVD One Step in Windows.

Figure 10.22
Choose Send To > DVD > QuickTime Reference on a Mac.

Note: A QuickTime reference movie is just a small link to the original files you captured in Media Composer. The reference movie contains no media. It only appears as a movie file but it points to the original media files that make up your sequence or clip. This option is great for a fast export with no quality loss, but it requires that the reference movie stays on the same computer where it can link to the original media files. What use is that? It's perfect when you are moving a sequence or clip portions to another application for DVD authoring. It also works for motion graphics creation that must retain its maximum image quality. The original media files are not recompressed into a QuickTime movie; they are referenced.

2. Choose any **SEND TO** menu item to open the Send To dialog box. Here you can choose different Export settings. The pre-defined template's default settings are your best option unless your workflow is very specific. This example uses the default; click **OK**. See Figure 10.23 and Figure 10.24.

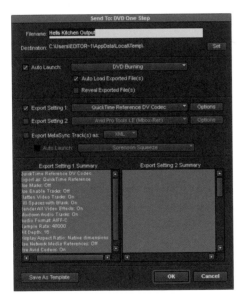

Figure 10.23
In Windows, Avid's default DVD template auto launches Avid DVD by Sonic.

3. If you auto launch an application, it will open. You can author a DVD from this point. For this exercise, close any other application except Media Composer.

The default location for the exported movie in Windows is C:/Users/Log In Name/ AppData/Temp. On a Macintosh, it's Users/Shared/AvidMediaComposer/Avid Users. In Windows, the DVD Send To templates automatically open Avid DVD by Sonic and import the QuickTime reference file. On a Mac, you can launch iDVD or another authoring app, but you must import the QuickTime reference file.

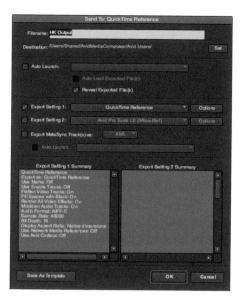

Figure 10.24
On the Mac, Avid's default DVD template can launch your authoring app of choice.

Media Composer includes a number of other Send To templates that auto-launch applications like Pro Tools for audio mixing and Avid DS for finishing. Next, you see how to create your own template to streamline a custom workflow.

Creating Your Own Send To Template

Media Composer includes a number of Send To templates for common workflows. If you are going to do additional audio mixing and mastering in Pro Tools, for example, there are five different Send To templates you can use, depending on your specific workflow. One workflow mixes down your video to DV25 and consolidates your audio, making an optimized sequence for a Pro Tools system that supports playback of Avid standard definition video. Another Pro Tools workflow is optimized for systems connected to shared storage and only exports metadata.

Although there are more than a half dozen workflows included, you might opt to create your own Send To template to optimize a workflow specific to your needs. Templates are quick and easy to make, and can save you a lot of time—even on a single project. You can customize a Send To template to output a review copy for the client or send clips to a motion graphics application, since these workflows may happen multiple times over the course of a large project. In this section, you'll create a Send To template perfect for sending high-quality clips to a motion graphics application on the same computer.

To create your own Send To template:

1. Choose **FILE** > **SEND TO** > **MAKE NEW** to open the Send To: Make New dialog box. This dialog box is the same one used in the previous section. Each template uses the same basic Send To dialog box with different options selected. In fact, you click the Save As Template button if you want to modify an existing template.

2. Click the **SET** button. Choose the **VIDEOS** directory (Windows) or the **MOVIES** folder (Mac) as the default location. See Figure 10.25.

Figure 10.25
Click the Set button to choose a spot for the exported file.

3. Since the motion graphics application is on the same computer, you would normally enable the **AUTO LAUNCH** check box and choose the application from the pop-up menu that appears. In this example, however, we won't auto-launch any applications, so don't enable this check box.

4. Choose **SEND TO QT MOVIE** from the **EXPORT SETTINGS 1** menu shown in Figure 10.26. This allows you to create a self-contained QuickTime movie that you can send to a different computer or a different studio.

Figure 10.26
Choose Send to QT Movie from the Export Setting 1 menu.

5. Click the **OPTIONS** button to open the QuickTime Movie Export Settings dialog box.

6. Click the **SAME AS SOURCE** button. Now Media Composer copies the files directly, without recompression, and using the same quality as the original media files.

7. Click the **VIDEO AND AUDIO** button to ensure that Media Composer exports both when you select this template. See Figure 10.27.

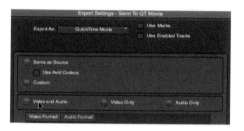

Figure 10.27
Choose to include video and audio.

8. Choose the aspect ratio you want the resulting file to have. For this exercise, choose **16:9 SQUARE PIXEL** in the **DISPLAY ASPECT RATIO** section, as shown in Figure 10.28. Media Composer works in a 601/709 color space, so leave that setting alone.

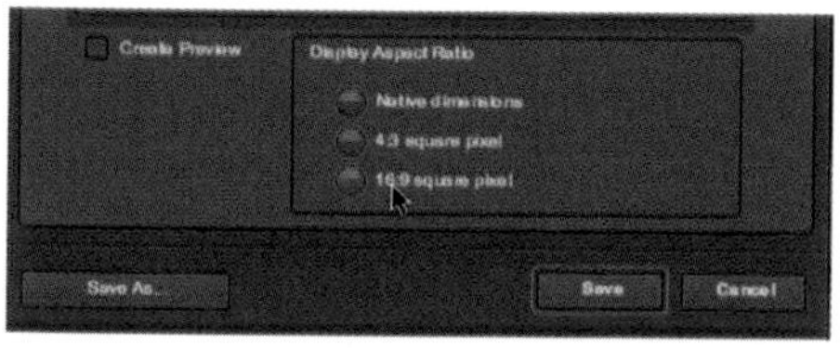

Figure 10.28
Choose the correct display aspect ratio for your content.

9. Click the **SAVE** button to save this QuickTime movie setting to the template.

10. In the Send To: Make New dialog box, click the **SAVE AS TEMPLATE** button. A Save dialog box opens so you can name the new Send To template and select a storage location.

11. Send To templates must go to specific locations on both Windows and Macintosh. In the Windows Save As dialog box, go to **C:/USERS/PUBLIC/ PUBLIC DOCUMENTS/AVID MEDIA COMPOSER/AVID TEMPLATES/SEND TO TEMPLATES**. In the Mac Save As dialog box, go to **MACINTOSH/LIBRARY/ APPLICATION SUPPORT/AVID/AVID TEMPLATES/SEND TO TEMPLATES**.

12. In the Save As dialog box, type **MOTION GRAPHICS 16X9.STT** in the **TEMPLATE NAME** field. Click **SAVE**.

13. In the Send To dialog box, click **CANCEL** to return to Media Composer.

You now have a custom Send To template in the File > Send To submenu, ready to speed up your output.

Congratulations! You have completed *Media Composer 6: Part I–Editing Essentials* and now you are ready to move on to *Media Composer 6: Part II–Effects Essentials*. These two courses combined help prepare you to obtain your Media Composer User Certification.

Review/Discussion Questions

1. How do you create audio tone media?

2. To create color bars in Media Composer, you must do which of the following?

    a. Create color bars from the Clip menu.

    b. Import a color bars graphic file.

    c. Visualize it in your mind and it will appear.

3. How do you change your sequence's start timecode?

4. True or false: To change sequence timecode from non-drop frame to drop frame, you must enter a : (colon) between the hours, minutes, seconds, and frames.

5. Describe the two methods that export a sequence.

6. True or false: You must always enable tracks and clear marks on a sequence before you begin an export.

7. What is a QuickTime reference movie?

8. How do you create a new Send To template?

9. What does the Same as Source button do in the QuickTime Movie Export Settings dialog box?

Lesson 10 Keyboard Shortcut

Key	Shortcut
Ctrl+1 (Windows)/Command+1 (Mac)	Opens the Audio tool

Preparing and Exporting a Sequence

With a cut sequence ready, it's time to use your skills to prepare the sequence for a digital cut and export it to the Web.

Media Used:
Hell's Kitchen

Duration:
30 minutes

GOALS

- Prepare a sequence with bars, tone, and filler
- Export a portion of a sequence for Web sharing

Preparing a Sequence

1. Load the **HK TRANSITIONS AND TITLES–START** sequence into the Record monitor.

2. Import the **COLORBARS_100PCT.PCT** test pattern into the **TEST PATTERNS AND TONE** bin with a duration of 60 seconds.

3. Using the **HK** sequence in the bin, edit in one minute of bars and tone and 30 seconds of black filler.

Exporting the Program Portion of the Sequence

1. Continue with the **HK TRANSITIONS AND TITLES–START** sequence from the previous exercise.

2. Without lifting or extracting any portions of the sequence, export only the actual program portion of the sequence—not the bars, tone, or filler.

3. Export the sequence as a QuickTime H.264 movie at half resolution and with AAC audio compression.

Technical Fundamentals

Working effectively on any editing system requires familiarity with certain technical concepts. These concepts form the foundation of everything that happens in an editing system, and understanding them will help you make educated decisions at key points in the life of a project—from production and acquisition to editing, finishing, output, and delivery.

This appendix is a primer, really. It will give you enough information to help you understand better some of the concepts taught in this book. It should also help you pinpoint topics with which you're unfamiliar and that merit deeper study if you are planning on a career in TV, film, or video production.

Media Used: Running the Sahara

Duration: One hour

GOALS

- Understand the basic functions of a codec and wrapper
- Change the project format to access preferred media resolutions
- Rewrap media on import rather than recompressing it
- Set the project format for maximum playback efficiency
- Locate media files associated with a clip
- Use the Media tool to identify all project media
- Troubleshoot offline media
- Relink offline master clips to online media
- Restore a saved bin from the Avid Attic

Understanding Compression, Codecs, and Wrappers

When editing video on any non-linear editing (NLE) system, you are looking at digital files rather than the actual film or videotape. The same is true for audio. But what exactly are those video and audio files? What determines the file format? How are they encoded? What's the difference between one file and another? Why do some media files play on one computer and not another?

A Compression Story

Let me start with an oversimplified analogy. Imagine you have a poster—an image—that you want to send to a friend. You can't simply slap a stamp on the back of it and expect to mail it. It's too big and would get damaged on the way. Obviously, it needs to be packaged for shipping.

At the post office, they tell you there are envelopes and cardboard boxes of all sizes. You can ship it either way, and you are choosing a method based on your friend's preferences (or which would fit in his mailbox). The smaller you can make the poster, the cheaper it is to ship and the worse it will look when it arrives. The postmaster says you can even cut it into little pieces and write a number on the back of each one. (But then your friend will have to put it back together when he gets it. "Oh look! A puzzle!")

As silly as the analogy seems, it clarifies two concepts.

■ The difference between a codec versus a wrapper

■ The decisions you face when compressing media

Compressing Media

When recorded, digital video and audio signals are almost always compressed—"folded up"—using a codec. A *codec* is a compression formula that defines how an image is compressed (*co-*) and decompressed (*-dec*). Compression happens when the file is created. Decompression happens every time the file is played back. In fact, for most codecs, each frame is decompressed individually, meaning the system is "unpacking" each individual image before presenting it.

Note: **Working with uncompressed media requires tremendous bandwidth and storage. If your system is high performance, you can edit with uncompressed video for maximum quality. Whether SD or HD, uncompressed video in Media Composer is identified by the resolution 1:1.**

When media is compressed, it is simultaneously put into a wrapper file. Like putting the poster into a box versus an envelope, though, the image itself doesn't change based on the packaging; the packaging only determines what it looks like from the outside. The wrapper defines the file format, and is reflected in the file extension, as shown in Figure A.1. Two of the most common are QuickTime and MXF.

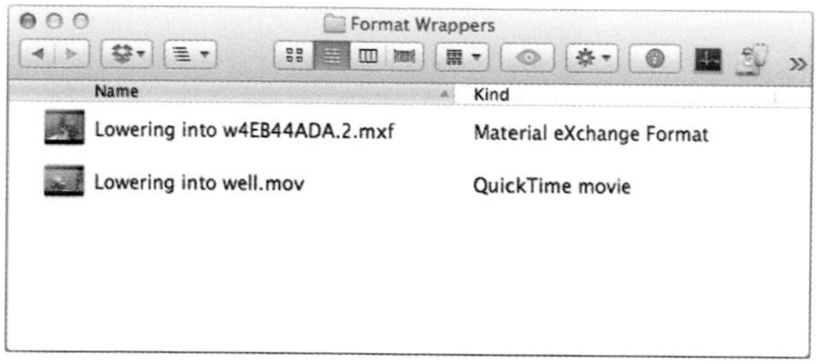

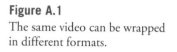

Figure A.1
The same video can be wrapped in different formats.

Some codecs are better than others at making images very small but maintaining the image quality. Again, the tradeoff is that those codecs generally are harder to process—like cutting up and reassembling the image instead of just folding and unfolding it. For example, DV is a relatively easy codec to process. Packing and unpacking DV images doesn't take much work. H.264, on the other hand (a very popular codec that uses the MPEG4 standard), makes the image much smaller, but is more processor intensive. It takes more processing cycles to compress and decompress an H.264 image.

In Media Composer, codec selection is listed in all settings as resolution. Avid standard definition (SD) codecs are listed as an easy-to-understand ratio, indicating the amount of compression (such as 2:1 or 15:1). The higher the ratio, the more compressed the image. Avid high-definition (HD) codecs are named DNxHD, and the number represents the data rate. In this case, the higher the number, the less compressed the image. Less compression equals more information, which means more data transferring for each frame.

Note: Codecs developed by other companies are listed by name (like XDCAM 35 or ProRes 422). The meaning of the number attached to each varies by manufacturer.

In the Media Creation–Current dialog box, for example, you can select the resolution for many editing tasks, including capture, import, and rendering. See Figure A.2.

Figure A.2
The Media Creation–Current dialog box lets you choose the codec used to compress the image.

Converting Versus Rewrapping Media

Lesson 3, "Ingesting File-Based Media," explains how to import media files and consolidate files linked through Avid Media Access (AMA). When you import, Media Composer does one of two things

■ Convert (that is, recompress) the media file to a new format.

■ Rewrap the file in the MXF wrapper.

The advantage of rewrapping is that you don't risk further damage by processing it a second time. Recompressing media can introduce *compression artifacts*, or defects in the image. It is always better to rewrap a file instead of recompressing it.

The key to making Media Composer rewrap a file on import is to use a matching codec. For example, if you are importing a QuickTime movie that was recorded using the Apple ProRes 422 codec, choose Apple ProRes MXF from the Resolution menu. If the codec you choose is similar, but not exactly the same, Media Composer will alert you to the difference and give you the option to change the setting automatically, as shown in Figure A.3. If a matching codec is chosen, Media Composer will perform a Fast Import operation, simply rewrapping the ProRes media from QuickTime into an MXF.

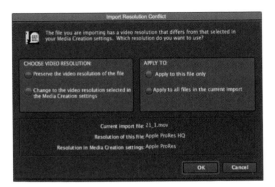

Figure A.3
Media Composer alerts you to a mismatched codec on import.

Tip: It's good to know the format of the file you are importing before you try to
      import it. To check the codec used to compress a QuickTime file:

      1. Open the file in QuickTime.

      2. Select Window > Show Movie Inspector or press Ctrl+I (Windows) or
          Command+I (Mac).

The wrapper and the codec are both important considerations. In most professional post-production workflows, several editing, effects, or compositing applications will be used. A workflow that is designed to only package the media once
saves time and preserves the image quality throughout post production. When
deciding which camera to use and how to capture or encode your media from tape
(and other similar quandaries), choosing a standard file format and codec will maximize efficiency.

Note: One of the key media-management tools in Media Composer is called
       Consolidate/Transcode. Consolidate copies the media from one location to
       another, rewrapping it as MXF if needed. Transcode does a format conversion.
       Media Composer is capable of high-quality, complex media conversions. This
       can solve problems in post production. To learn more about converting media
       and managing a post-production workflow, see the advanced editing book
       in this series, *Media Composer 6: Professional Picture and Sound Editing*.

Video Format and Your Project

Although related, the video format is distinct from both the codec and the file format.
The video format is defined by three factors:

■ Frame rate

■ Scan method for scanning the images

■ Raster dimension

Here's an example: 1080p/24, 1,920×1,080.

The *frame rate,* 24 fps (frames per second), is quite literally the number of frames
per second that are recorded and played back. Those frames are either scanned
progressively or interlaced; in this case, *p* indicates a progressive format. The *raster*
(1,920×1,080 in this example) is the image's frame size as measured horizontally
in pixels and vertically in scan lines.

Not long ago, the format options were pretty basic: NTSC or PAL for video; 24p
for film. The NTSC format has a frame rate of 30 fps interlaced and a raster of
720×486. PAL, on the other hand, had a frame rate of 25 fps interlaced and a
raster of 720×576. Numerous HD formats offer more format choices than ever.

This can lead to complications in production and post production. Discuss this with all the stakeholders and decision makers to alleviate many challenges before they arise. See Figure A.4 for a comparison of the format raster sizes.

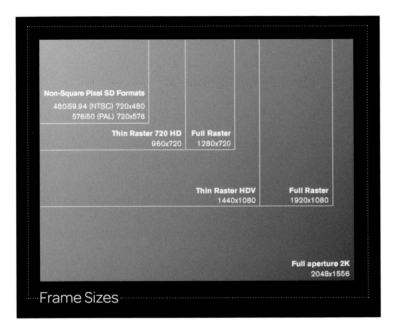

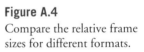

Figure A.4
Compare the relative frame sizes for different formats.

Media Composer, however, lets you work with video of different formats in the same project and Timeline. The only limitation is that video has to be captured, from tape, into a project of the same format, also called the *native format*. Otherwise, you can bring in video of any format through import or AMA linking, or borrowed from another project. You can cut together the mixed-format media; Media Composer automatically adapts it to the current project format.

For a free poster with useful reference information like what's shown in Figure A.4, see www.avid.com/static/resources/common/documents/
On the Web **f-r_poster_chnl_24x36_print.pdf**

Working with the Project Format Setting

The Project Format setting is a kind of master for the project. It dictates the options that are presented for creating media. If you want to import a file as SD, change the Project Format setting to an SD format. If you want to import a file as HD, make sure the Project Format setting is set to an HD format. See Figure A.5.

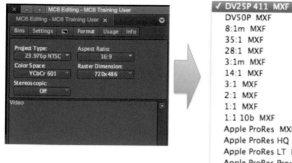

Figure A.5
Import resolution options change
based on the current project format.

The Project Format setting also controls the output signal coming from Media
Composer. To keep the signal consistent, any media played back on the Timeline
is scaled to fit the format raster displayed in the Format tab (shown in Figure A.6).

Figure A.6
Media played in the Timeline is scaled
to fit the current format raster.

This automatic scaling is a great convenience. Say you're cutting a documentary
and the researchers find some amazing archival footage. It won't matter if it's a
different format. Or, suppose the reality TV show you're cutting put helmet cameras on the contestants. You don't have to worry if you can get that footage in.

But, this has implications for system performance to consider. If you want maximum performance, don't give the system any extra work to do. You will get the best
performance out of Media Composer if the project format matches the format of
the *majority* of the media in your sequence. Since most of the media will already
match the output format, the system only has to decompress the frames for viewing. Only those shots that differ will need to be scaled.

For example, pretend that most of the RTS media was shot in the format AVC
Intra 50. You could configure the project to play AVC Intra media natively.

To configure the project format to the media's native format:

1. Open the **MC6 EDITING** project, if it's not already open.

2. Click the **FORMAT** button in the Project window to display the Format pane.

3. Click the **PROJECT TYPE** drop-down menu and choose **720P/23.976.** The project format changes to 720p. The **RASTER DIMENSION** setting indicates that the project is using the standard raster of 1,280×720.

4. Click the **RASTER DIMENSION** drop-down menu and choose **1,280×720.** The project raster changes to the *thin raster* format of 960×720. The Notes section in the Format pane lists the common formats that match the current Project Format setting, including AVC Intra 50. Nice job.

What is the sign of better performance after you have made this change? You can simultaneously play back more real-time effects, or layers of video, without dropping frames. How many more is hard to say, since overall performance differs from one system to another anyway. Why not run your own tests and see?

Understanding Metadata

Metadata is a term you will hear frequently in this industry. What is it? And, more importantly, what does it do for you? Metadata can mean different things. In the context of this book, and media production in general, *metadata* is simply information about your media.

The most basic metadata is the information that's written into the media file wrapper itself. For video, that includes frame rate, raster size, the codec, media timecode, the source, and the like. For audio, this includes bit depth, sample rate, source name, creation date, and so on.

The items that you see in the bin (master clips, audio files, sequences, and others) are another type of metadata used to identify and track your actual media files. This is clearly seen when you delete a clip from the bin. Your options include the clip information (metadata) and the associated media files, as shown in Figure A.7. (For more information about deleting media, see Appendix B, "Capturing Tape-Based Media.")

Note: Media Composer creates MXF files in the OP-1 atom format. That means three media files correspond to the average master clip. A separate file (such as V1, A1, or A2) is created for each audio and video track in the clip. For more information on MXF formats, search online for *MXF format.*

Figure A.7
You can delete the metadata (master clip)
or the associated media files.

Finally, you can add custom metadata to the project assets in the bin. This can include comments, color labels, focal length information, the quality of the take, and more. All of this is part of the metadata of a clip, and it's all tracked by Media Composer.

The Magic of Metadata

Many things we take for granted in editing are possible because of how Media Composer uses metadata. The metadata–media file relationship is what makes possible *non-destructive editing*—editing a clip into the Timeline without destroying the parts you didn't use. And it lets you edit the same clip into the Timeline multiple times. If you were using the actual video, you wouldn't be able to edit from the same clip more than once without creating a separate video file. Instead, you are creating a new link to the same media file. You do not need a second media file and you do not have to recapture the clip.

Collaborative Workflows

Metadata is small—tiny, really, when compared to video or audio files. For example, the bin in Figure A.8 is full of HD master clips and a completed sequence. The bin file is 2.9 MB. The MXF video and audio files for those clips measure 141 GB. That's almost 50,000 times larger! Yet, that bin file has full information about the clips, the media files they are supposed to be linked to, and the program that was created from them, complete with effects and audio mix.

Media files are so large that frequently it's still most efficient to copy them to a drive that is physically shipped rather than electronically transferred. A bin full of metadata, on the other hand, is so small it's really easy to e-mail, iChat, or Dropbox. If someone has the bin full of metadata, they only need a copy of the media files to reconstruct that sequence.

As a result, many filmmakers work remotely, collaborating with people across the country or around the world. After shooting has finished, two copies (or more) of the media are made: one for the director and one for the editor. To collaborate, they simply exchange bin files, relinking the master clips and sequences to the local copy of the media.

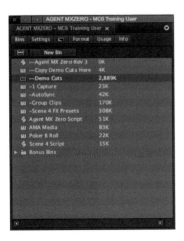

Figure A.8
Bin files full of metadata are still quite small.

Offline/Online Workflows

The metadata–media file link enables a very common workflow: *offline/online*. Traditionally, the offline stage consists of capturing large amounts of footage in a very compressed format. This preserves drive space and gives the editor access to the greatest number of edit choices possible. During the offline, the editor completes the creative stage of the edit and arrives at a completed edit, or *picture-locked* version of the sequence.

All the low-resolution media is deleted when the offline edit is complete. The metadata is preserved. The metadata—specifically the logged master clips, bins with organized subclips, numerous versions of the sequences, and so on—have all the work of the project to that point. It is incredibly valuable!

Using the completed sequence, the media is recaptured for the online at the highest resolution possible. The online, or *finishing*, stage is when you perform technical tasks that ensure the picture and sound are of the highest quality. This includes audio sweetening, color correction and grading, and effects and compositing.

Today, hard drives are good enough and cheap enough to allow many productions to work with high-resolution media through the entire edit. Nonetheless, this workflow is widely used as a way to help define the edit process and handle the demands of ever-increasing file sizes.

Metadata Versus Media Files

It should be clear by now that the master clip in your bin is not the same as your actual video file. One represents the other. They are separate items with a linked relationship.

It's important to note that you can have multiple copies of the clips (*metadata pointers*) pointing to the same media file. When you clone a clip from one bin to another, or duplicate a sequence, you're just creating another copy of that metadata. No new media is created; another set of pointers is created. See for yourself.

To see the media files linked to a clip:

1. Open the **MC6 EDITING** project.

2. Create a new bin and name it **MEDIA LINK TEST**.

3. Open the **CULTURE** bin and select the **SENEGAL, MOTHER AND BABY** master clip.

4. Alt-drag (Windows) or Option-drag (Mac) the clip to the **MEDIA LINK TEST** bin. A clone is created, with the same name as the original.

5. Right-click the master clip in the **CULTURE** bin and choose **REVEAL FILE**, as shown in Figure A.9. Media Composer opens an operating system (OS) window to show you the MXF file on the drive. On Macs, this is the Finder; on Windows, the Explorer.

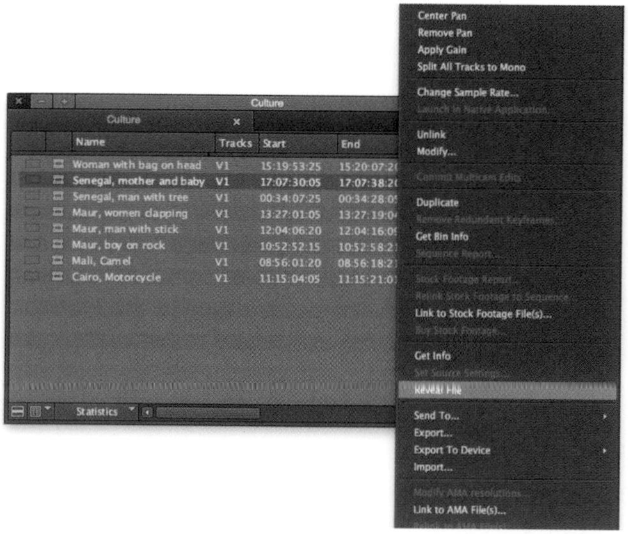

Figure A.9
Choose Reveal File to see the media file linked to a master clip.

6. Without closing the window, switch back to Media Composer. Right-click the master clip in the **MEDIA LINK TEST** bin and choose **REVEAL FILE**. The system reactivates the window, showing the same file highlighted the first time. See Figure A.10.

Media Composer tracks this media file–metadata relationship, and all the complex relationships that extend from a master clip, to the subclip you create from it, to the sequence you cut it into, to the duplicate version of that sequence, and on and on.

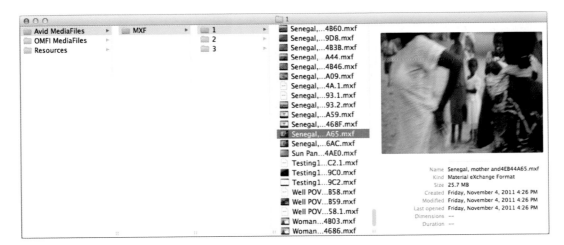

Figure A.10
A copied master clip shares the same media file as the original.

All assets that share that media file will show it as offline, too. Project assets that are linked together, sharing media, are referred to as *media relatives* in Media Composer.

To see what clips are used in a sequence:

1. Open the **MC6 EDITING** project.

2. Open the **2 FINISHED SEQUENCES** bin. Also open any source footage bins you want to see relatives in, such as **RTS SELECTS** or **CULTURE**. Arrange the bins so you can see them simultaneously without much overlap.

3. Highlight the **RTS EXTENDED VO AND MUSIC FINISHED** sequence.

4. Open the **FAST** menu and choose **SELECT MEDIA RELATIVES**. Media Composer highlights all related objects in all open bins.

Identifying media relatives can also be useful if you want to know:

■ From which master clip a subclip was drawn

■ Which subclips and media are related to a specific master clip

■ All the master clips, subclips, and precomputes associated with a sequence or project

■ Which media files to delete from a project without taking offline any media used in a sequence

Managing Your Media

Avid is famous for its robust media management. It uses a simple system that keeps the user from directly interacting with the media files. Instead, you are given simple, powerful tools to manage your media through Avid. If you are used to directly interacting with your media files, this can feel restrictive. You will soon come to appreciate the freedom you have to focus on the creative process of editing.

All media files created by Media Composer through capture, import, render, and so on go to the same place, as shown in Figure A.11: *Media drive*\Avid MediaFiles\ MXF\1.

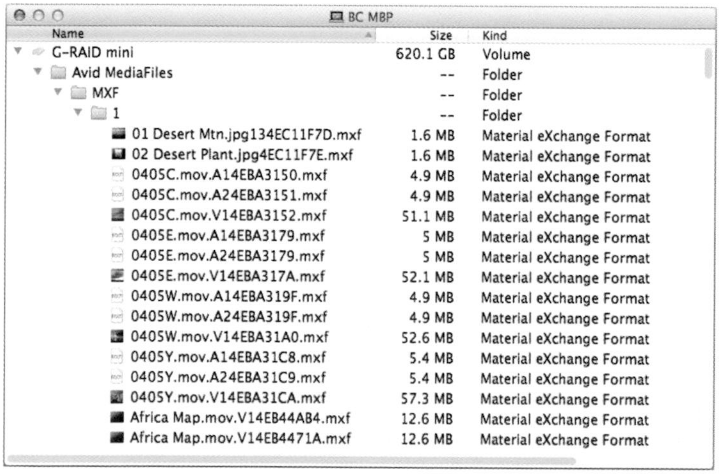

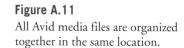

Figure A.11

All Avid media files are organized together in the same location.

Media Composer puts all the files it creates from all projects into the same folder, 1, until it reaches the limit—5,000 files. Then it starts a folder named 2, and so on. Besides the MXF media files, each folder has two database files: msmFMID.pmr and msmMMOB.mdb. See Figure A.12. Media Composer uses the database files to track each file's metadata and all the metadata links that relate to those media files.

You have no direct control over which file goes into which folder, nor can you separate the files by project. Again, this may be frustrating at first. You may want to double-click a media file to see which clip it is. Or, you may want to grab all the clips from one project and organize them into a folder. From Media Composer's viewpoint, you're working backward. Instead of going to the files, use the tools provided in Media Composer to manage your media more efficiently.

Maur, runners, tall4EB449CB.mxf		12.6 MB
Maur, runners, town4EB44B5C.mxf		22.5 MB
Maur, women clappin4EB44B26.mxf		53 MB
Maur, women clappin4EB446B1.mxf		53 MB
msmFMID.pmr	Avid Database File	55 KB
msmMMOB.mdb	Avid Database File	2.2 MB
Niger, camels.mov.V4EB44AAE.mxf		27.8 MB
Niger, camels.mov.V4EB44668.mxf		27.8 MB
Niger, dunes and su4EB44AED.mxf		54 MB
Niger, footsteps.mo4EB44A00.mxf		46.1 MB
Niger, runners, foc4EB44AAB.mxf		20.4 MB

Figure A.12
The two Avid database files catalog the media in the folder.

Using the Media Tool

You manage your media with the simply named Media tool. It allows you to see the media files on all hard drives online in a display that is similar to your bin formats. You can use the Media tool to view or delete the available media files or specific tracks in a media file. The Media tool also allows you to track down all media files used in a particular project or sequence. Right now, use the Media tool to see all the media files on your drive for the RTS project.

To identify all the media associated with a project:

1. Open the project whose media you want to see.

2. Choose **Tools > Media tool**. The Media Tool Display dialog box opens, as shown in Figure A.13. Here you can select the drives, projects, and media file types you want to see. (*Precomputes* are render files.)

Figure A.13
Select the drives and project for which you want to see media.

Note: Media files are associated with the project they are created in. Master clips borrowed from another project, or AMA-linked media, will not appear in the Media tool.

3. Click the **ALL DRIVES** button; then click the **CURRENT PROJECT** button.

4. Ensure that the **MASTER CLIPS** check box is checked, then click **OK**. The Media tool opens, displaying the online master clips associated with this project, as shown in Figure A.14.

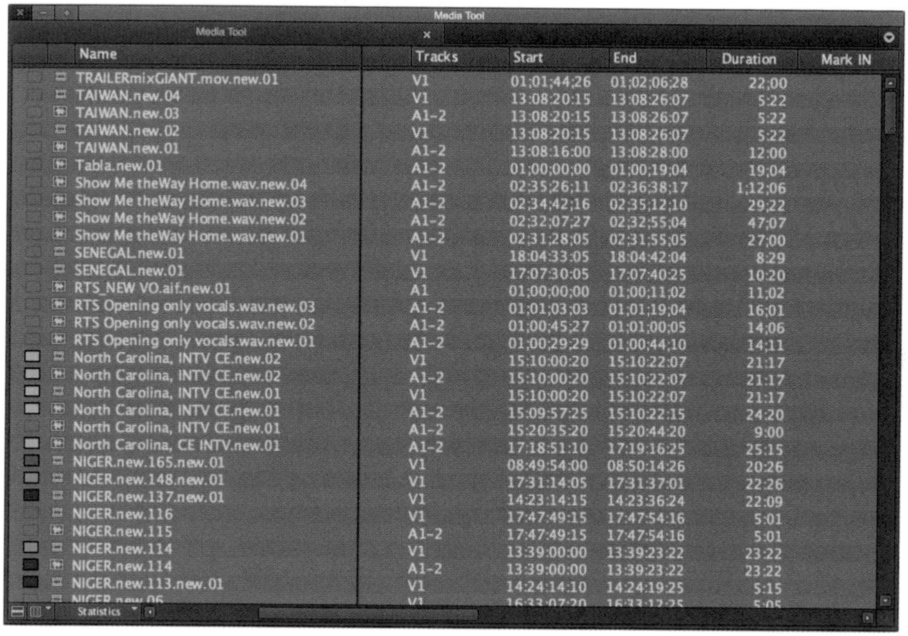

Name	Tracks	Start	End	Duration	Mark IN
TRAILERmixGIANT.mov.new.01	V1	01:01;44;26	01:02;06;28	22;00	
TAIWAN.new.04	V1	13:08:20:15	13:08:26:07	5:22	
TAIWAN.new.03	A1-2	13:08:20:15	13:08:26:07	5:22	
TAIWAN.new.02	V1	13:08:20:15	13:08:26:07	5:22	
TAIWAN.new.01	A1-2	13:08:16:00	13:08:28:00	12:00	
Tabla.new.01	A1-2	01:00:00:00	01:00:19:04	19;04	
Show Me theWay Home.wav.new.04	A1-2	02:35;26;11	02:36;38;17	1;12;06	
Show Me theWay Home.wav.new.03	A1-2	02:34;42;16	02:35;12;10	29;22	
Show Me theWay Home.wav.new.02	A1-2	02:32;07;27	02:32;55;04	47;07	
Show Me theWay Home.wav.new.01	A1-2	02:31;28;05	02:31;55;05	27;00	
SENEGAL.new.01	V1	18:04:33:05	18:04:42:04	8:29	
SENEGAL.new.01	V1	17:07:30:05	17:07:40:25	10:20	
RTS_NEW VO.aif.new.01	A1	01:00;00;00	01:00;11;02	11;02	
RTS Opening only vocals.wav.new.03	A1-2	01:01;03;03	01:01;19;04	16;01	
RTS Opening only vocals.wav.new.02	A1-2	01:00;45;27	01:01;00;05	14;06	
RTS Opening only vocals.wav.new.01	A1-2	01:00;29;29	01:00;44;10	14;11	
North Carolina, INTV CE.new.02	V1	15:10:00:20	15:10:22:07	21:17	
North Carolina, INTV CE.new.02	A1-2	15:10:00:20	15:10:22:07	21:17	
North Carolina, INTV CE.new.01	V1	15:10:00:20	15:10:22:07	21:17	
North Carolina, INTV CE.new.01	A1-2	15:09:57:25	15:10:22:15	24:20	
North Carolina, INTV CE.new.01	A1-2	15:20:35:20	15:20:44:20	9:00	
North Carolina, CE INTV.new.01	A1-2	17:18:51:10	17:19:16:25	25:15	
NIGER.new.165.new.01	V1	08:49:54:00	08:50:14:26	20:26	
NIGER.new.148.new.01	V1	17:31:14:05	17:31:37:01	22:26	
NIGER.new.137.new.01	V1	14:23:14:15	14:23:36:24	22:09	
NIGER.new.116	V1	17:47:49:15	17:47:54:16	5:01	
NIGER.new.115	A1-2	17:47:49:15	17:47:54:16	5:01	
NIGER.new.114	V1	13:39:00:00	13:39:23:22	23:22	
NIGER.new.114	A1-2	13:39:00:00	13:39:23:22	23:22	
NIGER.new.113.new.01	V1	14:24:14:10	14:24:19:25	5:15	
NIGER.new.06	V1	16:33:07:20	16:33:12:25	5:05	

Figure A.14
The Media tool looks and functions much like a bin.

Note: When you choose to view the master clips, Media Composer presents associated V1, A1, and A2 files together as a master clip for convenient viewing. You should not need to select media files for display in the Media tool. Displaying the actual media files is equivalent to looking at the files at the OS level, and typically only used for troubleshooting a problem with the assistance of Avid technical support staff.

The Media tool looks and functions very much like a bin, making it immediately familiar. It provides the same database functionality as a bin, including the ability to sort, sift, display column headings, and view clips in Frame, Text, or Script view.

You can even drag master clips from the Media tool into bins. This is very useful if you have accidentally deleted items from a bin, but have the media files saved on a backup media drive. You could simply mount the drive, use the Media tool to look at that drive, and drag the clips back to a bin.

Note: The Media tool makes it easy to view media, view clip associations, identify
drive locations, and more. To move media from one drive to another, the
Consolidate/Transcode function is used in conjunction with the Media tool.
Learn in-depth media-management techniques for professional post production in the book *Media Composer 6: Professional Picture and Sound Editing*.

Troubleshooting Missing Media Files

If Media Composer can't find the media file on any drive, it flags the clip in the
bin as *media offline*. This is displayed in several places. If the clip is loaded into
the Source monitor, Media Composer shows you the "media offline" slide in the
monitor. In the bin, an Offline column shows which tracks are missing, as shown
in Figure A.15. And, the Timeline can be set to display offline clips with a bright
red highlight, as described in Lesson 7, "Introduction to Multicamera Editing."

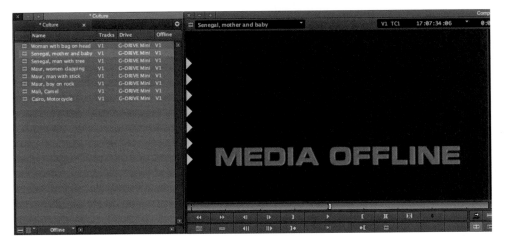

Figure A.15
The Offline column in the bin identifies the missing tracks.

Media can go offline for a few reasons: The files can be deleted, either intention-
ally or accidentally. The drive can be turned off or disconnected. Worst of all, the
drive could crash. For these reasons and more, you should always have a backup,
or duplicate copy, of the media files.

Tip: Some things in life are inevitable: death, taxes, and hardware crashes! It is
critical to back up your media files, especially if you are working with file-
based cameras that record to a disk or card instead of tape. After recording
the footage, back up the card. After capturing or transferring the footage to
your media drive, back up the drive. This will save your project, your sanity,
and your reputation.

Follow the steps to troubleshoot offline media. Each individual step may succeed in restoring the media. Proceed only as far as you need to bring the media back online.

To troubleshoot offline media:

1. Make sure all drives containing media are connected to the system and are visible to the OS. On Windows computers, choose **START > MY COMPUTER**. The drives should be next to the boot drive. On Macintosh computers, the drives should be on the desktop.

2. If a drive does not show up, follow the procedures for reconnecting your drive to the system as specified by the computer and drive manufacturers. Be sure to double-check the physical connections. A loose cable can prevent the drive from mounting properly.

3. Within Avid, you can go to the menu bar at the top of the screen and select **FILE > REFRESH MEDIA DATABASES**. This re-examines all the system's media databases (and can take some time to execute if you have large amounts of media).

4. If you moved the media drive or media files between two systems, the links may have been lost between the media files and the Avid application. Relink the material.

5. If none of the preceding procedures works, exit Media Composer. Open an OS window and double-click your media drive. Navigate to each numbered folder in the **AVID MEDIAFILES\MXF** directory. Delete the **MSMMMOB** and **MSMFMID** files. Repeat for each numbered folder, and on each media drive. Relaunch Media Composer. This forces the Avid application to rescan all media files and re-establish a link with the media files on your media drive. This may take some time.

Relinking Media Files

You can restore the pointers between the clip or sequence and the media files using the Relink command. When you select subclips or sequences and choose the Relink command, the system searches for master clips that contain the same material included in the selection. When you relink master clips, the system compares information such as source tape name, timecode information, and channels captured. If the search is successful, the system establishes new links to the available media files.

To relink offline items in a bin:

1. Click the bin with the offline items to activate it.

2. Click the bin **FAST** menu and choose **SELECT OFFLINE ITEMS**. All items with offline media files are selected automatically.

3. (Optional) If there are offline items in other bins that you also wish to relink, repeat steps 1 and 2 in those bins, without deselecting the items in the current bin.

4. Right-click a selected item in the bin; then choose **RELINK**. The Relink dialog box opens, as shown in Figure A.16. Use the settings in this dialog box to relink media in a wide range of workflow situations. You can relink to very specific resolutions or to any available media (as you do now).

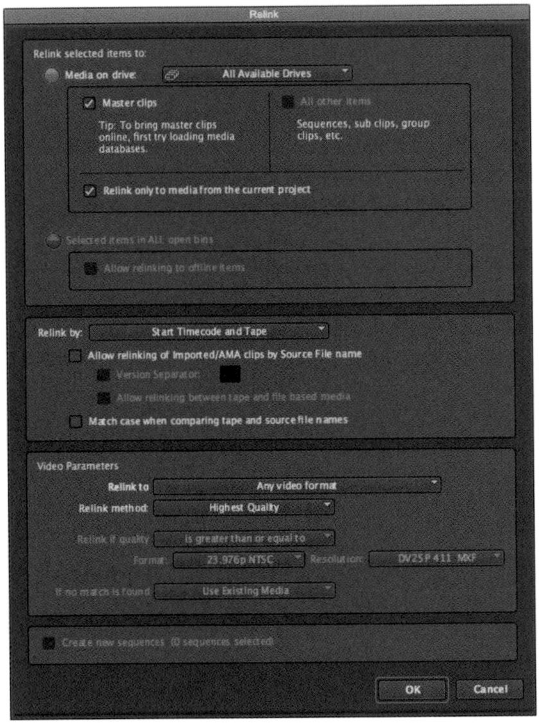

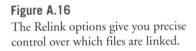

Figure A.16
The Relink options give you precise control over which files are linked.

5. In the top section (**RELINK SELECTED ITEMS TO**), ensure that the **MASTER CLIPS** check box is checked. If subclips or sequences are highlighted in the bin, also select the **ALL OTHER ITEMS** check box. From the **MEDIA ON DRIVE** menu, choose **ALL AVAILABLE DRIVES**.

6. Uncheck the **RELINK ONLY TO MEDIA FROM THE CURRENT PROJECT** option. If you have media in the sequence borrowed from another project, this will allow Media Composer to relink to that file as well.

7. In the **RELINK BY** section, deselect **MATCH CASE WHEN COMPARING TAPE AND SOURCE FILE NAMES**. Matching case is usually unnecessary; deselecting it ensures the widest range of possibilities when relinking, especially if media has been recaptured.

8. (Optional) If you're working with AMA media, select the **Allow Relinking of Imported/AMA Clips by Source File Name** check box.

9. In the **Video Parameters** section, choose **Any Video Format** for **Relink To**; then choose **Highest Quality** for **Relink Method**.

10. If you are relinking a sequence, deselect **Create New Sequence**. When finished, your settings should reflect those shown in Figure A.17.

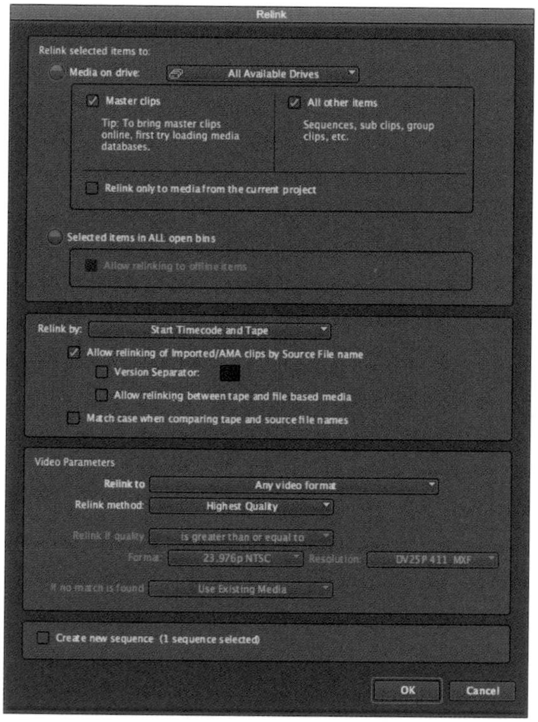

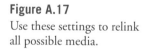

Figure A.17
Use these settings to relink all possible media.

11. Click **OK**. Media Composer reloads the database files and relinks your clips to any matching media files it finds.

Recovering Lost Work

It's a scary thing to lose media. It is worse to lose work you've done on a sequence.

Bins, like any computer file, can become corrupted. Technical problems can also cause a computer to crash. More frequently, you can lose work because you simply forgot to save at opportune times—like right before you tried that really great idea for the scene that didn't look so good in the morning. If you forgot to duplicate the sequence before trying the new idea, you may have no way to return to the previous version.

Media Composer has an automatic backup feature to protect your work in situations like these. The backup feature saves copies of all open bins at regular intervals and stores them in a special folder called the Avid Attic. The Auto-Save setting is part of the Bin settings, and is described in detail in Lesson 1, "Exploring the Interface and Preparing to Edit."

Here, you learn how to use the copies in the Attic to restore lost work.

To retrieve a bin from the Attic folder:

1. (Option) From within the Avid application, move any clips you will replace to another bin, and delete the bin you will replace. This places the bin in the **TRASH** folder, which is enough for this procedure.

2. Minimize or hide Media Composer. (If you are experiencing technical difficulties, you may wish to quit and restart the system, but this is not required.)

3. Navigate to the **\USERS\PUBLIC\PUBLIC DOCUMENTS\AVID EDITING APPLICATION\AVID ATTIC** folder (Windows) or the **MACHD/USERS/SHARED/AVID EDITING APPLICATION/AVID ATTIC** folder (Mac).

4. Find and open the project folder for the current project, and open the **BINS** folder within it. Inside the Bins folder, you will see a folder for every bin that was created in the project.

5. Open the folder for the bin you are restoring. The number of bin copies will vary. There may be several or even hundreds. The files are numbered sequentially.

6. Use the OS display settings to display the file details, as shown in Figure A.18. You need to see **DATE MODIFIED** information.

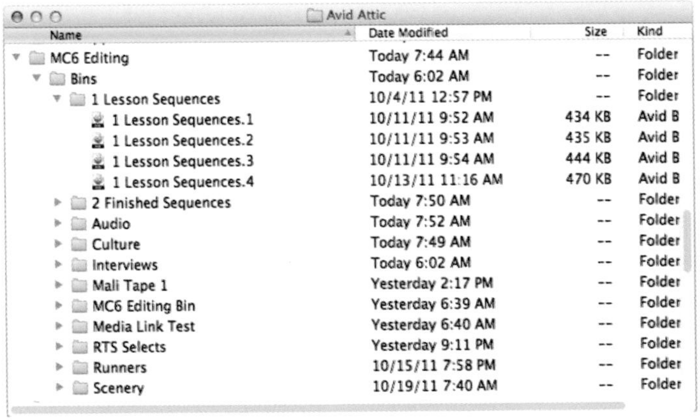

Figure A.18
Use the Date Modified information as a guide to which version of the bin to restore.

7. Select the file that roughly corresponds to the version of the sequence you want to restore. ("It was right after we went for coffee, so maybe 10:30?") Press **CTRL+C** (Windows) or **COMMAND+C** (Mac) to copy the file. Do not remove the file.

8. In the same OS window, navigate to the regular project folder. Remember, private projects are located in the **DOCUMENTS** folder for your OS user. Shared projects are located in the **SHARED DOCUMENTS** folder.

9. Paste the file into your project folder.

10. Reactivate Media Composer. The numbered bin file appears in the Project window. You will recognize it by the number extension on the bin name, as shown in Figure A.19.

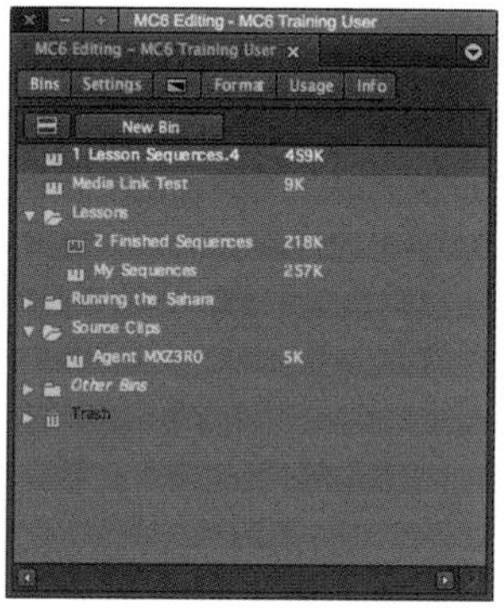

Figure A.19
The restored bin shows in the Project window with the number extension.

11. Open the bin and check the sequence to see if you restored the right one. If not, simply repeat the process, choosing another version of the bin.

Review/Discussion Questions

1. Which resolution is the most compressed?

   a. 20:1

   b. 10:1

   c. DNxHD 36

   d. DNxHD 145

2. Which function can be used to find the media for a clip?

   a. Match Frame

   b. Find Bin

   c. Find

   d. Reveal File

3. In which situation would you choose the Select Media Relatives option?
   a. To see what effects were used in a sequence
   b. To see what subclips come from a certain master clip
   c. To find the media files linked to a project
   d. To highlight the unused render files

4. What can you use to see render files?
   a. The Clear Renders command
   b. The Effect Editor
   c. The Smart tool
   d. The Media tool

5. If some of your media is offline, which of the following is a good trouble-shooting step?
   a. Delete the master clips.
   b. Delete the MXF folder.
   c. Delete the database files.
   d. Delete the sequence.

6. What are the names of the media database files?

7. What is the function of a codec?

8. What is the function of a wrapper file?

9. Which is more valuable in a project: the media or the metadata?

Capturing Tape-Based Media

When you use Media Composer to edit video, you are obviously not working with the physical source tapes, but rather with video and audio files. In this appendix, you'll learn how to get the video and audio off the tape and into the system. This process is referred to *digitizing* or *ingesting* the footage.

You have several capturing options when you are digitizing: capturing the entire tape, a single clip, or a series of clips (via *log and capture*), or capturing an incoming video signal from an uncontrolled source. this appendix covers them all, as well as a handy feature to streamline the process of capturing from DV tapes.

Finally, creating media is an important part of the editing process, but just as important is the process of deleting media. In this appendix, you look at deleting media from the bin.

Media Used: Your own videotape, pre-recorded, with footage to be captured

Duration: One hour

GOALS

- Set capture options and capture clips
- Examine DV scene extraction
- Log and batch capture clips
- Capture from a non-timecode source
- Delete unwanted master clips

Setting Up Your System for Capture

Before you are ready to capture media, several things need your attention, such as choosing the project format, connecting and configuring your capture deck, and so on. After your system is set up, the capture process goes quickly. In the future, you may need to adjust some settings rather than choosing all of them from scratch every time.

Creating the Project and/or Choosing the Format

Although Media Composer lets you edit material into your project Timeline regardless of format or frame rate, you can capture video from tape only in the tape's native format. In other words, the project format has to match the tape format. When you change a project's format, the hardware input and output, playback resolution, and new sequences change to support the new project.

Tip: If you need to capture a tape that has a format or frame rate that differs from the rest of your project, simply create a special project just to capture the media. After it is captured, you can use it in your main project via the Open Bin command.

Do one of the following to obtain the format for the media you want to capture:

■ Create a project in the format (such as 30i, 25i, 1080i, 1080p, or 720p) of the media you want to capture. (For more information about creating a project, refer to Lesson 3, "Ingesting File-Based Media.")

■ Open a project, click the Format tab in the Project window, and, from the drop-down menu, choose the related SD or HD format of the media you want to capture. If you choose an HD project type or format, also choose the appropriate raster dimension. (See Figure B.1.)

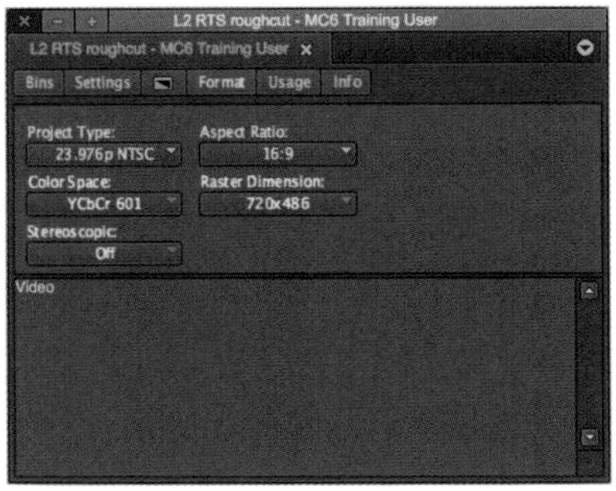

Figure B.1
Set the project format to match the tape you are capturing.

Connecting and Configuring Your Camera

The next step in the process is to configure Media Composer to communicate with the camera or deck connected to your system. This book assumes the camera or deck is already physically connected. If you need more information about connecting your deck or camera to your system, see the following articles from the Media Composer Help:

■ "Connecting Cameras, Decks, and Monitors"

■ "Connecting the Editing Equipment"

Most professional edit bays have one or more decks connected at all times, with separate connections to carry the audio, video, and control signals. On the other hand, you may be working with a camera directly attached to your laptop via FireWire cable. Either way, the configuration process is much the same.

To configure the connection to your camera:

1. Verify that you have made the right hardware connections for the deck(s).

2. Double-click **DECK CONFIGURATION** in the **SETTINGS** list in the Project window. The Deck Configuration dialog box opens, as shown in Figure B.2.

Figure B.2
Add a channel to start configuring Media Composer to control your camera or deck.

3. Click the **ADD CHANNEL** button to open the Channel dialog box. *Channel* refers to the signal path for deck control. (See Figure B.3.)

Figure B.3
Choose the channel type and port.

4. Click the **CHANNEL TYPE** menu and select your deck or camera connection type. Options include the following:

- **FireWire:** Choose this if you are controlling a DV camera or deck through a FireWire connection. OHCI is your computer's built-in FireWire port. This is the most common connection for software-only systems.
- **Direct:** Choose this if you are controlling a deck through an RS-422 connection to the serial port. This is the common channel type if you are using I/O hardware, such as an Avid Mojo DX, Nitris DX, or a third-party card.
- **VLAN VLX:** Choose this if you are controlling decks through a V-LAN/VLX*i* connection. This is typically only in larger facilities, and is the only channel type that allows multiple decks to be configured.

5. Click **OK** to close the Channel dialog box. Another dialog box asks if you want to automatically configure the channel now. This works well enough for basic deck control, but for best results, manually configure the deck.

6. Click **No** to manually configure the deck. Then click **ADD DECK**. The Deck Settings dialog box opens. Choose from the menus to identify your camera or deck. You can adjust the pre-roll if needed, but the default is typically a good place to start.

7. Choose your camera's manufacturer and model, then click **OK**.

Tip: Avid performs extensive testing on cameras and decks. Any performance issues they find are listed in the Notes section of the Deck Settings dialog box. Take a moment to read the notes. For instance, check out the notes in Figure B.4. Useful stuff, eh?

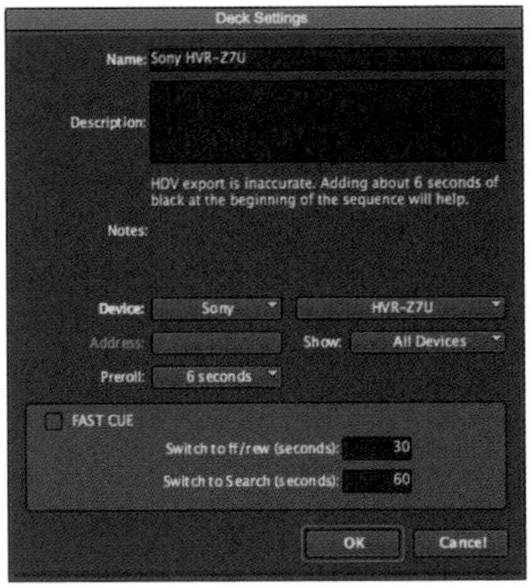

Figure B.4
Use the Deck Settings dialog box to identify your camera.

8. Click the **VERIFY CONFIGURATION AGAINST ACTUAL DECKS** check box to select it, as shown in Figure B.5. Then click **APPLY**. Enabling the check box will prompt Media Composer to immediately check for the deck.

If Media Composer can't find it or communicate properly with it, you will see an error message with some useful options. (See Figure B.6)

Figure B.5
Verify the communication with the camera.

Figure B.6
If Media Composer can't see the camera, it will tell you.

Tip: **If you're going to work for some time without the camera or deck connected, just turn off the Verify check box when you're done capturing to avoid repeated warnings.**

9. If you see the error message, double-check the connections between the camera and computer. Make sure the camera is turned on and that it is set to VCR mode. Click CHECK DECKS or click RE-VERIFY. Repeat this step until Media Composer finds the camera and clears the error message. If you consistently see the error message, click AUTO CONFIGURE to establish the most basic connection.

Tip: **You can configure only one deck for a FireWire or serial connection. But, if you work with multiple cameras or decks regularly, you may want to keep all your devices configured and ready to go at a moment's notice. No problem! Just duplicate and rename the Deck Configuration setting for each device. See Lesson 7, "Customizing Media Composer," for more information on duplicating and renaming settings.**

Configuring the Media Creation Setting

The aptly named Media Creation setting allows you to do the following:

■ Set the video resolution.

■ Select the destination drive for activities that create new media files, including capturing, creating titles, importing, performing mixdowns, and rendering.

Like all other settings, Media Creation is listed in the Project window's Settings pane. Because it is so important and frequently used, it is also in the Tools menu and has its own shortcut: Ctrl+5 (Windows) or Command+5 (Mac).

To set up the Media Creation settings:

1. Double-click MEDIA CREATION in the SETTINGS list or choose TOOLS > MEDIA CREATION.

2. Click MEDIA TYPE and select MXF.

Tip: Select OMF only if you're collaborating with someone on an old Media Composer or Pro Tools system that can't use MXF media. (This is uncommon.) Otherwise, MXF is the best choice. If your project uses HD media, you cannot select OMF as a file format. MXF is selected by default.

3. Click the CAPTURE tab. Then click the VIDEO RESOLUTION menu and select a video resolution, as shown in Figure B.7.

Figure B.7
Set the resolution and target drive for your captured clips.

4. Select video and audio drives.

5. Click APPLY TO ALL to set the same drive and media selections for all the Media Creation tabs.

6. Click OK to save your settings.

About the OMF and MXF File Formats

OMF and MXF are industry-standard, platform-independent file formats that let you exchange media and editing information for your sequence between applications. These formats are essentially wrappers for media files; your choice will not affect the quality of the media. Your choice will, however, affect which additional applications can use your media.

■ **OMF (or OMFI):** The OMF Interchange format exchanges files with Media Composer Adrenaline pre-2.0 or Avid Xpress Pro pre-5.0 (and earlier versions), Pro Tools, animation systems, and other applications that transfer complex metadata. OMF is now considered an "old" file format, and is hardly used in the industry for video media.

■ **MXF:** Material Exchange Format is the most popular file format for recording media today. It has become the dominant format in broadcast, post-production, asset management, and archiving applications throughout the industry. Most file-based cameras create MXF media files on disk, bypassing the capture process and accessing the files natively through AMA.

Configuring the Capture Settings

This setting is one you probably won't use every day, but it's important to set it up right—especially the first time you set up for capture. The capture settings, listed in the Project window's Settings pane and shown in Figure B.8, let you customize Media Composer's behavior during the capture process. Not all are covered here—just the particularly important options. Take a moment to consider these and enable the ones that make sense for you.

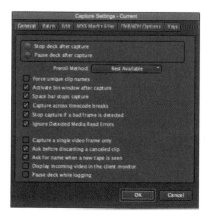

Figure B.8

Capture settings let you customize many capture options

- **General tab**
  - **Stop Deck After Capture:** The deck stops when the capture is complete. Recommended if you arc capturing an entire tape at once.
  - **Pause Deck After Capture:** The deck pauses when the capture is complete. Recommended if you are capturing multiple clips off a tape in a single session.
  - **Capture Across Timecode Breaks:** Media Composer attempts to capture sections of discontinuous timecode on a tape as separate clips. Media Composer stops capturing and reports an error when it encounters a timecode break. Mini DV and HDV tapes have many small timecode breaks that stop the capture process frequently if this is not enabled.

- **Batch tab**
  - **Switch to Emptiest Drive If Current Drive Is Full:** When this option is selected, Media Composer switches to a different media drive with the most available space when the current target drive becomes full during batch capturing. Media Composer will make the switch before starting to capture the clip, based on the number of minutes in the clip. For more information, see the section later in this appendix titled "Batch Capturing Logged Clips." When this option is deselected, Media Composer stops capturing when a drive becomes full.

- **MXF tab**
  - **Maximum (default) Capture Time:** Use this setting to set the maximum period of time the system will capture into a single master clip. It is recommended that you set it to a value slightly higher than your longest tape.

Capturing Your Footage

Now that you're system is set up, capture some footage! You can capture the entire tape on-the-fly, capture individual clips, or capture a series of clips in a batch.

Capturing a Tape on-the-Fly

Capturing an entire tape on-the-fly is a very common workflow. It's convenient because you simply load a tape and cue up the recording. It also gives you unrestricted access to all the footage on the tape. The downside? You may not need it all and unnecessarily use up drive space.

To capture a tape on-the-fly:

1. Load the tape you want to capture into the camera.

2. Open the bin where you want to store your clips (or create a new one and name it).

3. With that bin highlighted, choose BIN > GO TO CAPTURE MODE or press CTRL+B (Windows) or COMMAND+B (Mac). The Capture tool opens, as shown in Figure B.9, as does the Select Tape dialog box.

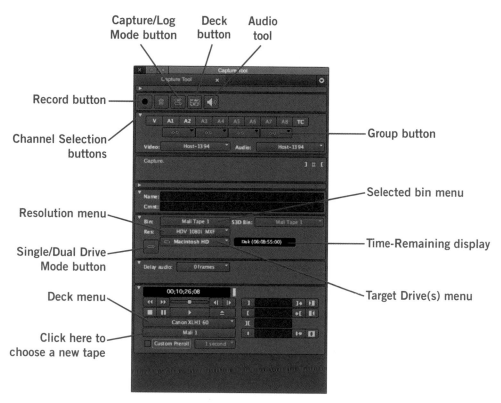

Figure B.9
The Capture tool contains all the controls to capture your media.

Note: The Capture tool is divided into panels, each with its own disclosure triangle. Each panel has a group of similar controls, for deck control, media resolution and drive selection, input selection, and so on. Hide any controls that you don't need at the moment.

4. In the Select Tape dialog box, shown in Figure B.10, click the NEW button. A new tape is listed in the Tape Name column and is highlighted.

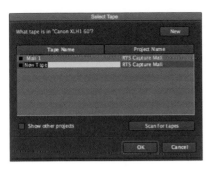

Figure B.10
Click New to add a new tape, then name it.

5. Name the tape, matching the name written on the label. (The tape is labeled, right?!) Then press **ENTER/RETURN**. This process is important for more than just staying organized. Media Composer tracks the media via the tape name. Don't get lazy and leave New Tape as the name. It's rare, but if media has matching tape names and timecode, Media Composer may confuse one media file for another, making a real mess. Besides, unnamed tapes just make you look unprofessional.

Tape-Naming Guidelines

Use a unique name for each new tape (and write the same name on the physical tape and on the tape box). The flexibility of Media Composer relies in part on its ability to correctly associate clips with the correct physical tapes. The system cannot distinguish between two tapes with the same name.

A typical naming convention looks like this: XXXYYY

XXX is the tape ID, starting with 001; YYY is the job ID, which might be a name (DINER) or date (260907).

Tape-naming schemes should reflect a project's finishing plan. A program that will be finished, or *onlined*, on Avid Symphony or Avid DS will have more flexibility in the length and format of tape names than some other systems. Check with your online house if you are unsure about how to name your tape.

6. Click **OK** to close the Select Tape dialog box and return to the Capture tool. In the future, if you are capturing additional material from a tape you have already used, simply highlight the correct tape name in the column. This way, Media Composer can accurately track which clips came from which tape.

7. In the top panel of the Capture tool, click the **V**, **A1**, **A2**, and **TC** buttons
   to enable the audio, video, and timecode tracks for capture, as shown in
   Figure B.11.

Figure B.11
Enable the video, audio, and timecode
tracks for capture.

8. Click the **VIDEO** and **AUDIO** menus to set the appropriate input source.
   This example's is **HOST-1394**. If you are using I/O hardware, the video
   input source may be component, composite, SDI, etc.

9. In the middle panel, double-check the **RES(OLUTION)** and **TARGET DRIVE**
   settings. These should already be set based on the Media Creation setting.
   Then verify the bin selection. Everything look good?

10. Click the **PLAY** button at the bottom of the Capture tool. The camera
    should start playing the tape, and the video should appear in the Composer
    window. You should hear the audio through your computer speakers.
    Playback buttons—Play, Pause, Stop, Fast Forward, Rewind, and 1-Frame
    Forward/Back—are at the bottom of the Capture tool (see Figure B.12).
    The slider above the Play button is a shuttle controller.

Figure B.12
The deck control buttons match the playback
buttons elsewhere in Media Composer.

Tip: **Click the speaker icon at the top of the Capture tool to open the Audio tool.
This is the same Audio tool discussed in Lesson 6, "Refining and Mixing
Audio." During capture, it is useful for checking audio levels. For example,
seeing the levels in the Audio tool gives you an objective way to tell if the
audio is too quiet or if your speakers are just turned down.**

11. Without stopping the tape, click the **RECORD** button (in the top left of the
    Capture tool). The light starts flashing and the Name field in the middle
    panel is highlighted. Congratulations! You are capturing video!

12. Immediately type a name for the clip. If you're planning to capture the
    entire tape, name the clip after the tape. If not, give it a name that repre-
    sents the scene or contents of the shot you're capturing here.

13. Press the **TAB KEY**, type in the **COMMENT** box (see Figure B.13), and press
    ENTER/RETURN. When capturing stops, the new name and Comment
    column appear in the bin.

Figure B.13
Name the clip and add comments while video is captured.

14. Sit back and watch your footage. No, seriously. The tape is going to be captured in real time. Because most tapes today are one hour, you may have some time on your hands while the tape is captured. You may be tempted to grab a cup of coffee, but watch the footage and familiarize yourself with it now to save time later. As you're watching, you can type in the **COMMENT** field. This comment will be visible in the bin after capture is complete.

Using DV and HDV Scene Extraction

DV and HDV Scene Extraction is a very convenient feature if you're working with the HDV, DV, or DVCAM video formats. Capture an entire tape with this feature enabled, and you'll end up with subclips and a master clip with markers, all relating to the places on the tape where the recording was started and stopped.

Discontinuities in the DV time-of-day (TOD) data indicate each place a new take was initiated on a DV camera. Using this feature, you can capture an entire DV tape as a single master clip and have the system automatically locate all the takes for you, which eliminates you logging manually.

Please note the following requirements and qualifications:

■ Your tape must have continuous timecode. To maintain continuous timecode when recording with a DV camera, roll long before stopping, and then roll back before you start to record again.

■ The DVCPRO format does not provide TOD metadata; you cannot use DV Scene Extraction with DVCPRO format.

■ DV Scene Extraction will not work on audio-only clips.

To set up DV Scene Extraction:

1. Double-click **CAPTURE** in the **SETTINGS** list to open the Capture Settings–Current dialog box; then click the **DV & HDV OPTIONS** tab.

2. Click the **DV & HDV SCENE EXTRACTION** check box, as shown in Figure B.14.

3. Select one of the options:

   ● **Add Markers:** This creates a master clip with markers where the TOD information breaks occur while capturing.

   ● **Create Subclips:** This creates a master clip and subclips where the TOD information breaks occur while capturing.

   ● **Both:** This creates master clips with markers and subclips where the TOD information breaks occur while capturing.

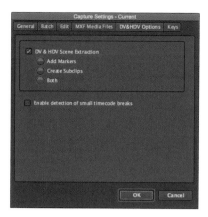

Figure B.14
Enable DV and HDV Scene Extraction
to save lots of time when capturing.

4. Click **OK**.

5. Click the **Record** button to start capture. When capture is complete, click the **Record** button again to stop capture. Subclips are created with the same source clip name and the following extension where TOD information breaks occurred: exercise.sub.01. Markers appear in the master clip where TOD information breaks occurred.

Note: To use DV Scene Extraction after capturing, select the clip(s) for which you want to create subclips or markers, select Bin > DV Scene Extraction, and choose the options you want.

Capturing Individual Clips

Many times in production, you will want to capture either a single clip or a series of clips rather than the entire tape. You can easily do this by using the Capture tool's marking controls. First, read about capturing a single clip, then read about capturing a series of clips (also referred to as *batch capturing*).

To capture a single clip, or section, of a tape, you simply need to set IN and OUT marks around the area you want to capture, as shown in Figure B.15.

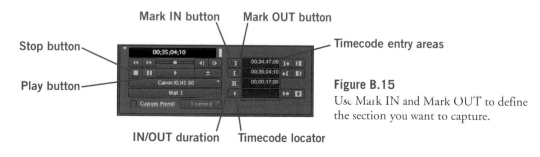

Figure B.15
Use Mark IN and Mark OUT to define
the section you want to capture.

The Importance of Timecode

Timecode helps track and count individual frames of video. Each video frame is assigned a timecode number in terms of hours, minutes, seconds, and frames. For example, 01:03:45:15 is read as one hour, three minutes, 45 seconds, and 15 frames.

Media Composer uses your videotape's timecode to navigate to various video frames. (Most videotapes have timecode, including Beta SP, Digi-Beta, and MiniDV; an exception is VHS. In reality, you will probably only deal with most of these formats as archival footage.) Timecode is also required for Media Composer to perform a batch capture, which is discussed later in this appendix.

Timecode is recorded onto the video cassette by most consumer and prosumer DV cameras. In general, after a camera is powered on, it starts recording at a specific start timecode. For example, most DV cameras start recording at 00:00:00:00.

To save battery power, you might turn off the DV camera several times over the course of shooting. However, if the camera is powered off in the middle of shooting and then powered back on again, the default recording start timecode might be reset. When the timecode is reset in the middle of the tape, the result is a discontinuity in timecode, called a *timecode break*.

Because these timecode breaks can prevent Media Composer from accurately seeking video frames and batch capture, be careful to avoid timecode breaks. Here are two techniques that might help:

- Pause the camera instead of stopping it. Pausing does not usually create a timecode break.
- If you have stopped the camera, prevent broken timecode by rolling the video back until you are parked on previously recorded material before starting to record again.

If your tape has a lot of timecode breaks, dub before capturing to achieve continuous time-code.

To capture a single clip:

1. Prepare the system for capture, including configuring any settings you need and loading and naming the tape you are working with.

2. Use the playback controls to find the beginning of the clip you want to capture.

3. Click the **MARK IN** button to set the clip's IN point. You will see the time-code entry for the mark, showing its position.

4. Play the tape until you see the end of the clip you want to capture. Click the **Mark OUT** button to set the OUT point for the clip. The Capture tool now displays the timecode position for the OUT mark, as well as the duration of the segment you have marked.

Tip: **Always set your IN and OUT points loose—that is, including slightly more footage than just the shot you want—so you have extra material for trimming and transition effects. This adds a small amount of extra media to your drive, but the flexibility it offers in editing is well worth it.**

5. Click the **Record** button or press **F4**. Media Composer will cue up the tape to the pre-roll point, play through, capture the designated clip with frame-accurate precision, and then stop playback.

6. Type a new name for the clip and press **Enter/Return**. As before, the name and comments appear in the bin after the capture finishes.

Logging and Batch Capturing

Many editors prefer to log all their clips (shots) first, and then use the Batch Capture function to capture their material automatically. This method is often considered the most efficient. As the name implies, the process has two parts:

■ Logging the footage, offline (metadata only) master clips in a bin

■ Capturing all the clips from the same tape, creating the media files that correspond to those offline master clips

Naming Bins

Naturally, you will need bins to store the master clips. Naming is important too. Your choice of bin names will affect the editing process. The simplest scheme is to name the initial bins you create by tape name. In other words, create a separate source bin for each source tape. For example, you would capture all the clips from tape 001 into a bin titled 001.

This strategy is helpful two ways:

■ The bin becomes a database for a specific tape. A printout of the bin can serve as a useful archiving tool.

■ Any scenes that were not logged and captured when the project was initially mounted will be easier to find because of visual associations with the clips in the bin bearing that tape's name.

Logging to a Bin from a Source Tape

When you log a series of clips, you follow a very similar process of marking clips (like you did to capture a single clip). Instead of capturing each clip right away, you'll do them all at once, as a group.

To log to a bin from a source tape:

1. Set up the Capture tool.

2. Click the **CAPTURE/LOG MODE** button to show the Log icon, as shown in Figure B.16.

Capture mode   Log mode

Figure B.16
Click to toggle between Capture and Log modes.

3. Go to where you want to mark an IN for the start of the clip.

4. Click the **MARK IN** button or press **F4**. The timecode for the IN point is displayed and the Mark IN button changes to an OUT mark with a pencil (see Figure B.17). The bar in the middle of the window also displays a mark OUT message, telling you that the system is waiting for an OUT point to be established.

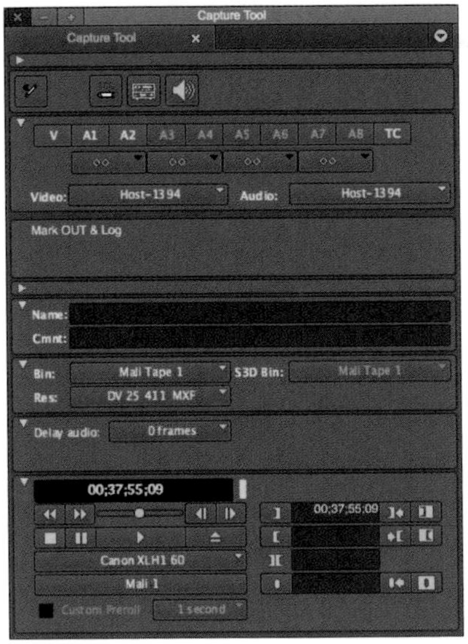

Figure B.17
After marking an IN point, the capture tool is ready for an OUT.

5. Shuttle or play to the place where you want to mark the OUT point of the clip.

Tip: **J-K-L shuttle controls work with the Capture tool. When you are logging clips, you are often advancing the tape over longer periods. It's the perfect time to go at 2× or 3× speed.**

6. Optionally, name the clip and add comments in the Capture tool.

7. Click the **Mark OUT/Log** button or press **F4**. Yes, you read that right. The F4 key is used for *both* marking an IN and an OUT. This makes the logging process very efficient—not to mention easily memorized.

8. If you didn't do so before, name the new clip that has appeared in the bin.

9. If you have been using the F4 key, press **Ctrl+7** (Windows) or **Command+7** (Mac) to return to the Capture window. Or, click the Capture tool to activate it again.

Tip: **You can log clips on-the-fly without stopping the tape. When you log a clip on-the-fly, the system pauses when the clip is added to the bin. It's the perfect opportunity to name the clip. Try it! You'll be surprised at how quickly it goes.**

10. Advance the tape to the beginning of the next shot and repeat the process.

11. Repeat these steps until you have logged all your clips. Then stop the tape.

Tip: **If you learn the keyboard shortcuts, you'll be very fast on Media Composer in no time. And when it comes to editing professionally, speed matters!**

Batch Capturing Logged Clips

After logging a group of clips, capture them automatically using Media Composer's batch capture capabilities.

To prepare for a batch capture, follow these steps:

1. Double-click **Capture** in the **Settings** list to open the Capture Settings–Current dialog box.

2. Click the **General** tab and select the **Capture Across Timecode Breaks** option.

3. Click the **Batch** tab and select the **Log Errors to the Console and Continue Capturing** option.

To batch capture your clips, follow these steps:

1. Click the **CAPTURE/LOG MODE** button in the Capture tool to return to Capture mode. The red Record button appears, as shown in Figure B.18.

Figure B.18
Toggle the Capture tool back to Capture mode when finished logging.

2. Activate the bin with the clips you want to capture.

3. Shift-click the group of clips you want to capture.

4. Choose **CLIP > BATCH CAPTURE**. A Batch Capture dialog box appears, as shown in Figure B.19.

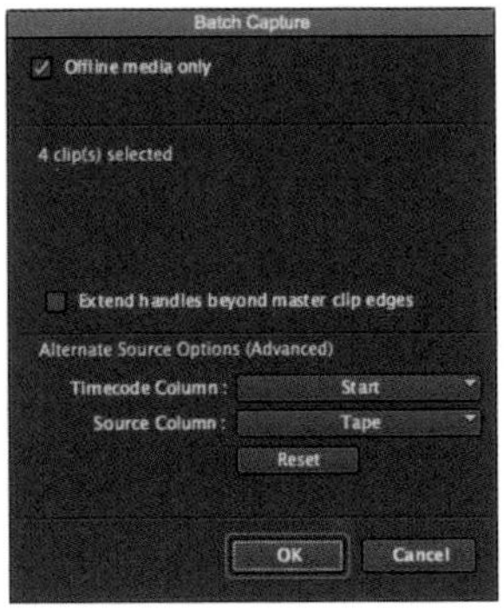

Figure B.19
Use these options to set up your batch capture.

Note: If the bin with the logged clips is not active, Batch Capture is unavailable in the menu.

5. Confirm that the **OFFLINE MEDIA ONLY** option is selected. That way, all selected clips that are offline will be captured. When this option isn't enabled, and some of the selected clips have media files, the system deletes the media files and recaptures new media files.

6. Optionally, select the **EXTEND HANDLES BEYOND MASTER CLIP EDGES** option. This lets handles extend before the beginning and after the ending of the original master clip. If you marked your clips tightly, this can give you some useful flexibility in adding effects and trimming.

7. Click **OK**.

8. If you have not inserted a tape into the tape deck, a dialog box will prompt you to do so. Insert the tape and click **MOUNTED**. The system will then know the correct tape is loaded and ready for capturing. A confirmation dialog box opens.

Tip: Be careful here. If you insert the wrong tape and Media Composer finds the required timecode, it will capture from this tape. If all your tapes start at 0:00:00:00, that may be quite easy. (Have I mentioned the importance of naming things?)

9. Click **OK** to confirm the tape and deck entries. The system captures each clip from the tape, in start timecode order. If you need another source tape, the system prompts you for it. At the end of the batch-capture process, a dialog box notifies you that the process is complete.

Note: You can stop the batch-capture process at any time by clicking the Trash icon in the Capture tool.

Capturing from a Non-Timecode Source

Sometimes you have to capture from an archive source such as VHS, DAT, or DVD that does not have timecode. Or you are capturing from a satellite or remote feed, where you have no deck control. Or you may capture without timecode simply to acquire video across a timecode break. In these cases, Media Composer will generate timecode based on the time of day. The time-of-day timecode is arbitrary; it does not actually match up to individual frames on the tape, so you cannot use it to batch capture or create an edit decision list (EDL).

Note: If the material needs to have timecode (for example, to recapture or create an EDL), dub it to tape or some other medium with timecode before you capture.

Capturing from a non-timecode source requires that you capture on-the-fly. When capturing a non-timecode source, you can adjust audio and video input levels and enter names and comments as usual. You cannot use the timecode that is generated when you are capturing from a non-timecode source for recapturing or in an EDL. The source never had real timecode.

To capture a non-timecode source:

1. Click the **DECK** button in the Capture tool. A red circle with a line through it over the button indicates that deck control will not be used in the following procedure. The system also removes the deck control buttons, as shown in Figure B.20.

2. Click once in the **TAPE NAME** box. The Select Tape dialog box appears.

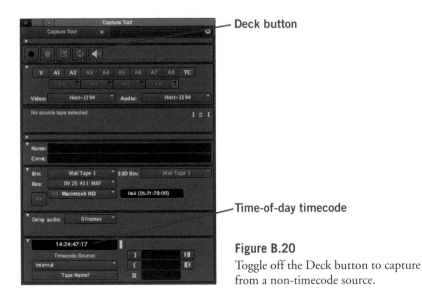

Deck button

Time-of-day timecode

Figure B.20
Toggle off the Deck button to capture from a non-timecode source.

3. Choose an existing tape name. Or, click **New**, type a new source tape name (**NTC [date]** is recommended), and press **Enter/Return**.

4. Click **OK** to return to the Capture tool.

5. Choose an option from the **Timecode Source** menu:

   - **Internal:** This is the default Avid system internal timecode, which is time-of-day (TOD) timecode.

   - **LTC Input:** This is timecode from any source (such as a facility's master clock) that is connected to the LTC IN port on the Nitris DX or Adrenaline box.

   - **Auto Detect:** This looks for LTC first. If it does not see it, it switches to internal.

   - **[Connected deck]:** This reads timecode for a connected deck so you can make a tape dub as you capture (for example, from a live feed).

6. Play the non-timecode source.

7. Click the **Record** button to start capturing on-the-fly.

8. Click the **Record** button again to stop capturing. Your clip appears in the bin and can immediately be used for editing.

9. Stop playback of your non-timecode source.

10. Click the **Deck** button to toggle it back on.

Deleting Clips and Media Files

Learning to ingest media—be it through AMA, import, or capture—is only half the story. You also need to know how to delete media as well. Whether it's to get rid of a clip that was accidentally imported or captured or to clean the media off a drive when the project is finished, you'll need to delete media at some point.

The capture process in general creates both the metadata in the bin and the media files on your media drives. The log and capture operation separates these two activities, but generally they happen at the same time. The same can be said for deleting clips. Generally, you delete both the master clip and the media file at the same time, but sometimes you want to delete only one or the other. Take a minute to read how to get rid of media.

Caution: **Deleting media is serious business. You cannot undo the deletion of media files. When you are working by yourself, needing to recapture a tape is a nuisance. When working with others, deleting their media accidentally can cost you your job. Make sure no one else needs the media files you are planning to delete, and make sure no other project is using these media files.**

Deleting Media Versus Metadata

Master clips, subclips, and sequences consist of statistical data (*metadata*) that occupies very little drive space on the internal disk, while the media files associated with them take up substantial room on the external media drives. If you need to free up a lot of drive space to work on a new project, you can delete the media used in an old project *as long as you save the master clips, subclips, and sequences.* Deleting media files will not harm the related master clips, subclips, and sequences—they simply go offline.

As long as you have the master clips, subclips, and sequences, you can always batch capture to bring the media back online. You can recapture media as long as it has timecode and you keep the clip information.

After deleting audio and video media files, the associated clips and sequence sections play silence and display the Media Offline frame. Offline audio-only clips will display a black frame and play without sound. They will not display the Media Offline message.

Tip: **If you are unsure if the audio is silent or offline, open the bin Fast menu and choose Select Offline Clips > Show Offline Clips.**

Deleting from a Bin

When deleting clips from a bin, you have the option to delete the master clip, its associated media files, or both.

■ Deleting associated media files clears space on the drives without losing any information about the clip. This enables you to recapture all the offline clips in the future based on their text information and timecode.

■ Deleting both the master clip and its associated media files is done when you no longer need a clip for a project.

To delete media files associated with master clips, sequences, and effects from a media drive:

1. Click the bin and select the clips whose media files you want to delete.

2. Choose **EDIT > DELETE** or press the **DELETE** key to open the bin's Delete dialog box.

3. Select the media objects that you want to delete, as shown in Figure B.21:

   ● To completely remove a media clip that you don't want (for example, a clip you captured by mistake), select both the master clip and the associated media files.

   ● Selecting Only Delete 3 Associated Media File(s) deletes the actual captured picture and sound associated with the clip. The master clip is retained. This results in an offline master clip, much like the ones you created when you logged clips. You could recapture this type of clip.

   ● Selecting Only Delete 1 Master Clip(s) deletes only the clip, which contains the text instructions such as its start and end timecode. The clip disappears from the bin but the media stays on the external drives. If this is the only copy of your master clip, you should avoid doing this.

 Select both check marks to completely remove a clip and its media

 Select only "associated media" to keep the master clip with its comments

Figure B.21
Choose the deletion options to delete the media only or both the media and the master clip.

Note: If you have no backups but delete the clips and sequences of the deleted
media files, you will not be able to recapture the material later unless you
log everything again. You should always make a backup copy of the project
and bins, just in case you need them some time in the future.

4. Click **OK**. A confirmation dialog box appears.

5. Click **DELETE**. The media files are permanently deleted from the drive.

Review/Discussion Questions

1. Identify the following items in the Capture tool:

    a. The button you click when you are ready to capture a clip

    b. The button you click to toggle between logging and capturing

    c. The button that displays the Audio tool

    d. The button you deselect if you are capturing a non-timecode source

    e. The button you click to mark an OUT point for a clip

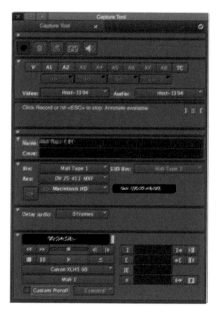

2. Name three things you need to do to prepare for batch capture.

3. Where can you quickly set the video resolution for all media, including captured media and titles?

4. After you log several clips in the bin, what is the process by which you capture that media?

5. What is time-of-day (TOD) timecode?

6. What is the disadvantage of using TOD timecode when capturing media?

7. If you want to delete media, but retain the option of recapturing it later, which options should you select in the Delete dialog box?

Appendix B Keyboard Shortcuts

Key	Shortcut
Ctrl+5 (Windows)/Command+5 (Mac)	Media Creation setting
Ctrl+7 (Windows)/Command+7 (Mac)	Capture tool
Ctrl+B (Windows)/Command+B (Mac)	Go to Capture mode (with bin active)
J-K-L	Deck shuttle (in Capture tool)
F4	Start/Stop Capture (in Capture mode)
F4	Mark In (in Log mode)
F4	Mark Out and Log (in Log mode)

Outputting to Tape

Videotape is still a common delivery format for TV broadcast, film festivals, and review copies for the client or director. Even though it is quickly being replaced by file-based delivery and play-out systems, you will no doubt have to deliver on tape at some point in your professional career. In this appendix, you use tools and techniques to ensure that your outputs are done right.

Media Used: Hell's Kitchen

Duration: 30 minutes

GOALS

- Prepare your sequence for output to tape
- Prepare your hardware for output
- Explore the Digital Cut tool
- Record a digital cut for tape-based delivery

Preparing a Sequence for Digital Cut

To get a sequence out of Media Composer and on to videotape, you perform a digital cut. During a *digital cut*, Media Composer plays the sequence and records the information onto a videotape recorder (VTR). You have three different ways to record a digital cut to tape:

■ Insert the edit onto the videotape.

■ Assemble the edit onto the videotape.

■ Manually edit onto the videotape.

Before any of that happens, you need to prepare the sequence and equipment for recording the digital cut. Just like capturing from tape, this may seem complicated the first time you do it. After you do it a couple times, it becomes easy and quick.

In this appendix, you go through the steps to output a sample sequence. If you don't have immediate access to a camera or deck to output the sequence to, you can still go through the steps of preparing the sequence and opening and reviewing the Digital Cut tool.

Note: This appendix assumes that your sequence has all the necessary elements already in the Timeline. If you haven't done so yet, you may want to add bars and tone, a slate, and a countdown prior to the program start. For more information on doing this, see Lesson 10, "Preparing for Output and Exporting a File."

Setting the Project and Timecode Format

The first step is to make sure the format and the timecode match the videotape for recording. In the same manner that media can only be captured into a project that matches the format of the tape—that is, the *native format*—you can only perform a digital cut from a project that is the native format of the tape. Here, the term *format* refers to the frame rate and raster size. For example, if the tape and deck to which you're outputting records full-frame HD at 59.94 frames per second, your project should be set to 1080i/59.94, and the raster set to 1,920×1,080.

To ensure the format and timecode match the videotape:

1. Launch Media Composer and select TRAINING USER. Then select the HELLS KITCHEN project and click the OPEN button.

2. In the Project window, double-click the HELLS KITCHEN SEQUENCES bin to open it.

3. In the **HELLS KITCHEN SEQUENCES** bin, double-click the **HK OUTPUT** sequence to load it into the Record monitor. See Figure C.1. This sequence has effects, titles, audio tracks, and various tracks enabled, as well as IN and OUT points. Some of these things matter when you perform a digital cut, and some you can address directly in the Digital Cut window.

Figure C.1
Load the HK Output sequence into the Record monitor.

4. If you are creating a tape for television broadcast in North America, Central America, Western South America, or Japan, the sequence should be set to drop-frame timecode. You can set the sequence timecode in the bin. In the **HELLS KITCHEN SEQUENCES** bin, click **BIN VIEW > STATISTICS**, as shown in Figure C.2. This view shows the start timecode, which you change to match your videotape.

Figure C.2
Choose Statistics from the Bin View menu.

5. Scroll through the **Hells Kitchen Sequences** bin window until you see the **Start** column. Click in the **HK Output Start** field and type **01;00;00;00**. Press **;** (**semicolon**) on the keyboard to change to drop-frame, as shown in Figure C.3. If you were required to perform a digital cut to a non-drop frame video tape, you would press **:** (**colon**) to change to non-drop frame.

Figure C.3
Type in the Start field for the HK Output sequence.

Note: Drop-frame timecode is a numbering system that keeps the video's timecode numbers in sync with real time (i.e., the clock on the wall). Drop-frame and non-drop frame timecode options only exist if your video was recorded using the NTSC television standard. All of Europe and most of Asia use the PAL standard, making it a non-issue. To read more about drop-frame time-code and how it came about, do a Web search on *SMPTE timecode*.

6. To confirm the change, press **Enter/Return**. Then click **OK** in the confirmation dialog box that appears.

Preparing the Sequence Video

Two things prepare your video images for playback:

■ Setting playback quality

■ Rendering any effects

Media Composer can change the quality of the playback image. The default is set to Draft Quality, which subsamples 50 percent of the raster width and height. Or, in other words, draft quality is one-quarter resolution. This works great for editing because it increases real-time performance, but it's not what you want for output. Because the playback quality setting also affects the image that goes out to the deck, set it to full quality now.

To set the playback quality:

1. In the Timeline's bottom toolbar, right-click the **Video Quality** button and select **Full Quality**, as shown in Figure C.4. This option provides the highest video playback quality by processing every image pixel of the full raster.

Figure C.4
Right-click the Video Quality button and select Full Quality.

Note: You can set the quality to the highest setting by clicking the Video Quality button and cycling through the settings until the button is entirely green. Or, right-click the button and choose Full Quality.

2. In the **HK OUTPUT** sequence in the Record monitor, mark an IN point at the start of the sequence and an OUT point at the end to define the render range. Then select the tracks with the effects on them: **V1**, **V2**, **V3**, and **V4**. The final step for video renders your effects and is important because real-time effects might exceed the capabilities of your hardware. That leads to dropped frames during a digital cut.

3. Choose **CLIP** > **RENDER IN/OUT** to open the dialog box; or right-click in the Timeline and choose **RENDER IN/OUT**. Rendering via this command is the easiest way to render all effects, but it can take a long time depending on the number of effects in your sequence. The Render In/Out dialog box shows the number of effects that require rendering and the drive that will store the rendered files.

Tip: Learn more efficient rendering techniques in the companion book *Media Composer 6: Part 2–Essential Effects* in the Avid Learning Series. Or, take the course MC110: Essential Effects from your nearest Avid Learning Partner.

4. Click **OK**. Media Composer displays a progress bar while it creates each effect. The progress bar disappears when rendering is complete.

Preparing the Sequence Audio

Audio is the last step in preparing your sequence for a digital cut output. All audio in a sequence should be at the same sample rate and bit depth when recording a digital cut. If the audio has different sample rates, you'll need to resample the sequence so it matches.

To convert the audio sample rate of the sequence:

1. Select and right-click the **HK OUTPUT** sequence in the bin. Then choose **CHANGE SAMPLE RATE** from the menu to open the dialog box, as shown in Figure C.5.

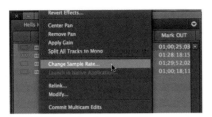

Figure C.5
Choose Change Sample Rate from the menu.

2. In the dialog box, choose **48 kHz** from the **Sample Rate** menu.

Tip: You must choose 48 kHz if you are going to a DV deck or using embedded SDI SD or HD audio.

3. Choose **High** and then click **OK**. New master clips and media are created for each converted clip. Those clips already at the correct sample rate remain unaffected. Our audio is already at 48 kHz.

Preparing Your Equipment for Output

Ensuring that your system and equipment are ready for output requires several steps.

Configuring the Deck

Naturally, if you're going to output to a deck, Media Composer must be configured to talk to that device. The process for connecting and configuring the deck for output is the same as capture. If you don't have the deck configured yet, see Appendix B, "Capturing Tape-Based Media."

If this is the same deck you used for capture, it should already be configured. If you have more than one deck configuration, activate the one that you're going to use for this output. See Figure C.6.

Figure C.6
Double-check that the Deck Configuration setting is configured and active.

To activate a setting:

1. Click the **SETTINGS** button in the Project window.

2. Open the **FAST** menu and choose **ALL SETTINGS**.

3. Click the space next to the setting name. This example activates the Canon XL-H1. The check mark moves, indicating that the setting you selected is now active, as seen in Figure C.7.

Correction	
Deck Configuration	Canon XL-H1
Deck Configuration	Sony HDCAM
Deck Preferences	

Figure C.7
The check mark indicates that the Canon is the active deck.

4. Double-check the cable connections and make sure the deck is turned on.

Blacking Your Tape

When you record a digital cut, you have to prep your tape by pre-blacking the entire tape or a portion of the tape. If you don't, you'll only be able to perform a manual edit. Insert edits, assemble edits, and crash record edits require a *pre-blacked tape*, which has a control track and timecode. You can lay down control track on your videotape by recording a black video signal to it. As you black your videotape, your record deck or camera can also record proper timecode to it.

The procedure to record black and stripe timecode to a cassette before performing the digital cut may be as simple as recording on your camera with the lens cap still in place. However, every deck and camera varies slightly in the procedure to engage the timecode. For more information on recording timecode on your video-cassette, consult your deck's or camera's operating manual.

■ **For an insert edit:** Black the entire tape. This is generally preferred.

■ **For an assemble or a crash record edit:** Black a short portion of the tape (preroll plus 10 seconds).

■ **For a manual edit:** Blacked tape is not required.

Note: In this appendix, you are outputting a sequence to standard videotape. Media Composer has several special output functions for working with other specific types of footage, or outputting to specific devices. Choose Output > Export to Device, as seen in Figure C.8.

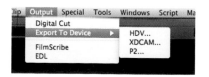

Figure C.8
Use the Export to Device options for specialized outputs.

For more information about using these options, see the Media Composer Help for these articles:

- ▪ "Generating Output"
- ▪ "Export to XDCAM"
- ▪ "Exporting to an HDV Device"
- ▪ "Exporting Your Clip or Sequence to a P2 Card"

Working with the Digital Cut Tool

The Digital Cut tool is similar to the Capture tool. It has buttons for controlling the deck and enabling audio and video tracks, and it has additional settings to customize the output to tape. Follow the most common output steps here so you can get familiar with the controls. Later, you can customize the controls to a variety of situations.

To set up the Digital Cut tool:

1. Choose **OUTPUT** > **DIGITAL CUT** to open the Digital Cut tool. Decide among options, including the output mode and the deck control edit type you want to perform, as covered in the following steps. See Figure C.9.

2. Click the **OUTPUT MODE** menu and choose a resolution, which varies depending on your project type and output hardware. Your Digital Cut tool's Output Mode menu may look different.

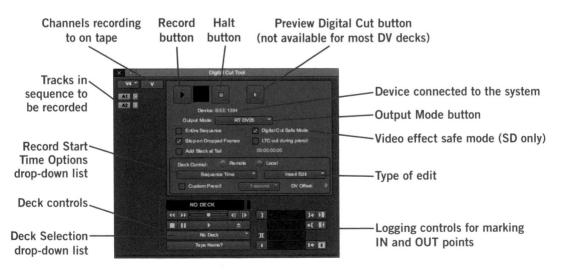

Figure C.9
Open the Digital Cut tool from the Output menu.

3. Enable the following settings, as shown in Figure C.10:

- **Entire Sequence:** This ensures that the entire sequence will be recorded out to the tape, regardless of any IN or OUT points you forgot to clear in the Timeline.

- **Digital Cut Safe Mode:** In SD projects only. The Safe mode warns you of any real-time effects or HD clips in an SD sequence (which might cause dropped frames). You can then render the problematic effects and transcode the HD clips. After you address these issues, Media Composer automatically initiates the digital cut.

- **Stop on Dropped Frames:** This stops the digital cut if a frame is dropped. This guarantees that if the process doesn't stop before the end of the program, the tape you are recording is clean.

- **Add Black at Tail:** (Optional) This is recommended for assemble edits or crash records, and 30 seconds is preferred. It ensures a clean area of black tape after the program finishes. Do not enable this for insert edits.

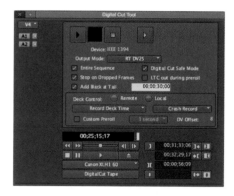

Figure C.10
Enable the output settings to customize your output.

4. Cue up the tape using the playback controls in the bottom section of the Digital Cut tool. This is an opportunity to make sure that Media Composer and the deck are properly communicating.

5. In the **DECK CONTROL** section, click **REMOTE** to control the record deck frame accurately from within Media Composer. Operating in Local mode disables remote deck control, requiring you to manually control the record deck. If you choose Remote, then decide between the available edit options to get your sequence to tape.

- **Insert Edit:** This is the preferred method of recording a digital cut. When you record an insert edit, you have to prepare your tape by blacking the entire thing. If you don't, you'll have to edit manually. Blacking the tape allows you to cleanly edit one or more sequences to tape. You can even cleanly overwrite sections of a recorded tape to fix a problem area.

- **Assemble Edit:** This gives you the same precise control over your start time as an insert edit but does not allow clean edits of additional sequences or overwriting portions of a recorded sequence on the tape. The benefit is that you have to black only a few seconds of the master tape—typically the duration of the preroll plus 10 seconds.

- **Crash Record:** During a crash record, the deck records over the audio, video, and control tracks on the tape. Unlike an assemble edit, crash records are not frame accurate. If your deck does not support insert editing, the Crash Record option appears automatically. (All DV cameras and decks connected via FireWire are automatically set to Crash Record, as seen in Figure C.11).

Figure C.11
A DV deck or camera attached via FireWire uses crash record.

Note: At the end of an assemble edit recording, the system automatically adds a freeze frame at the OUT point. The freeze frame lasts for one second or more, depending upon the record deck model. The freeze frame provides several frames of overlap for the next IN point before the control track and timecode end.

6. Choose **TIMECODE SETTING > SEQUENCE TIME**. This, the most common selection, cues the deck to record the program at the exact same timecode on the tape as the timecode currently on the sequence. (If instead you want to record the sequence to the tape at the position that the tape is cued to now, choose **RECORD DECK TIME**. This is preferred when doing a crash record.)

7. From the video track pop-up menu, select the topmost video track you want included in digital cut. In this case, click **V4**.

8. Make sure both audio tracks in the digital cut window are highlighted in the fuchsia color.

To perform the digital cut:

1. Click the **PREVIEW DIGITAL CUT** button. It's in the top-right corner of the tool, and has a yellow Play symbol on it. The preview runs all the equipment through the process of the digital cut without actually recording the video to the tape. This is really helpful! It gives you a chance to see if everything is working properly without risking a fresh tape.

Note: Preview Digital Cut is available for most professional decks using RS-422 deck control. It is not available on most DV decks or cameras.

2. The system prompts you to mount the destination tape, as shown in Figure C.12. If the tape is already in the deck, click **OK**. The deck cues to the preroll point, and the preview begins. During the preview, check that the tape cues to the right place, and the signal is flowing to the deck. If it is, you will be able to see and hear the video and audio through monitors attached to the deck. Everything go okay? Great, you're ready for the output! It's not necessary to preview the entire program, especially if it's long. If the tape cued to the right location and the signals were good, that's enough.

Figure C.12
A dialog box reminds you to put the tape in the deck.

3. Click the **HALT** button (a.k.a. Stop) to stop the preview.
4. Click the **PLAY DIGITAL CUT IN TO OUT** button.

When the digital cut is finished, review and eject the tape, pop out the record tab, and label the tape.

Review/Discussion Questions

1. What is the difference between preparing tape for an insert edit compared to preparing it for an assemble edit?

2. When might you have to record an assemble edit as opposed to an insert edit? What risk, if any, is involved?

3. If you need frame-accurate recording, should you record a manual edit?

4. If you are working with a DV camera or deck, what is the only type of edit available to you?

5. Name one reason to add black at the tail of the digital cut.

Glossary

Numbers

4:2:2 digital video A digital video system defined by the ITU-R 601 (CCIR 601) technical documentation. 4:2:2 refers to the comparative ratio of sampling of the three components of the video signal: luminance and two color channels.

A

A-mode A linear method of assembling edited footage. In A-mode, the editing system performs edits in the order they will appear on the master, stopping when the edit decision list (EDL) calls for a tape that is not presently in the deck.

add edit An edit added between consecutive frames in a sequence segment within the Timeline. An add edit separates segment sections so the user can modify or add effects to a subsection of the segment.

AES/EBU Audio Engineering Society/European Broadcasting Union. A standards-setting organization that defined a digital signal format for professional audio input to the Avid video-based editing systems using the SA 4 card. This signal format is typically used when you input sound directly to Avid video-based editing systems with a digital audiotape (DAT) machine, thereby bypassing the videotape capture process.

AIFF-C Audio Interchange File Format-Condensed. A sampled-sound file format that allows audio data storage. This format is primarily used as a data interchange format but can be used as a storage format. OMF Interchange includes AIFF-C as a common interchange format for uncompressed audio data.

alpha channel An 8-bit, grayscale representation of an image used to create a mask for keying images.

analog recording The common form of magnetic recording where the recorded waveform signal maintains the shape of the original waveform signal. All video-tape source footage is analog. When captured (via telecine transfer), footage is converted from analog format to digital format.

anti-aliasing A computerized process of digitally smoothing the jagged lines around graphic objects or titles.

aspect ratio The numerical ratio of a viewing area's width to its height. In video and television, the standard aspect ratio is 4:3, which can be reduced to 1.33:1 or 1.33. HDTV video format has an aspect ratio of 16:9. In film, some aspect ratios include 1.33:1, 1.85:1, and 2.35:1.

assemble edit An edit where all existing signals on a tape (if any) are replaced with new signals. Assemble editing sequentially adds new information to a tape and a control track might be created during the edit. The edit is made linearly and is added to the end of previously recorded material.

Attic folder The folder containing backups of your files or bins. Every time you save or the system automatically saves your work, copies of your files or bins go in the Attic folder, until the folder reaches the specified maximum. The Attic folder copies have the file name extension .bak and a number added to the file name. The number of backup files for one project can be changed (increased or decreased) in the Bin Settings dialog box.

audio timecode Longitudinal timecode (LTC) recorded on an audio track.

AutoSave A feature that saves your work at intervals you specify. Backups are placed in the Attic folder.

Avid disk The disk that contains the operating system files. The computer needs operating system information to run.

Avid Projects folder The folder containing your projects.

B

B-mode A "checkerboard" or nonsequential method of assembly. In B-mode, the edit decision list (EDL) is arranged by source tape number. The edit system performs all edits from the tapes currently assigned to decks, leaving gaps that will be filled by material from subsequent reels.

B-roll An exact copy of the A-roll original material, or new original material on a separate reel, for use in A-/B-roll editing.

backtiming A method of calculating the IN point by subtracting the duration from a known OUT point so that, for example, music and video or film end on the same note.

backup A duplicate copy of a file or disk in another location.

batch capture The automated process in which groups of clips or sequences, or both, are captured (recorded digitally).

Betacam Trademarks of Sony Electronics, Inc. Two component videotape and video recording standards. Sony Betacam was the first high-end cassette-based system, recording video onto ½-inch magnetic tape. Betacam SP arrived three years after the first Betacam, improving on signal-to-noise ratios, frequency responses, the number of audio channels, and the amount of tape available on cassettes. SP is now the only type sold.

bin A database in which master clips, subclips, effects, and sequences are organized for a project. Bins provide database functions to simplify organizing and manipulating material for capturing and editing.

black and code Video black, timecode, and control track that are prerecorded onto videotape stock. Tapes with black and code are referred to as *striped* or *blacked* tapes.

black burst A video signal that has no luminance or chrominance components (except burst) but contains all the other elements of a video signal. Black burst is the reference signal commonly used for timing audio and video samples.

black burst generator An electronic device that emits a signal that registers as pure black when recorded on videotape.

black edits 1. A video source with no image. 2. A special source you can fade into or out of, or use for other effects.

bumping up Transferring a program recorded on a lower-quality videotape to a higher-quality videotape (such as from ¾-inch to 1-inch videotape, or S-VHS to MII).

burn-in A visible timecode permanently superimposed (burned in) on footage, usually in the form of white numbers in a black rectangle. Burned-in timecode is normally used for tracking timecode during previews or offline editing. A videotape with burn-in is also called a *burn-in dub* or *window dub*.

C

C-mode A nonsequential method of assembly in which the edit decision list (EDL) is arranged by source tape number and ascending source timecode.

calibrate To fine-tune video levels for maximum clarity during capture (from videotape).

capture To convert analog video and audio signals to an Avid compressed digital signal format.

channel 1. A physical audio input or output. 2. One of several color components that combine to define a color image. An RGB image is made up of red, green, and blue color channels. In color correction, you can redefine color channels by blending color components in different proportions.

character generator An electronic device, or computer device and software combination, that creates letters and numbers that can be superimposed on video footage as titles.

chroma Video color.

chrominance The saturation and hue characteristics of a composite video signal; the portion of the video signal that contains color information. Adjust chrominance and other video levels before capturing.

clip 1. A segment of source material captured into your system at selected IN and OUT points and referenced in a project bin. The clip contains pointers to the media files in which the actual digital video and audio data are stored. 2. In a record in a log, which stands for one shot, the clip includes information about the shot's start and end timecode, the source tape name, and the tracks selected for editing. 3. In OMFI, a general class of objects in the OMF Interchange class hierarchy representing shared properties of source clips, filler clips, attribute clips, track references, timecode clips, and edge code clips. A clip is a subclass of a component.

codec *Co*mpressor/*deco*mpressor. Any technology for compressing and decompressing data. Codecs can be implemented in both software and hardware. Some examples of codecs are Cinepak, MPEG, and QuickTime.

color bars A standard color test signal, displayed as a video pattern of eight equal-width columns ("bars") of colors. SMPTE color bars are a common standard. You adjust video levels against the color bars on your source videotape before capturing.

component video The structuring of the video signal whereby color and luminance signals are kept separate from one another by using the color-subtraction method Y (luminance), B–Y (blue minus luminance) and R–Y (red minus luminance), with green derived from a combination. Two other component formats are RGB and YUV.

composite video A video signal in which the luminance and chrominance components have been combined (encoded) as in standard PAL, NTSC, or SECAM formats.

composition The standard term used by OMF Interchange to refer to an edited sequence made up of a number of clips. The OMF equivalent of a sequence in an Avid system.

compression 1. In audio, the process of reducing the dynamic range of the audio signal. 2. In video, a lack of detail in either the black or the white areas of the video picture due to improper separation of the signal level. 3. A reduction of audio or video (or both) signal detail to reduce storage requirements during transformation from analog to Avid digital format. In JPEG compression, for example, algorithms for variable frame length analyze the information in each frame and perform reductions that maximize the information retained. Compression does not remove any frames from the original material.

conform To prepare a complete version of your project for viewing. The version produced might be an intermediate working version or the final cut.

console A display that lists the current system information and chronicles recently performed functions. It also contains information about particular items you are editing, such as the shots in your sequence or clips selected from bins.

contrast The range of light-to-dark values present in a film or video image.

control track The portion of the video recording used to control longitudinal motion of the tape during playback. Control track can be thought of as electronic sprocket holes on the videotape.

CPU Central processing unit. The main computational section of a computer that interprets and executes instructions.

crossfade An audio transition in which the outgoing sound gradually becomes less audible as the incoming sound becomes more distinct. Also called an *audio dissolve*.

cue To shuttle a videotape to a predetermined location.

cut 1. An instantaneous transition from one video source to another. 2. A section of source or record tape.

D

D1, D5 Two digital videotape recording formats that conform to the ITU-R 601 (CCIR-601) standard for uncompressed 4:2:2 digital component video. D5 is very similar to D1 in that it is a component digital recorder. However, D1 records with 8-bit accuracy; D5 records with 10-bit accuracy.

D2, D3 Two digital videotape recording formats for composite video. The main difference between the two is that D2 uses ¾-inch digital videotape, and D3 uses ½-inch digital videotape.

D-mode An A-mode edit decision list (EDL) in which all effects (dissolves, wipes, graphic overlays) are performed at the end.

DAE Digidesign Audio Engine. A trademark of Avid Technology, Inc. The application that manages the AudioSuite plug-ins.

DAT Digital audiotape. A digital audio recording format that uses 3.8mm-wide magnetic tape in a plastic cassette.

decibel dB. A unit of measurement for audio volume level.

deck controller A tool that allows the user to control a deck by using standard functions such as shuttle, play, fast forward, rewind, stop, and eject.

depth shadow A shadow that extends solidly from the edges of a title or shape to make it appear three-dimensional.

digital cut The output of a sequence, which is usually recorded to tape.

digital recording A method of recording in which the recorded signal is encoded on the tape in pulses and then decoded during playback.

digital television DTV. The technology enabling the terrestrial transmission of television programs as data.

digitally record To convert analog video and audio signals to digital signals.

dip An adjustment to an audio track in which the volume gain level decreases, or "dips," to a lower level, rather than fading completely.

direct digital interface The interconnection of compatible pieces of digital audio or video equipment without conversion of the signal to an analog form.

dissolve A video or audio transition in which an image from one source gradually becomes less distinct as an image from a second source replaces it. An audio dissolve is also called a *segue*.

drop-frame timecode A type of SMPTE timecode designed to match clock time exactly. Two frames of code are dropped every minute on the minute except the tenth minute, to correct for the fact that color frames occur at a rate of 29.97 fps, rather than an exact 30 fps. Drop-frame timecode is recorded with semicolons between the digits; for example, 1;00;10;02.

drop shadow A shadow that is offset from a title or shape to give the feeling of spatial dimension.

dupe Duplicate. A section of film or video source footage that has been repeated (duplicated) one or more times in an edited program.

dupe reel A reel designated for the recording and playback of dupes (duplicate shots) during videotape editing.

DV Digital video that is transferred through equipment conforming to IEEE Standard 1394. This equipment is sometimes called *FireWire* or *I-Link*.

DVE Digital video effect.

dynamic range An audio term that refers to the range between the softest and loudest levels a source can produce without distortion.

E

E-mode A C-mode edit decision list (EDL) in which all effects (dissolves, wipes, and graphic overlays) are performed at the end.

EBU European Broadcasting Union. A standards-setting organization in which only users (not vendors) have a voice.

edit To assemble film or video, audio, effects, titles, and graphics to create a sequence.

edit rate In compositions, a measure of the number of editable units per second in a piece of media data (for example, 30 fps for NTSC, 25 fps for PAL, and 24 fps for film).

EDL Edit decision list. A list of edits made during offline editing and used to direct the online editing of the master.

effects The manipulation of an audio or video signal. Types of film or video effects include special effects (F/X) such as morphing; simple effects such as dissolves, fades, superimpositions, and wipes; complex effects such as keys and DVEs; motion effects such as freeze frame and slow motion; and title and character generation. Effects usually have to be rendered because most systems cannot accommodate multiple video streams in real time.

energy plot The display of audio waveforms as a graph of the relative loudness of an audio signal.

extract To remove a selected area from an edited sequence and close the resulting gap in the sequence.

F

fade A dissolve from full video to black video or from full audio to no audio, or vice versa.

field One-half of the scan lines in an interlaced video frame. In most systems, the odd-numbered lines form one field, and the even-numbered lines form the second.

NTSC video contains approximately 60 fields (30 frames) per second, and PAL video contains 50 fields (25 frames) per second.

file system   A way of organizing directories and files on a disk drive, such as FAT or NTFS for Windows computers.

filler clip   A segment of a sequence that contains no audio or video information. Filler can be added to the Source monitor (or pop-up monitor) and edited into a sequence.

format   To prepare a disk drive for use. For Windows computers, you format a disk drive by copying a file system (either FAT or NTFS) to the drive.

formatting   The transfer and editing of material to form a complete program, including any of the following: countdown, test patterns, bars and tone, titles, credits, logos, space for commercial, and so forth.

fps   Frames per second. A measure of the film or video display rates (NTSC = 30 fps; PAL = 25 fps; SECAM = 25 fps; Film = 24 fps).

frame   One complete video picture. A frame contains two video fields, scanned at the NTSC rate of approximately 30 fps or the PAL rate of 25 fps.

frame offset   A way of indicating a particular frame within the group of frames identified by the edge number on a piece of film. For example, a frame offset of +12 indicates the twelfth frame from the frame marked by the edit.

G

gain   1. A measurement of the amount of white in a video picture. 2. Audio levels or loudness.

gamma   A measurement of the midpoint in the luminance range of an image. Used in color adjustments to control the proportions of brighter and darker areas in an image. Also called the *gray point*.

gang   Any combination of multiple tracks that are grouped. An edit that is performed on one track is also performed on tracks that are ganged together.

generation   The number of times material has been rerecorded. The original videotaped material is the first generation. A copy of the original is a second-generation tape, and so on. Each generation shows a gradual loss of image quality. With digital copies, there is little or no loss in quality.

genlock   In broadcast, a system whereby the internal sync generator in a device (such as a camera) locks onto and synchronizes itself with an incoming signal.

gigabyte   GB. Approximately one billion (1,073,741,824) bytes of information.

H

handle Material outside the IN and OUT points of a clip in a sequence. The Avid system creates handles when you decompose or consolidate material. The Decompose and Consolidate features can create new master clips that are shorter versions of the original master clip. The handles are used for dissolves and trims with the new, shorter master clips.

hard disk A magnetic data recording disk that is permanently mounted within a disk drive.

hard recording The immediate recording of all audio, video, timecode, and control tracks on a magnetic recorder. Because hard recording creates breaks in any existing timecode or control track on the tape, this procedure is often performed on blank tape when an edit is not required or in emergency circumstances. Also called *crash recording*.

HDTV High-definition television. A digital video image having at least two times the resolution of standard NTSC or PAL video. The HDTV aspect ratio is 16:9. (Analog TV has a ratio of 4:3.)

head frame The first frame in a clip of film or a segment of video.

headroom 1. In video, the room that should be left between the top of a person's head and the top of the frame when composing a clip. 2. In audio, the amount of available gain boost remaining before distortion is encountered.

hertz Hz. The SI unit of frequency equal to one cycle per second.

hi con A high-contrast image used for creating matte keys.

hue An attribute of color perception. Red, green, and blue form the color model used, in varying proportions, to produce all the colors displayed in video and on computer screens. Also called a *color phase*.

I

IN point The starting point of an edit. Also called a *mark IN*.

initializing The setting of the computer edit program to proper operating conditions at the start of the editing session.

interface 1. The computer software or hardware used to connect two functions or devices. 2. The program access level at which a user makes selections and navigates a given system.

IRE A unit of measurement of the video waveform scale for the measurement of video levels, originally established by the Institute of Radio Engineers. The scale is divided into 140 IRE units, 100 above the blanking reference line and 40 below it.

ITU-R BT.601 The standard for standard-definition component digital video, published by the International Telecommunication Union as ITU-R BT.601-5 (formerly CCIR 601). This standard defines digital component video as it is derived from NTSC and PAL. It forms the basis for HDTV formats as well.

J

jam syncing The process of synchronizing a secondary timecode generator with a selected master timecode.

JFIF JPEG File Interchange Format. A file format that contains JPEG-encoded image data, which can be shared among various applications. JFIF resolutions store data at a constant rate; for example, JFIF 300 uses 300 KB for each frame it stores. JFIF resolutions comply with the ISO-JPEG interchange format and the ITU-R 601 standard.

JPEG Joint Photographic Experts Group. Also, a form of compression developed by Avid Technology, Inc.

K

kerning The spacing between text characters in print media, such as titles.

keyframes A control point used to define the value of an effect parameter at a given point in time; changes between two keyframes are automatically interpolated by the system to create an animation of the effect parameter over time.

kilobyte KB. Approximately one thousand (1,024) bytes of information.

kilohertz kHz. One thousand cycles per second.

L

layback The process of transferring a finished audio track back to the master videotape.

layered tracks The elements of an effect created by combining two or more tracks in a specified way, such as nesting one track as a layer within another.

leader A length of film, tape, or a digital clip placed at the beginning of a roll, reel, or sequence to facilitate the cueing and syncing of material.

level A quantitative measure of a video or an audio signal. A low level indicates the darker portions in video and the soft or quieter portions in audio; conversely, a high level indicates a brighter video image or a louder audio signal. The level of audio signal correlates directly with the volume of reproduced sound.

lift To remove selected frames from a sequence and leave black or silence in place of the frames.

line feed A recording or live feed of a program that switches between multiple cameras and image sources. Also known in sitcom production as the *director's cut*.

linear editing A type of tape editing in which you assemble the program from beginning to end. If you require changes, you must rerecord everything downstream of the change. The physical nature of the medium (for example, analog videotape) dictates how you place material on the medium.

locator A mark added to a selected frame to qualify a particular location within a sequence. User-defined comments can be added to locators.

log To enter information about your media into bins at the beginning of the editing process. Logging can be done automatically or manually.

looping 1. The recording of multiple takes of dialogue or sound effects. 2. Continuous audio playback.

lossless compression A compression scheme in which no data is lost. In video compression, lossless data files are usually very large.

lossy compression A compression scheme in which data is thrown away, resulting in loss of image quality. The degree of loss depends on the specific compression algorithm used.

LTC Longitudinal timecode. A type of SMPTE timecode that is recorded on the audio track of a videotape.

luminance The measure of the intensity of the combined color (white) portion of a video signal.

M

mark IN/OUT 1. The process of entering the start and end timecodes for a clip to be edited into a sequence. 2. The process of marking or logging timecode numbers to define clips during a logging or capturing session.

master The tape resulting from editing. The finished program.

master clip In the bin, the media object that refers to the media files captured from tape or other sources.

master shot The shot that serves as the basic scene, and into which all cutaways and closeups will be inserted during editing. A master shot is often a wide shot showing all characters and action in the scene.

match-frame edit An edit in which the last frame of the outgoing shot is in sync with the first frame of the incoming shot, such that the incoming shot is an extension of the outgoing shot.

matchback The process allowing you to generate a film cut list from a 30-fps video project that uses film as the source material.

media The video, audio, graphics, and rendered effects that can be combined to form a sequence or presentation.

media data Data from a media source. Media data can be analog data (film frames, Nagra tape audio, or videotape video and audio) or digital data (either data that was captured such as video frame data and audio samples, or data such as title graphics, DAT recordings, or animation frames created in digital form).

media files Files containing the digital audio or video data needed to play Avid clips and sequences.

megahertz MHz. One million cycles per second.

mix 1. A transition from one video source to another in a switcher. 2. The product of a recording session in which several separate sound tracks are combined through a mixing console in mono or stereo.

mixdown audio The process that allows the user to combine several tracks of audio onto a single track.

monitor 1. In video, a picture tube and associated circuitry without tuner or audio sections. The monitor includes the display of source media, clips, and sequences. In Avid products, virtual monitors are displayed on the screen in which source media, clips, and sequences can be edited. 2. In audio, to monitor specific audio tracks and channels, or another name for the speakers through which sound is heard.

MOS The term used for silent shooting. From the quasi-German, *mit out sprechen* —without talking.

multicamera A production or scene that is shot and recorded from more than one camera simultaneously.

multiple B-roll A duplicate of the original source tape, created so that overlays can be merged onto one source tape.

multitrack A magnetic tape or film recorder capable of recording more than one track at a time.

N

noise 1. In video, an aberration that appears as very fine white specks (snow) and that increases over multiple generations. 2. In audio, a sound that is usually heard as a hiss.

non-drop-frame timecode An SMPTE timecode format that continuously tracks NTSC video at a rate of 30 fps without dropping frames to compensate for the actual 29.97-fps rate of NTSC video. As a result, non-drop-frame timecode does not coincide with real time. Non-drop-frame timecode is recorded with colons between the digits (for example, 1:00:10:02).

nonlinear Pertaining to instantaneous random access and manipulation of any frame of material on any track and on any layer of an edit sequence.

nonlinear editing A type of editing in which you do not need to assemble the program from beginning to end. The nature of the medium and the technical process of manipulating that medium do not dictate how the material must be physically ordered. You can use nonlinear editing for traditional film cutting and splicing, and for captured video images. You can make changes at the beginning, middle, or end of the sequence.

NTSC National Television Standards Committee. The group that established the color television transmission system used in the United States, using 525 lines of information scanned at a rate of approximately 30 fps.

O

offline Pertaining to items that are unavailable to the computer, such as offline disks or media files.

offline edit The preliminary or rough-cut editing that produces an edit decision list (EDL).

OMFI Open Media Framework Interchange, a registered trademark of Avid Technology, Inc. A standard format for the interchange of digital media data among heterogeneous platforms. The format is designed to encapsulate all the information required to interchange a variety of digital media, such as audio, video, graphics, and still images, as well as the rules for combining and presenting the media. The format includes rules for identifying the original sources of the digital media, and it can encapsulate both compressed and uncompressed digital media data.

online edit The final edit using the master tapes and an edit decision list (EDL) to produce a finished program ready for distribution; usually associated with high-quality computer editing and digital effects.

OUT point   The end point of an edit, or a mark on a clip indicating a transition point. Also called a *mark OUT*.

outtake   A take that is not selected for inclusion in the finished product.

overwrite   An edit in which existing video or audio, or both, is replaced by new material.

P

PAL   Phase Alternating Line. A color television standard used in many countries. PAL consists of 625 lines of information scanned at a rate of 25 fps.

pan   An audio control that determines the left-to-right balance of the audio signal.

partition   A method of assigning disk space that creates two or more virtual disks from a single physical disk (similar to creating a directory).

patching   The routing of audio or video from one channel or track in the sequence to another.

pop-up monitor   An ancillary monitor used to view and mark clips and sequences.

position bar   The horizontal rectangular area beneath the Source monitor, Record monitor, Playback monitor, Composer monitor, and Source pop-up monitor that contains the position indicator.

position indicator   A vertical blue line that moves in the position bar and in the Timeline to indicate the location of the frame displayed in the monitor.

postroll   A preset period of time during a preview when a clip will continue to play past the OUT point before stopping or rewinding.

precomputed media   A computed effect stored in a file and referenced by a composition or sequence. Applications can precompute effects that they cannot create during playback.

preroll   The process of rewinding videotapes to a predetermined cue point (for example, six seconds) so the tapes are stabilized and up to speed when they reach the selected edit point (during capturing of source material from a video deck).

preview   To rehearse an edit without actually performing (recording) it.

progressive media   Media composed of single frames, each of which is vertically scanned as one pass.

project   A data device used to organize the work done on a program or series of programs. Bins, rundowns, and settings are organized in the Project window. The project bins contain all your clips, sequences, effects, and media file pointers.

R

RAM Random access memory. Computer memory that is volatile and unsaved; information in RAM clears when the computer is turned off.

random access The ability to move to a video point instantly, without having to shuttle.

real time The actual clock time in which events occur.

reel A spool with a center hub and flat sides on which magnetic tape is wound. Generally, a spool of tape is referred to as a *reel*, and a spool of film is referred to as a *roll*.

rendering The merging of effect layers to create one stream of digital video for playback in real time.

replace edit An edit in which a segment in the sequence is overwritten or replaced with source material of matching duration.

resolution 1. The amount and degree of detail in the video image, measured along both the horizontal and vertical axes. Usually, the number of available dots or lines contained in the horizontal and vertical dimensions of a video image. 2. The number of color or grayscale values that can be added, usually stated in bits (such as 8-bit or 24-bit). Sometimes dots per inch (dpi) is referred to as the *resolution*, although dpi is more properly called the *screen density*.

RGB Red, green, and blue. In computer systems, the additive primary colors used to create all other colors on a computer monitor.

rough cut A preliminary edit of a program, usually the result of an offline edit.

S

safe action area A region of the video image considered safe from cropping for either the action or onscreen titles, taking into account variations in adjustments for video monitors or television receivers. Safe action is 90 percent of the screen measured from the center. Used in conjunction with the safe title area.

safe title area A region of the video image considered safe from cropping for either the action or onscreen titles, taking into account variations in adjustments for video monitors or television receivers. Safe title is 80 percent of the screen measured from the center. Used in conjunction with the safe action area.

sample data The media data created by capturing from a physical source. A sample is a unit of data that the capturing device can measure. Applications can play digital sample data from files on disk.

sample plot The representation of audio as a sample waveform.

sample rate The frequency of the sample units.

saturation A measurement of chrominance. Saturation is the intensity of color in the video signal.

scale bar A control in the Timeline window that allows you to expand and contract the Timeline area centered around the blue position indicator.

scroll bar A rectangular bar located along the right side or the bottom of a window. Clicking or dragging in the scroll bar allows the user to move or scan through the file or window.

scrubbing The process of shuttling through audio at various speeds as the audio pitch changes.

SECAM Séquential Couleur à Memoire. A color television broadcast standard developed in France and several Eastern European countries.

segment A section of a track or clip within a sequence in the Timeline that can be edited.

sequence An edited composition that often includes audio and video clips and rendered effects connected by applied transitions. The Avid system contains a Timeline that graphically represents the edited sequence.

shot log A listing of information about a roll of film or a reel of videotape, usually in chronological order.

shuttling The viewing of footage at speeds greater than real time.

sifting The displaying of clips that meet specific criteria in a bin.

silence Blank (black) space in the audio tracks in a Timeline that contains no audio material.

SMPTE timecode A frame-numbering system developed by the Society of Motion Picture and Television Engineers that is used primarily for electronic editing and timing of video programs. It assigns a number to each frame of video, telling the elapsed number of hours, minutes, seconds, and frames (for example, 01:42:13:26).

soft wipe A wipe effect from one image to another that has a soft, diffused edge.

sorting The arranging of clips in a bin column in numerical or alphabetical order, depending on the column the user selects.

source clip One of the lowest-level building blocks of a sequence composition.

source mode A method of assembly that determines in what order the edit controller reads the edit decision list (EDL) and assembles the final tape. There are five different types of source mode: A-mode, B-mode, C-mode, D-mode, and E-mode.

speed The point at which videotape playback reaches a stable speed and there is enough preroll time for editing or capturing.

splice-in An edit in which the material already on the video or audio track is lengthened by the addition of new material spliced in at any point in the sequence.

split An edit in which the audio and video signals are given separate IN points or OUT points, so the edit takes place with one signal preceding the other. This does not affect audio and video synchronization. Also called an *L-cut*, *delay edit*, or *overlap edit*.

split-screen The video special effect that displays two images separated by a horizontal or vertical wipe line.

stepping The movement forward or backward one frame at a time. Also called *jogging*.

storyboard A series of pictures (traditionally sketches) designed to show how a production will look. Comic books are essentially storyboards. Storyboards and subsequent sequences can be created by manipulating images from the captured footage in a bin.

streaming A technology that allows users to watch a video clip or movie over the Internet while the video is being copied to their computers.

striped stock Film stock to which a narrow stripe of magnetic recording material has been applied for the recording of a sound track.

subclip 1. An edited part of a clip. In a sequence, a subclip can be bound by any variation of clip beginnings, endings, and mark points. 2. Created by marking IN and OUT points in a clip and by saving the frames between the points. The subclip does not contain pointers to media files. The subclip references the master clip, which alone contains pointers to the media files.

synchronization 1. The pulses contained within a composite video signal to provide a synchronization reference for signal sampling. Also, a separate signal that can be fed to various pieces of equipment. 2. The sound recorded on a separate audiotape but synchronized with videotape or film shot simultaneously. Also called *sync*.

T

tail frame The last frame in a clip of film or a segment of video.

TBC Time-base corrector. An electronic device that improves video signal stability by correcting time-base errors inherent in mechanical videotape recorders.

telecine 1. The process of transferring motion picture film to video. 2. Equipment used in the post-production process.

three-point editing The basic principle that an edit event requires only three marks between the source and record sides to automatically calculate the fourth mark and complete the edit.

TIFF Tag Image File Format. A tag-based system developed by Aldus Corporation for storing and interchanging raster images. The OMF Interchange standard includes TIFF as a common format for graphic interchange, and it includes TIFF with extensions as a common format for video frame data.

time-of-day timecode The timecode that approximately matches the actual time of day (clock time).

timecode An electronic indexing method used for editing and timing video programs. Timecode denotes hours, minutes, seconds, and frames (00:00:00:00) elapsed on a videotape. Address track timecode is recorded simultaneously with the video picture. Longitudinal timecode (LTC) is recorded on an audio track. Vertical interval timecode (VITC) is recorded in the vertical blanking interval of the video track. SMPTE timecode is the prevalent standard. Other timecodes exist that include film timecode and audio timecode used during film projects. During editing, the Avid system can display and track several types of timecode.

Timeline The graphical representation of every macroscopic and microscopic edit made to a sequence, including all nested effects and layered tracks.

title bar Located at the top of a window, it contains the name given to a project or bin.

tone A constant audio frequency signal recorded at the start of a tape at 0 VU (volume units) to provide a reference for later use. Usually recorded in conjunction with color bars.

track 1. The section of tape on which a signal is recorded. Also called a *channel*. 2. The sound portion of a video program. 3. A region of a clip or sequence on which audio or video is placed. 4. A playback channel represented in a sequence as either a video track or an audio track. Tracks are composed of one or more segments connected by transitions.

track selector A method of selecting one of the tracks from a track group; only the selected track is to be played. For example, a track selector can indicate which of four alternate views of the same scene is to be played.

tracking The positioning of video heads during tape playback so that the heads reproduce the strongest possible signal. Tracking is adjusted on the deck prior to capturing.

transition A representation of what is to take place as one segment ends and the next one begins. The simplest transition is a cut, which occurs in video when the first frame of the starting segment directly follows the last frame of the segment that is ending.

transition effect A wipe, dissolve, or digital video effect (DVE) applied to an edit transition.

trim The process of adjusting transitions in a sequence from the Timeline.

U

uncompressed video A captured video stream that is not processed by a data compression scheme. The video signal remains uncompressed at all stages of the process: input, storage, and output. Uncompressed video conforms to the ITU-R BT.601 standard.

undo/redo The process that allows a return to the state immediately preceding the last edit or a repeat of an "undo" edit.

up cut In editing, to cut the end of the previous scene, often by mistake. In general, to cut short.

V

VCR Videocassette recorder. A video recorder that uses consumer-grade videotape formats such as VHS, Betamax, and Hi8.

vectorscope A visual display that shows the electronic pattern of the color portion of the video signal. It is used to adjust the color saturation and hue by using a stable color reference such as color bars.

VHS Video Home System. The ½-inch videocassette format developed by JVC for consumer and industrial use.

video 1. The visual portion of a program or sequence. 2. All television other than broadcast television.

video stream 1. In analog editing systems, also called a *video playback source*. 2. In digital editing systems, a stream of data making up a digital video image.

VITC Vertical interval timecode. The timecode inserted in the vertical blanking interval.

volume level An objective measure of audio intensity.

VU meter Volume unit meter. An instrument used to measure audio levels.

W–Y

WAVE RIFF Waveform Audio File Format. A widely used format for audio data. OMF Interchange includes it as a common interchange format for audio data.

waveform 1. In video, a visual display that shows the electronic pattern of the video signal. It is used to adjust the setup and gain by using a stable reference such as color bars. The Avid waveform uses a single-line display. 2. In audio, a visual representation of changing frequencies.

white point The luminance value in a video image that you set equal to reference white when making a color adjustment.

wild sound A recording of sound on either videotape or audiotape made without an accompanying picture. Also called a *wild track*.

YUV The letter designations for luminance, luminance minus red, and luminance minus blue. YUV are the luminance and color difference signals of the component video standard for PAL. Also called *YCrCb*.

Answers to Review/Discussion Questions

Lesson 1 Answers

1. a, b, and c
2. d
3. b
4. False
5. a
6. d
7. c
8. a

Lesson 2 Answers

1. c
2. False. The correct answer is I and O.
3. b
4. 20
5. True
6. a
7. Splice-in
8. a and d

Lesson 3 Answers

1. d
2. c
3. b
4. a
5. a
6. b
7. d
8. a
9. c

Lesson 4 Answers

1. a and c
2. False. You can change the Splice-In default by clicking the red Lift/Overwrite Segment Mode button in the Smart Tool palette.
3. True. Positioning the pointer at the top of the segment in the Timeline will reposition the segment using Lift/Overwrite. Positioning the pointer at the bottom of the segment in the Timeline will reposition the segment using Extract/Splice-In.
4. c
5. a, b, and c
6. b
7. c
8. a

Lesson 5 Answers

1. c
2. b
3. a, b, and c
4. a
5. d
6. c
7. d
8. a

Lesson 6 Answers

1. The Quick Transition button is in the Timeline toolbar. The default shortcut key is the backslash (\).

2. If the second track is enabled and the keyframe is at the same location, the second keyframe will move when you drag the first keyframe.

3. Four keyframes are needed: two create the ramp down, and two create the ramp back up.

4. The Audio Mixer sets the volume level exactly to 3 dB. The volume keyframe adds the 3 dB to the Audio Mixer's level.

5. False. Yellow appears when the audio signal goes above the target. Audio is still acceptable to about −3 dB.

6. False. These marks specify the part of the sequence that plays back when you click Play in the Audio Punch-In tool. You can begin recording anywhere within the IN and OUT points.

7. Select the existing track in the New Track menu.

8. False. To save an effect template, drag the effect icon into a bin from the upper-left corner of the Effect Editor.

9. Click the Solo button in the Track Control panel for each track you want to solo. The remaining tracks automatically switch to mute.

10. Disable all tracks except the TC1 track; then click the Marker button.

Lesson 7 Answers

1. b, c, and d

2. b

3. a and d

4. d

5. b

Lesson 8 Answers

1. Open the Bin menu and choose Group Clips. Or access the command by pressing Ctrl+Shift+G (Windows) or Command+Shift+G (Mac).

2. A group clip appears in the bin with a square quad-split icon.

3. Open the Special menu and choose Multicamera Mode.

4. You must edit the group clip into a sequence before you can select Multicamera mode from the Special menu.

5. You can change the camera that appears in the Source monitor's full monitor display either by using the keyboard's Up Arrow or Down Arrow key or choosing a new camera from the Group menu.

6. You must use the Composer settings to show two rows of data above the Source and Record monitors.

7. When you select a V1 clip in the Group menu, the audio from that video is also selected.

8. False. Tracks are ignored when you switch cameras using the Up Arrow and Down Arrow keys or the Group menu.

Lesson 9 Answers

1. Make sure the V track is enabled and that no audio tracks are enabled in the Track panel.

2. The Object menu contains the Send Backward command, along with the Bring Forward command.

3. Select the rectangle shape with the Selection tool. Then pick a color by clicking the Fill box.

4. Choose Clip > New Video Track or press Ctrl+Y (Windows) or Command+Y (Mac).

5. False. The title must be created with the Video Background button enabled.

6. First enable the track that the title is on. Then place the position indicator over the title segment in the Timeline. Click the Effect Mode button (in the center of the Composer window's toolbar) to open the Effect Editor with the title parameters, including the Edit Title button.

7. False. First disable the Video Background button. Then click the Background Color (Bg) window to change the background color. The Title tool Color Picker dialog box opens and you can select a color.

8. The selection handles around a text object are only to resize the text box, not the text itself.

9. Select the text, choose Object > Soften Shadow, and enter a value for the softness.

10. The Save Title dialog box allows you to name the title as well as choose a bin, a drive to save it to, and media resolution.

Lesson 10 Answers

1. Select Tools > Audio tool. Click the PH (Peak Hold) menu in the Audio tool, and select Create Tone Media.

2. a

3. You can set the sequence start timecode using the Sequence Report dialog box.

4. False. To change sequence timecode from non-drop frame to drop frame, use a ; (semicolon) to indicate drop frame and a : (colon) to indicate non-drop frame.

5. Media Composer has two options for exporting your sequence out as a digital file. The Send To option uses templates (customized to workflow) to send selected clips or sequences to other applications. Alternatively, the Export option offers more flexibility at the expense of a more complicated interface.

6. False. Although it's a good habit to get into, you can enable tracks and use or ignore marks from within the Export dialog box.

7. A QuickTime reference movie is a small link to the original files you captured in Media Composer. The reference movie contains no media; it only appears as a movie file. It does point to the original media files that make up your sequence or clip.

8. Choose File > Send To > Make New to open the Send To: Make New dialog box. Change the settings as required and click the Save As Template button.

9. During export, Media Composer copies the media files directly, without recompression, using the same quality as the original media files.

Appendix A Answers

1. a

2. d

3. b

4. d

5. c

6. msmFMID.pmr and msmMMOB.mdb

7. To define how an image is compressed and decompressed

8. A wrapper is a container file that holds compressed media, and provides it a standard format for use by media player and editing applications.

9. This is a question that has no absolute right answer, making it an excellent discussion question. There may be significant costs to production, and therefore significant value placed on the media that is generated by it. Depending on the stage of post production, the value of the work represented by the project metadata may rival or exceed that of the original media.

Appendix B Answers

1. See callouts

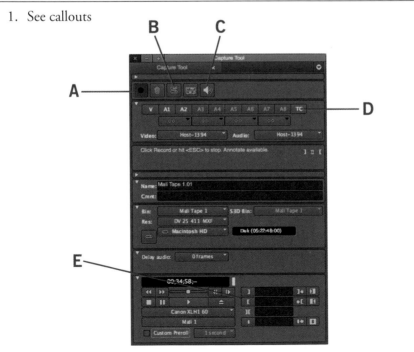

2. Set the project format, configure the deck, and configure the capture settings.

3. The Media Creation setting

4. Batch capture

5. TOD timecode is free-running timecode that matches the time of capture. It is not associated with specific frames on the source tape.

6. The disadvantage of TOD timecode is that it cannot be used to batch capture the master clips at a later time.

7. Associated media files only, not master clips

Appendix C Answers

1. To prepare a tape for an insert edit, you have to black the entire tape. To prepare a tape for an assemble edit, you only need to black the first few minutes.

2. Many decks are not capable of insert editing. The risk of recording an assemble edit is that you might break the continuity of the timecode. Assemble edits are also not clean, meaning the edits may be visible on the final tape.

3. No. Manual edits are never frame-accurate.

4. Crash record

5. To ensure clean, continuous timecode for a subsequent edit. Or, pad the tape with black so that when the program ends, the image doesn't immediately snow (turn to white noise).

INDEX

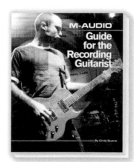

Like the Book?

Let us know on Facebook or Twitter!

facebook.com/courseptr

twitter.com/courseptr

Like us on Facebook or Follow us on Twitter to learn about upcoming books, promotions, contests, events and more!

License Agreement/Notice of Limited Warranty

By opening the sealed disc container in this book, you agree to the following terms and conditions. If, upon reading the following license agreement and notice of limited warranty, you cannot agree to the terms and conditions set forth, return the unused book with unopened disc to the place where you purchased it for a refund.

License:

The enclosed software is copyrighted by the copyright holder(s) indicated on the software disc. You are licensed to copy the software onto a single computer for use by a single user and to a backup disc. You may not reproduce, make copies, or distribute copies or rent or lease the software in whole or in part, except with written permission of the copyright holder(s). You may transfer the enclosed disc only together with this license, and only if you destroy all other copies of the software and the transferee agrees to the terms of the license. You may not decompile, reverse assemble, or reverse engineer the software.

Notice of Limited Warranty:

The enclosed disc is warranted by Course Technology to be free of physical defects in materials and workmanship for a period of sixty (60) days from end user's purchase of the book/disc combination. During the sixty-day term of the limited warranty, Course Technology will provide a replacement disc upon the return of a defective disc.

Limited Liability:

THE SOLE REMEDY FOR BREACH OF THIS LIMITED WARRANTY SHALL CONSIST ENTIRELY OF REPLACEMENT OF THE DEFECTIVE DISC. IN NO EVENT SHALL COURSE TECHNOLOGY OR THE AUTHOR BE LIABLE FOR ANY OTHER DAMAGES, INCLUDING LOSS OR CORRUPTION OF DATA, CHANGES IN THE FUNCTIONAL CHARACTERISTICS OF THE HARDWARE OR OPERATING SYSTEM, DELETERIOUS INTERACTION WITH OTHER SOFTWARE, OR ANY OTHER SPECIAL, INCIDENTAL, OR CONSEQUENTIAL DAMAGES THAT MAY ARISE, EVEN IF COURSE TECHNOLOGY AND/OR THE AUTHOR HAS PREVIOUSLY BEEN NOTIFIED THAT THE POSSIBILITY OF SUCH DAMAGES EXISTS.

Disclaimer of Warranties:

COURSE TECHNOLOGY AND THE AUTHOR SPECIFICALLY DISCLAIM ANY AND ALL OTHER WARRANTIES, EITHER EXPRESS OR IMPLIED, INCLUDING WARRANTIES OF MERCHANTABILITY, SUITABILITY TO A PARTICULAR TASK OR PURPOSE, OR FREEDOM FROM ERRORS. SOME STATES DO NOT ALLOW FOR EXCLUSION OF IMPLIED WARRANTIES OR LIMITATION OF INCIDENTAL OR CONSEQUENTIAL DAMAGES, SO THESE LIMITATIONS MIGHT NOT APPLY TO YOU.

Other:

This Agreement is governed by the laws of the State of Massachusetts without regard to choice of law principles. The United Convention of Contracts for the International Sale of Goods is specifically disclaimed. This Agreement constitutes the entire agreement between you and Course Technology regarding use of the software.